AMERICAN HEALTH CARE

Independent Studies in Political Economy

AMERICAN HEALTH CARE

Government, Market Processes, and the Public Interest

Edited by
Roger D. Feldman
Foreword by Mark V. Pauly

Transaction Publishers
New Brunswick (U.S.A.) and London (U.K.)

Library of Congress Catalog Number: 00-020662
ISBN: 1-56000-430-4 (cloth); 0-7658-0676-2 (paper)
Printed in the United States of America

Library of Congress Cataloging-in-Publication Data

American health care : government, market processes, and the public interest / edited by Roger D. Feldman ; foreword by Mark V. Pauly.
     p. cm.
  Includes index.
  ISBN 1-56000-430-4 (cloth : alk. paper) —ISBN 0-7658-0676-2 (pbk. : alk. paper)
  1. Medical policy—United States 2. Medical economics—United States.
 I. Feldman, Roger D.

RA395.A3 A523 2000
362.1'0973—dc21

                                                        00-020662

The INDEPENDENT INSTITUTE

The Independent Institute is a non-profit, non-partisan, scholarly research and educational organization that sponsors comprehensive studies on the political economy of critical social and economic problems.

The politicization of decision making in society has largely confined public debate to the narrow reconsideration of existing policies. Given the prevailing influence of partisan interests, little social innovation has occurred. In order to understand both the nature of and possible solutions to major public issues, The Independent Institute's program adheres to the highest standards of independent inquiry and is pursued regardless of prevailing political or social biases and conventions. The resulting studies are widely distributed as books and other publications, and publicly debated through numerous conference and media programs.

Through this uncommon independence, depth, and clarity, the Independent Institute pushes at the frontiers of our knowledge, redefines the debate over public issues, and fosters new and effective directions for government reform.

THE INDEPENDENT INSTITUTE
100 Swan Way, Oakland, CA 94621-1428, U.S.A.
Telephone: 510-632-1366 • Fax 510-568-6040
E-mail: info@independent.org • Website: http://www.independent.org

Contents

Part III: Drugs and Medication

Part IV: Health Care Personnel

Foreword

Mark V. Pauly

Is health care so different from other goods and services that a dominant role for government is inevitable or desirable? *American Health Care* addresses that important question, and answers it with a qualified "No." Instead, it makes a major contribution to the effort to find a mix between government and the market that reflects what each institutional arrangement can do best.

This effort is, in many ways a reasonable but radical way of describing ideal behavior (though it may not be so far from many aspects of actual behavior). Public policy in health most frequently assumes that the social purposes people correctly ascribe to health care can only and obviously be solved by government, with the market possibly supplying services, but in very much a subsidiary role. In this book, there is an effort instead to see how far the market can go in performing the critical functions of this industry—not to push it beyond its capabilities, but not to shortchange it either.

The book recognizes some things that have only lately dawned on many policy analysts: that the ability of actual governments to achieve ideal outcomes is limited, and that Americans fear government mistakes in health care financing and regulation as much as they fear market failure. That both government and market might be imperfect does not represent political prejudice. Rather, a great deal of modern political economy supports such a view. A trio of Nobel Prize winners have, in various ways, called attention to the obvious. Kenneth Arrow's "Impossibility Theorem" showed that no political process, however democratic and however well designed, can be guaranteed to reach outcomes that simultaneously satisfy some simple desirability criteria. James Buchanan's public choice theory (developed with Gordon Tullock) warns us not to be surprised when majorities sometimes discriminate against minorities, or politicians choose in their own self-interest. George Stigler initiated a positive theory of regulation based on the plausible assumption that government regulators sometimes pursue their own interests and those of the industries they regulate, rather than some vaguely defined public interest.

The upshot is that, in trying to decide what tasks government should perform and what tasks should be left to the market, conclusions do not come cheap. One cannot use armchair theorizing or journalistic anecdotes to spot imperfections relative to some ideal, and use that to rule out markets (or governments). Instead, analysts are faced with the more difficult task of trying to compare real and imperfect markets with real and imperfect governments—a task that requires such scarce commodities as data, judgment, and willingness to make choices without guarantees. This book helps choices (though obviously they do not settle matters) in this difficult process; they are all very much in the modern (and more realistic) tradition of policy analysis.

These are not unthinking arguments against government; quite the contrary, it is the recognition of the need for government, and of the power of its actions, which motivate the analysis. Assurance of adequate care for those we care about, preventing monopoly pricing, and helping to encourage the flow of good information are topics that come up over and over, and represent tasks in which government has an inevitable role. The book's authors recognize, however, that simply specifying what we would like to see happen and then asserting that "there ought to be a law" is not likely to work. Unintended consequences abound, regulators respond to the same temptations as do the rest of us, and government systems have no special claim on knowledge or wisdom.

Of these tasks, the assurance of adequate care is the one that most requires government, and which has proved the most stubbornly resistant to solution. The reason is simple: if some citizens cannot or will not pay for adequate care themselves, others will have to pay for them, but there will be controversy over how this burden should be distributed and what level and types of care are "adequate." Analysis of the failed Clinton plan shows in part how hard it is to assemble support for paying for others, in the face of a realistically skeptical middle class that knows it will have to pay.

The most subtle question is how to keep information flowing. Markets will not work well unless consumers have decent knowledge. The knowledge does not have to be perfect (and in health care, it never will be), but it should be of high quality. Perhaps there is a role for government in assisting in the production and distribution of knowledge, but inevitably this role must be meshed with the activities of private firms and health care providers in furnishing bits and pieces of information about themselves. We are fairly sure that the old fashioned medical economy in which government cooperated in the suppression of the flow of knowledge through advertising was not near the ideal, but we are not certain where we are going. This book helps to outline the kinds of markets that might be emerging, so that we can gauge their (and our) information needs.

Finally, there is the question of monopoly and market power. In my opinion, the provision of health care attracts more dedicated and selfless people than the typical commodity. Nevertheless, there is always the possibility of combinations of behavior to limit supply—for reasons of prestige, quality, or cross-subsidization of education or research, if not for reasons of higher profits. And yet high prices, regardless of the merit of the distribution of profits, themselves do substantial harm. Equally importantly, when competition is lacking, there is no assurance that citizens will get what they want. Permitting monopoly to exist but then regulating it might work reasonably well, if one could assume wise and just regulators. Such an assumption seems to contradict history and intuition. This book shows where to draw the line, how to prevent monopoly or regulation from doing harm where they are essential, and how to encourage competitive markets where they are not.

Much of the discussion of markets present and future in this book is hopeful, but much of it is avowedly tentative. That is as it should be, both because of the difficulty of judging among imperfect alternatives and because we have as yet had relatively little experience with something approximating a well-functioning health care market. We know already that markets can control cost growth, at least for a time, but that some aspects of quality will be lost (and the loss protested). There is much that we do not know, beginning with a judgment about whether the loss of such qualities as free choice of provider or easy access to inpatient care is smaller or larger in value than the costs saved, and continuing with the question of how markets will evolve over time.

American Health Care gives an excellent picture of the current state of knowledge (and informed speculation) about what is happening now or will happen in the near future. The book makes an important and articulate case for considering markets as an alternative to public regulation or expenditure, but it is honest in admitting that the argument is not settled, that the case is not open and shut, that there is still much we do not know and need to know.

Introduction

Roger D. Feldman

President Clinton's health care reform proposals of 1993 represented the most far-reaching program of social engineering to be attempted in the United States since the passage of Medicare and Medicaid in 1965. Under the guise of reforming the health care system, the Clinton plan would have herded almost all Americans under age sixty-five into large, government-sponsored health insurance purchasing alliances. Those alliances would have contracted with insurers that offered a standard set of benefits at regulated prices.

As the process dragged along, the President seemed increasingly uncomfortable with his own plan. He abandoned the notion of "play or pay" (forcing employers to pay a tax from which they could deduct the cost of health insurance), which had been adopted as a defensive measure during the primaries, and hastily embraced the strategy of managed competition—a market-oriented approach that had been advocated by a variety of academics and conservative Democratic politicians. At the same time, he continued to advocate universal coverage and spending controls to contain the cost of the new coverage. Senator Daniel Patrick Moynihan (D-N.Y.), reflecting the opinion of many experts, dismissed the Clinton budget numbers as "fantasy."[1]

By September 1994, the plan was in critical condition. With elections rapidly approaching, Senator Bob Dole (R-Kan.) threatened to withhold Republican support from the GATT trade agreement if the President continued to push his health care bill. Self-styled moderates in both parties, who appeared willing to fashion a compromise, complained that they were being ignored. Finally, on September 22, it was over. The plan had failed.

1

In the aftermath, House and Senate Democratic leaders rushed to blame someone for their own inaction. They found their target in greedy "special interests" and the health insurance industry, which had attacked the plan in a series of television commercials featuring Harry and Louise—a typical American couple who feared the plan would jeopardize their health insurance benefits. Academics also hashed over the failure of health care reform in their learned journals. Supporters of the plan, some on loan from universities and think tanks, continued to defend it while critics disparaged the plan from a variety of viewpoints. Alain Enthoven, for example, blamed the Clintonites for turning his "moderate" proposal of health insurance purchasing cooperatives into alliances with virtually everyone in them.[2]

These analyses miss the boat. Health care reform did not fail because of the "Harry and Louise" television commercials. In fact, 62 percent of the respondents to a *Newsweek* magazine poll rated those ads as dishonest.[3] Nor did it fail because of the sometimes arcane differences between various reform strategies advocated by the President's advisors.

To discover why health care reform failed, it's more enlightening to read the popular press than the academic journals. The press intuitively understood that the American people were not willing to entrust the government with running the health care system. *Washington Post* staff writers Dana Priest and Michael Weisskopf honed in on the "fatal miscalculation" that the White House brought to the process— "a vision of the government's role that does not fit with the high degree of skepticism with which the American public now views government solutions."[4] The *Wall Street Journal* noted that overwhelming initial support for the Clinton plan oozed away as people realized that decisions made through monopoly power, centralized planning, and a one-size-fits-all mentality allow no room for local innovation.[5] Robert Samuelson, writing in *Newsweek*, also commented that the plan failed because too many people concluded that it wasn't credible.[6]

The fundamental fact is that health care reform failed because people don't trust government to manage their medical care—a business that accounts for one of every seven dollars spent in the United States, and a healing art that touches the lives of almost every citizen. From this viewpoint, the primary flaw of the academic literature is its failure to offer a cogent analysis of why government control of health care does not work. In other words, why was the public's conclusion reasonable and proper?

This volume delivers that analysis. Thirteen experts—economists, lawyers, and a historian—explain why untoward consequences usually follow when the government sets out to do good things. I must caution the reader that this is not a polite bunch. You should not expect a dispassionate analysis of policy options, with heavily qualified appraisals of the various approaches. On the contrary, you will find passionate, "in your face" arguments—from Paul H. Rubin's polemic against the Food and Drug Administration (FDA) for withholding vital information on the health benefits of aspirin, to Richard Epstein's attack on community rating for making health insurance unaffordable to large numbers of young workers.

The result is a book that will challenge you to examine your fundamental convictions about the benefits of government intervention in health care. You will learn, for example, that hospital rate regulation raises hospital prices, that "no-fault" medical malpractice increases the occurrence of faulty medicine, and that FDA regulation is a major cause for the escalating cost of new drugs.

Despite the fact that this is a provocative and challenging book, the authors are well within the mainstream of economic thought, as it concerns the effects of government intervention in private economic endeavor. Before describing this mainstream and how the authors fit into it, I want to be more specific about the subject material of this book. Government intervention may take a variety of forms, including provision of *financing* for the private production of goods and services, as in Medicare or small business loans, direct *production*, as in Veterans Administration (VA) hospitals, or *regulation* of private economic activity. The authors of this book concentrate on the third form of government intervention: economic regulation.[7] Regulation consists of rules and orders prescribed by the government to control private economic activity.

The fundamental rationale for government regulation is to correct market failure in the private economy. Often this failure is related to information costs. As Ronald Hansen notes, FDA control of the claims that drug companies make for their products may reduce the need for physicians to verify those claims, thereby reducing information costs for physicians.

The authors would agree with this rationale. They also would agree that regulation should be pursued to the point where the marginal costs and marginal benefits to the public are equal. In the real world, however, regulation doesn't work this way. To understand how regulation really works, we need to invoke the names of two giants in the field: George Stigler and Sam Peltzman.

Prior to the work of these two economists, the prevailing view— held by sociologists and political scientists—was that regulation generally serves the public interest. Economists were skeptical of this view, having observed that several decades of airline regulation had prevented new carriers from entering the industry. The consequences of interstate trucking regulation also seemed at variance with the public interest theory. But economists didn't have an explanation of why regulation so often seemed to harm the public interest.

George Stigler supplied the missing explanation.[8] His central thesis is that there is a "political market" where regulation is bought and sold, subject to economic laws of supply and demand. In this political market the demand for regulations arises from the regulated industry, which seeks to utilize the state's power to coerce and to tax for its own interests. The state is the supplier of regulations, and it will supply more of them for a higher price.

A positive economic theory has to specify the arguments underlying the supply and demand functions. The central question for Stigler's positive theory of regulation is why a small group tends to dominate the regulatory process despite the widespread public interest to the contrary. His answer rests on two dominant characteristics of the political process: elections are held infrequently, and votes must be cast over a fairly short period of time. Consequently, the public does not vote separately on each issue; instead, it votes for representatives who express positions on a "package" of issues. Because they have only a small stake in each issue, most voters will find that the costs of learning how the issue affects them and how their representative stands on the issue outweigh the benefits of information. In contrast, the industry has a large stake in a few issues and is therefore more likely to be well informed. The industry also is better able to communicate its support to the representatives. This ability is facilitated by its small size, which minimizes the problem of "free-riding" on the efforts of others.

Stigler's theory accurately predicts the outcome of many regulatory ventures—such as the creation of entry barriers to the airline and trucking industries—that blatantly served the interests of incumbent firms. Another example is USDA inspection of meat and poultry products, which could be viewed as a publicly financed extension of the meat-packing industry, dedicated to promoting public confidence in the product while raising the costs of small firms. Regulation of health professions, such as physicians and registered nurses, also tends to be very solicitous of the professions' economic interests.[9]

The shortcoming of Stigler's theory is that it cannot account for instances where the regulatory agency does not serve the industry's interest. FDA regulation of drugs and medical devices is a case in point. Sam Peltzman supplied this missing piece of the puzzle.[10] To explain why the industry doesn't always win, Peltzman focuses on the regulator's need to mobilize a political coalition with at least a majority of voters in it. Coalition-building involves a tradeoff between higher profits, which benefit the industry, and lower prices, which build voter support for the regulator's political party. Thus, the usual political equilibrium will not deliver everything the regulated industry desires.[11]

In some cases it may be possible to create a coalition with more than enough profits to satisfy the industry, prices low enough to keep consumers happy, and something left over for the regulator. In such cases, the regulator's own preferences and ideology come into play. The regulator can pursue its self- interest, which might include amassing political power, redistributing income, or enlarging its budget.

Peltzman's extension of the theory creates a tension between two groups of analysts. In one camp are those who generally support the "regulatory capture" perspective espoused by Stigler. I'd place Mike Morrisey in this camp. As the title of his paper indicates, regulation protects the providers. For example, the majority of states have passed "certificate of need" (CON) laws which require prior approval for large hospital capital projects (e.g., construction of new hospitals or the purchase of expensive equipment by existing hospitals). The justification for CON is that by controlling hospital capital, regulators can control medical care costs. But research findings show that Medicare hospital costs and prices in CON states are higher, the longer CON has been in effect. Higher costs and prices benefit incumbent hospitals, so CON does exactly what Stigler's theory predicts: it protects the providers. Further support for this conclusion comes from the finding that CON laws reduce the for-profit hospital share in states dominated by nonprofit hospitals. Thus, CON keeps investor-owned hospitals out of those states where nonprofit hospitals control the political market for regulation.

Barbara Ryan's paper on hospital regulation and antitrust policy also falls into this category. Antitrust is a paradox for those who believe that regulation promotes the interests of the regulated industry. The ostensible goal of antitrust is to promote competition, and as Adam Smith reminds us, competition is never popular with the competitors.[12] But Ryan believes this paradox is more apparent than real. She shows that antitrust serves the interests of competitors who will be harmed by efficiency-promoting mergers. These firms exercise undue influence over the antitrust process and are able to block many mergers. Antitrust also protects other interest groups by obstructing changes in the ownership of firms. For example, hospital mergers in rural areas appear more likely to be challenged than mergers in urban areas. Ryan attributes this asymmetry in antitrust enforcement to the involvement of rural elites who don't want "their" hospital taken over by a faceless corporation or distant conglomerate.

In the other camp are those who emphasize the regulator's incentives to manipulate the system for its own self-interest, often with negative consequences for the industry. The aforementioned studies of the FDA by Ron Hansen, Paul Rubin, and Noel Campbell fall into the second category. Campbell accuses the FDA of arbitrarily garnering power, adding more layers of costly reporting, and interfering in the marketplace for medical devices. The FDA does this because it is a public agency answering to politicians, and the political heat from allowing an unsafe device to be marketed is always greater than the cost of delaying the introduction of safe and effective devices. Thus, the FDA has adopted the attitude that medical device manufacturers and their products are "guilty until proved innocent." Campbell cites one case where the introduction of a safe, painless, and permanent alternative to prostate surgery was delayed for six months in the United States after the device was available in Europe.

Although they disagree about the effects of regulation, members of both camps agree that regulation rarely hits the target of equal marginal benefits and marginal costs. More often than not it exacerbates the market failure it was designed to correct or creates problems where none previously existed. In place of regulation, the authors of this volume have an almost unlimited faith that unfettered private economic activity will promote the social good. Shirley Svorny, for example, questions the need for existing state licensing arrangements of medical professionals. She argues that professionals work together and are closely monitored by responsible private entities who have an interest in maintaining quality.[13] Thus, the private sector can supply the needed amount of discipline over medical professionals. Paul Rubin argues that regulation of drug advertisements may be unnecessary. Large firms have a strong interest in maintaining their reputations. This is especially true for large pharmaceutical firms, whose primary customers—physicians—are skilled buyers and repeat customers. It would be foolish to attempt to deceive those customers. In the same spirit, Noel Campbell would replace FDA regulation of medical devices with private certification, modeled on organizations such as Underwriters Laboratories (UL).

Clark Havighurst advocates the use of written contracts through which consumers could pre-commit themselves to use less medical care than they might wish to consume under open-ended health insurance policies. He contends that such contracts would provide market signals that consumers want self-restraint, as well as conferring the legal authority that health plans need to respond to those economizing signals. In a similar spirit, Gail Jensen argues that medical savings accounts (MSAs) would encourage consumers to choose health insurance policies with realistic levels of coinsurance and deductibles. Because most consumers would pay their medical bills out-of-pocket, they would have a strong incentive to use medical care carefully and effectively.

Richard Epstein's fine paper also displays a strong preference for "contractual" approaches to the allocation of health care resources. Epstein maintains that private parties should be free to enter into insurance contracts that discriminate among risks and that limit coverage for pre-existing medical conditions. Restricting the insurers' ability to match the premiums they charge with the risk they assume has led to unaffordable premiums that have pushed large numbers of younger workers into the ranks of the uninsured.

Patricia Danzon's paper on medical malpractice is an exception to the unconditional reliance on private resource allocation. In theory, by holding health care providers liable for medical injuries caused by their negligence, the tort liability system used in the United States provides a source of insurance for accident victims and a deterrent to future negligent behavior. However, tort liability is a grossly inefficient source of insurance, compared to either public or private first-party insurance. Only forty cents of the medical malpractice premium dollar reaches injured patients, compared with ninety cents for large first-party health insurance programs. Much of the difference is spent on litigation. If the tort liability system is justified, the reason has to be on the grounds that it deters future negligence.

One might question whether the tort liability, which relies on laws passed by public legislatures and enforced by public courts, should be classified as a private resource-allocation mechanism. I subscribe to this classification (and I believe Danzon does so implicitly) because it enables her to contrast the tort liability system with overtly public methods for resolving malpractice claims found in Sweden and New Zealand. Sweden uses a partial "no-fault" system that decouples patient compensation from deterrence. The Swedish system has a very low litigation rate compared with the U.S. But Danzon shows that the apparent reduction in medical malpractice is an illusion. Patients in Sweden have fewer rights than those in the U.S., so they would be less likely to sue in any case. Swedish physicians, having no personal stake in the outcome, generally cooperate rather than opposing compensation for an injured patient. The result is a general decrease in deterrence. New Zealand established a comprehensive no-fault program in 1974. Between 1975 and 1989, total expenditures under that program grew faster than the average rate of increase in U.S. medical malpractice premiums.

Danzon recommends some modest reforms in the tort system, such as limits on awards for non-economic losses. These would reduce litigation with minimal effects on deterrence. She also thinks that removing malpractice claims from the courts to a specialized administrative board is an option worth trying on an experimental basis. In the end, she counsels that there is no perfect system. The fundamental problem is imperfect information about what happened and who caused it. Neither public nor private approaches can completely solve this problem.

One of the strengths of this volume is that the authors don't simply analyze the current tug-of-war between competition and regulation—they look into the future to see where we're going. On this score this is no disagreement: the private sector is getting stronger and better able to correct instances where medical care markets fail. In the past, medical markets failed because of imperfect information, which usually meant that medical providers knew more than their patients. But private organizations are arising to exploit economies of scale in producing information for consumers. I think Shirley Svorny is most explicit about this trend. Under the "old" system, when physicians knew more than patients, Svorny actually concedes that medical licensure may have served the public interest. By guaranteeing a stream of profits for practicing physicians, licensure created an incentive for physicians to avoid malfeasance. But this incentive is no longer needed as hospitals, group practices, and Health Maintenance Organizations (HMOs) assume the watchdog role for consumers. And, as these organizations become more dominant in the medical care marketplace, the rationale for regulations of all kinds diminishes.

Ted Frech also understands the value of new health care purchasing arrangements such as Preferred Provider Organizations (PPOs), which negotiate prices with providers and steer patients toward those providers. In a system of competing PPOs, consumers who believe that the price agreements are too strict can switch to another PPO or insurance plan. These competitive options, unlike government price controls, are consistent with consumers' preferences and are sensitive to individual variation in consumer values for price and quality.

If the private sector is doing such a good job (and getting better all the time), how did we get into the mess of health care "reform?" This question brings us to Ronald Hamowy's paper on the history of Medicare. This is the longest contribution to the book, and in some respects the most interesting. Hamowy traces the history of Medicare back to the reforms of Otto von Bismarck. The theme that ties this excursion together is that public health insurance programs are fatally flawed because most voters want more health care than they are willing to pay for and socializing the insurance market is an excellent way to hide those costs. Self-interested politicians eagerly will supply this demand for public insurance. Since the dislocations caused by hiding the costs of health insurance are of no interest to politicians, the damage is not self-limiting and it may disrupt the whole economy.[14]

Charlotte Twight extends the analysis of political market failure to the Health Insurance Portability and Accountability Act of 1996 (HIPAA). While HIPAA was said to prevent health insurance loss triggered by job change, it contained strong provisions that may threaten innocent physicians with criminal prosecution and jeopardize the privacy of doctor-patient relationships. These provisions were enacted by a series of political maneuvers that included tying the act to a popular measure for health insurance access, and misrepresentation of the "federal health care offenses" that permeated the bill.

This type of behavior by politicians might seem pathological, but it is predicted by the theory of public choice. Two public choice theorists, William Mitchell and Randy Simmons, point out that "the politician spends other people's money and spends it on still others who may not have contributed to the common treasury."[15] If the politician has to choose between taxing everyone a small amount and taxing a small group of people a much greater amount, the politician will generally choose the former option because dispersed losses carry a lower electoral penalty. Instead of taxing anyone explicitly, it is even better to hide the costs of a public program through off-budget expenditures such as private-sector mandates.

The tendency of politicians to hide the costs of public health insurance was especially evident in President Clinton's proposals, the centerpiece of which was a mandatory employer contribution to premiums.[16] The fact that the cost of this mandate falls on individuals was disguised by the rhetoric of "security." The mandatory employer contribution capitalizes on the mistaken but widespread belief that the employer "pays" for the mandate. In reality, the mandate is a tax on labor that reduces the employee's wage.[17] The cost of health care reform was also hidden by promises to control overall health care spending through the use of global budgets imposed by the government. Those controls would have created excess demand for medical care (a gap between the amount of medical care providers are willing to supply and the amount that consumers demand).[18]

The President's proposals failed because these promises were too transparent, given the public's prevailing mistrust of government. I also believe the popular press played an important role in exposing the threadbare state of the emperor's new clothes. The press acted this way not because it wanted to serve the public interest but because there is a reasonably competitive market for information in the U.S. The public wanted to be informed about health care reform and the press satisfied that demand. Hopefully, the articles in this book will contribute to the stock of public knowledge on health care. By doing so, they will lessen the chance of another misguided episode resembling that of 1993-94.

Notes

1. "The Clinton Prescription for an Ailing Health System," *Medicine & Health*, 47:38 (September 27, 1993).

2. Alain Enthoven, "Why Not the Clinton Health Plan?" *Inquiry* 31:2 (summer 1994): pp. 129-35.
3. Robert J. Samuelson, "Health Care: The 'Con' That Failed," *Newsweek*, October 10, 1994, p. 35.
4. Dana Priest and Michael Weisskopf, "Health Care Reform: The Collapse of a Quest," *Washington Post*, October 11, 1994, A6.
5. Michael Rothschild, "Why Health Care Reform Died," *Wall Street Journal*, September 22, 1994, A10.
6. Samuelson, op. cit.
7. Public financing typically is accompanied by regulation, as in the Medicare program, which heavily regulates participating physicians and hospitals. Several papers in this volume discuss Medicare, but they focus on the regulatory aspects of Medicare rather than on how it finances medical care.
8. George J. Stigler, "The Theory of Economic Regulation," *Bell Journal of Economics*, 2:1 (spring 1971), pp. 3-21.
9. Roger Feldman and James Begun, "The Effects of Advertising Restrictions: Lessons from Optometry," *Journal of Human Resources*, 13:Supplement (1978), pp. 247-62.
10. Sam Peltzman, "Toward a More General Theory of Regulation," *Journal of Law and Economics*, 19:2 (August 1976), pp. 211-48.
11. For an excellent application of this theory, see Colleen Grogan, "The Political-Economic Factors Influencing State Medicaid Policy," *Political Research Quarterly*, 47:3 (September 1994), pp. 589-622. Grogan shows that each dimension of Medicaid policy is shaped by a different configuration of interest group and constituency interest in that policy.
12. Adam Smith, *The Wealth of Nations*, Book 1, chapter 7. Also see Mark Blaug's discussion in *Economic Theory in Retrospect*, 4th edition, Cambridge, MA: Cambridge University Press, 1985), pp. 43: "He [Smith] is aware of the fact that competition deprives the participants in the market process of the power to influence price and that the larger the number of sellers, the greater the obstacles to 'combinations'."
13. In this paper, Svorny focuses on supervision of physicians by hospitals. Supervision also may be applied by the large group practices in which many physicians now practice. In an analysis of data from 1991 to 1993, Svorny showed that the presence of group practices across states is positively related to the rate of disciplinary actions against physicians. See Shirley Svorny and Roger Feldman, "The Changing Structure of the Market for Health Services: Implications for Physician Discipline," draft paper, Department of Economics, California State University, Northridge, June 1997.
14. For example, consumers save less when they can rely on public insurance. A recent doctoral dissertation at the University of Minnesota showed that the introduction of Medicare could have been responsible for the well-documented decline in the U.S. savings rate since the early 1970s. See Ronald William Gecan, *A General Equilibrium Analysis of Medicaid and Medicare*, Ph.D. dissertation, University of Minnesota, Department of Economics, September 1997.
15. William C. Mitchell and Randy T. Simmons, *Beyond Politics: Markets, Welfare, and the Failure of Bureaucracy*, Boulder, CO: Westview Press, 1994, pp. 49.
16. The administration's proposal would have required employers to pay 80 percent of the weighted average premiums of plans offered by the regional purchasing alliance. For an excellent analysis of this proposal, see Bryan E. Dowd, "The Clinton Health Care Reform Proposal: Efficiency, Fairness, and the Role of Gov-

ernment," *Health Care Management: State of the Art Reviews,* 1:1 (August 1994), pp. 1-22.

17. Roger Feldman, "Who Pays for Mandated Health Insurance Benefits?" *Journal of Health Economics,* 12:3 (October 1993), pp. 341-48.

18. Roger Feldman and Felix Lobo, "Global Budgets and Excess Demand for Hospital Care," *Health Economics,* 6 (1997), pp. 187-96.

Part I

Health Insurance and Finance

1

The Genesis and Development of Medicare[1]

Ronald Hamowy

In June 1883 Otto von Bismarck, then Chancellor of a newly united Germany, was successful in gaining passage of a compulsory health insurance bill covering all factory and mine workers. This, together with a series of reform measures including accident insurance, disability insurance, and an old-age bill, formed the core of Bismarck's state socialist policy that was crafted both to outflank the entrepreneurial class and the liberal, laissez-faire party it supported and to detach labor from the social democratic left.[2] The original act was later amended to include workers engaged in transportation and commerce and, in 1911, was extended to almost all employees, including agricultural and domestic workers, teachers, actors, and musicians.[3]

The motives that impelled the German government to enact a compulsory, state-run medical insurance law were not inconsistent with the views of most social reformers of the period, who regarded a powerful, centralized, bureaucratic state as capable of being a kind and beneficent institution. Bismarck's attempts to enact his social insurance bill did not, of course, go unopposed. A substantial portion of the imperial and Prussian bureaucracy held strong free-market views and resisted the Chancellor's attempts to introduce measures that so dramatically intruded into the marketplace. However, the opposition to Bismarck's program proved unsuccessful and his victory encouraged reformist elements in other countries to agitate for similar legislation. As a consequence, compulsory national health insurance was hailed throughout

Europe as a model of progressive legislation and, over the course of the next thirty years, was emulated by a number of other nations.[4]

In Great Britain, David Lloyd George, Chancellor of the Exchequer from 1901 until 1914 was sufficiently animated by Bismarck's success to introduce a national health insurance scheme on the part of the Liberal government in 1911. Lloyd George, who had visited Germany in 1908 and had returned to Britain greatly excited by its social welfare legislation, hoped to introduce a similar series of measures at home. Indeed, he viewed compulsory health insurance as only the first installment in a far more ambitious plan of social reform.[5] The National Health Insurance Act that passed Parliament in 1911 provided for two types of benefits, a cash payment in the event of maternity or disability, and medical services, should the worker fall ill. All manual workers between the ages of sixteen and sixty-five, as well as nonmanual workers earning below a stipulated maximum, were required to contribute to and participate in the program;[6] in return, every participant was entitled to the services of a physician anywhere in Great Britain. Patients were free to select their doctor while doctors, who were compensated on a capitation basis, were free to refuse any individual seeking treatment.[7]

While at the outset there appears to have been some resistance by the medical profession to the introduction of health insurance legislation, opposition to the Act quickly disappeared as physicians' incomes increased under National Health. In addition, doctors, who felt their autonomy compromised by the restrictions imposed by the voluntary health insurance groups (known as Friendly Societies) that were replaced by the Act, no longer regarded themselves as constrained in determining the courses of treatment and the medications they prescribed to their patients.[8] Indeed, many hoped for a closer and more extended relationship with the government.

Early positive reports regarding the British compulsory health insurance program did much to encourage reformers in the United States in the belief that it would prove politically feasible to enact similar legislation here. In 1911, immediately after passage of the National Health Act in Britain, Louis D. Brandeis, who was later to be appointed to the Supreme Court but was at the time an attorney in private practice in New York, urged the National Conference on Charities and Corrections to vigorously support a national program of mandatory medical insurance.[9]

A compulsory system of health insurance soon became a subject of American presidential politics. Affronted at having been denied the Republican nomination for President against the incumbent William Howard Taft, Theodore Roosevelt, in June 1912, decided to enter the Presidential race at the head of the Progressive, or Bull Moose, Party. On August 6, 1912, Roosevelt, after having learned that the Democrats had adopted a liberal platform and chosen Woodrow Wilson as their candidate, delivered what later came to be called his "Confession of Faith," a long and somewhat tedious speech calling for, among a number of other paternalistic measures, a national compulsory health care scheme for all industrial workers.[10] He had been strongly influenced by a group of progressive economists from the University of Wisconsin, protégés of the labor economist John R. Commons who taught at the University from 1904 to 1932.

Commons was a tireless and determined advocate of the welfare state and of economic planning. A staunch crusader for "social justice," he regarded massive state intervention in the economic and social lives of Americans as absolutely essential to the nation's welfare.[11] In 1906, Commons, together with the other Progressive social scientists at Wisconsin, founded the American Association for Labor Legislation (AALL) to lobby for reforms at both the state and federal level. Commons served as secretary of the new organization from 1908 to 1909 and was succeeded in this position by his former student John B. Andrews.

Roosevelt and other members of the Progressive Party were convinced, especially in light of recent passage of a national health program in Great Britain, that compulsory national health insurance would be heavily endorsed by working-class Americans. The American Association for Labor Legislation regarded enactment of a bill along the lines of that passed in Great Britain as a priority. Indeed, the author of the health insurance plank in the 1912 Progressive Party platform was one of the leading members of the Association, Dr. Isaac M. Rubinow,[12] who was in fact a member of the Socialist Party.[13]

Andrews' efforts to expand the membership of the AALL and to gain passage of the kinds of legislation the organization sought proved surprisingly successful. By 1913 he had managed to increase membership from a few hundred to more than 3,000.[14] More important, in 1912 the AALL was awarded its first legislative victory when Congress voted to adopt an AALL-sponsored bill that prohibited the match industry from using phosphorus in its manufacturing process. This success appears to have "catapulted the Association into a position of leadership in the movement for protective labor legislation and social insurance."[15] Indeed, so prominent did the AALL become that it was able to attract a large number of academics and social workers to its ranks, some of great eminence. Among its earliest presidents were such notable academicians as Richard T. Ely of Wisconsin, Irving Fisher of Yale, Henry Seager of Columbia, and William F. Willoughby of Princeton.[16] (Willoughby, in fact, had authored a comprehensive report on European government health insurance schemes in 1898).

The AALL next turned its attention to the question of a mandatory health insurance bill. Aware that terms such as "mandatory" or "compulsory" would almost certainly alienate prospective supporters and hoping to capitalize on the cooperative fellowship suggested by the term "social," the Association adopted the term "social insurance" in its place.[17] At its annual meeting in Boston in December 1912 the AALL established a Committee on Social Insurance to, among other things, "prepare carefully for needed legislation."[18] By 1914 the Committee had drafted a model bill, ostensibly a combination of the best elements in the German and British systems. It called for the mandatory enrollment of all workers earning less than $1,200 per year and voluntary enrollment of any self-employed person with incomes no higher than that amount. Premiums were ostensibly divided among employers, employees, and the government, with the government paying twenty percent and the employer paying a minimum, depending on the employee's earnings, of forty percent.[19]

The AALL was naturally anxious to obtain the support of the American Medical Association (AMA) in its campaign for enactment of a compulsory health insurance bill. Having limited its legislative lobbying to the state level prior to the turn of the century,[20] the AMA, following its reorganization in 1901, had discovered that it was equally possible to gain passage of federal legislation that would benefit its membership. Thus it had campaigned for pure food and drug legislation and, less successfully, for a cabinet-level Department of Health. There appeared every reason to believe that if it could be shown that the introduction of a mandatory national health insurance program would in fact profit physicians, then the AMA would throw its weight behind the proposed legislation. Toward this end, the AALL secured the aid of several prominent physicians in revising its draft bill, which was circulated to physicians' groups for possible further revision.[21]

As a consequence, the AMA established a Committee on Social Insurance in 1915 to study the issue and appointed Dr. Alexander Lambert, physician to former President Roosevelt, a member of the AALL's Committee on Social Insurance and chairman of the AMA's Judicial Council, as chairman. Doubtless Lambert's connections with the AALL account for his selecting Isaac Rubinow as the AMA committee's secretary. Lambert had earlier reported to the annual meeting of the AMA that the European experiment with national health insurance had proven good for both doctor and patient. Among other leading AMA figures who supported the AALL's program were George H. Simmons, who had been editor of the *Journal of the American Medical Association (JAMA)* since 1899, Abraham Jacobi, president of the AMA in 1912 and 1913, and, most important, Frederick R. Green, secretary of the AMA's Council on Health and Public Instruction.[22]

Green was a tireless campaigner for a national system of compulsory health insurance and had editorialized in the *JAMA* for its passage.[23] At one point he had written the secretary of the AALL that the Association's model bill and its plans to lobby for its enactment were "exactly in line with the views that I have held for a long time regarding the methods which should be followed in securing public health legislation."[24] Certainly one of the benefits that would accrue to medical practitioners, it was thought, was an increase in their incomes. The London correspondent for the *JAMA* reported in 1914 that the incomes of British doctors had risen substantially with the introduction of national health insurance, sometimes doubling in the case of physicians in the poorer industrial districts of the country and increasing by as much as 20 to 50 percent in the more prosperous areas.[25] Indeed, in the same year the secretary of the British Medical Association advised a visiting American physician that the incomes of general practitioners had in many instances quadrupled.[26]

With large numbers of physicians eager to reap the increased incomes that would likely follow in the wake of a health insurance plan in which payment of patients' charges would be underwritten by government, the AALL's model bill at first received little opposition from the medical profession. A commission appointed by the California legislature to consider the measure reported favorably on it, as did commissions in New Jersey and Ohio. It was introduced into the legislatures of Massachusetts and New Jersey, and the New York Senate went so far as to pass the bill, although it was defeated in the

Assembly.[27] Of greater significance, a few months prior to the 1916 elections, Congress began holding hearings on a national plan. What appears to have particularly buoyed the spirits of the measure's supporters was Woodrow Wilson's shift to a more "liberal" position on social reform issues in preparation for his second election.[28] Certainly with passage of the War Risk Insurance Act of 1917—which for the first time extended medical and hospital care to veterans—serving as a precedent, it would be unlikely that a universal health insurance plan would fail in Congress.

Despite these favorable signs, however, a compulsory government health insurance plan was not enacted, either at the state or national levels. The model bill put forward by the AALL apparently had one grievous flaw; it did not clearly stipulate whether physicians enrolled in the plan would be reimbursed on the basis of a capitation fee, as was the case in Great Britain, or fee-for-service, nor did it insure that medical practitioners be represented in ample numbers on the administrative boards to be established under the contemplated health insurance authority.[29] The effect of this was to seriously erode medical support for the bill.[30] In addition, insurance firms were bitterly opposed to the scheme. Not only did the model bill contain a provision for the payment of funeral benefits, thus competing directly with the coverage offered by private insurance companies, but it also explicitly excluded private firms from acting as health insurance carriers.

Beyond physicians, who saw in the proposed legislation weaknesses that might lead to a substantial erosion in their incomes, and insurance companies, who objected to the bill's funeral insurance provisions, important members in organized labor regarded the proposal with suspicion. Samuel Gompers, the head of the American Federation of Labor, in particular, opposed a compulsory system of national health insurance on the grounds that its passage would deprive the labor movement of an extremely effective issue with which to organize workers.[31] Finally, there appears to have been opposition on the part of some to covering the medical expenses of those whose illnesses were the product, not of work or accident, but of intemperate and wanton lives.[32]

With American entry into the First World War, interest in passage of compulsory health insurance waned. The anti-German hysteria originally incited by government propaganda and so ably carried forward by more doltish Americans proved an ally of those who opposed the measure. Its adversaries were not above stressing the German origins of mandatory medical insurance and referring to the AALL's bill as "un-American."[33] Indeed, the proposal's defenders were forced to imply that the scheme's origins were British rather than German and began referring to it as "health insurance," its British designation, rather than the German "sickness insurance."[34] Even the president of the American Surgical Association, in speaking of the plan, warned that "with a clear understanding of German methods in molding public sentiment and with utter detestation of that sinister thing—German *Kultur*—we should hesitate long before subscribing to a dictum or a doctrine emanating from such a source."[35]

As opposition to the AALL bill became more organized and with the increasing popularity of the view that mandatory health insurance was in reality the product of a German conspiracy to impose Prussian values on America,[36] the movement to enact the measure disappeared until it again resurfaced during the New Deal era.[37] Renewed interest in mandatory health insurance emerged primarily as a consequence of the report of the Committee on Economic Security, a cabinet-level committee appointed by President Roosevelt in 1934. Eager to offer an alternative social welfare package to compete with those of Upton Sinclair,[38] Senator Huey Long of Louisiana,[39] and Dr. Francis E. Townsend,[40] whose popularity appeared to be increasing as the Depression worsened, Roosevelt's advisors, particularly the membership of this Committee (Frances Perkins, the Secretary of Labor, Henry Morganthau, Jr., Secretary of the Treasury, Homer Cummings, Attorney-General, Henry Wallace, Secretary of Agriculture, and Harry Hopkins, Administrator of the Emergency Relief Administration),[41] advised the passage of a comprehensive social security system to include unemployment insurance, old-age security, and government-administered health-care insurance. Given the political biases of the committee, their recommendations can hardly be regarded as surprising.[42]

Support for a mandatory health insurance bill had earlier gained impetus with issuance of the final report of the Committee on the Costs of Medical Care in 1932. The Committee, organized four years earlier under the chairmanship of Dr. Ray Lyman Wilbur, former Secretary of the Interior under President Hoover and former President of the AMA, had concluded that both the medical infrastructure and medical services in the United States were inadequate and recommended that physicians and other health care personnel be organized around a hospital or clinic and that they be reimbursed through group payment financed either through insurance or taxes.[43] In addition, in 1935, the American Federation of Labor endorsed compulsory health insurance, thus reversing its earlier position.

But despite the favorable climate among social scientists, labor leaders, and politicians and the philosophical leanings of its members, the report of the President's Committee on Economic Security did not include among its recommendations passage of a health insurance bill. While it did urge enactment of an unemployment insurance bill and of social security it failed to put forward a compulsory health insurance measure despite persistent pressure from Harry Hopkins, an indefatigable proponent of state medicine.[44] The reasons for this are clear. A substantial segment of the medical profession was adamantly opposed to any compulsory government-run health insurance program and made their views known, both in editorials in the major medical journals including the *JAMA*[45] and through a torrent of representations to members of Congress. While the President's committee wished to recommend a health insurance plan in addition to a comprehensive system of unemployment insurance and old-age security the opposition of the AMA proved decisive and rather than jeopardize his other reforms the President advised that the issues be severed and that health insurance legislation be postponed until after passage of the social security bill.[46]

In an attempt to keep the subject of health insurance alive, Roosevelt established an Interdepartmental Committee to Coordinate Health and Welfare Activities immediately following passage of the Social Security Act and at the same time ordered his staff to keep the matter before the public. The result was that it became a major topic of public debate, both in speeches and in a host of articles in the nation's press; by 1938, no fewer than fifteen books were published on the subject.[47] At the same time, the federal government completed an extensive study of the nation's health that purported to show that 90 percent of the population was receiving inadequate medical care, the inescapable conclusion of which was that enactment of a national health care system was imperative.[48]

All this activity culminated in the convening of a National Health Conference under the auspices of the Interdepartmental Committee, which had earlier approved a report of its Technical Committee on Medical Care, predictably urging a huge extension of federal control over health matters. The conference, which took place in Washington in July 1938 opened with a statement by President Roosevelt which one report describes as marking "the first definite affirmation by an American chief executive of the ultimate responsibility of the government for the health of its citizens."[49] Among the conference's participants was the full complement of Roosevelt's closest advisors concerned with expanding the government's role in the area of medical care together with numbers of social workers, public health officials, and representatives of women's and farmers' groups and labor unions. In addition, acting under instructions from its House of Delegates, the AMA sent several representatives including its president, Dr. Irvin Abell, and the editor of the *JAMA*, Dr. Morris Fishbein.[50]

The Conference, acting on the advice of its "technical committee," ultimately recommended that the federal government enact legislation in several areas including (1) an expansion of the public health and maternal and child health programs included in the original Social Security Act; (2) a system of grants to the various states for direct medical care programs; (3) federal grants for hospital construction; (4) a disability insurance scheme that would insure against loss of wages during illness; and (5) grants to the states for the purpose of financing compulsory statewide health insurance programs.[51] The total cost of these programs was estimated at about $850,000,000 a year.[52]

While the Conference had proposed legislation that would provide for a tax-funded system of compulsory health care insurance, it had urged adoption of these programs at the state level in an attempt to placate the majority of medical practitioners. It was thought that the reason why physicians so adamantly opposed such programs, especially at the national level, was that they feared, at best, that they were unlikely to have much say in their administration and, at worst, that physicians would eventually become salaried employees of the government.[53] This was, of course, less likely to be the case, were the plans managed by the various states.[54] However, it was clear to all, including the membership of the AMA, that any legislation introduced in Congress aimed at putting into effect the Conference's recommendations would call for a national program of health insurance. And indeed this is precisely what occurred. When, in 1943 Senator Robert Wagner of New York,[55] together with Senator James Murray of Montana and Representative John Dingell of Michigan, introduced a bill reflecting the recommendations of the National Health Conference, it called for, among other things, a compulsory national health insurance program. The bill was exceedingly ambitious. Not only did it provide for mandatory health insurance, but also for a federal system of unemployment insurance, broader coverage and extended benefits for old-age insurance, temporary and permanent disability payments underwritten by the federal government, unemployment benefits for veterans attempting to reenter civilian life, a federal employment service, and a restructuring of grants-in-aid to the states for public assistance.[56]

Although Roosevelt had no objections to the Wagner-Murray-Dingell bill[57] he was not yet prepared to endorse a measure quite so sweeping and, as a consequence, the bill died in committee. There is evidence that he once again wished to reserve the issue of national health care for the next presidential campaign in 1944 and for his fourth term, when he could personally sponsor the measure. During the campaign he called for an "Economic Bill of Rights," which included "the right to adequate medical care and the opportunity to achieve and enjoy good health" and "the right to adequate protection from the economic fears of old age, sickness, accident, and unemployment" and in his budget message of January 1945 he announced his intention of extending social security to include medical care.[58]

The idea of a government-administered health insurance scheme appears to have been received with so much popularity in some areas of the country that it was even taken up by some prominent Republican politicians in an effort to curry favor with the voters. In 1945, Governor Earl Warren of California, who was to become the Republican vice-presidential nominee in 1948, proposed passage of a compulsory health insurance bill to the California legislature. The California Medical Association expended substantial resources to defeat the measure but the events in California had brought the issue to national prominence.[59]

With Roosevelt's death in April 1945 Harry Truman took over the presidency committed to most of the same domestic policies as his predecessor. Truman was determined to carry through with Roosevelt's intentions respecting national health insurance and he made it a crucial part of his "Fair Deal" program. A few weeks after Japan's surrender in October 1945 Truman submitted a health message to Congress, accompanied by a slightly reworked version of the Wagner-Murray-Dingell bill for its consideration.[60] However, the revised bill was unable to obtain hearings in the House Ways and Means Committee prior to the elections of 1946, at which point the Republicans, for the first time since 1932, held majorities in both the Senate and the House of Representatives. Nevertheless, one title of the Wagner-Murray-Dingell bill, relating to federal grants for hospital construction, was enacted into law in 1946. The Hill-Burton Hospital Survey and Construction Act was to have an enormous impact on the shape, direction, and extent of American hospital care for the next twenty-five years.

The 1948 election, in which Truman was reelected and which returned control of Congress to the Democrats, revived the hopes of those supporting national health insurance. This was especially true since the Democratic Party had called for passage of a health insurance bill in their platform and Truman had made congressional inaction on the proposal a major campaign issue. However, a coalition of Republicans and conservative Democrats was able to block yet another revision of the Wagner-Murray-Dingell bill once again. The AMA's unyielding opposition to any form of federal control of the nation's health delivery system, coupled with waning support from the labor unions who had switched their efforts to trying to obtain private health insurance coverage from employers, certainly made this decision more politically palatable.[61]

Attempts to enact a health insurance bill during the Truman era came to a definitive end with the election of 1950. A number of prominent proponents of the measure in Congress, including Senators Elbert D. Thomas of Utah and Glen H. Taylor of Idaho, were defeated, in large measure because of a vigorous and costly campaign by the American Medical Association. The AMA, as the preeminent lobbyist against compulsory health insurance, had succeeded in associating Truman's plan in the mind of the public with notions of socialism, now in disrepute thanks to the Cold War mentality Truman himself had so energetically encouraged. By mid-1951 the Association was confident enough that it had made impossible any serious attempt to reintroduce the measure it began reducing the scale of its propaganda operations.[62] Nor was the issue raised in President Truman's State of the Union address in 1952.

Despite these setbacks, there remained substantial support both among politicians and the public for some form of government-administered compulsory health insurance. While Truman's closest advisors agreed that there was little chance of enacting legislation of the sort called for in the Wagner-Murray-Dingell bill, whose provisions would have universal applicability, two officials in the Federal Security Agency,[63] Wilbur J. Cohen—instrumental in drafting the original Social Security Act of 1935 and later to become Secretary of Health, Education, and Welfare—and I. S. Falk, conceived of resurrecting a health insurance scheme by limiting its coverage to social security beneficiaries.[64] The proposal was enthusiastically received by Oscar Ewing, the director of the Federal Security Agency and, according to one analyst, "shaped the entire strategy of health insurance advocates in the period after 1951."[65] The idea of restricting coverage to the elderly was politically brilliant. Among the principal criticisms leveled against a general compulsory health insurance plan were that it did not distinguish between the deserving and undeserving poor and that it covered those who were well off as well as those in need. Since it appeared intuitively obvious that the elderly as a group were less likely to afford, while at the same time more apt to have need of, medical care, no means test would be necessary to determine which recipients required assistance.[66] In addition, Americans had been gulled into accepting the notion that social security was in fact a funded program in principle no different from any other savings plan, thus depriving it of much of the onus of a welfare measure. Finally, in order to assuage the fears of physicians that a government-administered health insurance plan would eventually lead to control of the medical system by a health care bureaucracy, the new plan's coverage excluded physicians' services.[67]

In 1952, the Social Security Administration's annual report recommended enactment of health insurance for social security beneficiaries and this recommendation was echoed by the President's Commission on the Health Needs of the Nation later that year. The issue was soon to become moot, however, since General Eisenhower, who was soon to take office as President, had made clear his opposition to government health insurance. Yet, despite the Eisenhower administration's antipathy to an extension of government involvement in medical care, a series of occurrences in 1956 once again brought the issue of health insurance to public prominence. In that year Congress enacted a permanent program of health care coverage for the dependents of servicemen (what has been described as a military "medicare" program) and at the same time began debate on adding to the Social Security Act cash benefits to totally and permanently disabled persons over the age of fifty. Inasmuch as the proposed legislation required some government supervision of those private physicians who would be making the determination of medical disability, the AMA opposed the amendment. The battle between those supporting and opposing this extension of the social security program was viewed by many as a test of strength between physicians and health reformers and when the measure passed, supporters of government health insurance were elated.[68] Buoyed by passage of a disability insurance measure, a Democratic member of the House Ways and Means Committee, Aime J. Forand, introduced a medicare bill just prior to adjournment of the House in late 1957.

The public hearings on the bill, held in June 1958 before the House Ways and Means Committee, proved inconclusive. By this point a number of national groups had lined up on either side of the issue. Supporting the bill were the AFL-CIO, the National Farmers Union, the Group Health Association of America, the American Nurses Association, the American Public Welfare Association, and the National Association of Social Workers. Those opposed included the National Chamber of Commerce, the National Association of Manufacturers, the Pharmaceutical Manufacturers' Association, the American Farm Bureau Association, the Health Insurance Association of America, and, of course, the American Medical Association.[69]

The National Insurance Association of America had been recently formed and represented some 264 insurance companies. These firms had good reason to be fearful that a further extension of government insurance would again cut into their sales,[70] as had been the case with government life insurance for servicemen during the First and Second World Wars and, most dramatically, with the passage of social security and its extensions. Its spokesman at the Forand bill hearings in 1958 estimated that the costs of the measure would exceed $2 billion per year, not the $850 million predicted by its proponents.[71] In the event, of course, this proved a colossal underestimate.

Given the controversial nature of the Forand bill and the President's opposition the outcome of the proposal was inevitable and the measure died in committee. Hearings were again held in 1959, but with the same result. Finally, in March 1960 Forand was able to obtain a vote on the bill in the Committee, where it was defeated by a vote of 17 to 8. Yet, in spite of its defeat, momentum in support of the proposal seemed to be increasing. Both House Speaker Sam Rayburn and Senate Majority Leader Lyndon Johnson spoke in favor of the measure and lobbying on behalf of the bill increased substantially.[72]

Confronted with what appeared to be increasing popularity for a government-administered health insurance plan for the elderly the chairman of the Ways and Means Committee, Wilbur Mills, introduced a bill that would provide medical assistance—through the states—to a new class of recipients, the "medically indigent," to comprise the elderly who might not otherwise qualify for state welfare payments but who required help with their medical bills.[73] The proposal had the advantage of having been approved by the AMA, who saw no reason to oppose government-sponsored medical benefits if they were limited to those who were unlikely to seek medical help in the absence of a subsidy. In addition, Mill's proposal met the complaints of those who objected to instituting a tax-supported measure that would benefit the well-to-do and had the further advantage of being a Democratic bill. The bill was quickly approved by the Ways and Means Committee and by the full House and sent to the Senate. In the Senate, the measure was somewhat modified, renamed the Kerr-Mills bill after its Senate sponsor, Senator Robert Kerr of Oklahoma, and, in August 1960 passed by a vote of 91-2.[74]

Passage of Kerr-Mills by no means ended the agitation for a comprehensive health insurance program for the elderly and the defeat of the Forand bill provided a ready-made campaign issue for the Democratic Presidential candidate, John F. Kennedy. Kennedy, together with Clinton P. Anderson of New Mexico, had introduced a measure similar to the Forand bill in the Senate that summer and although the Kennedy-Anderson proposal was defeated in favor of Kerr-Mills the 1960 Democratic platform contained a provision supporting an extensive hospital insurance scheme for the aged. Indeed, to the surprise of both candidates, so much public interest appears to have been generated by the proposal that Kennedy made it a subject of his speeches far more often than he had originally intended.[75] Even prior to the new administration's taking office, a White House Conference on Aging again brought the issue of government health insurance to prominence and its advocates were encouraged by the fact that Eisenhower's Secretary of Health, Education, and Welfare, among several other prominent Republicans, joined them in supporting enactment of a comprehensive measure.[76]

On February 9, 1961, almost immediately following his inauguration, President Kennedy sent a message to Congress calling for the extension of social security benefits to cover hospital and nursing home costs. Sponsored by Senator Anderson and Representative Cecil King of California, the bill would have covered fourteen million recipients of social security over the age of sixty-five and provided for ninety days of hospital care, outpatient diagnostic services, and a hundred and eighty days of nursing home care. Curiously, the measure did not include the costs of medical or surgical treatment.[77] The annual costs of the program were estimated to be approximately a billion and a half dollars. However, in light of Kennedy's thin margin of victory in November and the fact that the Democrats had lost twenty seats in the House, it was deemed expedient not to press for passage of the measure until the following year.

The reaction of the American Medical Association was swift and vigorous. In April 1961 the Association had placed a seven-column advertisement in thirty-one newspapers attacking the King-Anderson bill. And one month later its Board of Trustees gave formal approval to the creation of a political action committee, the American Medical Political Action Committee (AMPAC).[78] Joining in opposition to the bill were the commercial health insurance carriers and Blue Cross-Blue Shield,[79] who questioned the cost estimates put forward by the Kennedy administration. Over the course of 1961 the AMA distributed millions of pamphlets and advertised extensively on radio and TV against government health insurance. Posters attacking the King-Anderson bill were sent to all members for display in their offices and physicians were encouraged to send leaflets containing the same text to all their patients. There seems little doubt that what particularly exercised the Association was that the measure included a fee schedule for hospitals, nursing homes, and nurses which could serve as a precedent should government insurance be expanded to include physicians' services.[80]

Despite strong support for a Social Security-supported plan of limited hospital care for the elderly both within the administration and among Democrats in Congress, the King-Anderson bill faced strong opposition from the powerful House Ways and Means Committee, the majority of whose members were either Republicans or Southern Democrats who opposed the measure. Unable to bring direct pressure on the membership of the Committee, the Kennedy administration decided to demonize the American Medical Association's opposition in the hope that the bill's critics would fear being branded as equally mean-spirited. The AMA was accused of thwarting the public will in the interests of lining the pockets of its membership and of employing the worst scare tactics against a government whose only concern was to extend to the aged and infirm needed medical benefits which otherwise would be denied them.

Supporting the efforts of the administration was organized labor, which lobbied extensively in favor of the measure, and several new organizations whose creation was, in large part, aided by the White House and the Democratic National Committee. Among them was the Physicians' Committee for Health Care through Social Security, whose formation was in part an outgrowth of the support extended King-Anderson by the American Public Health Association. The organization's chairman was Dr. Caldwell Esselstyn, former personal physician to Eleanor Roosevelt and president of the Group Health Association of America, and boasted among its members several well-known physicians including Drs. Benjamin Spock, Michael E. DeBakey, and Arthur Kornberg and Dickinson W. Richards, both Nobel laureates.[82]

In July 1961 organizers for the AFL-CIO aided in establishing the National Council of Senior Citizens, an outgrowth of the earlier Senior Citizens for Kennedy, once again chaired by retired Congressman Aime Forand. With a nucleus of union retiree organizations[83] as its base, the Council soon attracted other associations of seniors, among them a number of union and church groups, whose affiliation brought the Council's membership to more than one million people. The size of its membership and the fact that older voters had played a decisive role in Kennedy's victory in a number of key districts led to the Council receiving financial support from the Democratic National Committee. The Council's agitation culminated in a rally in Madison Square Garden in May 1962 at which President Kennedy himself spoke. Before twenty thousand enthusiastic supporters of the administration's health care bill and a TV audience estimated at more than twenty million people, the President proceeded to deliver one of the worst speeches of his political career. Not only did it fail to rouse the general public in support of the King-Anderson bill, but it left the impression in the minds of many that the President's own support for the measure was at best lukewarm.[84]

Meanwhile, during the spring of 1962 there appears to have been some small movement in favor of some form of health care bill in the House Ways and Means Committee. Hearings before the Ways and

Means Committee the previous year had proved inconclusive; the testimony reflected the same divisions as had existed earlier, and in the late summer of 1961 the House Speaker reported that fifteen Congressmen opposed King-Anderson while only ten supported it.[85] However, a proposal to limit coverage to instances where the elderly were faced with "catastrophic" charges appears to have won the tentative support of three Representatives who would otherwise have voted against the bill, changing the tally to thirteen in favor with twelve against. In return for their support the Committee members involved demanded that the Kerr-Mills program be repealed and that the elderly who had earlier retired be required to contribute premiums in order to qualify for benefits, conditions the White House was not prepared to concede.[86] As a consequence no compromise was reached in the end. After three weeks of executive sessions on King-Anderson in the late spring of 1962, Committee support and opposition to King-Anderson remained exactly as before.

The congressional stalemate continued following the congressional elections of 1962. While the Democrats maintained control of Congress, the King-Anderson bill, by now commonly referred to as Medicare, still did not command a majority in the House.[87] Both opponents and supporters of the measure had made determined efforts to influence the electorate but foreign policy appears to have been of far greater importance in the minds of most voters in November 1962 than was the government's health insurance plan. Indeed, the AMA's campaign against those candidates who had supported Medicare was a failure and not one seat in either the Senate or the House was lost by a candidate who had endorsed the bill.[88]

In the wake of the assassination of President Kennedy in November 1963, Congressional support for Kennedy's legislative program swelled. Large numbers of politicians rushed to embrace many of the proposals Kennedy had put forward as if by doing so they could more clearly distance themselves from the actions of his murderer. President Johnson, a longtime master of legislative manipulation, was able to play upon these simpleminded sentiments to push for enactment of a host of reform measures, among them Medicare. In one of his earliest speeches to Congress Johnson referred to Medicare as "one of his top priorities"[89] and in March 1964 the *Wall Street Journal* predicted that the measure was "a good bet to come out of Congress this year."[90] Under intense pressure from President Johnson, the Senate Finance

Committee finally agreed to hold public hearings on the King-Anderson bill in August 1964. And, although the measure again failed in committee, its supporters were able to bring it to the floor of the Senate without committee sanction as an amendment to a bill authorizing increased social security benefits. On September 2, 1964, the full Senate passed the amendment by a vote of 49 to 44, thus putting the Senate on record as approving a mandatory federal health insurance scheme for the elderly.[91] The vote was a particularly bitter defeat for the Republican presidential candidate, Barry Goldwater, who had flown back from Arizona solely for the purpose of casting his vote against the measure.

Meanwhile, support for Medicare was gaining headway in the House Ways and Means Committee. By 1964 two Democratic seats on the Committee previously held by anti-Medicare Southerners had opened up as a consequence of retirement. These were filled by Representatives who ultimately pledged themselves to support a Medicare bill, thus narrowing the division against mandatory health insurance for the elderly to twelve votes for as opposed to thirteen against.[92] In light of the actions of the Senate in September, however, the Johnson administration conceived the notion of bypassing the Committee entirely. Since Senate passage of Medicare had taken the form of a rider to a previously enacted House bill, the differences between the two measures would have to be reconciled by a Senate-House conference committee. Were the House to pass a resolution instructing its conferees on the Senate-House committee to vote for the Medicare provisions earlier enacted by the Senate, a vote in the Ways and Means Committee would no longer be necessary before presenting the reconciled bill to the full House for a vote. This would, of course, have meant that the Ways and Means Committee would lose control over the content of any Medicare bill finally enacted by the House. Anticipating this, Wilbur Mills, Ways and Means' chairman, was able to prevail upon the pro-Medicare Democrats on the Committee to reject the rider in return for his promise that a Medicare bill would "be the first order of business" in the following year.[93]

The November election proved decisive in the history of Medicare. President Johnson's campaign underscored the central importance of extending social security benefits to cover health care costs, while Barry Goldwater was adamantly opposed to the plan. It became a central issue in the campaigns of many congressional candidates who supported the measure while at the same time organized medicine devoted substantial sums either directly or through political action committees in an attempt to defeat Medicare's chief defenders.[94] In the event, the election proved a disaster for Medicare's opponents. In the House, the Democrats gained thirty-eight seats while the pro-Medicare majority appears to have increased by forty-four seats.[95] In almost every instance organized medicine had been unsuccessful in defeating those candidates who had made passage of a Medicare bill a key aspect of their campaign. Of the fourteen physicians who ran for Congress in the election eleven lost, and of the three that were elected one was a Medicare supporter.[96] More important, as a consequence of the election and of changes to House rules brought in by the new Congress, the composition of the Ways and Means Committee was altered from fifteen Democrats and ten Republicans to seventeen Democrats and eight Republicans.[97]

There seems little question that the electoral outcome was due in large part to the strong support given pro-Medicare candidates by older voters. It has been estimated that approximately 22 percent of Americans who voted in the 1964 election were over the age of sixty and that two million of these had switched from voting Republican to voting Democratic. In addition, all ten states with the highest percentage of elderly voters, seven of which were traditionally Republican, voted Democratic.[98] The prominence given the prospective passage of a Medicare bill during the campaign led to its being given pride-of-place in the 89th Congress. The King-Anderson bill was the first bill introduced into each chamber (H.R. 1 and S. 1) when Congress convened on January 4, 1965. Three days later the President, in a Special Message to Congress, urged swift passage of the measure. The bill thus brought before Congress at the beginning of 1965 was, in almost every important respect, similar to the measure earlier introduced by Representative King and Senator Anderson in 1963 and approved by the Senate in 1964.[99] The measure was thus a hospital insurance scheme only and did not cover physicians' services, although apparently most voters believed that physicians' fees were included among the bill's benefits.[100]

Since it now appeared inevitable that Congress and the Administration would proceed to enact a bill mandating compulsory health insurance for the elderly, the American Medical Association was confronted with the option of either acceding to the provisions of King-Anderson or of trying to amend the measure so that its shape was more to organized medicine's liking. As a consequence, in early January 1965 the AMA proposed an alternative, which it called "Eldercare," that would have expanded the Medical Assistance (MAA) for the Aged program established under the Kerr-Mills Act.[101] The Eldercare bill would have allowed MAA funds to be used for either partial or full payment of the premium costs of private health insurance while at the same time substantially easing the means test requirements imposed by Kerr-Mills. On 27 January two members of the Ways and Means Committee, Thomas B. Curtis (R-Mo.) and A. Sydney Herlong (D-Fla.), introduced legislation along these lines, underscoring the fact that King-Anderson limited benefits to hospital services while their proposal provided far more sweeping coverage.

The AMA's campaign in support of Eldercare,[102] which concentrated on the comprehensive coverage afforded by the bill, appears to have struck a sympathetic chord among the electorate. In a survey financed by the AMA during January and February 1965 it was found that about 72 percent of respondents agreed that any government health insurance plan should cover physicians' fees.[103] Far from weakening support for King-Anderson, however, the survey served to encourage the bill's more ardent adherents to expand its provisions to include a whole range of medical services. Most Congressional backers of a government health insurance plan were in fact secretly delighted with the results of the AMA poll since it signaled widespread popular support for extending the coverage offered by King-Anderson.

To further complicate matters, yet a third bill was introduced in the Ways and Means Committee by its ranking Republican member, John Byrnes of Wisconsin. Fearful of being deprived of any credit for a health insurance law, the Republicans on the Committee proposed what amounted to an extension of the private health insurance plan then offered by the Aetna Life Insurance Company to federal employees. The plan called for the creation of a government-administered insurance scheme for the elderly that covered not only hospital expenses but both physicians' services and the costs of drugs and permitted older Americans to either opt out of the scheme or not, as they saw fit.

Rather than choose between these various alternatives, Wilbur Mills, the Committee's Chairman, hit upon the idea of combining the most ambitious components of all three bills into a new proposal. Mills' suggestion was quickly embraced by the Administration, who regarded it as insurance against any Republican attack.[104] On March 23, 1965, the Ways and Means Committee voted 17 to 8 to substitute Mills' bill for King-Anderson and on the following day the bill was introduced on the House floor. Finally, on April 8, after only one day of floor debate, the Mills bill was passed without amendment by a vote of 313 to 115. The features of the new bill were incorporated into two amendments to the Social Security Act which provided in Title 18 for a universal hospital insurance program for the elderly and for optional coverage of physicians' services while Title 19 (since known as Medicaid) expanded the Kerr-Mills program of medical coverage for the needy.

The Mills bill was then referred to the Senate for its consideration. There was no question that the more liberal Senate would enact some form of health insurance but exactly what its shape would be remained uncertain. The Finance Committee, chaired by Russell Long of Louisiana, held public hearings on the bill during late April and early May and met in executive session to consider the measure during the following month. The Mills bill was eventually reported out of committee on June 24 by a vote of 12 to 5, having been amended no less than seventy-five times.[105] The full Senate, having considered a further 250 amendments, passed the measure on July 9 by a 68 to 21 vote and the bill, as amended, was then sent to a Senate-House conference committee whose task it was to resolve the over 500 differences between the two chambers.[106]

On July 27 the House passed the bill as finally revised, officially part of the Social Security Amendments of 1965, by a vote of 307 in favor with 116 opposed and the next day the Senate approved the measure by a vote of 70 to 24. Finally, on July 30, 1965, President Johnson, having flown to Independence, Missouri, to append his signature to the Medicare bill in the presence of former President Truman, signed the measure into law.

The main provisions of the 1965 legislation were as follows:[107]

Title XVIII, Part A: Hospital Insurance (HI) provided that all persons over the age of sixty-five otherwise entitled to benefits under the Social Security or Railroad Retirement Acts were eligible and were automatically covered. Benefits were to be measured in sixty-day periods, each period ending sixty days following discharge from a hospital or extended-care facility. During each benefit period subscribers were entitled to up to ninety days in a hospital, one hundred days in an extended care facility, and home-care benefits for up to one year after the most recent discharge from either a hospital or extended-care facility. (In 1967, Congress amended this provision to add to each beneficiary's coverage an additional lifetime reserve period of sixty days of hospital care.) Care in either a psychiatric or tuberculosis hospital was limited to a lifetime amount of 190 days, provided the patient was certified by a physician as being "reasonably expected to improve." Subscribers were required to impose a "front-end" deductible for each hospital stay of up to ninety days (initially $40, by 1997 this amount had risen to $760 for the first sixty days and an additional $190 for days 61-90). No front-end deductibles were imposed for the use of extended care facilities for the first twenty days but after that point a daily copayment was levied (in 1997 this amount was $95.00). The program was financed by earmarked payroll taxes levied on employers and employees and disbursements were made from this fund either directly to providers or through an intermediary insurance company who then reimbursed the provider. The rate of reimbursement was ostensibly based on "reasonable costs."

Title XVIII, Part B: Supplementary Medical Insurance (SMI). All persons over sixty-five were eligible for participation in this program on a voluntary basis, without the requirement that they had earlier paid into the Social Security program. Benefits included physicians' services at any location and home health services of up to one hundred visits per year. Coverage also included the costs of diagnostic tests, radiotherapy, ambulance services, and various medical supplies and appliances certified as necessary by the patient's physician. Subscribers were at first required to pay one-half the monthly premium, with the federal government underwriting the other half. After July 1973 premium increases levied on subscribers were limited to "the percentage by which Social Security cash benefits [had] been increased since the last . . . premium adjustment." Each enrollee was subject to a front-end deductible ($50 per year originally, $100 in 1997). After having met this payment, patients were responsible for a coinsurance of 20 percent of the remaining "reasonable" charges. Limits were set on the amount of psychiatric care and routine physical examinations. Among the exclusions were eye refraction and other preventive services, such as immunizations and hearing aids. The cost of drugs was totally excluded. Similar financing arrangements as prevailed for Part

A coverage were put in place for Part B for the payment of benefits. Premium payments were placed in a trust fund, which made disbursements to private insurance companies—carriers—who reimbursed providers on a "reasonable cost" or, in the case of physicians, "reasonable charge" basis. Physicians were permitted to "extra bill" patients if they regarded the fee schedule established by the carriers as insufficient payment.

Title XIX: Medicaid. The 1965 legislation provided states a number of options regarding their level of participation in Medicaid, ranging from opting out of the program entirely to including all covered services for all eligible classes of persons. The federal government provided matching funds for two of the three groups stipulated in the legislation (the "categorically needy" and those "categorically linked," while in the case of the third group ("not categorically linked but medically indigent") only administrative funds (and no medical expenses) were matched. Each state was required to include members of the first group, the categorically needy, in a medical care program acceptable to the Department of Health, Education, and Welfare, while inclusion of the other groups was optional. Eligibility standards varied (and continue to vary) from state to state, depending on state legislation.[108] The three groups were:

1. The Categorically Needy. This group included all persons receiving federally matching public welfare assistance, including Families with Dependent Children, the permanently and totally disabled, the blind, and the elderly whose resources fell below welfare-stipulated levels. The federal government matched state expenditures from 50 to 80 percent, depending on the state's per capita income.

2. The Categorically Linked. This class included persons who fell into one of the four federally assisted categories whose resources exceeded the ceiling for cash assistance. Should the state designate members of this class as medically indigent, benefits had to be extended to all four subgroups. The amount of federal matching funds was determined by the same formula as was used for the Categorically Needy.

3. Not Categorically Linked but Medically Indigent. Members of this group could include those eligible for statewide general assistance and those between the ages of twenty-one and sixty-five deemed medically indigent. State operating expenses were not matched by the federal government, who confined their grants to matching the costs of administering the program if the benefits extended to members of this group were comparable to those provided to other groups.

Among the benefits that the various states were required to provide recipients were (1) inpatient hospital care (other than in an institution for tuberculosis or mental disease), (2) outpatient hospital services, (3) laboratory and x-ray services, (4) nursing facility services for those over the ages of twenty-one (and, after July 1, 1970, to home health services), and (5) physicians' services, regardless of location of treatment. In addition, states could underwrite a host of other services, including physical therapy, dental care, diagnostic, preventive, and rehabilitative services, and the cost of prescribed drugs, dentures, prosthetic devices, and eyeglasses. The elderly insured by Medicare who were also eligible by virtue of their incomes for Medicaid had their hospital deductibles and copayments paid by Medicaid.[109]

In 1967, the Johnson administration proposed amendments to the Social Security program that included extending Medicare benefits to the disabled who were otherwise eligible for cash payments. To pay for this extension, a higher earnings base on which Medicare taxes would be levied was recommended. From the then current $6,600, the amount was to rise to $7,800 in 1968, $9,000 in 1971, and $10,800 in 1974 and thereafter. Despite strong support from the administration, the House Ways and Means Committee voted to defer consideration of the extension in light of the substantial costs associated with the amendment. While it had been the administration's contention that medical costs per disabled beneficiary would prove to be about the same as those associated with Medicare recipients over the age of sixty-five, a study released while the bill was before the committee indicated that in fact these costs would be about two and a half to three times as high.[110]

It was clear following the first full year of operation of the Hospital Insurance program that its costs significantly exceeded the estimates put forward by the program's proponents.[111] The main purpose of enacting a national health insurance bill had been, after all, to encourage greater use of health care facilities by the elderly. It was therefore not surprising that with the measure's passage there should have been an increased demand for hospital and medical services. However, not only was there greater utilization of medical facilities on the part of those covered by the Medicare program, but there followed a far higher increase in the prices of covered services than had been expected. The following table gives some idea of the disparity between the original estimates for hospital insurance and supplementary medical insurance programs and their actual costs for 1966 and 1967:

TABLE 1.1

Comparison of Estimates (E) with Actual Costs (A) of Hospital Insurance and Supplementary Medical Insurance, Calendar Years 1966-1967[a]
(in millions of dollars)

| | Hospital Insurance | | | | Medical Insurance | | | |
| | 1996 | | 1967 | | 1966 | | 1967 | |
	(E)	(A)	(E)	(A)	(E)	(A)	(E)	(A)
Benefit payments	1,023	891	2,477	3,353	324	128	1,124	1,197
Administrative expenses	54	107	77	77	87	74	97	110
Total	1,077	998	2,554	3,430	411	202	1,221	1,307

Source: Robert J. Myers, Medicare (Bryn Mawr, PA: McCahan Foundation, 1970): Tables 11-16 and 11-17 (pp. 253-254).

[a] Cost estimates are intermediate and are determined by averaging low-cost and high-cost estimates.

In light of these data, Congress increased the contribution schedule along the lines suggested by the administration despite its not having incorporated the disabled among the program's beneficiaries.

By 1972 the costs associated with Medicare had increased at such a rate that even the administration and Congress were expressing concern.[112] As a consequence a number of studies were undertaken to examine whether the cause of this rise was attributable primarily to the increased use of medical facilities or to the higher prices that followed in the wake of increased demand.[113] Among the conclusions reached was that hospital service charges rose much faster than the Consumer Price Index and additionally faster than the medical care component of that index. Further, over the course of the first five years of Medicare that ended in 1971 physicians' charges rose 39 percent, compared with a 15 percent rise in the five years before the advent of Medicare. In real terms (that is, adjusted for the increase in the Consumer Price Index), Medicare physicians' charges rose by 11 percent from 1966 to 1971. Equally important, the proportion of total health care expenditures of the elderly that originated in public sources rose far more sharply than had been expected prior to Medicare's passage. In fiscal year 1966, government programs provided 31 percent of the total expended on health care for the elderly. Just one year later this proportion had risen to 59 percent and Medicare alone accounted for thirty-five cents of every dollar spent on health services by or for those over the age of 65.

Even more dramatic increases occurred in the Medicaid program during its first few years. The wording of Title XIX provided that the federal government had an open-ended obligation to help underwrite the costs of medical care for a wide range of services to a large number of possible recipients, depending on state legislation. There was therefore no accurate way of predicting the ultimate costs of the program. In 1965 the House Ways and Means Committee had estimated that if all the states were to take full advantage of the program—that is, if each state were to include all the services to which each possible beneficiary could receive assistance and if all categories of possible beneficiaries were included at the highest level of eligibility—the additional federal cost of medical assistance (beyond that already provided by previously existing programs) would amount to $238,000,000. However, in fiscal year 1967 total Medicaid payments amounted to $1,944,000,000, about half of which were federal funds, in a program that was operating in only twenty-eight states. It is true that with the introduction of Medicaid, federal funding for other programs (for example, Medical Assistance for the Aged) sharply declined. Yet even if the drop in expenditures for these other programs are factored in, federal outlays increased dramatically. By the end of the calendar year 1968 forty-one states had opted into the Medicaid program and total expenditures (of which about 50.1 percent were federal) amounted to $3,783,000,000. (As a point of comparison, total federal outlays for all medical assistance programs in fiscal year 1965, prior to the introduction of Medicare and Medicaid, amounted to $1,239,000,000.)

In 1971, the House Ways and Means Committee, still under the chairmanship of Wilbur Mills, began hearings on a new H.R. 1, whose goal was to contain the spiraling costs of Medicare and Medicaid. Among the large number of individuals and organizations that testified before the committee were members of the Nixon administration who suggested a whole series of cost-control measures, among them that new legislation promote a system of capitation payments to health maintenance organizations (HMOs) and that Medicaid introduce cost sharing while Medicare expand its own cost sharing policies. Many of these recommendations eventually found their way into the final bill to reform these programs, which became law in October 1972. Among the changes to the Medicare program was (1) the inclusion of the totally disabled as eligible for Medicare benefits. Workers of any age and widows and disabled dependent widowers over the age of fifty were eligible to receive Medicare benefits after having received APTD (Aid to Permanently and Totally Disabled) assistance for twenty-four months. This added approximately 1,700,000 beneficiaries to the Medicare rolls and was the first instance of any group under the age of sixty-five being made eligible for benefits. Additionally, (2) beneficiaries of Part B (Supplementary Medical Insurance) who otherwise were ineligible for Part A (Hospital Insurance) by virtue of not qualifying for Social Security coverage could now voluntarily enroll in Part A by paying a monthly premium, and (3) provision was made for capitation payments to HMOs and certain limits were placed on the items that a health care facility could include in calculating its cost.

Perhaps the most significant change to the Medicaid program contained in the 1972 amendments was the repeal of a provision contained in the 1965 legislation that made it mandatory that each state expand its Medicaid program each year until it offered comprehensive coverage for all the medically needy by 1977. When Medicare and Medicaid were first introduced, Congress had hoped to establish a universal hospital and medical insurance scheme for the needy using Medicaid as its foundation but largely as a result of the swelling costs of the program this design was abandoned in 1972.[115]

A further provision of the 1972 legislation was the establishment of Professional Standards Review Organizations (PSROs), whose function it was to assume responsibility for monitoring the costs, degree of utilization, and quality of care of medical services offered under Medicare and Medicaid. It was hoped that these PSROs would compel hospitals to act more efficiently.[116] In keeping with this goal, in 1974 a reimbursement cap was instituted that limited hospitals from charging more than 120 percent of the mean of routine costs in effect in similar facilities, a limit later reduced to 112 percent.[117] Despite these attempts at holding down costs, they continued to escalate inasmuch as hospitals were still reimbursed on the basis of their expenses and the caps that were instituted applied only to room and board and not to ancillary services, which remained unregulated.[118] The following table will give some idea of the costs associated with the Medicare program from its inception to the mid-1980s:

TABLE 1.2

Medicare Benefit Payments and Annual Percentage Change, 1966-1984

Year	Total (billions)	Hospital Insurance (billions)	Supplementary Medical Insurance (billions)	Annual Change (%)
1966	$ 1.0	$ 0.9	$ 0.1	—
1967	4.6	3.4	1.2	346.5
1968	5.7	4.2	1.5	25.2
1969	6.6	4.7	1.9	15.9
1970	7.1	5.1	2.0	7.5
1971	7.9	5.8	2.1	10.8
1972	8.6	6.3	2.3	9.9
1973	9.6	7.1	2.5	10.9
1974	12.4	9.1	3.3	29.6
1975	15.6	11.3	4.3	25.5
1976	18.4	13.3	5.1	18.2
1977	21.8	15.7	6.0	18.2
1978	24.9	17.7	7.3	14.5
1979	29.3	20.6	8.7	17.6
1980	35.7	25.1	10.6	21.7
1981	43.5	30.3	13.1	21.7
1982	51.1	35.6	15.5	17.6
1983	57.4	39.3	18.1	12.4
1984	62.9	43.3	19.7	9.5
ACRG[a]	16.6%	16.1%	17.9%	
ACRRG[b]	9.1%	8.6%	10.3%	

---

a Annual compound rate of growth.
b 1967 to 1984: Annual compound rate of real growth (that is, the rate of growth adjusted for changes in the Consumer Price Index, 1967-1984).

Source: Marian Gornick, Jay N. Greenberg, Paul W. Eggers, et al., "Twenty Years of Medicare and Medicaid: Covered Populations, Use of Benefits, and Program Expenditures," *Health Care Financing Review, 1985, Annual Supplement,* 43.

It had been surmised by some analysts during the 1970s that escalating hospital expenditures could be largely accounted for by increases in input prices that exceeded the general increase in consumer prices and that price controls on hospital expenditures might prove effective in limiting Medicare costs. This theory, that an inflation in the price of hospital input prices was the driving force behind rising Medicare costs, was tested by, among others, John Virts and George Wilson, who concluded that somewhat less than half the change in hospital expenditures between 1965 and 1972 could be attributed to changes in price, while over 40 percent was attributable to changes in utilization. The following table summarizes their findings:

TABLE 1.3

Sources of Change in Hospital Expenditures, 1965-1981

	1965-1981 $ billions	%	1965-1972 $ billions	%	1972-1981 billions	%
Change in prices	67.3	64.6	10.1	48.1	57.2	68.8
Change in utilization	28.2	27.1	9.2	43.8	19.0	22.9
Change in population	8.6	8.3	1.7	8.1	6.9	8.3
Total	04.1	100.0	21.0	100.0	83.1	100.0

Source: Jack A. Meyer, *Passing the Health Care Buck: Who Pays the Hidden Cost?* (Washington, DC: American Enterprise Institute for Public Policy Research, 1983): 48.

Virts and Wilson further found that of the $57.2 billion in increased hospital expenditures that could be attributed to price changes during the ten years from 1972 to 1981 no more than $7.1 billion (somewhat less than 10 percent of the total increase in hospital expenditures) could be ascribed to inflationary rises peculiar to the health care sector. The implications of the Virts-Wilson study are clear: beyond a general increase in all prices, increased utilization was the single most important factor responsible for the unrelenting rise in Medicare hospital costs.

In 1974 new legislation was enacted whose goal was to reduce the construction of new hospitals in the hope that this would diminish overall utilization of hospital facilities and thus lessen the rate of increase in Medicare-Medicaid expenditures. The National Health Planning and Resource Development Act mandated that certificate-of-need (CON) programs be instituted in each of the states to regulate the construction of new health care facilities. Since little could be done to limit the demand for medical services that were effectively underwritten by the government, it was hoped that limiting the supply of these services might act as a brake on rising costs. This program too was of limited value despite its huge costs, having had little impact on new hospital construction.

With the election of Ronald Reagan some attempt was made to cut Medicare and Medicaid funding. Toward this end the PSRO program, which had proved a disaster, was all but abolished and, with passage of the Omnibus Budget Reconciliation Act (OBRA) of 1981, limits were placed on reimbursements for a large number of inpatient and outpatient services. The main thrust of OBRA however, was not Medicare but Medicaid. Under the Act's provisions, federal transfers to the states were to be reduced over the course of three years and the states themselves were empowered to limit the services extended to beneficiaries. The Tax Equity and Fiscal Responsibility Act (TEFRA), enacted in 1982, introduced a flat payment per hospital patient based on the historic average cost of care and instituted a ceiling on increases in hospital revenue. This act also permitted states to require copayments from most Medicaid recipients, altered the terms under which HMOs entered into risk-sharing contracts to make them more attractive, and made Medicare the secondary, rather than the primary, insurer in the case of workers under the age of seventy covered by a company health insurance plan.

The combined effect of the OBRA and TEFRA reforms was to introduce hospital budget caps for Medicare patients. These caps, which reimbursed medical facilities on the basis of average cost without regard to variations in severity of illness, were regarded as unworkable by the nation's hospitals, who lobbied for some change in these provisions. Denied any flexibility by TEFRA, hospitals were left with no room to benefit from any increases in efficiency they might introduce. As a consequence, most hospitals in 1982 regarded almost any change in Medicare's method of payment as preferable to the existing arrangements and it was this that appears to have eased the way for radical payment reform. The result of their lobbying was the Social

Security amendments of 1983, which replaced Medicare's cost-based system of reimbursement for hospitals (which in 1983 accounted for more than 68 percent of total Medicare expenditures) with a Prospective Payment System (PPS), under which the program currently operates.

Henceforth, hospitals were to be paid a prospectively determined rate per patient per stay, based on a diagnosis of each Medicare patent's illness. Upon discharge each patient is categorized as having fallen into a Diagnosis-Related Group (DRG) which in turn determines the amount of reimbursement Medicare is prepared to make. Payments to hospitals are adjusted for the average wage rate in the community in which the hospital is located, whether the facility is situated in an urban, large urban, or rural area, and whether it is a teaching hospital. Given that fairly large regional differences existed in hospital expenses and fearful that what amounted to national pricing for hospital care might result in substantial transfers of federal dollars from high to low-income areas, these national rates were to be phased in over a period of four years. Under this new system of payment, hospitals would no longer have an incentive to encourage long hospital stays and to perform unnecessary tests and medical procedures, as seems to have been the case when they were reimbursed retrospectively on the basis of their costs. Rather, these facilities would now be able to garner any rewards for increases in efficiency in the delivery of medical care or for reducing the costs per patient while he was undergoing treatment.

The most effective way of cutting costs is, of course, to limit the length of a patient's hospital stay for any particular illness. While the length of stay had been decreasing for Medicare beneficiaries (and for the population as a whole) for several years, this trend accelerated following the introduction of PPS; from 1983 to 1985 the average hospital stay for Medicare patients declined from 9.7 days to 8.7 days. In 1985 there were 22.8 million fewer hospital days as compared with 1983, no doubt in part in response to the incentives generated by Medicare's new method of calculating payments to health care facilities. Despite this decline, however, Medicare expenditures continued to increase. This appears to have resulted largely from shifting some procedures that had been routinely performed on an inpatient basis to the outpatient departments of hospitals and to doctors' offices. Thus, certain tests and some surgery (for example, cataract surgery) are now conducted almost exclusively on an outpatient basis and it is the policy of most hospitals to "unbundle" tests performed on Medicare patients either immediately before their admission or immediately after their discharge from a hospital.

The PPS reforms did not address the question of Medicare's physician reimbursement costs under Supplementary Medical Insurance, which had been increasing substantially. In fact, over the course of the 1980s, the growth in physician payments had actually outpaced the growth in hospital costs, which had been moderating in response to the Prospective Payment System. Between 1975 and 1982, the number of physicians' services employed by the average Medicare beneficiary increased by 6 percent per year. In 1970, Medicare spent $1.8 billion on physicians' services; by 1983 this amount had reached $14 billion. Indeed, during this period, expenditures for physicians' services were growing more rapidly than any other component of the Medicare program or, in fact, any other program in the federal domestic budget. Between 1970 and 1983, Medicare payments to doctors grew at a rate of over 17 percent per year. As a consequence of this dramatic increase, a freeze was put on the "prevailing charge"—the absolute cap on physicians' charges allowed by Medicare. However, in the wake of intense lobbying by physicians' groups, this freeze was lifted in 1986. Not only did the administration support reform in Medicare's payment structure for physicians, but a large number of practitioners supported some reform because of the system's perceived inequities. For example, physicians were paid far more for high-technology services than for basic care and, more important, practitioners in rural areas were compensated at substantially lower rates than those practicing in cities, thereby encouraging physicians to congregate in urban areas.

Agitation for reform led Congress in 1986 to establish a Physician Payment Review Commission whose function was to recommend to Congress and the Reagan administration how the payment system should be altered. Among the Commission's recommendations was a resource-based, relative value scale that was later to form the basis of the fee schedule passed into law in 1989. Under the terms of the relevant provisions of the Budget Reconciliation Act of 1989, payments for surgical interventions and other expensive procedures were reduced while reimbursements for office visits were substantially increased. The legislation called for these reforms to be phased in starting in January 1992, and to be fully in place by 1996. The new fee schedule is based on an incredibly complex system of "relative value units" awarded to each procedure on the basis of the time and complexity (and desirability) of the service performed. Beyond establishing the fee schedule the 1989 legislation further limited physicians' ability to extra-bill Medicare patients. Physicians who decline to "accept assignment" may bill their Medicare patients no more than 10 percent above the fee schedule. While the new fee schedule is far from simple (it contains over 7,000 codes and 233 geographic areas and occupies 317 pages in the Federal Register), the Health Care Financing Administration has attempted to calculate its impact on various medical specialties when compared with the method of payment in place prior to 1992.

TABLE 1.4

Impact of Medicare Fee Schedule by Physician Speciality

Speciality	Change in Payments per Service (%)
Family practice	28
General practice	27
Cardiology	-17
Internal medicine	5
Gastroenterology	-18
Neurology	- 4
Psychiatry	3
Urology	- 8
Radiology	-22
Anesthesiology	-27
Pathology	-20
General surgery	13
Ophthalmology	-21
Orthopedic surgery	-11
Thoracic surgery	-27
All specialities	- 6

Source: Marilyn Moon, *Medicare Now and in the Future* (Washington, DC: The Urban Institute Press, 1993) Table 3.5 (p. 70).

As had been the case with the introduction of a PPS method of reimbursement for hospital care, the effect of these reforms in payments to physicians appears to have been to moderate the increase in the costs of physicians' services and to decrease disbursements to physicians as a percent of total Medicare costs. However, payments to physicians continued to increase and are projected to reach $104 billion by the year 2000.

TABLE 1.5

Medicare Expenditures for Physicians' Services, Selected Years

Year	Amount (billions)	Percent of Total Supplementary Insurance Expenditures
1970	1.8	90.6
1975	3.4	79.9
1983	14.1	77.7
1984	15.4	78.5
1985	17.3	75.4
1986	19.2	73.2
1987	22.6	73.4
1988	24.4	71.7
1989	27.1	70.7
1990	29.6	69.6
1991	32.3	68.3
1992	32.4	65.7
1993	35.3	65.4
1994	38.1	n/a
1995 (FY est.)	40.0	n/a
1996 (FY est.)	45.6	n/a

Source: 1970 to 1993: Health Care Financing Administration, *Health Care Financing Review, Medicare and Medicaid Statistical Supplement, 1995*: Table 55 (pp. 280-81); 1994: Katharine R. Levit, et al., "National Health Expenditures, 1994," *Health Care Financing Review,* 17:3 (spring 1996): Table 17 (pp. 239-40); 1995 and 1996: "National Health Care Expenditures: Medicare Benefit Outlays," Washington, DC, October 1996 (http://www.hcfa. gov/stats/nhce96.htm).

In light of the Reagan administration's ostensible concern to reintroduce market forces into the various government programs affecting hospital and medical services and in the face of the spectacular growth in Medicare and Medicaid costs, it is almost beyond comprehension that the largest expansion of the Medicare program since its inception occurred under Reagan's presidency. In June 1988, Congress enacted the Medicare Catastrophic Coverage Act, which was signed amid the

usual pageantry in the Rose Garden on July 1. The Act was the product of recommendations put forward by the Bowen Commission, which
had earlier been empaneled by the President. The Commission, chaired
by a former Secretary of Health and Human Services, Otis Bowen,
was charged with the task of studying the issue of catastrophic health
costs, including both acute and long-term care. This problem appears
to have been particularly severe in the case of the elderly who, by
1987, were spending about the same proportion of their incomes on
health care as had obtained before the advent of Medicare. The Bowen
Commission released its final report in the fall of 1986 and limited
itself to recommendations respecting acute care for Medicare beneficiaries, which it regarded as most amenable to a solution. The report
proposed expanding Medicare by placing an annual $2,000 limit on
beneficiaries' out-of-pocket expenses for hospital and physician charges.
Any expenditures above that amount would be absorbed by Medicare.
The program would be financed by increasing Medicare's existing
Part B premium by $59/year.

The Reagan administration agreed to support the recommendations
of the Commission since it regarded this extension of the Medicare
program as revenue-neutral. It was thought that projected additional
annual costs of $2 billion would be made up by the $59 annual charge
levied on beneficiaries and it was only on that condition that the
administration agreed to support the proposal. The House Ways and
Means Committee, however, insisted on adding further benefits to the
package. These additions at first were somewhat modest (i.e., improved home health care and skilled nursing home care coverage) but
were soon extended to include further benefits to the Medicaid program and the addition of prescription drugs to Medicare's coverage.
While the Senate Finance Committee's recommendations were not
quite as ambitious as were these, they did end up reporting out a
scaled-down version of the House bill, minus the drug benefit. In July
1987 the Congressional Budget Office reassessed the cost of the original Bowen proposal at $78 per Medicare enrollee and $226 per enrollee should the House version be enacted. In addition, the House
version called for the payment of an additional graduated premium
based on income, rising to $580 annually for those with adjusted gross
incomes of more than $14,166. The "premium"—Congress was insis-
tent that this was not an increase in taxes— was to be collected by the
IRS and was mandatory.

The act as finally passed in June 1988 contained several adjustments to Part A of the Medicare program, including a reduction in the liability of Medicare beneficiaries for hospital care to one deductible per year. In addition, hospital benefits were calculated for the full year, without regard to sixty-day blocks, and provided for unlimited inpatient care while eliminating all copayments and deductibles except for the one annual amount. The skilled nursing facility benefit was extended to 150 days per year and required no prior hospital stay, as in the past. A coinsurance payment was limited to the first eight days per year, at 20 percent of the average daily cost. Hospice and home health benefits were expanded and requirements for participation eased. With respect to Part B, the new legislation placed a limit on deductibles and copayments for physicians' services, including payments to surgeons. Additionally, Medicare reimbursements were extended to cover outpatient prescription drugs above a $600 deductible, which were to be phased in over a period of several years with decreasing copayments by the beneficiary. Finally, Part B coverage was expanded to biennial mammography screening. Changes to Medicaid were much along the lines recommended by the House Ways and Means Committee, including exempting low-income Medicare beneficiaries from deductibles and copayments and protecting the assets of spouses of nursing home residents. In sum, according to the Congressional Budget Office, the changes brought about by the Medicare Catastrophic Coverage Act would have increased Medicare benefits for each beneficiary by about 7 percent. Catastrophic benefits would have added an average of approximately $194 to the $2,801 in benefits per enrollee under the old law.[136]

These extensions of Medicare and Medicaid coverage were to be financed by a flat premium levied on all beneficiaries except Medicaid recipients plus an income-related supplement, to be paid by all enrollees with an income tax liability of $150 or more at the rate of $22.50 per $150 of tax liability (or 15 percent). The maximum liability was set at $800 per person. The surtax rate was scheduled to increase over time to a maximum of 28 percent by 1993. As in the House version, "premiums" were mandatory and collected by the IRS.

While the American Association of Retired Persons was pleased with the legislation, a number of groups had serious reservations about one or another of its provisions. The Pharmaceutical Manufacturers Association was fearful that the inclusion of coverage for prescription drugs would eventually lead to cost controls on pharmaceuticals and the National Committee to Protect Social Security and Medicare was strongly opposed to the supplemental premium as an additional tax on the elderly. Indeed, since many of the benefits of the new legislation were to be phased in over a period of several years while premiums were set to begin immediately, critics of the new legislation could with some justification claim that the Act was in reality aimed at reducing the deficit at the expense of the elderly. This conclusion seemed to be supported by the Treasury, who reported in the spring of 1989 that collections of the supplemental premium would be higher than anticipated and would generate a substantial increase in the Catastrophic Coverage Trust Fund.[137] On the heels of this report, the Congressional Budget Office released figures showing that the costs of some benefits under the 1988 legislation had been seriously underestimated. This was particularly true of the costs associated with skilled nursing facilities, where average stays increased from twenty-seven to thirty-four days between 1988 and 1989, while the number of persons covered rose from 392,000 to 591,000 during the same period. The cost of the prescription drug benefit was also revised upward, to more than double the original estimates. These new figures now suggested that not only would the Trust Fund not show a surplus, but that a huge shortfall would likely occur. These data served the Act's opponents well, who were able to capitalize on the legislation's profound shortcomings. For some reason, the media appear to have been somewhat skeptical about the value of this extension of Medicare and this added to the general discontent about the increase in taxes (that is, "mandatory premiums") by which the Act was funded.

There followed a period of vigorous lobbying in Congress by interest groups representing the elderly to amend the Catastrophic Coverage provisions in such a way that the benefits contained in the Act would be retained while the supplemental premium was eliminated. However, in the face of the federal government's huge deficit, this "compromise" was not politically feasible and there appeared no option but to repeal the Act. In October 1989 the House of Representatives voted to repeal all but the Medicaid provisions of the Medicare Catastrophic Coverage Act and in the following month the Senate followed suit. This appears to be the first instance in the legislative history of national health care insurance that Congress was forced to confront the realities of the program's increasingly heavy expenditures.

Indeed, while both Congress and the various administrations have made modest attempts to moderate the growth in Medicare and Medicaid spending that have marked these programs since their birth, the lure of votes has been far stronger. There seems little doubt that the majority of Americans want far more health care than they are individually willing to pay for and socializing the costs associated with health care is an excellent way of disguising its real costs. That this brings in its wake further dislocations in the economy as costs are shifted is of no interest or concern to most politicians. Indeed, even the attempts that have been made to set rates in the form of a Prospective Payment System for hospitals and a Medical Fee Schedule for physicians simply disguise the true costs of Medicare programs by shifting and masking them. Indeed, there is evidence that one of the effects of placing effective caps on hospital charges below what they would otherwise have been leads to hospitals subsidizing Medicare beneficiaries at the expense of their other patients and their insurance companies. The same thing, of course, holds for physicians' services. Nor is increasing Medicare premiums the solution since its effect is to raise business costs and lower real incomes for workers. In 1966, the maximum Medicare tax imposed on employees and the self-employed was $23.10; by 1993, this amount had increased to $1,957.50 and double that, $3,915.00, for self-employed workers. In 1993, employees with earnings of $26,382, the annual average pay, had $382.25 withheld from their paychecks while their employers contributed another $382.25 on their behalf, a total of $764.50. Yet, despite these increases in Medicare taxes (which have since again been raised) Hospital Insurance (Part A) expenditures exceeded the Hospital Insurance Trust Fund's annual income in 1995. The Fund's income was estimated to meet only 93 percent of expenditures in 1996 and 72 percent in 2001. Projections for income and expenditures for the Fund indicate that the shortfall in the year 2005 will reach over $400 billion and that in seventy-five years the Fund's income will cover less than one-third of the costs of the program.[138]

The lessons of Medicare seem clear. The program is currently spending all that it receives in premiums and payroll taxes and expenditures are increasing; indeed, at current rates of growth expenditures on hospital insurance alone will consume 3 percent of the nation's GDP by the year 2070. The nation can ill afford a health insurance program that constitutes such a drain on the nation's resources and distorts individual costs such that there is simply no incentive to economize on health care. Nor are we encouraged to economize. We are enjoined to consult a physician for almost every possible ailment or in connection with even the most minor decisions affecting our health. And physicians themselves, eager to recommend the best care money can buy, often recommend expensive diagnostic procedures and elaborate surgical interventions even for the extremely old. It is now theoretically possible to keep the bodily organism functioning almost interminably, although often at huge cost. We are naturally reluctant to call an end to our own lives and those of the people we love. But the truth is that we simply cannot afford unlimited health care coverage under a program that draws no distinction in terms of out-of-pocket expenses between the most comprehensive options and a more modest level of care. It is unfortunate that politicians, whose horizons rarely extend beyond the next election, are so little concerned with these problems. Limiting oneself to making the occasional judicious-sounding statement about the need to restructure the government's health programs to halt waste and increase efficiency will not solve Medicare's deficiencies nor will an infinite amount of tinkering with the program's details, inasmuch as a government-operated mandatory national health insurance scheme is fatally flawed. Nothing better misrepresents the actual effects of government control over the health care system than the following claim:

> The more services are made free to the patient at time of receipt of service, and the more the system is planned and regulated by the state in the public interest, the better is the quality of service, the better the health of the people—and the less it costs.[140]

Such sentiments are a recipe for disaster and display an appalling ignorance both of the most rudimentary conclusions of economics and the empirical data on government health care programs. Only the market allows consumers to make these tradeoffs, in which we can weigh the benefits of elaborate medical procedures against their cost. Medicare masks these costs and distorts our choices while packaging the program in a massive regulatory system subject to the decisions of bureaucrats rather than consumers.

Notes

1. I am grateful to the Social Philosophy and Policy Center at Bowling Green

State University, Bowling Green, Ohio, whose generosity in providing me with a grant and research facilities made this essay possible.

2. The details of this state-socialist program and the motives that impelled Bismarck to craft these measures can be found in Otto Pflanze, *Bismarck and the Development of Germany*, Vol. III: *The Period of Fortification*: 1880-1898, Princeton, NJ: Princeton University Press, 1990, pp. 145-84. Bismarck's sentiments in placing this legislation before the Reichstag were best expressed in his Motive that accompanied the first accident insurance bill: "That the state should assist its needy citizens to a greater degree than before is not only a Christian and humanitarian duty, of which the state apparatus should be fully conscious; it is also a task to be undertaken for the preservation of the state itself. The goal of this task is to nurture among the unpropertied classes of the population, which are the most numerous as well as least informed, the view that the state is not only a necessary but also a beneficent institution." Quoted in Pflanze, *Bismarck*, III: 159.

3. For a detailed examination of the provisions of the health insurance bill and its amendments by one of its chief admirers, see William Harbutt Dawson, *Social Insurance in Germany, 1883-1911*, London: T. Fisher Unwin, 1912. In writing of Bismarck's policies, Dawson, at his most repellent, notes of German politics, "long before the era of constitutional government and Parliamentary systems, wise rulers and far-seeing Ministers were always ready, when social evils became acute and new conditions and needs arose, to take occasion by the hand and readjust discordant relationships even in the absence of the active pressure of popular demand" (p.2). Dawson's book contains not one word of criticism of Bismarck's policies and the chapter that is devoted to the "attitudes of employers and workpeople" towards the social insurance act is an unrelieved litany of praise.

4. Austria enacted similar legislation in 1888; Hungary, in 1891; Luxembourg, in 1901; Norway, in 1909, Serbia, in 1910; Great Britain, in 1911; Russia, in 1912; and Romania, in 1913. Ronald Numbers, *Almost Persuaded: American Physicians and Compulsory Health Insurance, 1912-1920*, Baltimore, MD: Johns Hopkins University Press, 1978, pp. 10.

5. Daniel M. Fox, *Health Policies, Health Politics: The British and American Experience, 1911-1965*, Princeton, NJ: Princeton University Press, 1986, pp. 5.

6. The Act covered about one-third of the population of Great Britain. J. Rogers Hollingsworth, *A Political Economy of Medicine: Great Britain and the United States*, Baltimore, MD: Johns Hopkins University Press, 1986, p. 24.

7. Details of the original program are contained in Hollingsworth, *Political Economy of Medicine*, 19-25.

8. Fox, Health Policies, Health Politics, 8.

9. Richard Harris, *A Sacred Trust*, Baltimore, MD: Penguin Books Inc., 1966, pp. 4. In fact, a compulsory government-administered health insurance scheme had a long history. In 1798 Congress enacted legislation that provided hospital care for merchant seamen, the cost of which was originally underwritten by compulsory monthly contributions from those covered. The "care" to which they were entitled was provided by the Marine Hospital Service, forerunner of the United States Public Health Service. The plan as originally conceived proved unworkable and soon degenerated into hospital care for indigent seamen, financed out of general revenues (Herman Miles Somers and Anne Ramsay Somers, *Medicare and the Hospitals: Issues and Prospects*, Wash-

ington, D.C.: The Brookings Institution, 1967, pp. 1-2).

10. Henry F. Pringle, *Theodore Roosevelt*, New York: Harcourt, Brace, 1956, pp. 396-97.

11. See Lafayette G. Harter, John R. Commons: His Assault on Laissez-Faire, Corvallis: Oregon State University Press, 1962. From his base at the University of Wisconsin Commons was able to successfully lobby for three of Wisconsin's pathbreaking reforms: (1) the regulation of the state's public utilities by an administrative commission; (2) the creation of the Wisconsin Industrial Commission to regulate safety in the workplace and to administer a workmen's compensation program; and (3) the institution of unemployment compensation. Harter argues that Commons' "greatest contribution to government was his share in the development of the administrative commission" (p. 4). Indeed, Commons was one of the originators of the regulatory and administrative agency that would be possessed of sufficient flexibility to determine the outcome of specific cases that came before it on an ad hoc basis, a flexibility ordinarily denied the courts. See Edward Berkowitz and Kim McQuaid, *Creating the Welfare State: The Political Economy of Twentieth-Century Reform*, 2nd ed., rev., New York: Praeger, 1988, p. 47.

12. James G. Burrow, *Organized Medicine in the Progressive Era: The Move Toward Monopoly*, Baltimore, MD: Johns Hopkins University Press 1977, p. 140.

13. The Socialist Party had called for the establishment of a national system of health insurance in 1904.

14. Numbers, *Almost Persuaded*, pp. 15-16.

15. Lloyd F. Pierce, "The Activities of the American Association for Labor Legislation in Behalf of Social Security and Protective Labor Legislation" (Ph.D. diss., University of Wisconsin, 1953), quoted in Numbers, *Almost Persuaded*, p. 16.

16. Numbers, *Almost Persuaded*, p.15.

17. The term was understood to incorporate a whole series of government-administered compulsory insurance schemes, including accident insurance, unemployment insurance, old age insurance, disability insurance, and, of course, medical insurance.

18. Numbers, Almost Persuaded, p. 16. Among the Committee's members were Edward Devine, Director of the New York School of Philanthropy, Henry R. Seager, Professor of Economics at Columbia University, and Isaac M. Rubinow.

19. Robert J. Myers, *Medicare*, Bryn Mawr, PA: McCahan Foundation, 1970, pp. 4-7.

20. See Ronald Hamowy, "The Early Development of Medical Licensing Laws in the United States, 1875-1900." *Journal of Libertarian Studies*, 3 (Spring, 1979), pp. 73-119.

21. Burrow, *Organized Medicine in the Progressive Era*, p. 142.

22. Numbers, *Almost Persuaded*, p. 33. In mid-1917 the Committee on Social Insurance admonished those in the medical profession who opposed any compulsory government-administered health insurance scheme in the following words: "To work out these problems [that might arise with such a plan] is a most difficult task. The time to work them out, however, is when the laws are molding, as now, and the time is present when the profession should surely study earnestly to solve the questions of medical care that will arise under various forms of social insurance. Blind opposition, indignant repudiation, bitter denunciation of these laws is worse than useless; it leads nowhere and it

leaves the profession in a position of helplessness as the rising tide of social development sweeps over it" (*JAMA* 68 [9 June 1917]: 1755).

23.   "A Model Bill for Health Insurance," JAMA 65 (20 November 1915): 1824.

24.   Quoted in Numbers, *Almost Persuaded*, p. 34.

25.   London correspondent, "Mr. Lloyd-George on the Insurance Act," *JAMA* 62 (1914): 789, and "Medical Remuneration under the Insurance Act," *JAMA* 62 (1914): 945, quoted in Numbers, *Almost Persuaded*, p. 32.

26.   *Journal of the South Carolina Medical Association* 12 (1916): 260, quoted in Numbers, *Almost Persuaded*, p. 125, fn. 28.

27.   James Rorty, *American Medicine Mobilizes*, New York: W. W. Norton & Co., Inc., 1939, pp. 74-75.

28.   Peter A. Corning, *The Evolution of Medicare . . . from Idea to Law*, Washington, DC: U.S. Department of Health, Education, and Welfare, Social Security Administration, Office of Research and Statistics, 1970, p. 9.

29.   Substantial representation on such boards was, of course, crucial since the prospective health authority was empowered to draw up the fee schedules determining physician compensation.

30.   The response of the medical profession to the proposal to institute a national compulsory health insurance plan, both favorable and unfavorable, is discussed in some detail in Numbers, *Almost Persuaded, passim*, and Burrow, *Organized Medicine in the Progressive Era*, pp. 133-53.

31.   Howard Wolinsky and Tom Brune, *The Serpent on the Staff: The Unhealthy Politics of the American Medical Association*, New York: G. P. Putman's Sons, 1994, p.18.

32.   These views were apparently voiced by, among others, George MacAdams, "Do We Want to Pay the Health Insurance Bill?," *New York Times Magazine*, March 11, 1917, p. 11, quoted in Burrow, *Organized Medicine in the Progressive Era*, p. 153.

33.   Numbers, *Almost Persuaded*, p. 77.

34.   *Ibid.*, p. 76.

35.   Thomas W. Huntington, "Address of the President," *American Surgical Association, Transactions* 36 (1918): 5-6, quoted in Numbers, *Almost Persuaded*, p. 77.

36.   That the campaign to institute a mandatory national system of medical insurance proved unsuccessful in large part because Americans still embraced free market and Social Darwinist views has no historical warrant. See Peter A. Corning, *The Evolution of Medicare*, pp. 12-13.

37.   It is worth noting that the cost of physicians' services for most American workers was not prohibitively high prior to the 1920s. A substantial number of proprietary medical schools graduated an abundance of practitioners until release of the Flexner Report in 1910 encouraged the various state licensing boards to set their criteria for acceptable medical education at a level that most of these schools were unable to meet. Nor indeed was medical care itself particularly efficacious for most ailments before the late 1930s, when the sulfonamide drugs came into common use, while it was only in World War II that penicillin was introduced as a therapeutic agent. And what held for physicians' services was equally true for hospital care, which most Americans regarded as necessary only in cases of surgery or tuberculosis. Finally, to the extent that private health insurance policies were available, most offered benefits in terms of cash payments for disability or illness rather than medical services. For a comprehensive discussion of the financing of medical care in

the United States prior to the introduction of Medicare, see Herman Miles Somers and Anne Ramsay Somers, *Doctors, Patients, and Health Insurance: The Organization and Financing of Medical Care*, Washington, DC: The Brookings Institution, 1961.

38. The socialist muckraker and author Upton Sinclair won the Democratic nomination for governor of California in 1933 on a platform which he called End Poverty in California (EPIC). His supporters, organized into the End Poverty League, embraced Sinclair's plan to have the state of California institute a state-wide system of production and exchange, in which the state would set up land colonies in which farmers would live and produce the state's food while at the same time the state would employ all the urban unemployed in government factories and "great productive units." Sinclair was defeated for the governorship, largely through the defection of manufacturers and other businessmen who would otherwise have supported the party. Excerpts from Sinclair's plan appear in Edward H. Merrill, *Responses to Economic Collapse: The Great Depression of the 1930's*, Boston: D. C. Heath and Co., 1964, pp. 101-104.

39. With an eye to running for the Presidency in 1936 Long, in 1934, set out an economic program for the country which he called the Share Our Wealth Plan. It called for the confiscation of all large fortunes and the redistribution of this wealth to all those in need (that is, those with an estate worth less than $5,000). Each family would be guaranteed a "household estate" of $5,000 (sufficient to provide each recipient with a house, an automobile, a radio, and other "necessities"), together with a guaranteed annual income of $2,500 per year. Share Our Wealth Clubs became extremely popular, especially in the South and West, and Long's slogan "Every man a king, but no one wears a crown" became a rallying cry for hundreds of thousands of American workers and farmers. See Alan Brinkley, *Voices of Protest: Huey Long, Father Coughlin, and the Great Depression*, New York: Alfred A. Knopf, 1982, passim.

40. Townsend's Old Age Revolving Pension Plan was based on the crackpot program earlier put forward by Major C. H. Douglas, founder of the Social Credit movement. Townsend's plan called for the federal government to pay every unemployed American over the age of sixty a pension of $200 per month (estimates put this amount at approximately twice the average income of workers). Pensioners were required to spend the full amount each month in order to be eligible for the next month's payment. Payments were to be financed by a 2 percent federal sales tax. The proposal was received with such enthusiasm that thousands of Townsend clubs were established, not only in Townsend's home state of California, but throughout the country. A bill to enact Townsend's scheme was actually put before the House of Representatives in 1939 and received 101 votes! See Edward Merrill, *Responses to Economic Collapse*, pp. 97-100.

41. The committee's executive director was Edwin E. Witte, chairman of the economics department of the University of Wisconsin. Witte, like Hopkins and Wallace and, indeed, like the President himself, embraced a "purchasing-power" thesis respecting the cause of the Depression: that what lay at its root was an inequitable distribution of purchasing power which, in turn, led to consumptive capacity lagging behind productive capacity. The result was over-production and unemployment. Recovery, it was thought, rested on increasing total purchasing power and this required that a larger share of the

national income go to wages rather than profits. For a discussion of this "explanation" and its adherents, see Theodore Rosenof, *Dogma, Depression, and the New Deal: The Debate of Political Leaders over Economic Recovery*, Port Washington, NY: Kennikat Press, 1975, pp. 39-43.

42. Fearful that a national mandatory social security system would be struck down by the Supreme Court, Frances Perkins is reported to have asked Justice Harlan F. Stone, then on the Court, whether he thought the program might fail, to which Stone is reputed to have replied, "The taxing power of the federal government, my dear; the taxing power is sufficient for everything you want and need." Frances Perkins, *The Roosevelt I Knew*, New York: Viking Press, 1946, p. 286. As a result, the legislation eventually enacted by Congress provided that unemployment insurance be based on a tax placed on employers and that old-age pensions be ostensibly paid for through payroll taxes levied on both employer and employee. Lewis E. Weeks and Howard J. Berman, eds., *Shapers of American Health Care Policy: An Oral History*, Ann Arbor, MI: Health Administration Press, 1985, p. 53.

43. For brief discussions of the Committee's work, see James G. Burrow, *AMA: Voice of American Medicine*, Baltimore, MD: Johns Hopkins Press, 1963, pp. 180-83; and, James Rorty, *American Medicine Mobilizes, passim*.

44. Hopkins had at one time directed the New Orleans Red Cross and had been the director of the New York Tuberculosis and Health Association before being appointed to head the Federal Emergency Relief Administration.

45. The campaign against enactment of a compulsory health insurance bill was led by the *JAMA*'s editor, Dr. Morris Fishbein, probably the most powerful medical lobbyist in the country. Not only was Fishbein considered the leading spokesman on questions relating to the medical profession and its relation to government policy but as the editor of the *JAMA* from 1924 to 1949 his views came to dominate the meetings of the AMA's Board of Trustees.

46. The decisive issue for Roosevelt appears to have been the 1936 presidential election. He apparently felt it essential to get a social security bill enacted prior to the campaign and was advised that it was unlikely to be passed expeditiously if health insurance were included as a part of the legislation. Weeks and Berman, eds., *Shapers of American Medical Policy*, p. 53. The social security bill did, in fact, pass Congress in August 1935.

47. Corning, *The Evolution of Medicare*, p. 44.

48. Among the findings of the National Health Survey of 1935-36 were: (1) those with incomes below $1,000/year suffered from 47 percent more acute illnesses and 87 percent more chronic illnesses than did those with incomes above $3,000/year; (2) the duration of illness for those on relief was 63 percent longer than for the rest of the population; (3) 30 percent of those on relief were not receiving medical care for disabling illnesses lasting a week or longer (vs. 17 percent for those with an income above $3,000/year); (4) annual mortality rates from accidents and infant mortality rates exceeded that of any other industrialized nation; (5) 40 percent of the nation's counties, containing 18,000,000 people, possessed no registered general hospital; and, finally, (6) a substantial portion of the American population simply could not afford the costs of medical care. The Survey concluded that it would cost approximately $850,000,000 a year to provide adequate medical coverage for the lowest income groups. Excerpts from the Survey's conclusions are quoted in Rorty, *American Medicine Mobilizes*, pp. 22-24.

49. Rorty, *American Medicine Mobilizes*, p. 21.

50.   Burrow, AMA: *Voice of American Medicine*, p. 216.

51.   The recommendations are printed in full in Rorty, *American Medicine Mobilizes*, pp. 312-19.

52.   This amount would have increased the federal government's expenditures on health by a factor of seventeen! In 1940, federal expenditures on health, exclusive of the Veterans Administration, amounted to approximately $55,000,000.

53.   See Burrow, AMA: *Voice of American Medicine*, pp. 205-27. The AMA's representatives at the Conference apparently had no objection to the other four recommendations and a delegation of AMA leaders, meeting with the members of the Interdepartmental Committee to Coordinate Health and Welfare Activities, offered to support the other recommendations if the government were prepared to drop its insistence on passage of a compulsory health insurance scheme. Corning, *The Evolution of Medicare*, p. 48.

54.   In 1935, the California legislature had established a committee to study the creation of a statewide compulsory health insurance plan and the California Medical Association had agreed to cooperate with the committee in drafting an acceptable program. The plan that was eventually recommended provided for compulsory medical insurance for all employees (including agricultural and domestic workers) earning less than $3,000/year while allowing voluntary enrollment to those earning over that amount. Employers who provided suitable alternate medical-care plans were permitted to opt out of the government program. The plan's medical care coverage was extensive and included almost all hospitalization and prescription drug costs. Provision was even allowed for including dental care, should sufficient funds be available. The plan was to be financed by contributions of 1 percent of income from the employer and 3 percent from each employee, with persons voluntarily covered paying the full 5 percent, up to a $3,000 annual maximum. The proposal, which called for no regulation of physicians' fees, was considered by the California State Assembly in 1939 and, despite the fact that the state medical association had played a role in its drafting, was decisively defeated. Myers, *Medicare*, pp. 16-17.

55.   Senator Wagner had introduced similar legislation in 1939 and, in fact, had arranged for hearings on the bill that April but the attempt to gain support for its passage failed, in large part because Roosevelt hoped to make national health insurance a campaign issue when the President came up for re-election in 1940. Corning, *The Evolution of Medicare*, pp. 48-49. It thus seems clear that Roosevelt had determined to run for a third term as early as 1938.

56.   It appears that by 1943 most Americans, influenced by a decade of government propaganda, believed that market forces were responsible for the economic ills that the nation had suffered in the 1930s and that government intervention alone was able to provide a social safety net to protect the great mass of people from the horrors of an unrestrained capitalist system. As a consequence, public opinion shifted in favor of a compulsory national health insurance program. While in 1938 only 53 percent of the public supported health insurance of any kind, either public or private, by 1942 no less than 74 percent favored national health insurance. See Corning, *The Evolution of Medicare*, 48n, and Monte Poen, *Harry S. Truman Versus the Medical Lobby: The Genesis of Medicare*, Columbia: University of Missouri Press, 1979, p. 30.

57.   In 1942 the Social Security Board announced its support for a comprehensive system of social insurance including health benefits and in fact was instrumental in drafting the Wagner-Murray-Dingell bill.

58. See Corning, *The Evolution of Medicare*, p. 56. Roosevelt appears to have been outraged that Sir William Beveridge was being credited with having authored the blueprint for the modern welfare state. When the Beveridge Report (under the title *Social Insurance and Allied Services*) was released in November 1942 Roosevelt is reported to have whined to his Secretary of Labor, Frances Perkins, "Why does Beveridge get his name on this? Why does he get credit for this? You know that I have been talking about cradle to grave insurance ever since we first thought of it. It is my idea. It is not the Beveridge plan. It is the Roosevelt plan." Frances Perkins, *The Roosevelt I Knew*, p. 144.

59. Somers and Somers, *Medicare and the Hospitals*, p. 4.

60. The provisions respecting veterans' benefits were eliminated inasmuch as the GI Bill had been enacted in the meantime.

61. Apparently the public was less enthusiastic about a compulsory national insurance scheme than had been the case earlier. A Gallup poll taken in late 1949 showed only 51 percent supported the measure. Corning, The Evolution of Medicare, p. 67. In the same year all the major welfare organizations of the Catholic church opposed the notion of government insurance, as did the General Federation of Women and the National Medical Association, both earlier supporters. Poen, *Harry S. Truman Versus the Medical Lobby*, p. 161-62.

62. Burrow, *AMA: Voice of American Medicine*, p. 374.

63. The Federal Security Agency was created in 1939 to bring together most of the health, welfare, and education services of the federal government and, in turn, became the core component of the Department of Health, Education, and Welfare when it was established in 1953.

64. See Theodore R. Marmor, *The Politics of Medicare*, London: Routledge & Kegan Paul, 1970, pp. 13-14.

65. Marmor, *The Politics of Medicare*, p. 14.

66. The health commission established by President Truman in 1952 had concluded that Americans over sixty- five were indeed poorer and in greater need of medical care for which they lacked insurance than was the average American and these data were often cited in support of linking hospital insurance to social security. However, as one analyst has observed: "Proof that the aged were the most needy was based on calculation for all persons over 65. Yet social security financing would in 1952 have restricted Medicare benefits to seven million pensioners out of the twelve and one-half million persons over 65. This would have meant not insuring five and one-half million aged whose medical and financial circumstances had been used to establish the "need" for a Medicare program in the first place. " Marmor, *The Politics of Medicare*, p. 22.

67. The political implications of this new approach to government health insurance are discussed at length in Marmor, *The Politics of Medicare*, pp. 13-28.

68. Corning, *The Evolution of Medicare*, p. 75.

69. *Ibid.*, pp. 80-81.

70. Private health insurance had witnessed a spectacular growth during the postwar years. The Secretary of Health, Education, and Welfare, Marion B. Folsom, testified before hearings on the Forand bill that between 1952 and 1958 the number of people covered by hospitalization policies had increased from 91 million to 121 million; those covered by surgical insurance had risen from 73

million to 109 million; and those covered by medical insurance had doubled, from 36 million to 72 million.

Percent of Individuals with Health Insurance Prior to the Introduction of Medicare By Type of Coverage

Type of Coverage	1953 (%)	1958 (%)	1963 (%)
Hospital	57	65	68
Surgical-medical	48	61	66
Outpatient doctor visits[1]	2	2	35
Major medical	2	2	22
Outpatient drugs[3]	2	2	26
Dental	2	2	2

Source: U.S. Department of Health, Education, and Welfare, Public Health Service, Health Resources Administration, National Center for Health Statistics, *Health: United States 1975* (Washington, DC, 1976): Table A-3 (p. 51).

1. Includes first dollar doctor visit coverage as written by prepaid group practice plans, unions, and certain other insurers, and all major medical policies whether or not connected with a base plan.
2. Not available.
3. Includes first dollar drug coverage as written by some prepaid group practices, unions, and certain other insurers, and major medical policies.

71.   Richard Harris, *A Sacred Trust*, Baltimore, MD: Penguin Books, Inc., 1966, p. 78. Apparently the Eisenhower administration's own estimates showed that the bill would cost less than $1 billion a year and that there was little likelihood of its unbalancing the social security budget (p. 78).
72.   Corning, *The Evolution of Medicare*, p. 84. It appears that when, in the spring of 1960, Walter Reuther, the President of the United Auto Workers and one of the leading proponents of a national health insurance bill, urged Lyndon Johnson to publicly endorse the Forand bill, Johnson agreed to do so only on condition that Reuther support Johnson's bid for the Presidential nomination. Despite the fact that Reuther is reported to have been unwilling to commit himself, Johnson did speak in favor of the proposal. Harris, *A Sacred Trust*, p. 108.
73.   Congress appeared deadlocked between Democrat-sponsored measures that sought to extend hospital insurance to all the elderly, and the approach favored by Republicans (and embodied in a bill proposed by Senator Jacob Javits of New York) that limited federal grants for medical care to the lower-income elderly only. One analyst has charted the distinctions between the two approaches in the following way:

	Forand Social Security Approach	Welfare Approach
Beneficiaries:	Only the aged who were covered under social security	Anyone over 65 whose resources were insufficient to meet his medical expenses
Benefits:	Hospitalization, nursing, home and in-hospital surgical insurance (Medicare bills introduced after 1959 specified hospitals and nursing home insurance only).	Comprehensive benefits for physicians' services, dental care, hospitalization, prescribed drugs, and nursing home care.
Source of financing:	Regressive social security taxes	Progressive federal income tax revenues, plus state matching funds
Administration and setting of standards:	Uniform national standards administered by the Social Security Administration	Standards varying by state administered by state and local officials

Theodore R. Marmor, *The Politics of Medicare*, p. 38. Marmor points to the irony of the two approaches. While the Forand backers wished to extend benefits to all social security beneficiaries, it proposed limiting benefits to hospital and surgical insurance, to be paid for by a regressive social security tax. The more conservative welfare advocates, on the other hand, proposed a broader package of benefits for a smaller group, to be financed by progressive federal tax revenues (p. 37).

74. Only Senators Barry Goldwater of Arizona and Strom Thurmond of South Carolina opposed the measure.
75. Harris, A Sacred Trust, p. 117. A group known as Senior Citizens for Kennedy, headed by none other than newly retired Congressman Aime Forand, was formed to keep the issue before the public (Corning, *The Evolution of Medicare*, p. 87).
76. Corning, *The Evolution of Medicare*, p. 87.
77. Certainly such a provision would have won the immediate enmity of the medical profession which remained adamantly opposed to any government determination of the fees paid doctors. In any case this appears to have made no difference since physicians regarded the King-Anderson proposal as a first step towards a completely socialized medical system.
78. Frank D. Campion, *The AMA and U.S. Health Policy Since 1940*, Chicago: Chicago Review Press, 1984, p. 216. No political action committee existed prior to the creation of AMPAC except the Committee on Political Education (COPE) of the AFL-CIO, formed in 1943 for the purpose of achieving organized labor's political objectives.
79. Blue Cross had its origins in the depression, when hospitals hit upon the scheme of instituting prepayment plans for hospital care as a cure for the large number

of empty beds with which they were faced. The movement, which started at the Baylor University Hospital in Dallas, Texas in 1929, soon spread to other cities and expanded into community-wide programs. In 1934, the American College of Surgeons formally endorsed such prepayment plans for medical and surgical services and four years later the American Medical Association approved them. In 1940, there were over 6,000,000 enrollees in Blue Cross plans covering hospitalization and 370,000 enrollees in Blue Shield plans covering surgical expenses. By 1958 these numbers had grown to 52,000,000 and 40,400,00 respectively and there is every reason to believe that both plans would have continued to sign up new members at the same rate. If one were to add all those covered by commercial medical insurance, the totals in 1958 show that approximately 128,000,000 people, or about 72 percent of the civilian population, had some form of hospital insurance. This figure probably includes a 5 to 6 percent overlap while of those covered about 75 to 80 percent held group rather than individual coverage. However, in the early 1950s, insurance companies had started offering benefits programs that covered all major medical expenses whether the enrollees were part of a group or not and by the close of the decade both Blue Cross-Blue Shield and the commercial carriers began designing programs to provide comprehensive medical coverage for the elderly (Somers and Somers, *Doctors, Patients, and Health Insurance*, p. 364). The history of private attempts to provide medical insurance to the public belies Wilbur Cohen's self-serving claim that "the political threat of Federal legislative action on health insurance in the 1930's and early 1940's and the economic impact of wage and price controls during World War II and the Korean War [were what] stimulated private and commercial health insurance plans to expand their coverage" (Wilbur J. Cohen, "Policy Planning for National Health Insurance," in U.S. Department of Health, Education, and Welfare, *Health in America: 1776-1976* [DHEW Pub. No. (HRA) 76-616], Washington, DC, 1976: 175). It is true that the introduction of wage and price controls and the absence of controls on corporate profits during World War II encouraged firms to increase wages in the form of fringe benefits including health insurance, but this is hardly sufficient to account for the spectacular growth of medical prepayment plans after 1945.

80. Harris, *A Sacred Trust*, p. 125.
81. For an extended discussion of the composition of this committee in the context of the Anderson-King bill, see Marmor, *The Politics of Medicare*, pp. 44-53.
82. Corning, *The Evolution of Medicare*, p. 91; Harris, *A Sacred Trust*, pp. 132-33. The Committee hardly represented the wishes of most physicians. In the spring of 1961, the *Medical Tribune* reported that no less than 81 percent of American physicians were opposed to the King-Anderson bill (Harris, *A Sacred Trust*, p. 130).
83. Including the United Auto Workers, the United Steel Workers, and the International Ladies Garment Workers Union (Corning, *The Evolution of Medicare*, p. 91).
84. Harris, *A Sacred Trust*, p. 142.
85. Corning, *The Evolution of Medicare*, pp. 92-93.
86. *Ibid.*, pp. 95-96.
87. HEW's congressional liaison staff estimated in 1961 that the House breakdown on Medicare was about 23 votes short of the 218-seat majority (Marmor, *The Politics of Medicare*, p. 58).
88. Harris, A Sacred Trust, p. 149.
89. Corning, *The Evolution of Medicare*, p. 107.

90. Wall Street Journal, 25 March 1964, quoted in Harris, *A Sacred Trust*, 1652.
91. Corning, *The Evolution of Medicare*, p. 108.
92. *Ibid.*, p. 104.
93. Marmor, *The Politics of Medicare*, p. 60. Wilbur Mills' role during the conference committee's deliberations is recounted in Harris, *A Sacred Trust*, pp. 167-71.
94. The American Medical Association was not above suggesting in some of its election propaganda that supporters of Medicare were playing into the hands of the world communist conspiracy. There is, however, no evidence to support the contention that "as many as a third of the members of the A.M.A.'s House of Delegates [were] also members of the John Birch Society." Harris, *A Sacred Trust*, p. 172.
95. Somers and Somers, *Medicare and the Hospitals*, p. 12.
96. Harris, *A Sacred Trust*, p. 174.
97. Marmor, *The Politics of Medicare*, p. 63.
98. Harris, *A Sacred Trust*, p. 174.
99. For a detailed discussion of the provisions of the various health insurance proposals and modifications introduced into Congress between 1961 and 1964, see Myers, *Medicare*, pp. 42-50.
100. Marmor, *The Politics of Medicare*, p. 64.
101. Besides increasing federal matching grants to the states for medical vendor payments, Kerr-Mills also provided for public assistance with medical bills for the medically indigent. Medical Assistance for the Aged (MAA) was extended to those whose incomes and assets might be sufficient to cover their normal living expenses but who were unable to meet the substantial costs of medical care. Federal financing was available to help with the costs of the full range of medical services, including hospitals, nursing homes, physicians, dentists, nurses, physical therapists, laboratory work, prescribed drugs, home health care, and so on.
102. Total costs to the AMA of their campaign to promote Eldercare during 1965 amounted to $1,669,0000 (Campion, *The AMA and U.S. Health Policy*, p. 274).
103. Marmor, *The Politics of Medicare*, p. 65.
104. *Ibid.*, p. 68.
105. The most significant event that occurred during these sessions was a series of surprise amendments put forward by Senator Long to eliminate time limits on the use of hospitals and nursing homes. To underwrite the increased costs associated with this change Long's revisions called for a sliding scale of deductibles to be paid by the patients themselves based on their incomes. These changes were approved by the Committee—in part because of Long's misuse of a proxy earlier provided to him by Senator J. William Fulbright—but the Administration eventually prevailed on those who had supported the Long amendments and the Committee reversed itself some days later. See Harris, *A Sacred Trust*, pp. 196-205,
106. Theodore Marmor (*The Politics of Medicare*, pp. 77-78) has ably summarized the decisions of the Senate- House conference committee as follows:
   "Benefit duration—House provided sixty days of hospital care after a deductible of $40. Senate provided unlimited duration but with $10 co-insurance payments for each day in excess of sixty. Conference provided sixty days with the $40 House deductible, and an additional thirty days with the Senate's $10 co-insurance provision.
   "Posthospital extended care (skilled nursing home)—House provided twenty

days of such care with two additional days for each unused hospital day, but a maximum of 100 days. Senate provided 100 days but imposed a $5 a day co-insurance for each day in excess of twenty. Conference adopted Senate version. "Posthospital home-health visits—House authorized 100 visits after hospitalization. Senate increased the number of visits to 175, and deleted requirements of hospitalization. Conference adopted House version.

"Outpatient diagnostic services—House imposed a $20 deductible with this amount credited against an inpatient hospital deductible imposed at the same hospital within twenty days. Senate imposed a twenty per cent co-insurance on such services, removed the credit against the inpatient hospital deductible but allowed a credit for the deductible as an incurred expense under the voluntary supplementary program (for deductible and reimbursement purposes). Conference adopted Senate version.

"Psychiatric facilities—House provided for sixty days of hospital care with a 180-day lifetime limit in the voluntary supplementary program. Senate moved these services over into basic hospital insurance and increased the lifetime limit to 210 days. Conference accepted the Senate version but reduced the lifetime limit to 190 days."

107.   An extended summary of the law's provisions appears in William Shonick, *Government and Health Services: Government's Role in the Development of U.S. Health Services, 1930-1980*, New York: Oxford University Press, 1995, pp. 285-91, from which this account is taken.

108.   The following data give some idea of the variation in Medicaid eligibility in a selection of states.

Medicaid Eligibility Requirements: Family of Four, 1986

	Eligibility Standard ($)	Eligibility as a Percentage of the Federal Poverty Level (%)
Alabama	1,764	16
California	11,208	100
Indiana	4,356	39
New York	8,484	76
Texas	3,612	32
Average of all 50 states	5.665	51
Federal Poverty Level, Family of Four	11,203	100

Source: Ullrich K. Hoffmeyer and Thomas R. McCarthy, eds., Financing Health Care, 2 vols., Dordrecht: Kluwer Academic Publishers, 1994: Table 15.1 (II:1194).

109.   By March 1971 all states except Alaska and Arizona had joined the Medicaid program. The participation of twenty-five of the forty-eight states receiving matching grants from the federal government was limited to offering the minimal required five services—and perhaps a few others—solely to the obligatory group of public assistance recipients. In the remaining jurisdictions Medicaid coverage was extended to the categorically linked medically needy as well. Shonick, *Government and Health Services*, 296.

110.   Myers, *Medicare*, pp. 64-65.

111.   Estimates of income and expenditures for the Hospital Insurance Trust Fund

and the Supplementary Medical Insurance Trust Fund under the original 1965 Act were as shown in the table below. These estimates should be compared with the actual data as shown in the appendix.

Original Estimates of the Hospital Insurance Trust Fund, 1965 Act
Intermediate Cost Estimates
(in millions)

Year	Contributions	Benefit Payments	Administrative Expenses	Interest on Fund	Balance in Fund at End of Year
1966	$ 1,617	$ 987	$ 50	$ 18	$ 618
1967	2,756	2,210	66	25	1,123
1968	3,018	2,406	72	46	1,709
1969	3,123	2,623	79	66	2,196
1970	3,229	2,860	86	82	2.561
1971	3,329	3,077	92	91	2,812
1972	3,433	3,303	99	95	2.938
1973	3,891	3,540	106	100	3,283
1974	4,096	3,788	114	108	3,585
1975	4,260	4,047	121	112	3,789
1980	6,113	5,307	159	166	5,790
1985	7,026	6,860	206	259	8,341
1990	9,015	8,797	264	323	10,426

Original Estimates of the Supplementary Medical Insurance Trust Fund, 1965 Act High Cost Estimates (95 Percent Participation)
(in millions)

Year	Premiums from Participants	Government Contributions	Benefit Payments	Administrative Expenses	Interest on Fund	Balance at End of Year
1966	$ 325	$ 325	$ 410	$ 100	$ 5	$ 145
1967	665	665	1,260	110	5	110

Source: Robert J. Myers, *Medicare*, Bryn Mawr, PA: McCahan Foundation, 1970: Tables 10-4 and 10-6 (pp. 200-203).

112. Shonick, *Government and Health Services*, p. 291,
113. A number of these studies appeared in the *Social Security Bulletin*. See especially Regina Loewenstein, "Early Effects of Medicare on the Health Care of the Aged," *Social Security Bulletin*, 34:4 (April 1971): 3-20; Howard West, "Five Years of Medicare—A Statistical Review," *Social Security Bulletin*, 34:12 (Dec. 1971): 17-27; Loucele A. Horowitz, "Medical Care Price Changes in Medicare's First Five Years," *Social Security Bulletin*, 35:3 (March 1972): 16-29; Barbara S. Cooper, "Medical Care Spending for Three Age Groups: 1966-1971" *Social Security Bulletin*, 35:5 (May 1972): 3-16; and, Julian. H. Pettengill, "Trends in Hospital Use by the Aged," *Social Security Bulletin*, 35:7 (July 1972): 3-15. A summary of these authors' findings appear in Shonick, *Government and Health Services*, pp. 292- 94, to which this account is indebted.
114. Shonick, *Government and Health Services*, p. 299. Inasmuch as HMOs are

paid in advance to provide a range of medical benefits to its subscribers, there is a strong incentive for them to conserve on the delivery of services, either by increasing preventive care, avoiding unnecessary duplication and overutilization of services, substituting less costly for more expensive forms of health care, and, finally, by simply not providing certain services that would otherwise be available in the marketplace.

115. William Shonick's discussion of the 1972 legislation forms the basis of this account. See Shonick, *Government and Health Services*, pp. 300-303.

116. The PSRO program proved to be worse than useless. According to a Congressional Budget Office analysis undertaken in 1980, the program operated at a net loss of between thirty and sixty cents for each dollar it spent (U.S. Congressional Budget Office, *The Impact of PSROs on Health Care Costs: 1980 Update of the CBO Evaluation*, Staff Draft Analysis, May 2, 1980 [Washington, DC: Congressional Budget Office, 1980]).

117. These came to be known as Section 223 limits, named after the Social Security statute.

118. Marilyn Moon, *Medicare Now and in the Future*, Washington, DC: The Urban Institute, 1993, p. 48.

119. John R. Virts and George W. Wilson, "Inflation and the Behavior of Sectoral Prices," *Business Economics*, 18:3 (May 1983): 45-54. Their findings are summarized in Jack A. Meyer, *Passing the Health Care Buck: Who Pays the Hidden Cost?*, Washington, DC: American Enterprise Institute for Public Policy Research, 1983, pp. 47-49. The conclusions reached by Virts and Wilson confirmed the findings arrived at as early as 1976. See Martin Feldstein and Amy Talor, *The Rapid Rise of Hospital Costs*, Washington, DC: Council on Wage and Price Stability, January 1977, p. 20.

120. Excess demand would thus be translated into queues. This appears to be the method of choice for limiting expenditures on health care in Canada, where long waits in doctors' offices and for "non-emergency" diagnostic and surgical procedures are the norm.

121. Judith Bentkover, Philip Caper, Mark Schleslinger, and Joel Suldan, "Medicare's Payments of Hospitals," in David Blumenthal, Mark Schlesinger, and Pamela Brown Drumheller, *Renewing the Promise: Medicare and Its Reform*, New York: Oxford University Press, 1988. p. 93.

122. Shonick, *Government and Health Services*, pp. 328-329.

123. At the outset there were 468 different categories of diagnosis, covering all possible discharge diagnoses listed in the International Classification of Diseases. The number of DRGs has since been somewhat reduced by the Health Care Financing Administration.

124. A number of facilities were either partially or completely exempted from the PPS provisions, including psychiatric hospitals, children's hospitals, and sole community hospitals.

125. National Center for Health Statistics, *Health, United States, 1990*, Hyattsville, Md.: U.S. Public Health Service, 1991.

126. Joe Feingold and James J. Holloway, "The Initial Impact of the Medicare Prospective Payment System on U.S. Health Care," *Medical Care Review*, 48 (Spring 1991), quoted in Moon, *Medicare Now and in the Future*, p. 92. There is evidence to suggest that this reduction in average length of hospital stay has, in some cases, been at the expense of the health of some Medicare recipients. A study conducted by the Rand Corporation in 1990 concluded that of the four health conditions studied, hospital readmissions, while falling for the other

three, increased for those with myocardial infarctions. Additionally, the proportion of beneficiaries discharged in an unstable condition increased by 22 percent after PPS was initiated. Of those patients discharged home, as opposed to some institution, the discharge rate for unstable patients rose to 43 percent. Katherine Kahn, Lisa V. Rubenstein, David Draper, et al, "The Effects of the DRG-Based Prospective Payment System on Quality of Care for Hospitalized Medicare Patients," *Journal of the American Medical Association*, 264: 15 (1990): 1953-1955, quoted in Moon, *Medicare Now and in the Future*, pp. 93-94.

127. Moon, *Medicare Now and in the Future*, p. 95.
128. United States Congress, Senate, Special Committee on Aging, *Medicare: Paying the Physician—History, Issues, and Options*, quoted in David Blumenthal and William Hsiao, "Payment of Physicians Under Medicare," in Blumenthal, Schlesinger, and Drumheller, *Renewing the Promise*, p. 116.
129. *Health Care Financing Review, Medicare and Medicaid Statistical Supplement: 1995*, 280-281 (Table 55). During the five-year period 1979 to 1984 the increase in these expenditures had accelerated to an annual rate of 21 percent! David Blumenthal and William Hsiao, "Payment of Physicians Under Medicare," p. 116.
130. Other factors considered in calculating the "relative values" of various physicians' services were the physician's expenses and whether use of the particular procedure had grown at an undesirable rate. It should be underscored that the "relative values" of each procedure are determined not by the consumers of physicians' services but by academics and bureaucrats and that these values are not subject to quick and simple change, as are market prices.
131. That is, those physicians who agree to bill Medicare directly rather than billing their patients.
132. Sally T. Burner, Daniel R. Waldo, and David R. McKusick, "National Health Expenditures Projections Through 2030," *Health Care Financing Review*, 14:1 (fall 1992): Table 10 (pp. 26-27). Projections of Medicare expenditures on physicians' services into the twenty-first century are truly mind-numbing. In 1996 they were projected to reach $324.3 billion in 2010, $733.9 billion in 2020, and $1,533.5 billion in 2030, in part because the first of the baby boomer generation will have reached sixty-five years of age by 2015 and by 2030 will have entered their seventies and eighties. At that point it was estimated that those over the age of sixty-five will account for slightly more than 20 percent of the population, with those over seventy-five accounting for 9 percent.
133. The account which follows relies heavily on that contained in Moon, *Medicare Now and in the Future*, pp. 107-37.
134. A sizeable proportion of these costs were associated with the increased deductible and coinsurance payments under the Medicare program in addition to increased fees for those services not covered by Medicare (nursing home care, prescription drugs, dental and vision care, and home services). It has been estimated that the average annual liability of Medicare beneficiaries, not including out-of-pocket expenses associated with the Medicare program, was $1,278 in 1987. Moon, *Medicare Now and in the Future*, p.108.
135. Among them, that Medicaid pay all coinsurance, deductible, and premium costs for all Medicare beneficiaries whose incomes were below federal poverty levels—which tended to be substantially higher than state Medicaid eligibility requirements—and raising the income and asset maximums of the spouses of nursing home residents below which these residents could receive Medicaid

support. Attempts by Congressman Claude Pepper to add a comprehensive home care package to the bill, however, failed.

136. Congressional Budget Office, "The Medicare Catastrophic Coverage Act of 1988," Staff Working Paper (Washington, DC, August 1, 1988), quoted in Moon, *Medicare Now and in the Future*, pp. 119-20.
137. Moon, *Medicare Now and in the Future*, p. 124.
138. Board of Trustees, Federal Hospital Insurance Trust Fund, *1996 Annual Report* (Washington, DC, June 1996): 2 and Table I.E1 (p. 11).
139. Federal Hospital Insurance Trust Fund, *1996 Annual Report*, p. 2.
140. Gordon H. Hatcher, Peter R. Hatcher, and Eleanor C. Hatcher, "Health Services in Canada," *Comparative Health Systems: Descriptive Analyses of Fourteen National Health Systems*, University Park: Pennsylvania State University Press, 1984, p. 90. While this claim reflects a startling degree of ignorance and dishonesty, the general sentiment is, alas, shared by most social planners.

Appendices

Appendix 11:

---

1.   *National Health Expenditures* are defined as comprising all spending for individual health care, including the administrative costs of non-profit and government health programs, the net cost to consumers of private health insurance, non-profit health research, and construction of medical facilities.

Sources: Data for 1929 through 1979: Robert M. Gibson and Daniel R. Waldo, "National Health Care Expenditures, 1980," *Health Care Financing Review*, III (September, 1981): pp. 1-54.

   Data for 1980 through 1984: Daniel R. Waldo, Katharine R. Levit, and Helen Lazenby, "National Health Expenditures, 1985," *Health Care Financing Review*, VIII (Fall, 1986): pp. 1-21.

   Data for 1985 through 1989: Helen Lazenby and Suzanne W. Letsch, "National Health Expenditures, 1989," *Health Care Financing Review*, XII (Winter, 1990): pp. 1-26.

   Data for 1990 through 1994: Katharine R. Levit, Helen C. Lazenby, etc., "National Health Expenditures, 1994," *Health Care Financing Review*, XVII (Spring, 1996): pp. 205-242.

   Data for 1995 through 1997 and Projections for 2000:: Health Care Financing Administration, Office of the Actuary, National Health Statistics Group, "National Health Care Expenditures, 1960-1997" (Cited 7 October 1999), available from the World Wide Web @ *http://medicare.hcfa.gov/stats/nhe-oact/tables/nhegdp97.txt*

APPENDIX 1

Medicare: Tax Rates and Maximum Tax Bases

Year	Maximum Tax Base	Tax Rate (Percent of Taxable Earnings)		Maximum Tax	
		Employee and employer, each	Self-employed	Employee portion	Self-employed
1966	$ 6,600	0.35	0.35	$ 23.10	$ 23.10
1967	6,600	0.50	0.50	33.00	33.00
1968	7,800	0.60	0.60	46.80	46.80
1969	7,800	0.60	0.60	46.80	46.80
1970	7,800	0.60	0.60	46.80	46.80
1971	7,800	0.60	0.60	46.80	46.80
1972	9,000	0.60	0.60	54.00	54.00
1973	10,800	1.00	1.00	108.00	108.00
1974	13,200	0.90	0.90	118.80	118.80
1975	14,100	0.90	0.90	126.90	126.90
1976	15,300	0.90	0.90	137.70	137.70
1977	16,500	0.90	0.90	148.50	148.50
1978	17,700	1.00	1.00	177.00	177.00
1979	22,900	1.05	1.05	240.45	240.45
1980	25,900	1.05	1.05	271.95	271.95
1981	29,700	1.30	1.30	386.10	386.10
1982	32,400	1.30	1.30	421.20	421.20
1983	35,700	1.30	1.30	464.10	464.10
1984	37,800	1.30	2.60	491.40	982.80
1985	39,600	1.35	2.70	534.60	1,069.20
1986	42,000	1.45	2.90	609.00	1,218.00
1987	43,800	1.45	2.90	635.10	1,270.20
1988	45,000	1.45	2.90	652.50	1,305.00
1989	48,000	1.45	2.90	696.00	1,392.00
1990	51,300	1.45	2.90	743.85	1,487.70
1991	125,000	1.45	2.90	1,812.50	3,625.00
1992	130,200	1.45	2.90	1,887.90	3,775.80
1993	135,000	1.45	2.90	1,957.50	3,915.00
1994	no limit	1.45	2.90	no limit	
1995	no limit	1.45	2.90	no limit	
1996	no limit	1.45	2.90	no limit	
1997	no limit	1.45	2.90	no limit	
1998	no limit	1.45	2.90	no limit	
1999	no limit	1.45	2.90	no limit	
2000	no limit	1.45	2.90	no limit	

Source: Board of Trustees, Federal Hospital Insurance Trust Fund, *1999 Annual Report* (Washington, D.C., 1999): Table II.B1 (p. 20).

APPENDIX 2

Number of Enrollees in the Medicare Hospital and/or Supplementary Medical Insurance Programs, by Type of Coverage and Type of Entitlement, Calendar Years 1966-1998
(in thousands)

	Hospital Insurance and/or Supplementary Medical Insurance			Hospital Insurance			Supplementary Medical Insurance		
	Total	Aged Enrollees	Disabled Enrollees	Total	Aged Enrollees	Disabled Enrollees	Total	Aged Enrollees	Disabled Year Enrollees
1966	19,109	19,101	—	19,082	19,082	—	17,736	17,736	—
1967	19,521	19,521	—	19,494	19,494	—	17,893	17,893	—
1968	19,821	19,821	—	19,770	19,770	—	18,805	18,805	—
1969	20,103	20,103	—	20,014	20,014	—	19,195	19,195	—
1970	20,491	20,491	—	20,361	20,361	—	19,584	19,584	—
1971	20,915	20,195	—	20,742	20,742	—	19,975	19,975	—
1972	21,332	21,332	—	21,115	21,115	—	20,351	20,351	—
1973	23,545	21,815	1,731	23,301	21,571	1,731	22,491	20,921	1,570
1974	24,201	22,273	1,928	23,924	21,996	1,928	23,167	21,421	1,745
1975	24,959	22,790	2,168	24,640	22,472	2,168	23,905	21,945	1,959
1976	25,663	23,371	2,392	25,313	22,920	2,392	24,614	22,446	2,168
1977	26,458	23,838	2,619	26,094	23,474	2,619	25,363	22,991	2,373
1978	27,164	24,371	2,793	26,777	23,984	2,793	26,074	23,531	2,543
1979	27,859	24,948	2,911	27,459	24,548	2,911	26,757	24,098	2,659
1980	28,478	25,515	2,963	28,067	25,104	2,963	27,400	24,680	2,719
1981	29,010	26,011	2,999	28,590	25,591	2,999	27,949	25,182	2,759
1982	29,494	26,540	2,954	29,069	26,115	2,954	28,412	25,707	2,705
1983	30,026	27,109	2,918	29,587	26,670	2,918	28,975	26,292	2,682
1984	30,455	27,571	2,884	29,996	27,112	2,884	29,415	26,764	2,651
1985	31,083	28,176	2,907	30,589	27,683	2,907	29,989	27,311	2,678
1986	31,750	28,791	2,959	31,216	28,257	2,959	30,590	27,863	2,727

APPENDIX 2 (cont.)

	Hospital Insurance and/or Supplementary Medical Insurance			Hospital Insurance			Supplementary Medical Insurance		
	Total	Aged Enrollees	Disabled Enrollees	Total	Aged Enrollees	Disabled Enrollees	Total	Aged Enrollees	Disabled Year Enrollees
1987	32,411	29,380	3,031	31,853	28,822	3,031	31,170	28,382	2,788
1988	32,980	29,879	3,102	32,413	29,312	3,101	31,617	28,780	2,837
1989	33,579	30,409	3,171	33,040	29,869	3,171	32,099	29,216	2,883
1990	34,213	30,961	3,252	33,731	30,479	3,252	32,636	29,691	2,945
1991	34,870	31,485	3,385	34,429	31,043	3,385	33,237	30,185	3,052
1992	35,598	32,019	3,579	35,159	31,581	3,578	33,956	30,722	3,234
1993	36,339	32,477	3,863	35,924	32,063	3,862	34,643	31,162	3,480
1994	36,935	32,801	4,135	36,543	32,409	4,135	35,167	31,447	3,720
1995	37,535	33,142	4,393	37,135	32,742	4,393	35,685	31,742	3,942
1996	38,064	33,424	4,640	37,662	33,022	4,640	36,140	31,984	4,155
1997	38,445	33,630	4,815	38,052	33,237	4,815	36,460	32,164	4,296
1998	38,825	33,802	5,023	38,432	33,410	5,023	36,781	32,308	4,472

SOURCE: 1966-1993: Medicare and Medicaid Statistical Supplement, 1995, *Health Care Financing Review* (1995): Table 5 (page 161). 1994-1998: Medicare Enrollment Trends, 1966-1998, "Medicare Aged and Disabled Enrollees by Type of Coverage" (Cited 8 October 1998), available from the World Wide Web @ *http://www.hcfa.gov/stats/enrltrnd.htm*

APPENDIX 3

Medicaid Users, by Eligibility Group, Fiscal Years 1975-1997
(thousands)

Year	Total	Low-Income Children	Low-Income Adult	Low-Income Aged	Low Income Disabled	Other
1975	22,007	9,598	4,529	3,615	2,464	1,801
1976	22,815	9,924	4,773	3,612	2,669	1,837
1977	22,862	9,651	4,785	3,636	2,802	1,958
1978	21,965	9,376	4,643	3,376	2,718	1,852
1979	21,520	9,106	4,570	3,364	2,753	1,727
1980	21,605	9,333	4,877	3,440	2,911	1,044
1981	21,980	9,581	5,187	3,367	3,079	766
1982	21,603	9,563	5,356	3,240	2,891	553
1983	21,554	9,535	5,592	3,372	2,921	134
1984	21,607	9,684	5,600	3,238	2,913	172
1985	21,814	9,757	5,518	3,061	3,012	466
1986	22,515	10,029	5,647	3,140	3,182	517
1987	23,109	10,168	5,599	3,224	3,381	737
1988	22,907	10,037	5,503	3,159	3,487	721
1989	23,511	10,318	5,717	3,132	3,590	754
1990	25,255	11,220	6,010	3,202	3,718	1,105
1991	27,967	12,855	6,703	3,341	4,033	1,035
1992	31,150	15,200	7,040	3,749	4,487	674
1993	33,432	16,285	7,505	3,863	5,016	763
1995	36,200	17,600	7,800	4,200	6,000	600
1996	37,500	18,200	8,000	4,400	6,300	600
1997	38,700	18,700	8,300	4,600	6,600	500

SOURCE: Data for 1975 through 1993: Medicare and Medicaid Statistical Supplement, 1995 *Health Care Financing Review* (1995): Table 105 (page 359).
Data for 1995 through 1997: Medicaid recipients, HCFA Statistics: *Populations*, Table 11, available from the World Wide Web @ *http://www.hcfa.gov/stats/hstats96/blustats.htm*

APPENDIX 4

Operations of the Hospital Insurance Insurance Trust Fund, Calendar Years 1970-2008
(millions)

Year	Income				Disbursements			Balance at end of Year
	Payroll Taxes	Reimbursement for Uninsured Persons	Interest and other income[1]	Total	Benefit Payments	Administrative Expenses	Total	
Historical Data:								
1970	$ 4,881	$ 863	$ 235	$ 5,979	$ 5,124	$ 157	$ 5,281	$ 3,202
1975	11,502	621	857	12,980	11,315	266	11,581	10,517
1980	23,848	697	1,552	26,097	25,064	512	25,577	13,749
1985	47,576	766	3,055	51,397	47,580	834	48,414	20,499
1986	54,583	566	4,117	59,267	49,738	664	50,422	39,957
1987	58,648	447	4,969	64,064	49,496	793	50,289	53,732
1988	62,449	475	6,315	69,239	52,517	815	53,331	69,640
1989	68,369	515	7,837	76,721	60,011	792	60,803	85,558
1990	72,013	413	7,946	80,372	66,239	758	66,997	98,933
1991	77,851	605	10,383	88,839	71,549	1,021	72,570	115,202
1992	81,745	621	11,469	93,836	83,895	1,121	85,015	124,022
1993	84,133	367	13,687	98,187	93,487	904	94,391	127,818
1994	95,280	506	13,784	109,570	103,282	1,263	104,545	132,844
1995	98,421	462	16,144	115,368	116,368	1,236	117,604	130,267
1996	110,585	419	13,598	124,603	128,632	1,297	129,929	124,942
1997	114,670	481	15,003	130,154	137,762	1,690	139,452	115,643
1998	124,317	34	16,196	140,547	133,990	1,782	135,771	120,419

APPENDIX 4 (CONT.)

| Year | Income | | | | Disbursements | | | Balance at end of Year |
	Payroll Taxes	Reimbursement for Uninsured Persons	Interest and other income[1]	Total	Benefit Payments	Administrative Expenses	Total	
Intermediate Estimates								
1999	128,880	652	16,134	145,666	143,140	2,051	145,191	120,894
2000	133,464	470	16,835	150,769	140,238	2,223	142,461	129,202
2001	139,172	202	17,944	157,318	148,215	2,344	150,559	135,962
2002	145,134	170	18,576	163,880	154,759	2,451	157,210	142,632
2003	151,571	158	19,223	170,952	163,082	2,553	165,635	147,949
2004	158,636	156	19,851	178,643	171,821	2,606	174,427	152,165
2005	166,685	161	20,488	187,334	181,949	2,667	184,616	154,883
2006	174,808	168	21,117	196,093	193,252	2,737	195,989	154,987
2007	183,966	175	21,746	205,887	205,309	2,816	208,125	152,749
2008	193,100	179	22,411	215,690	217,910	2,901	220,811	147,628

SOURCE: Board of Trustees, Federal Hospital Insurance Trust Fund, 1999 *Annual Report* (Washington, D.C., June, 1999): Table II.D2 (p. 34-35).

[1] Other income includes railroad retirement account transfers, premiums from voluntary enrollees, payments for military wage credits and, beginning in 1994, the income from the taxation of benefits.

[2] For the period 1998 to 2008, benefit payments include monies transferred to the Supplementary Medical Insurance Trust Fund for home health agency costs, as provided for in Public Law 105-33.

APPENDIX 5

Total Benefits Under the Supplementary Medical Insurance Program, Calendar Years 1967-2008

Year	Aggregate Benefits (millions)	Percent Change	Per Capita Benefits [1]	Percent Change	SMI Benefits as a Percent of GDP
Historical Data:					
1967	$ 1,197	—	$ 66.97	—	0.14
1968	1,518	26.8	82.27	22.8	0.17
1969	1,865	22.9	97.86	19.0	0.19
1970	1,975	5.9	101.30	3.5	0.19
1971	2,117	7.2	106.68	5.3	0.19
1972	2,325	9.8	114.91	7.7	0.19
1973	2,526	8.6	122.02	6.2	0.18
1974	3,318	31.4	144.47	18.4	0.22
1975	4,273	28.8	179.96	24.6	0.26
1976	5,080	18.9	207.39	15.2	0.28
1977	6,038	18.9	239.27	15.4	0.30
1978	7,252	20.1	279.58	16.8	0.32
1979	8,708	20.1	326.86	16.9	0.34
1980	10,635	22.1	389.87	19.3	0.38
1981	13,113	23.3	471.15	20.8	0.42
1982	15,455	17.9	545.55	15.8	0.48
1983	18,106	17.2	627.79	15.1	0.52
1984	19,661	8.6	670.77	6.8	0.50
1985	22,947	16.7	768.25	14.5	0.55
1986	26,239	14.3	861.37	12.1	0.59
1987	30,820	17.5	992.69	15.2	0.68
1988	33,970	10.2	1,076.64	8.5	0.67
1989	38,294	12.7	1,195.42	11.0	0.70
1990	42,468	10.9	1,305.14	9.2	0.74
1991	47,336	11.5	1,426.90	9.3	0.80
1992	49,260	4.1	1,454.81	2.0	0.79
1993	53,979	9.6	1,562.66	7.4	0.82
1994	58,618	8.6	1,670.03	6.9	0.85
1995	64,972	10.8	1,824.03	9.2	0.90
1996	68,599	5.6	1,901.88	4.3	0.90
1997	72,756	6.1	1,998.68	5.1	0.90
1998	76,125	4.6	2,074.65	3.9	0.89

APPENDIX 5 (cont.)

Year	Aggregate Benefits (millions)	Percent Change	Per Capita Benefits [1]	Percent Change	SMI Benefits as a Percent of GDP
Intermediate Estimates:					
1999	83,403	9.6	2,258.03	8.8	0.94
2000	95,666	14.7	2,567.11	13.7	1.04
2001	101,539	6.1	2,669.46	5.2	1.06
2002	110,098	8.4	2,899.25	7.4	1.10
2003	119,448	8.5	3,111.05	7.3	1.14
2004	128,035	7.2	3,294.56	5.9	1.16
2005	136,799	6.8	3,475.22	5.5	1.18
2006	147,169	7.6	3,686.45	6.1	1.21
2007	158,882	8.0	3,914.20	6.2	1.24
2008	172,071	8.3	4,156.51	6.2	1.28

SOURCE: Data for 1967 through 1984: Board of Trustees, Federal Supplementary Medical Insurance Trust Fund, *1996 Annual Report* (Washington, D.C., June, 1996): Table II:D3 (pp. 34-35).

Data for 1985 through 2008: Board of Trustees, Federal Supplementary Medical Insurance Trust Fund, *1999 Annual Report* (Washington, D.C.: June, 1999): Table II:D3 (p. 31).

[1] All Part B enrollees.

APPENDIX 6

Operations of the Supplementary Medical Insurance Trust Fund, Calendar Years 1970-2008

(millions)

Year	Income				Disbursements			Balance at end of Year
	Premiums from enrollees	Government Contributions[1]	Interest and other income	Total	Benefit Payments	Administrative Expenses	Total	
Historical Data:								
1970	$ 1,096	$ 1,093	$ 12	$ 2,201	$ 1,975	$ 237	$ 2,212	$ 188
1975	1,918	2,648	107	4,673	4,279	462	4,735	1,444
1980	3,011	7,455	408	10,874	10,635	610	11,245	4,530
1985	5,613	18,250	1,243	25,106	22,947	933	23,880	10,924
1986	5,722	17,802	1,141	24,665	26,239	1,060	27,299	8,291
1987	7,409	23,560	875	31,844	30,820	920	31,740	8,394
1988	8,761	26,203	861	35,825	33,970	1,260	35,230	8,990
1989	12,263	30,852	1,234	44,349	38,294	1,489	39,783	13,556
1990	11,320	33,035	1,558	45,913	42,468	1,519	43,987	15,482
1991	11,934	37,602	1,688	51,224	47,336	1,541	48,877	17,828
1992	14,077	41,359	1,801	57,237	49,260	1,570	50,830	24,235
1993	14,193	41,465	2,021	57,679	55,78	2,000	57,784	24,131
1994	17,386	36,203	2,018	55,607	58,618	1,699	60,317	19,422
1995	19,717	39,007	1,582	60,306	64,972	1,627	65,599	13,130
1996	18,763	65,035	1,811	85,609	68,598	1,810	70,408	28,332
1997	19,289	60,171	2,464	81,924	72,757	1,368	74,124	36,131
1998	20,933	64,068	2,711	87,711	76,125	1,505	77,630	46,212

APPENDIX 6 (cont.)

	Income				Disbursements			Balance at end of Year
Year	Premiums from enrollees	Government Contributions[1]	Interest and other income	Total	Benefit Payments	Administrative Expenses	Total	
Intermediate Estimates:								
1999	18,655	58,096	2,821	79,572	83,403	1,549	84,953	40,832
2000	21,689	70,009	2,779	94,477	95,666	1,596	97,261	38,047
2001	23,607	76,056	2,686	102,348	101,539	1,650	103,188	37,207
2002	25,747	83,236	2,668	111,650	110,098	1,708	111,805	37,052
2003	28,335	91,426	2,677	122,438	119,448	1,771	121,219	38,272
2004	30,919	96,831	2,730	130,480	128,035	1,840	129,875	38,877
2005	33,019	103,627	2,773	139,419	136,799	1,915	138,715	39,581
2006	35,834	112,247	2,854	150,934	147,169	1,994	149,163	41,452
2007	38,968	122,086	3,018	164,071	158,882	2,078	160,960	44,464
2008	42,226	132,242	3,250	177,719	172,071	2,167	174,238	47,944

SOURCE: Board of Trustees, Federal Supplementary Medical Insurance Trust Fund, *1996 Annual Report* (Washington, D.C., June, 1996): Table II.D2 (p. 28).

[1] Government contributions constitute transfers from the general fund of the Treasury and are determined by calculating the expected cost per beneficiary less expected premium collections, following a formula set down by statute.

[2] Benefit payments less monies transferred from the Hospital Insurance trust fund for home agency costs, as provided by the Balanced Budget Act of 1997.

APPENDIX 7

National Health Care Expenditures: Aggregates and Per Capita Amounts by Type of Expenditure and Source of Funds, Selected Calendar Years 1929-1965

Type of Expenditure	1929	1940	1950	1955	1960	1965
National Health Expenditures ($ billions)	3.6	4.0	12.7	17.7	26.9	41.7
As a percentage of GNP	3.5%	4.0%	4.4%	4.4%	5.3%	6.0%
Source of Funds						
Private Expenditures ($ billions)	3.2	3.2	9.2	13.2	20.3	30.9
Public Expenditures ($ billions)	.5	.8	3.4	4.6	6.6	10.8
Federal Expenditures ($ billions)	—	—	1.6	2.0	3.0	5.5
State/Local Expenditures ($ billions)	—	—	1.8	2.6	3.6	5.2
Per Capita Expenditures ($)	29.49	29.62	81.86	105.38	146.30	210.89
Source of Funds						
Private Expenditures	25.49	23.61	59.62	78.33	110.20	156.32
Public Expenditures	4.00	6.03	22.24	27.05	36.10	54.57
Federal Expenditures	—	—	10.49	11.90	16.42	27.97
State/Local Expenditures	—	—	11.75	15.15	19.69	26.60
Percentage Distribution of Funds	100.0%	100.0%	100.0%	100.0%	100.0%	100.0%
Private Funds	86.4	79.7	72.8	74.3	75.3	74.1
Public Funds	13.6	20.3	27.2	25.7	24.7	25.9
Federal Funds	—	—	12.8	11.3	11.2	13.3
State/Local Funds	—	—	14.4	14.4	13.5	12.6
Annualized Percentage Change from previous year shown						
National Health Care Expenditures	—	.8%	12.2%	7.0%	8.7%	9.2%
Private Expenditures	—	.1%	11.2%	7.4%	9.0%	8.8%
Public Expenditures	—	4.6%	15.5%	5.8%	7.8%	10.2%
Federal Expenditures	—	—	—	4.3%	8.5%	12.9%
State/Local Expenditures	—	—	—	7.0%	7.2%	7.7%

APPENDIX 8

National Health Care Expenditures: Aggregates and Per Capita Amounts by Type of Expenditure and Source of Funds, Calendar Years 1966-1973

Type of Expenditure	1966	1967	1968	1969	1970	1971	1972	1973
National Health Expenditures ($ billions)	45.1	51.3	58.2	65.7	74.7	83.3	93.5	103.2
As a percentage of GNP	6.1%	6.4%	6.7%	7.0%	7.5%	7.0%	7.9%	7.8%
Source of Funds								
Private Expenditures ($ billions)	32.5	32.4	36.1	40.8	46.9	61.6	58.1	63.9
Public Expenditures ($ billions)	13.6	19.0	22.1	24.9	27.8	31.7	35.4	39.3
Federal Expenditures ($ billions)	7.4	11.9	14.1	16.1	17.7	20.3	22.9	25.2
State/Local Expenditures ($ billions)	6.1	7.0	8.0	8.8	10.1	11.3	12.5	14.1
Per Capita Expenditures ($)	230.29	253.73	284.97	318.50	357.90	394.23	437.77	478.34
Source of Funds								
Private Expenditures	162.47	159.98	176.82	197.78	224.68	244.36	271.89	296.19
Public Expenditures	67.82	93.75	108.15	120.72	133.22	149.87	165.88	182.15
Federal Expenditures	37.19	58.90	69.05	77.95	84.69	96.18	107.13	116.75
State/Local Expenditures	30.63	34.84	39.10	42.77	48.54	53.68	58.75	65.40
Percentage Distribution of Funds	100.0%	100.0%	100.0%	100.0%	100.0%	100.0%		
Private Funds	70.6	63.1	62.0	62.1	62.8	62.0	62.1	61.9
Public Funds	29.4	36.9	38.0	37.9	37.2	38.0	37.9	38.1
Federal Funds	16.1	23.2	24.3	24.5	23.7	24.4	24.5	24.5
State/Local Funds	13.3	13.7	13.7	13.4	13.6	13.6	13.4	13.7
Annualized Percentage Change from previous year shown								
National Health Care Expenditures	10.5%	11.4%	13.4%	12.9%	13.6%	11.5%	12.3%	10.3%
Private Expenditures	5.1%	[-.5%]	11.6%	13.0%	14.8%	10.1%	12.5%	10.0%
Public Expenditures	25.7%	39.7%	16.5%	12.7%	11.6%	13.9%	11.9%	10.9%
Federal Expenditures	34.5%	60.1%	18.4%	14.0%	9.8%	15.0%	12.6%	10.0%
State/Local Expenditures	16.5%	15.0%	13.3%	10.5%	14.7%	12.0%	10.6%	12.4%

APPENDIX 9

National Health Care Expenditures: Aggregates and Per Capita Amounts by Type of Expenditure and Source of Funds, Calendar Years 1974-1981

Type of Expenditure	1974	1975	1976	1977	1978	1979	1980	1981
National Health Expenditures ($ billions)	116.4	132.7	149.7	169.2	189.3	214.6	248.1	287.0
As a percentage of GNP	8.1%	8.6%	8.7%	8.8%	8.8%	8.9%	9.1%	9.4%
Source of Funds								
Private Expenditures ($ billions)	69.3	76.5	86.7	99.1	110.0	124.5	142.9	165.8
Public Expenditures ($ billions)	47.1	56.2	62.9	70.1	79.4	90.1	105.2	121.2
Federal Expenditures ($ billions)	30.4	37.1	42.6	47.4	53.7	60.8	71.0	83.3
State/Local Expenditures ($ billions)	16.6	19.1	20.3	22.7	25.7	29.3	34.2	37.9
Per Capita Expenditures ($)	534.63	603.57	574.14	754.81	835.57	936.92	1054.0	1207.0
Source of Funds								
Private Expenditures	318.18	348.08	390.63	442.14	485.29	543.61	607.0	697.0
Public Expenditures	216.44	255.49	283.51	312.67	350.27	393.31	447.0	510.0
Federal Expenditures	139.86	168.61	191.73	211.39	236.84	265.41	302.0	350.0
State/Local Expenditures	76.58	86.88	91.78	101.28	113.44	127.70	145.0	159.0
Percentage Distribution of Funds	100.0%	100.0%	100.0%	100.0%	100.0%	100.0%		
Private Funds	59.5	57.7	57.9	58.6	58.1	58.0	57.6	57.8
Public Funds	40.5	42.3	42.1	41.4	41.9	42.0	42.4	42.2
Federal Funds	26.2	27.9	28.5	28.0	28.3	28.4	28.6	29.0
State/Local Funds	14.3	14.4	13.6	13.4	13.6	13.7	13.8	13.2
Annualized Percentage Change from previous year shown								
National Health Care Expenditures	12.8%	14.0%	12.8%	13.1%	11.9%	13.4%	15.6%	15.7%
Private Expenditures	8.4%	10.5%	13.3%	14.3%	10.9%	13.2%	15.1%	16.0%
Public Expenditures	19.9%	19.2%	12.0%	11.4%	13.2%	13.5%	16.2%	15.2%
Federal Expenditures	20.9%	21.8%	14.8%	11.4%	13.2%	13.3%	16.4%	17.3%
State/Local Expenditures	18.2%	14.6%	6.6%	11.5%	13.2%	14.0%	15.8%	10.9%

APPENDIX 10

National Health Care Expenditures: Aggregates and Per Capita Amounts by Type of Expenditure and Source of Funds, Calendar Years 1982-1989

Type of Expenditure	1982	1983	1984	1985	1986	1987	1988	1989
National Health Expenditures ($ billions)	323.6	357.2	390.2	420.1	452.3	492.5	544.0	604.1
As a percentage of GNP	10.2%	10.5%	10.3%	10.5%	10.7%	10.9%	11.2%	11.6%
Source of Funds								
Private Expenditures ($ billions)	188.4	209.7	230.7	245.7	260.9	282.9	315.8	350.9
Public Expenditures ($ billions)	135.3	147.5	159.5	175.1	191.3	209.6	228.2	253.3
Federal Expenditures ($ billions)	93.2	102.7	111.7	123.6	132.6	143.5	156.7	174.4
State/Local Expenditures ($ billions)	42.1	44.8	47.8	51.5	58.8	66.2	71.5	78.8
Per Capita Expenditures ($)	1348	1473	1595	1700	1813	1955	2139	2354
Source of Funds								
Private Expenditures	784	865	943	992	1046	1123	1242	1367
Public Expenditures	563	608	652	709	767	832	898	987
Federal Expenditures	388	424	456	500	532	570	616	680
State/Local Expenditures	175	185	195	208	236	263	281	307
Percentage Distribution of Funds	100.0%	100.0%	100.0%	100.0%	100.0%	100.0%	58.1	58.1
Private Funds	58.2	58.7	59.1	58.3	57.7	57.4	58.0	58.1
Public Funds	41.8	41.3	40.9	41.7	42.3	42.6	42.0	41.9
Federal Funds	28.8	28.8	28.6	29.4	29.3	29.1	28.8	28.9
State/Local Funds	13.0	12.5	12.3	12.3	13.0	13.4	13.1	13.0
Annualized Percentage Change from previous year shown								
National Health Care Expenditures	12.8%	10.4%	9.2%	8.9%	7.7%	8.9%	10.5%	11.1%
Private Expenditures	13.6%	11.3%	10.0%	8.5%	6.5%	8.4%	11.6%	11.1%
Public Expenditures	11.6%	9.1%	8.1%	9.6%	9.3%	9.6%	8.9%	11.0%
Federal Expenditures	11.9%	10.2%	8.7%	11.4%	7.3%	8.2%	9.2%	11.3%
State/Local Expenditures	11.1%	6.4%	6.8%	5.3%	14.2%	12.6%	8.1%	10.2%

APPENDIX 11

National Health Care Expenditures: Aggregates and Per Capita Amounts by Type of Expenditure and Source of Funds, Calendar Years 1990-1997 and Projected Estimates for the Year 2000

Type of Expenditure	1990	1991	1992	1993	1994	1995	1996	1997	2000
National Health Expenditures ($ billions)	697.5	761.3	833.6	892.3	949.4	993.7	1042.5	1092.4	1316.2
As a percentage of GNP	12.6%	12.9%	13.3%	13.6%	13.7%	13.7%	13.6%	13.5%	14.6%
Source of Funds									
Private Expenditures ($ billions)	413.1	441.0	477.0	505.1	528.6	536.5	561.1	585.3	722.6
Public Expenditures ($ billions)	284.3	320.3	356.5	387.2	420.8	455.2	481.4	507.1	593.6
Federal Expenditures ($ billions)	195.8	224.4	254.8	278.5	303.6	326.0	348.0	367.0	423.9
State/Local Expenditures ($ billions)	88.5	95.8	101.8	108.6	117.2	129.2	133.4	140.0	169.7
Per Capita Expenditures ($)	2688	2902	3144	3331	3510	3637	3781	3925	4611
Source of Funds									
Private Expenditures	1592	1681	1799	1886	1954	1970.7	2034.9	2103.1	2531
Public Expenditures	1096	1221	1345	1445	1556	1665.9	1745.5	1822.0	2079
Federal Expenditures	754	856	961	1040	1122	1193.0	1262.0	1318.9	1485
State/Local Expenditures	341	365	384	406	433	472.9	483.7	503.1	594
Percentage Distribution of Funds	100.0%	100.0%	100.0%	100.0%	100.0%	100.0%	100.0%	100.0%	100.0%
Private Funds	59.2	57.9	57.2	56.6	55.7	54.2	53.8	53.6	54.9
Public Funds	40.8	42.1	42.8	43.4	44.3	45.8	46.2	46.4	45.1
Federal Funds	28.1	29.5	30.6	31.2	32.0	32.8	33.4	33.6	32.2
State/Local Funds	12.7	12.6	12.2	12.2	12.3	13.0	12.8	12.8	12.9
Annualized Percentage Change from previous year shown									
National Health Care Expenditures	11.6%	9.1%	9.5%	7.0%	6.4%	4.9%	4.9%	4.8%	7.1%
Private Expenditures	10.6%	6.7%	8.2%	5.9%	4.7%	2.6%	4.2%	4.3%	8.0%
Public Expenditures	13.2%	12.7%	11.3%	8.6%	8.7%	7.7%	5.7%	5.3%	6.1%
Federal Expenditures	11.9%	14.6%	13.5%	9.3%	9.0%	8.2%	6.8%	5.5%	6.0%
State/Local Expenditures	16.0%	8.3%	6.2%	6.7%	7.9%	6.2%	3.2%	5.0%	6.4%

2

Medicare's Progeny:
The 1996 Health Care Legislation

Charlotte Twight

On August 1 and 2, 1996, Congress cleared for the president's signature the Health Insurance Portability and Accountability Act of 1996, known in the press as the Kennedy-Kassebaum bill. There was little dissent: the House vote approving the conference report on the bill was 421 to 2, the Senate vote 98 to 0. The press response was muted but unquestioningly favorable. After all, this bill was said to bring about health insurance "portability" and "accountability." President Clinton signed the bill into law on August 21, 1996.[1]

Unbeknownst to most Americans, the 1996 act contained major provisions of the Clinton administration's previously rejected 1993 Health Security Act. How did some of the most feared provisions of the 1993 proposal—potentially threatening innocent physicians with federal criminal penalties and jeopardizing the privacy of doctor-patient relations through a nationwide electronic database—become law in 1996 virtually without opposition? The remarkable truth is that the political strategies that facilitated passage of this bill are the same as those that allowed the original Medicare law to be passed in 1965 after decades of public rejection of federal health insurance measures. In both cases advocates achieved their goals by manipulating political transaction costs to deflect and silence public opposition.

Imagine a well-publicized congressional vote on a widely understood single issue: whether to mandate creation of a uniform national electronic database requiring the recording and transmission of personal health information revealed by private individuals to their doctors, with no privacy protection required to be put in place for three and a half years. That one cannot imagine passage of such a measure highlights the importance of transaction-cost manipulation in facilitating and sustaining government encroachments on what people long regarded as inviolable rights. Congress in 1996 passed exactly such a privacy-threatening database law—but not as a stand-alone measure and without either publicity or public understanding of its substance. The trick used by proponents of such measures is to raise the transaction costs to voters (and to congressmen) of resistance—a trick performed as ably in 1996 with the Health Insurance Portability and Accountability Act as in 1965 with the Medicare legislation. In both cases transaction-cost-increasing political strategies such as tying, incrementalism, and misrepresentation were used to establish new governmental powers whose implementation, in turn, would raise the transaction costs to citizens resisting this expanded federal authority.

I shall consider the 1965 Medicare legislation and the 1996 Health Insurance Portability and Accountability Act as linked case studies of the accretion of federal power over U.S. health care. The facts of the individual cases and the theory linking them reveal a political process of greater regularity and generalizability than a consideration of either law in isolation would suggest. Readers concerned about the future of freedom may find my conclusions disturbing. Advocates of expanded federal authority persist, and manipulation of political transaction costs combined with induced ideological change allows them to work their will in the longest of long runs.

A Theory of Institutional Change

For many years I have worked to develop and test a theory of government manipulation of constitutional-level transaction costs (Twight 1983, 1988, 1994). That theory will serve as a backdrop for the analysis of health care legislation that follows. Although it would be inappropriate to reiterate the full theory here, some definitions and a brief summary will be useful.

I define constitutional-level transaction costs as the costs to individuals of negotiating and enforcing collective political agreements that influence the scope of government authority—the line dividing what is handled by government from what is regarded as outside its purview. Constitutional-level political transaction costs so defined encompass both costs of *perceiving* relevant political information (information costs) and costs of *acting* on those perceptions (which I term "agreement and enforcement costs").[2]

Animating the theory is the idea that government officials as individuals often have both the incentive and the capacity to manipulate the political transaction costs facing private citizens (and each other) so as to achieve more of what officeholders want with less resistance from the public. This quest often involves transaction-cost augmentation—artificially increasing the costs to private citizens of resisting authority-changing measures favored by particular officeholders. The motive for this behavior is readily understandable: if government officials can increase the marginal costs to voters of understanding or taking political action to oppose a measure that changes the scope of government authority, they can reduce political resistance. For example, officeholders may mitigate resistance by misrepresenting a bill's contents, using incremental strategies, tying controversial measures to popular ones, using tax strategies that obscure a program's cost, and the like. The theory strongly rejects the supposition that government always functions to minimize politically relevant transaction costs.

Artificially increased political transaction costs thus drive a wedge between voter preferences and political action that reflects those preferences. The theory identifies various determinants influencing an individual officeholder's decision to favor a transaction-cost-increasing measure: executive and party support for the measure, impact on officeholder job security and perquisites, third-party payoffs, officeholder ideology, the measure's complexity and perceived importance to constituents, publicity, time, and the existence of an appealing rationale for the measure (Twight 1983, 1988).

Once in place, institutional changes that increase the public's transaction costs of resisting expanded federal authority set in motion a process of accommodative ideological change that further lessens the likelihood of restoring the status quo ante (Higgs 1985, 1987; Kuran 1995). Twentieth-century U.S. politics has supplied countless examples of government manipulation of constitutional-level transaction costs fostering institutional changes followed by sympathetic ideological change. The legislative histories of Social Security, income-tax withholding, public education, and other government-expanding measures have proved consistent with this interpretation (Twight 1993, 1995, 1996). What about Medicare?

Medicare's Passage in 1965: Tactical Blueprint for 1996

Medicare did not emerge spontaneously in 1965.[3] Its passage had been sought continuously since 1934 by a group of advocates within the federal government. For three full decades the concept of compulsory national health insurance had been rejected, year after year, by Congress and the public (Twight 1997). Of interest here are the strategy proponents employed to overcome this demonstrated public opposition.

National health insurance first appeared on the federal government's agenda in a serious way in 1934,[4] when President Franklin Roosevelt established the Committee on Economic Security (CES) and charged its members with formulating recommendations for a social security bill. Included in their initial recommendations, with Roosevelt's approval, was a provision for the study of national health insurance. That provision caused such resistance that President Roosevelt successfully sought its removal from the resultant bill in order to secure passage of the Social Security Act of 1935 (Corning 1969, 38; Chapman and Talmadge 1970, 342).

Nonetheless, the president and the Social Security Board proceeded as if the original statutory language had been retained. The day after the Social Security Act was signed, Roosevelt appointed the Interdepartmental Committee to Coordinate Health and Welfare Activities to consider health insurance. That committee created the Technical Committee on Medical Care, whose 1938 report led to the "climate-building" National Health Conference and Interdepartmental Committee recommendations that included, inter alia, a "general program of medical care, paid for either through general taxation or social insurance contributions" (Poen 1979, 19).

Thereafter, bills on this subject were introduced in virtually every session of Congress. Beginning in 1943, the Wagner-Murray-Dingell bills sponsored by Senator Robert Wagner (D-N.Y.), Senator James Murray (D-Mont.), and Representative John Dingell (D-Mich.) explicitly proposed universal compulsory national health insurance. Advocates from the Social Security Board often drafted the bills and cajoled willing legislators into introducing them. These executive-branch officials' names echo across the pages of thirty years of legislative history: Isidore Falk, Wilbur Cohen, and Robert Ball, among others. Though their positions changed when reorganizations occurred and when inclement political conditions arose, they were never far from the drafting of the bills. Throughout this period, government officials tried hard to change public opinion on this topic (surveys in 1942 showed 76.3 percent of the public opposed to government provision of free medical care), in one case successfully intervening prior to publication to persuade the authors of a *Fortune* magazine article to change their conclusions regarding the Wagner-Murray-Dingell bill (Poen 1979, 45; Cantril 1951, 440). Martha Derthick (1979, 317) remarked that "Nowhere is the aggressiveness of social security program executives better demonstrated than in these early campaigns for national health insurance."

Deliberate reliance on incremental strategies began in earnest in 1951. It was a turning point. After discouraging results for advocates of compulsory national health insurance in the 1950 elections, program executives including Social Security officials Cohen and Falk realized that they could not succeed with a *universal* compulsory health insurance plan. As a result, in the spring of 1951 they began to work for a narrower program specifically targeted at the elderly. Such bills were introduced repeatedly throughout the Eisenhower years, as advocates tried to keep the idea alive. In 1956, in a political development that Derthick (1979, 319) regarded as a "necessary prelude" to Medicare, a statute providing disability coverage was passed, whereupon the AFL-CIO recommitted itself to the fight for compulsory national health insurance. Along with Cohen, Falk, and Ball, Nelson Cruikshank (head of the AFL-CIO's Department of Social Security) spearheaded the drafting of a bill proposing hospital, surgical, and nursing home benefits for social security recipients. Their bill became the Forand bill, introduced by Aime J. Forand (D-R.I.) but rejected by the House Ways and Means Committee in 1959. In 1960, in an effort to forestall more comprehensive legislation, House Ways and Means Committee chairman Wilbur Mills (D-Ark.) and Senator Robert Kerr (D-Okla.) introduced and secured passage of the Kerr-Mills program of needs-based medical assistance for the aged.

This preemptive effort failed to stem the tide. In 1961 and again in 1963 Representative Cecil King (D-Calif.) and Senator Clinton Anderson (D-N.M.) introduced another bill patterned on the Forand bill. When the landslide election of President Lyndon Johnson changed the political calculus in 1964, the King-Anderson bill became the basis for the administration's health care proposals, H.R. 1 and S. 1.

Incrementalism in its various forms—including the decision to target the elderly in the belief that they represented the most sympathetic group—was a deliberate and sustained strategy that increased the costs to the public of resisting compulsory national health insurance. After the 1964 elections, when for the first time all of the determinants discussed earlier favored pro-Medicare transaction-cost augmentation, Congress used additional transaction-cost-increasing strategies to pass and entrench the Medicare bill (Twight 1997).

First, the Medicare bill was included within—and tied to—the Social Security Amendments of 1965. Chief among the politically irresistible features of the broader package was a 7 percent across-the-board increase in social security cash benefits—not to mention maternal and child-health services and the like. To vote against Medicare, a legislator had to vote against that 7 percent social security benefit increase, made retroactive to January 1, 1965. Congressmen in a 1964 conference deadlocked on the Medicare issue had decided to forgo a Social Security benefit increase agreed to by both houses of Congress in order to permit this tie-in and thereby give Medicare another chance in 1965 (Twight 1997).

Some legislators objected to the linkage. Representative John Byrnes (R-Wisc.) decried the fact that Medicare's "proponents are unwilling to let [it] stand on its own feet and rise or fall on its own merits," instead choosing to "tie [it] to the now controversial amendments to the Social Security Act" (*Cong. Rec.*, House, April 7, 1965, 7220). Representative Delbert Latta (R-Ohio) asked his colleagues "why the administration and the Medicare backers were afraid to let this so-called Medicare part of this bill come to the floor of the House by itself . . . and be voted up or down on its own merits. What were they afraid of?" (*Cong. Rec.*, House, April 8, 1965, 7420). When the Senate vote drew near, Senator Milward L. Simpson (R-Wyo.) spoke bluntly about his personal unwillingness to succumb to the incentives created by the tie-in: "I choose not to prostitute my vote in this matter and because portions of this bill are objectionable to me, I am compelled to vote against the total bill, even though I support parts of it" (*Cong. Rec.*, Senate, July 8, 1965, 15874). In the end, however, most did succumb.

Second, legislators and others in government misrepresented the Medicare bill's contents. Although private citizens were led to believe that Medicare was designed in part to avoid the financial devastation associated with extended illness in old age, catastrophic illness was not covered by the bill. As originally introduced in 1965, H.R. 1 and S. 1 covered only sixty days of hospital care, sixty days of nursing-home care, and some laboratory and X-ray services. Senator Russell Long (D-La.) challenged Department of Health, Education, and Welfare (HEW) Secretary Anthony Celebrezze for his duplicity on this point, stating, "Well, in arguing for your plan you say let's not strip poor old grandma of the last dress she has and of her home and what little resources she has and you bring us a plan that does exactly that unless she gets well in 60 days" (U.S. Senate 1965, 183). Ordinary physicians' visits, therapeutic drugs, and the like were not covered by H.R. 1 and S. 1. Nonetheless, the public widely believed that the proposal represented comprehensive coverage of all medical needs of the elderly as suggested by use of the term "Medicare," a label originally applied to a comprehensive medical program for military dependents.

There were other misrepresentations as well. To counter the public's fear that Medicare would allow government control over the provision of medical care, government proponents of Medicare included a provision in the bill specifically disavowing such control. The disavowal was a charade. As Representative Thomas Curtis (R-Mo.) remarked, "If you look at the bill, right at the very beginning there is a great big label. . . . It says there will be no Federal interference, and that free choice by the patient is guaranteed. Then the next 70 pages tell you how the Federal interference will be carried out" (*Cong. Rec.,* House, April 7, 1965, 7231). Nonetheless, the statutory language made it more difficult for the public to understand that control was inevitable if government was empowered to determine and pay "reasonable" charges for medical services.

In addition, legislators and program executives falsely represented the Medicare bill as a way to "avoid dependence" in old age. As already noted, the omission of coverage for catastrophic illness guaranteed that the elderly would not be protected against this most feared condition. More important politically, the appeal of "avoiding dependence" put a favorable gloss on an unspoken rationale for much public support for Medicare—the desire of adult children to avoid responsibility for their aging parents' medical bills.

Other transaction-cost-increasing strategies involved cost conceal-ment associated with Medicare's financing. Because the program was to be financed through the payroll tax, employer withholding of the Medicare taxes would make it more difficult for employees to per-ceive their magnitude. Moreover, the Medicare tax was nominally split between employers and employees, further obscuring the employee's full tax burden (Browning 1975). Even today few people understand that the payroll taxes nominally paid by employers are largely borne by employees. Government officials downplayed the regressivity of the payroll tax and ignored the protests of congressmen such as Senator Russell Long (D-La.), who asked, "Why should we pay the medical bill of a man who has an income of $100,000 a year or a million dollars a year income?" (*Cong. Rec.,* Senate, July 9, 1965, 16096). Although people were told that their money would be put in a separate Medicare trust fund and that they would be paying for "insur-ance" to defray the cost of illness in their later years, many legislators understood that there would be no such prepayment, referring to the "myth" of prepayment and "the subterfuge of a separate tax and a separate trust fund" (U.S. House 1965b, minority views, 251; *Cong. Rec.,* House, April 8, 1965, 7405). Only the public was fooled.

Finally, there was Wilbur Mills's "three-layer cake." Having blocked passage of Medicare legislation in previous years, Representative Mills (D-Ark.) decided after the 1964 election that passage of a Medicare bill was inevitable. Accordingly, he would use his copious power as chairman of the House Ways and Means Committee to shape it to his liking.

Mills did so through transaction-cost manipulation. He refused to allow open public hearings on the 1965 bill. Instead, he invited only select technical experts to testify in executive sessions of the commit-tee, allowing them to discuss only the technical aspects of the pro-posed bills. Discussion of "philosophy" or ideology was ruled out. After the suggestions of the experts had been heard, the executive sessions were closed; the public and the press were barred. No printed record of the closed sessions was made available to Congress or the public. In addition to discussing the administration's King-Anderson bill, Mills and his committee also debated alternative proposed bills, including Representative John Byrnes's (R-Wisc.) "better-care" bill proposing coverage of physicians' services and the AMA bill ("elder-care") suggesting improvements in the Kerr-Mills program.

To many people's surprise, what emerged from the House Ways and Means Committee with a recommendation for passage was a composite bill that combined the three approaches—a "three-layer cake" along lines first suggested by Wilbur Cohen (U.S. House 1965a, 123-24). The first layer was the King-Anderson approach, financing compulsory federal hospital insurance for the elderly under the Social Security program through additional payroll taxes. The second layer was "voluntary" medical insurance ("supplemental medical insurance") for the elderly that would cover physicians' services, with 50 percent of the premium paid by the subscriber and—despite the ostensibly voluntary nature of the insurance—50 percent paid for out of general revenues of the federal government. The third layer was an expansion of the Kerr-Mills program for the aged poor, partly financed by the federal government and partly financed by state governments.

This bundle was tied together as the recommended Medicare legislation, which in turn was tied to the other components of the Social Security Amendments of 1965 such as the 7 percent cash benefit increase. Rechristened as H.R. 6675, the committee-recommended bill went to the House floor under a closed rule, which did not permit amendments.

The closed hearings, closed rule, and tying—along with incrementalism, misrepresentation, appealing rhetoric, and cost concealment—were significant components of the transaction-cost augmentation leading to the passage of Medicare (Twight 1997). So constructed, the package was politically irresistible, as confirmed by House and Senate action on the bill in the summer of 1965.[5] Once in place, Medicare institutionalized transaction-cost barriers for the future. As Senator Carl Curtis (R-Neb.) expressed it:

> [I]f we button it into social security we will write it into perpetuity and will never have another opportunity to consider another plan voluntary in nature involving the private enterprise concept, once the proposed legislation is enacted. Once we start the procedures of taxation and withholding on the basis of a social security withholding tax, it then becomes too late to unscramble the omelet. (*Cong. Rec.,* Senate, July 9, 1965, 16121).

Button it in they did. Thirty years later, some of the same strategies would be used to further increase federal authority over U.S. health care.

The Health Insurance Portability and Accountability Act of 1996

"I don't see the logic . . . of how we could keep that confined to that aged group. The logic looks like once we have done this we are going to have to extend it further. That is why I think logically people say this will lead to socialized medicine, not saying those who advocate it are Socialists—I want to emphasize that again—but would lead to the technique of the Government moving heavily into the entire field of health care."
—*Representative Thomas B. Curtis (R-Mo.)*
(U.S. House 1963-64, 137)

Representative Curtis was right about the logic. As he predicted over thirty years ago, government has continued to move ever more heavily into the "entire field of health care." Steps taken in the intervening years, such as the Health Maintenance Organization Act of 1973, will not be discussed here. Instead, I shall focus on the sequence of events beginning with the Clinton administration's proposal of the Health Security Act in 1993.

The Clinton administration's 1993 proposal, if passed, would have mandated a virtual federal takeover of health care delivery in the United States, mandating ubiquitous price and service controls administered by regional alliances subordinate to a "National Health Board." The bill was 1,342 pages long, developed in secret by a group of Hillary Clinton's friends and associates.[6] It was presented to the American public with great fanfare, the president touting every American's entitlement to a "health security card" and the comprehensive health benefits said to accompany it. Despite the fanfare, many people became alarmed about the bill's implications when articles were published detailing extensive criminal sanctions to be applied to physicians and regimentation to be mandated throughout U.S. health care markets under the Health Security Act. The bill died, and many people breathed a great sigh of relief.

That sigh of relief was premature. Intentionally or unintentionally, advocates of more invasive government controls over U.S. health care took a page from the 1965 Medicare strategy book. Many of the strategies used to pass Medicare in 1965 were deployed again in 1996 to secure passage of the Health Insurance Portability and Accountability Act.

Although the title of the Health Insurance Portability and Accountability Act of 1996 sounds wholly benign, its content is not. By using the strategies of transaction-cost manipulation that served Medicare's proponents so well in 1965, advocates of government control over U.S. health care secured passage of a law that includes some of the most feared provisions of the Clinton administration's 1993 Health Security Act. Many of the 1993 provisions that potentially threaten innocent physicians with federal criminal penalties and jeopardize the privacy of doctor-patient relations through a nationwide electronic database literally were copied from the earlier bill and included verbatim in the 1996 law. Yet dissent—or even attention to these provisions—scarcely arose. With little notice in the press, the House and Senate gave virtually unanimous final approval to the Health Insurance Portability and Accountability Act in early August 1996.[7]

Little-Known Provisions of the 1996 Bill

Without doubt, the Health Insurance Portability and Accountability Act of 1996 contains some features that most Americans value highly, including portability provisions to prevent loss of health insurance triggered by job changes, significant health insurance access and renewability guarantees, and—on an experimental basis—medical savings accounts to establish greater individual financial stakes (and hence cost consciousness) in making health care choices.[8] Ironically, during the 1996 bill's consideration few acknowledged that some of the problems at which its provisions were aimed—job lock, inadequate portability—themselves arose from earlier government interventions.[9] This history notwithstanding, the appeal of the core ideas of portability and renewability cannot be overstated: the *Congressional Record* is rife with the stories of people whose long-standing insurance coverage was canceled after serious illness occurred and others whose continued coverage, due to family illness, depends on staying in their present job. Highlighted in congressional and media statements, the portability and renewability issues figured importantly in political strategies used to secure the bill's passage, as will be discussed later.

But Congress and the press did not openly tell the public about other provisions, including a bevy of federal criminal sanctions potentially threatening innocent physicians and a national electronic database threatening the privacy of individuals' medical records. Most of these provisions appear in Title II of the new law under the heading "Preventing Health Care Fraud and Abuse; Administrative Simplification."[10] Although many congressmen's fears about these provisions were quieted as proponents insisted that "[t]his is not 'Clinton Lite,'" such acquiescence was misguided (*Cong. Rec.*, Senate, April 18, 1996, 3543).

One of the purposes of the new law is to limit Medicare fraud, said to cost Americans approximately $18 billion annually (*Cong. Rec.*, Senate, April 18, 1996, 3568). Accordingly, the new law establishes a "fraud and abuse control program" to be administered by the Department of Health and Human Services (HHS) and applied to any "federal health care program," defined as "any plan or program that provides health benefits, whether directly, through insurance, or otherwise, which is funded directly, in whole or in part, by the United States Government" as well as any "state health care program" [§204(f)].

In provisions cribbed from §5401 of Clinton's 1993 bill, the 1996 act empowers the secretary of HHS, inter alia, "to conduct investigations, audits, evaluations, and inspections relating to the delivery of and payment for health care in the United States," to "arrange for the sharing of data with representatives of health plans," and to secure "qualified immunity" for those who provide information to the secretary or the attorney general [§201]. Like the rejected 1993 bill's §5402, it establishes a "Health Care Fraud and Abuse Control Account." In a section labeled "Beneficiary Incentive Programs," the 1996 law authorizes the secretary of HHS to "encourage" informants and to pay them a portion of amounts collected as a result of their disclosures [§203(b)].[11]

Civil Penalties

Civil penalties under the 1996 act apply to medical practice involving federal health care programs, including Medicare and other federal programs, as well as state health care programs. Preexisting civil penalties are increased (in general from $2,000 to $10,000 per violation) and broadened in ways that may include innocent efforts by practitioners to render appropriate health care services to patients. For example, a new provision makes a physician's miscoding of insurance claims filed with any federal or state agency subject to civil penalties of up to $10,000 for each instance. Under a provision of the new law headed "Claim for Item or Service Based on Incorrect Coding or

Medically Unnecessary Services," civil sanctions can be applied to any person who "engages in a pattern or practice of presenting or causing to be presented a claim for an item or service that is based on a code that the person knows or should know will result in a greater payment to the person than the code the person knows or should know is applicable to the item or service actually provided" [§231(e)]. Dr. Jane Orient, a private practitioner and the executive director of the Association of American Physicians and Surgeons, reports that "there are thousands of codes and no consistent interpretation" of them (Orient 1996). Yet the secretary of HHS and the courts are now empowered to determine after the fact what the doctor should have known about them.[12]

Civil sanctions also are to be applied if a health care provider makes a claim "for a pattern of medical or other items or services that a person knows or should know are *not medically necessary*" [§231(e), my emphasis]. Again, the HHS secretary is empowered to determine *ex post* whether something was or was not "medically necessary." Under such rules, every physician who serves patients participating in any federal or state health care program is potentially subject to governmental second-guessing and the threat of concomitant civil penalties.

Reminiscent of the Medicare controversy in the 1960s over the "control" issue, again in 1996 official disclaimers were written into the record about the intended scope of the legislation. Because disclaimers in conference or committee reports, though part of the bill's legislative history, are not part of its language and did not become statutory law, they often served chiefly to disarm opposition to questionable provisions without in fact limiting the bill's scope.

A case in point involves the civil sanctions just described. In response to fears expressed by practitioners of alternative medicine, the conferees stated in the conference report that they "do not intend to penalize the exercise of medical judgment of health care treatment choices made in good faith and which are supported by significant evidence or held by a respectable minority of those providers who customarily provide similar methods of treatment," adding that the act "is not intended to penalize providers simply because of a professional difference of opinion regarding diagnosis or treatment" (U.S. House 1996b, 255). Statutory language broad and ambiguous enough to trigger such a disclaimer highlights the dangerous scope of authority granted by the new law.

Physicians' experience under prior Medicare law heightens these concerns. During the late 1980s and early 1990s the Medicare bureaucracy threatened to penalize nonparticipating physicians whose patients over age sixty-five contracted with them to obtain services outside the Medicare system, even though no reimbursement would be sought from Medicare in these cases. Physicians received official correspondence from Medicare carriers and administrators stating that such private contracting was largely inconsistent with Medicare law. Many patients were furious. As one patient stated, "Why should I wake up with fewer rights on turning 65 than I had the day before?" (Copeland 1993, 9).

In 1991, Dr. Lois Copeland and five representative patients brought suit against the secretary of HHS, Dr. Louis Sullivan, challenging this interpretation of Medicare law.[13] Judge Nicholas Politan dismissed the case, ruling that the evidence did not establish that the HHS secretary had a clearly articulated "policy" interpreting the Medicare law to prohibit private contracting.[14] Attorneys for HHS were unable to identify the source of the Medicare carriers' statements. As Dr. Copeland (1993, 10) put it, "physicians actually [had been] coerced into following a regulation that did not exist."

Although the case was dismissed, Dr. Copeland stated that the plaintiffs "considered this ruling to be an absolute victory" (Copeland 1993, 10). By upholding the plaintiffs' standing to sue in this case, the judge opened the door for their return to court if the HHS secretary subsequently issued an explicit policy against private contracting. In the meantime, their primary objective was achieved: physicians were now free to establish private contracts with their elderly patients outside of Medicare.

This victory was short-lived. As part of the Balanced Budget Act of 1997 (Public Law 105-33, 111 Stat. 251), Congress included a provision that makes such private contracts between doctors and elderly patients virtually impossible. The Balanced Budget Act effectively kills private contracting by requiring any physician who contracts privately (wholly outside Medicare) with even one patient over age sixty-five to file a signed affidavit with the federal government stating that he will not submit *any* claims to Medicare for *any* patient "during the 2-year period beginning on the date the affidavit is signed" [§4507(a)(3)]. That is, to form a voluntary contract outside of Medicare with one elderly patient, a physician must renounce any and all

Medicare patients for a full two-year period. Commentators have pointed out that this gives elderly Americans fewer rights to pay for their medical care than British retirees possess under their country's largely socialized system of medicine (Brown 1997).

House and Senate bills already have been drafted seeking to reverse this outrageous statutory deprivation of liberty. Court challenges also are expected. Nonetheless, the systematic efforts by the Medicare bureaucracy and compliant legislators to restrict people's right to pay for their own health care—despite statutory language in the original Medicare legislation disavowing such control—make it clear that the federal government cannot be relied on to interpret narrowly the broad discretionary authority in the 1996 act.

New Health Care Crimes

Equally disturbing, the 1996 act threatens innocent physicians with potential prosecution for loosely drawn new crimes accorded the Orwellian designation of "federal health care offenses," investigation of which confers broad subpoena power on the U.S. attorney general [§248]. Unlike the new law's civil sanctions, the criminal penalties discussed here reach all private contracts for medical services: they are not limited to medical practice in connection with Medicare and other federal or state health care programs.

In provisions copied almost verbatim from the 1993 Health Security Act, the 1996 law establishes as crimes "health care fraud," "theft or embezzlement in connection with health care," "false statements relating to health care matters," and "obstruction of criminal investigations of health care offenses"[15] [§§242–45]. These labels suggest that the forbidden behavior is Bad Stuff, and some of it clearly is. The question is, can any Good Stuff be prosecuted under the language of the new rules—and, if so, what effects will the threat of federal criminal prosecution have on honest medical practitioners?

The new rules penalize actions relating to "health care benefit programs," defined in the statute to include every "public or private plan or contract" in which "any medical benefit, item, or service is provided to any individual," specifically including "any individual or entity who is providing a medical benefit, item, or service for which payment may be made under the plan or contract" [§241]. Private fee-for-service physicians most definitely are included. The criminal penalties established for violation of the new crimes typically involve up to ten years in prison in addition to large fines and property forfeiture.

Consider the new crimes. Copied almost verbatim from the Clinton administration's 1993 bill, §5431(a), the new federal crime of "health care fraud" specifies criminal penalties of up to ten years in prison plus fines for anyone who "knowingly and willfully executes, or attempts to execute, a scheme or artifice (1) to defraud any health care benefit program; or (2) to obtain, by means of false or fraudulent pretenses, representations, or promises, any of the money or property owned by, or under the custody or control of, any health care benefit program" [§242(a)]. The prison sentence is up to twenty years if the violation "results in serious bodily injury" and up to life in prison if anyone dies. Even an *attempt* to undertake the proscribed behavior could land a physician in jail for ten years. Because determination of what constitutes "knowing" and "willful" behavior can come only after the fact, innocent behavior potentially falls under the broad umbrella of this language. Moreover, attempting to secure payment for a procedure that the physician considered to be medically necessary (and that helped the patient) but that later was deemed unnecessary by government officials could be deemed a "false representation." If a patient died in such a situation, the doctor could face a potential sentence of life in prison.

Again the conference report, though not the statute, contains a disclaimer. The conference report states regarding §242 that the act "is not intended to penalize a person who exercises a health care treatment choice or makes a medical or health care judgment in good faith simply because there is a difference of opinion regarding the form of diagnosis" (U.S. House 1996b, 258). The very existence of such a disclaimer again shows that the language of the statute is broad enough to allow federal authorities to initiate prosecution in situations involving controverted medical judgments.

The second new federal crime, "Theft or embezzlement in connection with health care," was lifted in its entirety from §5437 of the Clinton administration's 1993 bill. Fines and imprisonment of up to ten years (or up to one year if the amount in question is *$100 or less!*) await anyone who "knowingly and willfully . . . without authority converts to the use of any person other than the rightful owner, or intentionally misapplies any of the moneys, funds, securities, premiums, credits, property, or other assets of a health care benefit program" [§243].

The third new federal crime, making "false statements relating to health care matters," specifies fines and up to five years of prison time for anyone who "knowingly and willfully—(1) falsifies, conceals, or covers up . . . a material fact; or (2) makes any materially false . . . statements or representations . . . in connection with the delivery of or payment for health care benefits, items, or services" [§244]. Again the language was copied almost verbatim from the Clinton administration's 1993 bill, §5433. Because what is "knowing and willful" ultimately can be determined only in court, every fee-for-service physician becomes vulnerable under these provisions, and mistakes or controverted judgments of medical necessity may portend criminal prosecution.

Finally, there is the new federal crime of "Obstruction of criminal investigations of health care offenses." In a provision that threatens not only physicians but also the privacy of medical records, the 1996 law specifies fines and up to five years in prison for anyone who "willfully prevents, obstructs, misleads, delays or attempts to prevent, obstruct, mislead, or delay the communication of information or records relating to a violation of a Federal health care offense to a criminal investigator" [§245]. The proscribed behavior need not be "knowing," only "willful." Accordingly, under this language a deliberate decision to withhold medical records for whatever reason—due to concerns about patients' privacy or even uncertainty about the requesting party's authority—could be used to threaten a physician with prison time.

Thus, physicians engaged in fee-for-service practice will live under constant threat of the criminal penalties that permeate this new law. The property forfeiture provision alone is noteworthy, requiring the court to order anyone convicted of a federal health care offense "to forfeit property, real or personal, that constitutes or is derived, directly or indirectly, from gross proceeds traceable to the commission of the offense" [§249]. A doctor's house and other assets could be at risk. Like the other provisions cited, this too was copied from the 1993 Clinton administration proposal [§5432].

Electronic Database

American citizens have more to fear in this act than the consequences of potential misapplication of the criminal penalties described. Under the heading of "Administrative Simplification," the Health Insurance Portability and Accountability Act of 1996 mandates creation of a uniform electronic database that jeopardizes the privacy of medical records and intrudes upon doctor-patient relationships nationwide to a degree unprecedented in the United States. In circumstances to be explained later, these provisions allow the federal government to require private practitioners to divulge information about their patients, even though no federal health care program such as Medicare is involved. Contrary provisions of state law are largely superseded [§262(a), sec. 1178].

The 1996 act empowers the federal government to require detailed information, at its discretion, on what lawmakers call "encounters" between doctors and patients. The lawmakers' stated purpose in so doing is "to improve the Medicare program . . . , the Medicaid program . . . , and the efficiency and effectiveness of the health care system, by encouraging the development of a health information system through the establishment of standards and requirements for the electronic transmission of certain health information" [§261]. "Standards and requirements" will abound. The plan of the statute is to require medical practitioners to comply with data encoding and transmission standards, to require the secretary of HHS to establish such standards, to identify covered transactions, to require the electronic transfer and sharing of information as ordered by the secretary of HHS, and to impose penalties for failure to comply with the secretary's standards for data recording and transmission.

The language of the statute is broad. Central to the interpretation of key sections is the meaning of the phrase "health information," which is defined to include just about everything:

The term "health information" means any information, whether *oral or recorded* in any form or medium, that

(A) is created or received by a health care provider, health plan, public health authority, employer, life insurer, school or university, or health care clearinghouse; and

(B) *relates to the past, present, or future physical or mental health or condition of an individual,* the provision of health care to an individual, or the past, present, or future payment for the provision of health care to an individual. [§262(a), sec. 1171; my emphasis]

Subsequent language requires the secretary of HHS, within eighteen months in most cases, to "adopt *standards* for *transactions,* and data elements for such transactions, to enable *health information* to be exchanged electronically . . . [and] establish specifications for implementing each of the standards adopted" [§262(a), secs. 1172(d), 1173(a); my emphasis]. Compliance with the standards is mandatory for all health plans, health care clearinghouses, and any "health care provider who transmits any health information in electronic form in connection with a transaction" referred to in the preceding provision. That is, if a private physician transmits *any* patient medical information pertaining to such a transaction in electronic form (which may include most physicians who use computers in their medical practice), then the physician can be compelled to comply with "standards" that the secretary of HHS creates. Where will such information go? At a minimum, anywhere it is required by government or by private contract to be sent. Indeed, the secretary of HHS is specifically mandated to establish "standards for transferring among health plans appropriate standard data elements" [§262(a), sec. 1173(f)]. Moreover, despite intended safeguards to be described, once the information is received in electronic format it can be retransmitted at will.

The secretary's standards are to apply to "transactions," defined to include, among others, "Health claims or equivalent encounter information" and "Health claims attachments." These are labeled as "financial and administrative transactions," despite the broader reach suggested by the provision's "encounter information" and "health claims attachments" language. Standards must be "appropriate for" any "financial and administrative transactions determined appropriate by the secretary, consistent with the goals of improving the operation of the health care system and reducing administrative costs" [§262(a), sec. 1173(a)]. Open-ended discretionary authority in these matters is given to the secretary of HHS.

Again disclaimers appear, this time in the House Ways and Means committee's original report on the bill. The committee there stated that these provisions are "limited to financial and administrative transactions" and that the committee did "not intend for these requirements [to] apply to information collected that is beyond this scope such as . . . *personnel records* of employers who provide health plan benefits or *medical records of patients*" (U.S. House 1996a, 99; my emphasis). No similar statement about medical records of patients appears in the conference report or in the statute.

The statutory language casts doubt on this disclaimer for at least two reasons. First, the law requires "standards for transactions . . . to enable *health information* to be exchanged electronically, that are *appropriate for"*—not limited to—financial and administrative transactions. Second, as already noted, the term "health information" as used in this provision is defined broadly, and standards are allowed to govern "transactions" that include doctor-patient "encounter information." Had lawmakers intended to create firm limits on the targeted information, such provisions would have been easy to draft. As the 1996 act stands, because "encounter information" and "health information" clearly reach private conversations between doctors and patients, the law seems to create a federal power much broader than the House Ways and Means Committee's disclaimer suggests.

But the secretary's authority is greater still. As noted, a key part of the power in this provision is power to adopt standards that will enable "health information"—everything a doctor or employer or university or life insurer ever learns about you—"to be exchanged electronically." To facilitate such exchange, another provision lifted from the Clinton administration's 1993 proposal requires the secretary of HHS to adopt standards "providing for a standard *unique health identifier* for each individual, employer, health plan, and health care provider for use in the health care system" [§262(a), sec. 1173(b), patterned after 1993 §5104; my emphasis]. Congressmen understood in passing the bill that the mandated standard health identifier might turn out to be people's social security numbers.

There are civil monetary penalties (not to exceed $25,000 per calendar year) for noncompliance with the secretary's standards, with broad discretionary authority given to HHS in applying them [§262(a), sec. 1176]. Threatening more federal intrusion in the future, the new law requires an advisory committee to "study the issues related to the adoption of *uniform data standards for patient medical record information and the electronic exchange of such information,*" requiring the committee to make "recommendations and legislative proposals for such standards and electronic exchange" within four years [§263(4); my emphasis].

Almost as an afterthought, lawmakers instructed the secretary to make recommendations within twelve months regarding "standards with respect to the privacy of individually identifiable health information," while explicitly permitting a total of forty-two months to elapse before privacy regulations need be applied [§264]. Another provision requires the secretary of HHS to establish limited "security standards" for health information, taking into account costs as well as the capabilities of small health care providers [§262(a), sec. 1173(d)]. Those subject to the secretary's database-related standards also are admonished to maintain "reasonable and appropriate" safeguards. A separate provision gives nominal deference to privacy by authorizing fines and imprisonment for unlawful disclosure of individually identifiable health information or unlawful use of a unique health identifier [§262(a), sec. 1177]. But these provisions are empty boxes: violations are to be defined by standards not yet formulated.

The threats to the private practice of medicine and to doctor-patient relationships contained in the Health Insurance Portability and Accountability Act of 1996 are evident. Privacy regulations coming as much as three and one-half years after the bill's passage may be futile, as by then people's medical histories will likely be ensconced in databases held by insurance companies, government agencies, hospitals, and private consultants. Given the public outcry in 1993, how could these provisions have been approved in 1996 without substantial resistance within Congress and by the public?

Role of Political Transaction-Cost Manipulation in the 1996 Bill's Passage

The answer is, by the skillful use of transaction-cost manipulation. Its use in this case was not surprising. The theory outlined earlier predicts that government officials' incentives to support transaction-cost-increasing measures depend on specific variables. With the 1996 act, changes in these determinants were consistent with use of these strategies in passing the new law. President Clinton's renewed executive support pushed in that direction, as did the increased support of both political parties for some type of health care legislation. Accordingly, the ideology variable more pervasively supported transaction-cost augmentation to blunt resistance to the measure. Moreover, there existed an appealing rationale: the specter of "job lock" and individuals' being denied insurance due to preexisting medical conditions evoked widespread public sympathy. Legislators perceived the measure's portability provisions as vitally important to constituents. The complexity of the 168-page single-spaced bill suggested further transaction-cost increases. Also pushing toward transaction-cost augmentation on this issue was the new law's promise of enhanced job security and potential third-party payoffs for government officials, likely products of expanded government power and increased dependence of the populace on the federal government. The passage of time since 1993 had served more to entrench relevant interest groups than to inform the public. Part of the reason for the widespread public ignorance on this topic in 1996—and perhaps the biggest change in the relevant variables since 1993—was the utter failure of the popular press to publicize negative features of the proposed legislation.

During consideration and passage of the Health Insurance Portability and Accountability Act of 1996, public resistance to its authorization of governmental encroachments on the private practice of medicine and people's private relationships with their physicians was virtually nonexistent. Gone were the outspoken protests of 1993. Dr. Jane Orient, one of the few who warned the public of the impending power shift, said she believed the passivity existed because people "don't read" (Orient 1996). I believe the explanation is more complex. Strategies used in 1996 closely paralleled those used to pass the original Medicare statute in 1965 and, like the earlier techniques, relied heavily on government manipulation of political transaction costs facing the public. Again in 1996, incrementalism, tying, misrepresentation, and appealing rhetoric were fundamental to the bill's passage. Consider the similarities.

Incrementalism

Having failed to win in the 1940s, advocates of universal national health insurance narrowed their compulsory health insurance proposals in the 1950s to cover only the elderly. A piece at a time, they got disability insurance (1956), medical assistance for the aged poor (1960), and finally Medicare.

Likewise, in the years leading up to 1996, when advocates of comprehensive federal government control over the U.S. health care system found that they couldn't win on their broad 1993 Health Security Act proposal, they narrowed it. As with Medicare, they deliberately focused on the most appealing and popular aspects of their proposals—in this case the portability, accessibility, and renewability of health insurance and (for some) medical savings accounts.

In congressional debates, members admitted their intent to proceed incrementally. As Senator Arlen Specter (R-Pa.) expressed it, the bill "should be viewed as the first step of an incremental approach to health care reform" (*Cong. Rec.,* Senate, April 23, 1996, 3818). On the day of final House passage of the bill, Representative Anthony C. Beilenson (D-Calif.) conveyed his hope that "this is just a first step" (*Cong. Rec.,* House, August 1, 1996, 9777), and Representative Harris W. Fawell (R-Ill.) said that "we will be back next year fighting . . . with renewed vigor" for further reforms (*Cong. Rec.,* House, August 1, 1996, 9779). On the Senate floor, Senator Edward M. Kennedy (D-Mass.) stated that the "passage of the legislation is the beginning of a journey, not an end," anticipating that in the near future Congress would "move on to the broader field of universal health care coverage in one way or another"—what Senator John D. Rockefeller IV (D-W.Va.) called "the next round of health care reform" (*Cong. Rec.,* House, August 1, 1996, 9504, 9508, 9513).

The next round already has occurred. As part of the August 1997 Balanced Budget Act (Public Law 105-33, 111 Stat. 251), legislators approved a child-health-insurance program that has been called "the biggest new social program since Medicare" (Goldberg 1997). Though said to provide federal funds for state programs to provide health care for low-income children, the new law actually allows assistance to be provided for families whose income is up to 200 percent or more above the poverty line [§4901, sec. 2110(c)]. Between fiscal years 1998 and 2007, the law appropriates $39,650,000,000—roughly $40 billion—in nominal dollars for this program [§4901, sec. 2104(a)]. Anticipating that the "new 'kid care' plan will be available to every child in families with income of up to $50,000 a year," Goldberg (1997) warns that the purpose and likely outcome of the program are to "consolidate government control over health care by moving as many middle-class children into federally funded and regulated health programs as quickly as possible," an assessment consistent with Senator Kennedy's recent statement that "'this is a major step forward' toward national health insurance." We can expect legislators' deliberate use of incrementalism to continue.

Tying

The 1965 compulsory hospital insurance for the elderly was tied to other legislation at two levels. On one level it was tied to the other two layers of Mills's three-layer cake, supplemental medical insurance and liberalization of Medicaid. Moreover, the whole Medicare package was tied to the 7 percent increase in cash benefits for Social Security recipients and bundled with the Social Security Amendments of 1965, with the House of Representatives not even allowing a vote on the issue of deleting Medicare from the Social Security amendment package.

Similarly, in 1996, legislators tied the popular measures for health-insurance access, portability, and renewability (as well as provisions increasing self-employed people's tax deductions for health care) to the electronic database and criminal/civil penalty provisions. This package deal made it politically impossible to vote against the 1996 bill. Voting against it would have required a senator or representative to go on record appearing to support insurance-related "job lock," Medicare fraud, and continued use of widely abhorred exclusions for preexisting medical conditions. In 1996 as in 1965, tying the popular with the controversial dramatically increased the cost to voters and to dissatisfied lawmakers of resisting the proposed legislation.

Misrepresentation

Misrepresentation was fundamental to passage of the 1965 Medicare bill. Similar misrepresentation occurred with passage of the Health Insurance Portability and Accountability Act of 1996, permeating the language of the bill and official statements about its content.

The appealing language in the act's title set the tone: who could oppose such apparently desirable ends as health-insurance "portability" and "accountability"? Legislators described the bill as "consensus" legislation. Senator Nancy L. Kassebaum (R-Kans.) stated that "There is no controversy about the central elements of the bill" (*Cong. Rec.*, House, March 28, 1996, 3034; *Cong. Rec.*, Senate, August 2, 1996, 9502). Government officials repeatedly told the press that this bill concerned health-insurance "access, portability, and renewability" and medical savings accounts (MSAs). According to official sources, the only issue was whether the House and Senate could agree on a MSA provision.

Hardly anyone spoke about the proliferation of loosely drawn new "federal health care offenses" with criminal penalties that permeated the bill. Senator Orrin G. Hatch (R-Utah), one of the few who alluded to the issue, stated that "we need to ensure that these [antifraud] efforts do not penalize innocent behavior or unintentionally bog down the delivery of health care." He reminded his colleagues that

> The practice and delivery of health care is overwhelmingly conducted by honest and well meaning individuals who should not be suspected of wrongdoing merely because they are physicians, hospital administrators or other health care providers. Creating a cloud of suspension [sic] over the entire health care community will not solve the fraud problem when only a few are guilty of wrongdoing. . . . Equally important is that antifraud provisions avoid penalizing innocent individuals for inadvertent or clearly innocent behavior. (*Cong. Rec.*, Senate, August 2, 1996, 9524)

Although Senator Hatch acknowledged that judgments regarding "medical necessity" may differ—in my judgment making every physician governed by the 1996 act potentially subject to prosecution under its rules that forbid false claims of "medical necessity"—he acted as if the requirement for "knowing and willful" behavior to establish criminal liability provided an adequate safeguard. He did not mention the act's imposition of civil penalties for claims that a physician "knows or should know are not medically necessary" [§231(e)]. Nor did his colleagues raise these issues as passage neared. Only Representative Sheila Jackson-Lee (D-Tex.) in the House protested that she was "disturbed" that the bill "would burden physicians with overly burdensome fraud provisions," asserting that eliminating fraud "should not be at the expense of making criminals of physicians that provide us good health care across the Nation" (*Cong. Rec.*, House, August 1, 1996, 9790).

Neither did most congressmen talk publicly about the provisions for a national electronic database. Representative Jim McDermott (D-Wash.) was almost alone in identifying the threat to privacy created by the national electronic database, reminding colleagues on the day of the bill's passage that as a result of the provisions on administrative simplification "this is the day that we voted to give the insurance companies the right to use your Social Security number and gather all the information in a clearinghouse for which there is no privacy protection in this bill." He added:

> Now people want to think that it is called "administrative simplification," but simply what it does is give the insurance companies the ability to shift information back and forth, use it against applicants for life insurance, auto insurance, homeowners insurance. Anything they want to do, they can do in this bill because there is not one single shred of protection of your privacy. . . . That means if a

patient goes to see the doctor and tells the doctor anything that has gone on in their [*sic*] life, the doctor could be compelled by the insurance company data system to release that information because there is nothing, nothing in here that protects the doctor-patient relationship. . . . [W]e are taking away people's privacy." (*Cong. Rec.*, House, August 1, 1996, 9792)

In the House of Representatives, a substitute measure that omitted the antifraud and electronic database provisions failed on a vote of 192 to 226 (fourteen not voting) (*Cong. Rec.*, House, March 28, 1996, 3137-38).

On the day of the Senate's passage of the bill, only two senators commented on its threat to privacy. Senator Paul Simon (D-Ill.) criticized the database provision for accelerating "the creation of large data bases containing personally identifiable information" that might be perused by "prying eyes," describing the bill's allowance of a potential forty-two-month time lag before adopting privacy protection as "put[ting] the cart before the horse" (*Cong. Rec.*, Senate, August 2, 1996, 9516). Senator Patrick J. Leahy (D-Vt.) added that "[w]hen the American people become aware of what this law requires and allows by way of computer transmission of individually identifiable health information without effective privacy protection, they should demand, as I do, prompt enactment of privacy protection" (*Cong. Rec.*, Senate, August 2, 1996, 9523).

In addition to these larger misrepresentations of the bill's content, the 1996 Health Insurance Portability and Accountability Act is rife with misleading language. "Beneficiary incentive programs" include the paying of informants, "federal health care programs" include state health care programs, and "administrative simplification" cloaks national electronic-database mandates. Threats to liberty are alternately covered with pleasant-sounding phrases or obscured by stigmatizing language of criminal misconduct ("fraud and abuse," "health care fraud"). Lip service in the new law to privacy and the protection of individually identifiable health information parallels the nominal statutory deference to avoidance of government "control" in 1965.

Likewise, few inside or outside of Congress cited the costs associated with the legislation. Senator Phil Gramm (R-Tex.), an economist, asked if it was "somehow magic that through Government edict we can bestow billions of dollars of benefits on our fellow citizens at no cost . . . whatsoever?" Based on the bill's requirements for insuring higher-risk individuals, Senator Gramm predicted that "at the end of the first full year of its implementation, the cost of individual private health insurance policies will rise by a minimum of 10 percent," which he called a "conservative estimate" (*Cong. Rec.*, Senate, April 18, 1996, 3538).

Even the health-insurance portability, renewability, and access provisions are not what they seemed. Senator Nancy Kassebaum (R-Kans.) stated that the new law "will guarantee that those who need coverage the most are not shut out of the system." Echoed by many supporters of the bill, she said that the bill will eliminate health-insurance barriers to changing jobs ("job lock") and "will mean the world to millions of Americans who will no longer live in fear that they will lose their health coverage when they change jobs or lose their job" (*Cong. Rec.*, Senate, August 2, 1996, 9502).

Although the new law undoubtedly will reduce job lock, its portability mandates are not as broad as many proponents implied. Its portability provisions prohibit insurance companies only from denying coverage for preexisting medical conditions and from singling out specific individuals, based on their medical history, for higher premiums.[16] Less widely communicated to the public was that the law—properly from an economic point of view—allows insurance companies to raise premiums to the group as a whole or, in certain circumstances, to eliminate particular benefits entirely, so long as it is done uniformly. As Senator Kassebaum (R-Kans.) stated:

> This provision is meant to prohibit insurers or employers from excluding employees in a group from coverage or charging them higher premiums based on their health status and other related factors that could lead to higher health costs. *This does not mean that an entire group cannot be charged more.* But it does preclude health plans from singling out individuals in the group for higher premiums or dropping them from coverage altogether. (*Cong. Rec.*, Senate, April 23, 1996, 3832; my emphasis).

Representative McDermott (D-Wash.) put it more succinctly: "No one listening to this should think that portability means what I have now I will have tomorrow, because it simply is not so" (*Cong. Rec.*, House, March 28, 1996, 3087).

Moreover, some of the provisions enhancing people's access to insurance are more limited than the public in general has been told. Although the bill does not benefit people who have never had group health insurance, it is said to assure that people who lose their coverage through a group policy will have access to individual health insurance. Yet Senator J. Robert (Bob) Kerrey (D-Nebr.) noted that the bill will do

much less: "The conference agreement will allow insurance companies to offer only two policies—and even though the bill includes
some requirements for these plans, I am concerned that insurers may
be able to charge these individuals exorbitant rates" (*Cong. Rec.*, Senate, August 2, 1996, 9523). In addition, access provisions aimed at the
group-insurance market apply only to small businesses having fifty or
fewer employees [§102, sec. 2711]. As Representative Fortney Pete Stark
(D-Calif.) noted, the bill "limited the guaranteed issue to small businesses
of 50, so a firm of 51 people does not have guaranteed access while a
firm of 50 does" (*Cong. Rec.*, House, August 1, 1996, 9786).

Along with the tying and the incremental strategies, misrepresentation on these key issues helped to secure passage of the act, establishing a structure that would permanently increase the transaction costs
to private citizens of resisting an expanding role for the central government in their personal medical affairs.

Conclusion

> *"Sometimes . . . I wonder who we Senators think we are when we sit in our
> seats and pompously say we know so much more about the affairs of the
> average family in America than anyone else that we can compel them to
> make financial determinations which they themselves think are unwise for
> them to make. I somehow doubt that we have the Olympian wisdom that
> enables us to pontificate for all of society."*
> —*Senator Karl Mundt (R-S.D.)*
> (Cong. Rec., *Senate, July 9, 1965, 16121-22*)

Most were not as modest as Senator Mundt (R-S.D.) about
Congress's "Olympian wisdom" enabling members to "pontificate for
all of society" in passing Medicare. After the tying and misrepresentation that made possible its enactment, the 1965 Medicare law created
built-in transaction-cost-increasing mechanisms that assured the
program's growth. The insurance imagery, payroll taxes, and incentives of current recipients to foist off costs on future generations all
worked to increase the transaction costs of taking political action to
"unscramble the omelet." Once Medicare became part of the U.S.
institutional structure, an entitlement mentality, ideological change,
and baser political and economic interests combined to assure its en-
trenchment—regardless of costs or consequences.

The Health Insurance Portability and Accountability Act of 1996
will have similar consequences. Produced by means of transaction-

cost-increasing strategies, the 1996 law authorized a superstructure of new regulations that will spawn ever-increasing federal controls over medical practice and formerly private doctor-patient relationships. Cost increases caused by forced alteration of insurers' risk pools will trigger demand for such controls, even as increased regulatory compliance costs and vulnerability to federal prosecution drive more doctors out of private practice.

The dangers transcend the immediate ones represented by the national electronic database, mandated distribution of confidential patient information, and the web of new federal civil and criminal penalties threatening honest doctors. If this law stands, people gradually will become accustomed to the new federal intrusiveness: future generations will know nothing else. Ideological change will follow, making it increasingly difficult to reestablish a system in which the privacy of medical information and the primacy of doctors' medical judgments are sacrosanct. As Representative Jim McDermott (D-Wash.) warned his colleagues about the threat to privacy, "You are going to come to rue the day that you pass this bill without talking about it" (*Cong. Rec.,* House, March 28, 1996, 3038). Rather than talk about it, they gained short-run political benefits by uncritically applauding a measure said only to establish health insurance "portability" and "accountability." Unfortunately, the new levers of government power thereby created will long outlast those transitory personal political gains, and all Americans who cherish freedom will "come to rue the day."

Notes

1. Health Insurance Portability and Accountability Act of 1996, Public Law 104–191 (August 21, 1996). This bill was agreed to by the House-Senate conference committee appointed following passage of differing bills by the two chambers: the House of Representatives had passed H.R. 3103, the Health Coverage Availability and Affordability Act of 1996, on March 28, 1996 (267 to 151); the Senate had amended the House bill with substitute language passed as S. 1028, the Health Insurance Reform Act of 1996, on April 23, 1996 (100 to 0).
2. The phrase "political transaction costs" also is used to denote these constitutional-level transaction costs.
3. I analyze the history of Medicare in greater detail in Twight (1997).
4. For discussion of the history of the federal government's treatment of health care issues in the United States from 1793 forward, see Chapman and Talmadge (1970). See Wasley (1992, 49-50, 55-58) for discussion of the federal government's role in stimulating employer-provided, first-dollar-coverage health

care and in shaping the health insurance market.

5. The House of Representatives passed the Social Security Amendments (H.R. 6675) on April 8, 1965, by a vote of 313 to 115, approving the conference report by a similar margin (307 to 116) on July 27. The Senate passed a different version of H.R. 6675 on July 9, 1965, by a vote of 68 to 21 and subsequently adopted the conference report on July 29 by a vote of 70 to 24. President Lyndon Johnson signed the Social Security Amendments of 1965 into law on July 30, 1965 (Public Law 89-97).

6. Intellectual candor requires acknowledgment that it was 1,342 pages in *double-spaced* format. Perhaps in future years there will be a movement to distribute bills to the public only in single-spaced format.

7. As noted earlier, the votes giving final approval to the conference report were 421 to 2 in the House and 98 to 0 in the Senate (August 1-2, 1996). Prior votes occurred in the spring, the House of Representatives passing H.R. 3103 by a vote of 267 to 151 on March 28, 1996, and the Senate passing its version of the bill by a vote of 100 to 0 on April 23, 1996.

8. Medical savings accounts (MSAs) were hotly debated during consideration of the 1996 bills. A provision authorizing MSAs was included in the original House bill (H.R. 3103) but not in the substitute Senate bill (S. 1028). The MSA provision included in a Senate amendment offered by Senator Robert Dole (R-Kans.) was deleted on a recorded vote of 52 to 46 (*Cong. Rec.*, Senate, April 18, 1996, 3568). During floor consideration, proponents clearly stated the positive role of MSAs in increasing patient choice: Senator Rick Santorum (R-Pa.) suggested that they be called "Patient Choice Accounts." Senator Phil Gramm (R-Tex.) identified MSAs as one of two fundamental reforms capable of improving the existing health care system (*Cong. Rec.*, Senate, April 18, 1996, 3539, 3566). Professor Milton Friedman's (1996) article supporting MSAs was entered into the record on more than one occasion (*Cong. Rec.*, Senate, April 18, 1996, 3540-41, 3555-56). The House-Senate conference committee compromised by authorizing a four-year experiment with MSAs as described in the text.

9. Citing the origin of today's employer-provided health care in World War II's wage and price controls, Milton Friedman (1996) noted that "[b]ecause private expenditures on health care are not exempt from income tax, almost all employees now receive health care coverage from their employers, leading to problems of portability, third-party payment and rising costs that have become increasingly serious" (A20). Even the push for a federal solution to many insurance-coverage problems flowed from earlier legislation. Senators and the General Accounting Office (GAO) said that states could not solve key problems because earlier Employee Retirement Income Security Act of 1974 (ERISA) legislation had preempted state insurance regulation for a large category of health benefit plans, namely, employer self-funded health plans. As Senator James M. Jeffords (D-Vt.) put it, "ERISA preemption effectively blocks States from regulating most employer-based health plans. . . . [E]mployer plans that cover 44 million people have elected to self-fund and avoid the State insurance laws" (*Cong. Rec.*, Senate, April 18, 1996, 3519-20).

10. Although the outcome might have been different had the heading been phrased "Criminalizing Private Medical Practice; Compulsory Electronic Database," such forthrightness would have been altogether inconsistent with transaction-cost manipulation theory.

11. Other provisions reflect lawmakers' bias in favor of health maintenance organizations (HMOs). The new law authorizes "intermediate sanctions" for HMOs

that have failed to live up to their contracts with the federal government and specifically requires that the secretary of HHS "first provid[e] the organization with the reasonable opportunity to develop and implement a corrective action plan to correct the deficiencies" [§215(a)]. No such opportunity is accorded private fee-for-service physicians.

12. The term "should know" is defined in the statute to mean "deliberate igno-rance" or "reckless disregard of the truth or falsity of the information" [§231(d)]. The relevant code sets will change with full implementation of the 1996 act. As part of new governmental authority to require creation of an electronic database (discussed later), the act requires the secretary of HHS to select or establish code sets for data elements describing "transactions" included in the database [§262(a), sec. 1173(c)].

13. I thank Professor Edward Zajak (University of Arizona) for calling my atten-tion to this case and the issues it raised.

14. *Stewart et al. v. Sullivan et al.*, 816 F.Supp.281, U.S. District Court, District of New Jersey, No. 92-417, October 26, 1992. The plaintiffs' evidence consisted of various bulletins to physicians from the official state Medicare carrier (Blue Cross/Blue Shield) and letters to physicians from various officials in the Health Care Financing Administration (HCFA), Medicare's administrative arm.

15. "Investigative demand procedures" authorized in such cases include subpoena power to require production of relevant records [§248].

16. In general, the maximum allowable waiting period before coverage of a pre-existing condition begins is twelve months. The law specifies circumstances in which this waiting period may be reduced by years of "creditable coverage" under another health plan [§102, sec. 2701].

References

Brown, Kent Masterson. 1997. "Want to Pay for Something Medicare Doesn't Cover? Forget It." *Wall Street Journal,* October 1, A23.

Browning, Edgar K. 1975. "Why the Social Insurance Budget is Too Large in a Democracy." *Economic Inquiry* 13:373–87.

Cantril, Hadley. 1951. *Public Opinion 1935–1946.* Princeton, NJ: Princeton Univer-sity Press.

Chapman, Carleton B., and John M. Talmadge. 1970. "Historical and Political Back-ground of Federal Health Care Legislation." *Law and Contemporary Problems* 35 (2):334–47.

Congressional Record 1965. 89th Cong., 1st sess. Vol. 111.

———.1996. 104th Cong., 2d sess. Vol. 142.

Copeland, Lois J. 1993. "Please Do No Harm: A Doctor's Battle with Medicare Price Controllers." *Policy Review* 65:4–11.

Corning, Peter A. 1969. *The Evolution of Medicare: From Idea to Law.* Research Report no. 19, U.S. Department of Health, Education, and Welfare, Social Security Administration, Office of Research Statistics. Washington, DC: U.S. Government Printing Office.

Derthick, Martha. 1979. *Policymaking for Social Security.* Washington, DC: Brookings Institution.

Friedman, Milton. 1996. "A Way Out of Soviet-Style Health Care." *Wall Street Journal,* April 17, A20.

Goldberg, Robert M. 1997. "The Birth of Clintoncare Jr. . . ." *Wall Street Journal,* August 5, A18.

Higgs, Robert. 1985. "Crisis, Bigger Government, and Ideological Change: Two Hypotheses on the Ratchet Phenomenon." *Explorations in Economic History* 22:1–28.

———. 1987. *Crisis and Leviathan: Critical Episodes in the Growth of American Government.* New York: Oxford University Press.

Kuran, Timur. 1995. *Private Truths, Public Lies: The Social Consequences of Preference Falsification.* Cambridge, MA: Harvard University Press.

Orient, Jane M. 1996. "Health Bill Would Shackle Doctors—Literally." *Wall Street Journal,* May 30, A14.

Poen, Monte M. 1979. *Harry S. Truman versus the Medical Lobby: The Genesis of Medicare.* Columbia and London: University of Missouri Press.

Twight, Charlotte. 1983. "Government Manipulation of Constitutional-Level Transaction Costs: An Economic Theory and Its Application to Off-Budget Expenditure through the Federal Financing Bank." Ph.D. diss., University of Washington, Seattle.

———. 1988. "Government Manipulation of Constitutional-Level Transaction Costs: A General Theory of Transaction-Cost Augmentation and the Growth of Government." *Public Choice* 56:131–52.

———. 1993. "Channeling Ideological Change: The Political Economy of Dependence on Government." *Kyklos* 46 (4):497–527.

———. 1994. "Political Transaction-Cost Manipulation: An Integrating Theory." *Journal of Theoretical Politics* 6 (2):189–216.

———. 1995. "Evolution of Federal Income Tax Withholding: The Machinery of Institutional Change." *Cato Journal* 14 (3):359–95.

———. 1996. "Federal Control over Education: Crisis, Deception, and Institutional Change." *Journal of Economic Behavior and Organization* 877:1–35.

———. 1997. "Medicare's Origin: The Economics and Politics of Dependency." *Cato Journal* 16 (3): 309–38.

U.S. House. 1963–64. Committee on Ways and Means. *Medical Care for the Aged: Hearings on H.R. 3920,* 88th Cong., 1st sess., November, and 2d sess., January.

———. 1965a. Committee on Ways and Means. *Medical Care for the Aged: Executive Hearings,* 89th Cong., 1st sess., January–February.

———. 1965b. *Social Security Amendments of 1965: Report of the Comm. on Ways and Means on H.R. 6675.* House Report no. 213, 89th Cong., 1st sess., March 29.

———. 1996a. Committee on Ways and Means. *House Report no. 104–496* [To accompany H.R. 3103], 104th Cong., 2d sess. March 25.

———. 1996b. *House Conference Report no. 104–736* [To accompany H.R. 3103], 104th Cong., 2d sess., July 31.

U.S. Senate. 1965. Committee on Finance. *Social Security: Hearings on H.R. 6675,* 89th Cong., 1st sess.

Wasley, Terree P. 1992. *What Has Government Done to Our Health Care?* Washington, D.C.: Cato Institute.

3

Making Room for Medical Savings Accounts in the U.S. Health Care System

Gail A. Jensen

Introduction

Now that Congress has abandoned efforts at comprehensive health system reform, attention has focused on possible incremental changes to restrain health care costs. One reform receiving serious consideration is to change the tax laws to foster the emergence of Medical Savings Accounts among Americans of all ages. MSAs, as they are called, would give consumers a strong financial incentive to control their own health care costs. An MSA is an individual savings account specifically for uninsured medical expenses, which is combined with a catastrophic health insurance policy. The policy is designed to protect the individual against very large medical bills, while the savings account provides the personal funds needed to pay smaller bills. The idea of MSAs, and of using the tax code to encourage them, was first developed by John Goodman and others at the National Center for Policy Analysis (Goodman and Musgrave 1994).

The key advantage of MSAs over conventional insurance is their cost-containment potential. MSAs would significantly increase the cost-consciousness of consumers in purchasing medical services, because their out-of-pocket costs at the point of purchasing services would be much higher than under most of today's health care plans. If more persons had catastrophic health insurance, as they would if MSAs

119

were more common, medical expenditures would be lower. This we know from the Rand Health Insurance Experiment (RHIE).

Indeed, the intent of MSA legislative proposals is to give individuals a financial incentive to accept insurance plans with much greater cost-sharing at the point of purchase. Most proposals would do this by providing a larger tax subsidy (than currently) to persons electing this arrangement, while leaving intact the current subsidy for other types of health insurance. Some, however, would limit the tax subsidy provided for all types of health insurance, whether an MSA with catastrophic coverage or more standard health plans. In particular, MSAs have been proposed together with a tax-cap applicable to plans of all types, and also with fixed-dollar tax credits. Under the later reform, any individual who acquires an adequate package of insurance and savings for uninsured expenses would be eligible for a tax credit.

In 1996 and 1997, Congress authorized two very limited "demonstrations" of MSAs, one which provided a federal tax exemption to some very small employers, self-employed persons, and the uninsured who set them up, and the other, which offered MSAs to some Medicare beneficiaries as an alternative to traditional Medicare. The demonstrations, however, are limited in their size and scope. Considered together, they will extend a larger tax subsidy for MSAs (than presently) to fewer than half of 1 percent of all Americans, while leaving intact the current tax treatment of MSAs for the rest of us.

General knowledge about MSA arrangements and various tax-reform approaches is limited, primarily because the idea is new—MSAs are largely untried in the private sector, and—with the exception of these two recently authorized demonstrations—the federal tax reforms proposed are also untried. Nonetheless, a few companies have set up MSAs, and the RHIE does provide some insight as to what would likely occur if they were more common.

The purpose of this chapter is to describe what MSAs are, review employers' experiences with these plans to date, discuss the potential benefits of these plans, drawing largely on findings from the RHIE, describe the two demonstrations which Congress recently authorized, and raise some policy questions regarding MSAs. In particular, the different tax approaches to MSAs are discussed and compared, both in terms of the distortions likely to occur in the markets for health insurance and medical care and in terms of how equitable the tax-treatment would be across persons with different economic circumstances.

What Are MSAs?

An MSA is an individual savings account to pay uninsured medical expenses, which is coupled with a catastrophic health insurance policy. The MSA, also sometimes called a Medisave Account, can be tapped to pay medical expenses not covered by the insurance plan. With an MSA, individuals are personally responsible for paying most of their medical bills, but they have insurance should health care bills be very high.

Unlike a conventional plan, which often has a deductible of $150 per individual or $300 per family, a catastrophic policy tied to an MSA would have a deductible of, say, $1,500 per individual or $3,000 per family. Expenses below this amount would be paid from funds accumulated in the MSA or out of pocket. In either case, individuals would buy many routine medical services with their own money, and funds not spent for medical care would be theirs to keep. This plan contrasts sharply with conventional fee-for-service (FFS) plans, preferred provider organizations (PPOs), health maintenance organizations (HMOs), and point-of-service (POS) plans, which tend to heavily subsidize care at the point of purchase. With most FFS and PPO policies, for example, once the low deductible is met, most subscribers pay only twenty cents on the dollar. Remaining expenses are paid by a third party—the insurance plan. With HMOs and POS plans, on the other hand, care is effectively "free" to members when provided (or approved) by their assigned primary care physician, and the only restraints on the use and cost of services come from the provider side.

With deductibles of $1,500 to $3,000, the large majority of persons would pay all of their health care expenses with their own money. Currently, about 80 percent of persons who are privately insured spend less than $2,000 a year on all of their medical care, as shown in Figure 1 (by the black bars). Fifty-two percent spend less than $500. Thus, with MSAs most persons would face the full price of services at the point of purchase, not 20 percent of the price as with conventional coverage or no cost as with most HMO plans. MSAs would clearly provide most persons an incentive to carefully weigh the benefits of health services against their cost, whereas in our current situation they do not.

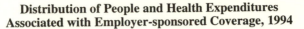

FIGURE 3.1

**Distribution of People and Health Expenditures
Associated with Employer-sponsored Coverage, 1994**

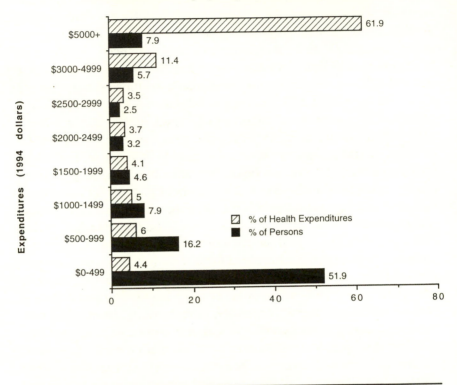

Source: Len Nichols, Tabulations of the 1987 NMES data, reported in 1994 Dollars, The
Urban Institute, Washington, DC, April 1995.

On the other hand, most spending for health care occurs on behalf
of a small percentage of persons who are very sick. In Figure 1 the
light bars illustrate this point. They show the distribution of aggregate
health expenditures by person in 1994, which follows a pattern opposite the distribution of persons according to spending level (the black
bars). MSAs would not have much effect on expenditures for the care
of these very sick individuals, since much of their expenditures would
occur above the deductible and hence be fully covered by the catastrophic plan. Although the savings potential of high cost-sharing is
clearly limited by the nature of the expenditure distribution, savings

would still result. Therefore, even though most persons (80 percent) would fall under a $2,000 deductible, in the aggregate they would account for only a relatively small share (20 percent) of total health care spending. (In the next section, research from the Rand Health Insurance Experiment is reviewed to ascertain just how much could be saved by switching to high-deductible coverage.)

A group catastrophic policy—one with a deductible of, say, $2,500 and full coverage above that—typically costs only two-thirds as much as conventional and HMO coverage, according to the Health Insurance Association of America (HIAA) (Hammond 1993). Thus, MSA arrangements could easily be set up with what employers and employees now spend on health insurance—about $6,000 a year for family coverage and $2,300 for individual coverage. While MSA deposits in the first year would probably not cover the deductible fully, by year two most account balances would exceed this level because, as noted earlier, most persons incur few health care expenses over the course of a year.

What about excess balances in an MSA? It would be reasonable to allow workers to withdraw funds that exceed their deductible as taxable income, to spend or save as they please. Such a policy would further the incentives for MSA-holders to consume health care prudently, because any savings they achieved would become income they could spend on other things. For most persons, in the second and subsequent years of an MSA, smaller contributions to the account would be possible as average account balances increased to secure levels. Hence, over time total outlays for health benefits in many cases could decline.

Alternatively, if constant contributions to the account were maintained, the balance would grow substantially over the long term. This has been demonstrated by Jensen and Morlock (1994) and Eichner et al. (1996) using MSA simulation models. Jensen and Morlock, for example, showed that if the money saved from switching from standard health insurance to a catastrophic policy (e.g., an annual deductible of $2,500 and full coverage above that) were deposited each year in a Medisave account, then in twenty-five years (assuming an 8 percent annual interest rate), the average Medisave balance would grow to about $120,000 (1993 dollars). These calculations assumed that average annual withdrawals of $250 were made to pay for out-of-pocket medical expenses. They also found that even with withdrawals of $1,000 annually (which is probably on the high side), an individual's balance would be over $60,000 (1993 dollars) after twenty-five years. Likewise, Eichner and colleagues simulated the size of MSA accounts upon retirement, and found that 80 percent of enrollees would likely retain over 50 percent of their contributions by the time they retired. Further, only 5 percent would retain less than 20 percent of their contributions. This study too suggests that the large majority of MSA participants would be able to pay their out-of-pocket health expenses with their MSA.

MSAs together with catastrophic insurance could be set up either for a group of persons, for example, by a firm for its workers and their families, or by individuals who obtain insurance on their own. In an employment setting, the catastrophic policy would be group coverage, just as standard employer policies are group coverage, but each MSA would be for an individual (or family). The account would belong to the worker, the balance rolling over from one year to the next, and would be totally portable if he or she were to change jobs. With employer-sponsorship, the firm would provide the catastrophic group coverage and make an annual contribution to each worker's Medisave account.

MSAs and Health Care Expenditures

How effectively would MSAs contain expenditures for health care? Information on this issue is available from two sources: from reports of the experience of employers who have set up MSA-type plans for their workers, and from a large body of literature on the effects of cost-sharing for health care, more generally.

Employer Experiences with MSAs

The evidence on employers' experiences with these plans is largely anecdotal. A number of U.S. firms currently have health insurance programs that give workers a direct incentive to reduce their claims under the company plan. Some are true MSAs. Others simply create a financial incentive not to file insurance claims. Four case studies show how such arrangements have worked in practice.

Dominion Resources, a utility holding company, has offered its workers a high-deductible indemnity plan option since 1989. The plan's annual deductible is $1,500 per individual or $3,000 per family, and full coverage is provided once the deductible is met. For the 80 percent of its workers who have chosen this plan, the firm deposits $1,620 a year into a bank account in the worker's name. The funds are intended to help employees cover medical expenses below the plan's deductible. Tax laws require that workers pay tax on these deposits.

Dominion also provides year-end rebates to workers who stay healthy. Under this program, if the firm spent less than was budgeted for health care, it gives workers a cash payment at the end of the year. Half of whatever the firm saved is divided equally among workers who did not exceed their annual deductibles. In 1992, Dominion spent 31 percent less than it had budgeted for medical expenses, and distributed checks of $680 to 100 employees who participated in the program. Between 1989, when it first set up its MSA, and 1992, the firm's health benefit outlays increased by about 1 percent a year (Bennett 1993, Spencer 1993). This was far lower than the national average over this time period, which was about 12 percent growth in premium outlays per year (Jensen et al. 1997).

Reports on the experiences of other companies that have switched to high-deductible plans are also favorable. For more than ten years, Quaker Oats has offered its 11,000 employees a high-deductible plan and has paid an annual $300 contribution toward a "personal health account" for any worker electing the plan. Unspent funds in the account are given to the worker at year-end to spend as he or she pleases. Between 1982 and 1992, the company's health benefit outlays increased at an average annual rate of 6.3%, while premiums for the rest of the nation grew at nearly twice that rate (Johnson 1993).

In 1993, Golden Rule Insurance Company in Indianapolis switched from a conventional FFS plan with a $250 deductible to a catastrophic $3,000 deductible plan. By making the change the company was able to save enough in premium costs to give each worker a $1,750 annual Medisave account. In 1994 it found that its outlays for health benefits were unchanged from their 1993 level (Merline 1994).

Forbes magazine in New York does not offer an MSA, but provides a cash incentive program for workers to stay healthy and not file insurance claims. The firm offers a single indemnity plan, which is self-insured, and varies the annual deductible according to a worker's gross income. Specifically, it is set at one percent of income. Under the program, if a worker's annual medical claims are less than $600, the firm pays him double the difference between $600 and his claims. Thus, it is in the worker's interest *not* to file claims against the plan unless he accumulates $1,200 or more in claims during the year. An example will illustrate how the Forbes program works. Suppose a worker earns $50,000 a year, and he and his family have $700 in medical expenses. With this income, the family's deductible is $500. Thus, if he files the claims, he will be reimbursed $200 by the plan ($700 minus his deductible). If instead, he does not file them, *Forbes* will pay him $1,200 ($600 minus zero claims doubled is $1,200). In essence, he is reimbursed the $700 plus $500 more for having not filed the claims.

Health care costs have dropped significantly under the program, and *Forbes* has more than made up for what it has paid out in bonuses. Its insurance costs fell 23 percent in 1992 and 18 percent in 1993. Roughly, for every dollar *Forbes* has saved in claims paid, it has paid out sixty cents in bonuses, so overall it has saved money (Wildavsky 1993).

All of these companies contained health care costs by giving their workers a personal financial motive to control their own expenses. Although I have described only four firms' experiences here, other firms that have switched to MSA-type arrangements have reported similar benefits (Barchet 1995). While case studies can be only suggestive, all of these reports suggest that employees can and will reduce their health care expenditures if they can keep the savings.

Research on the Effects of Cost-Sharing for Health Care

A substantial body of empirical research suggests that cost-sharing at the point of purchase significantly reduces health care expenditures. The Rand Health Insurance Experiment (RHIE) provides some of the best evidence that MSAs might significantly lower health care expenditures. The experiment, which was conducted over several years in six areas of the country, studied the relationship between consumers' use of health care services and their health insurance plans. Families who participated were randomly assigned to different insurance plans, which varied the price of services to them. All medical services were covered by the different plans; only the family's cost-sharing provisions for medical care varied. One of the plans was a catastrophic policy with a family deductible of roughly $3,000 (in 1994 dollars).

The RHIE found that total health care expenditures for persons in the catastrophic plan were 15 percent less than expenditures for persons with 25 percent coinsurance (Newhouse et al. 1993). And those savings were achieved in an economic environment much like today's, that is, individuals had little information on the prices charged by different providers. With increased information, the savings resulting from widespread catastrophic coverage would be even greater. In Seattle, the RHIE compared catastrophic insurance with HMO coverage. The savings under catastrophic coverage equaled those achieved with HMOs—both reduced expenses about fifteen percent, relative to a 25 percent coinsurance plan (Newhouse et al. 1993).

Would MSAs encourage people to neglect or postpone important visits for physician office care, so that they would ultimately require more expensive hospital care? The Rand experiment found no evidence of this phenomenon. Persons in the catastrophic plan had the same inpatient expenses as persons in the 25 percent coinsurance plan. The reductions in overall expenditures were achieved through savings on less expensive items.

Would MSAs cause health status to suffer? If a person were to avoid necessary care in order to keep from spending the MSA funds, then conceivably health might suffer. The RHIE, however, found little evidence to support this conjecture. Catastrophic health insurance had little or no measurable adverse effects on health status for the average person.

Other Advantages of MSAs

MSAs have other advantages besides savings on health expenditures. They include covering uninsured spells associated with job changes, reducing the administrative costs of health insurance, increasing personal savings for long-term care expenses, and reducing the tax distortion between consumer spending on conventional health care and "alternative" treatments, which tend to be covered less generously, if at all, under today's insurance plans.

Individuals with MSAs would have a source of funds to purchase health insurance for themselves and their families during periods when they would otherwise go uninsured, such as between jobs. Currently, most persons who lose private health insurance become uninsured for about four to five months (Swartz and McBride 1990). And although most uninsured spells involve a loss of employer coverage, very few persons take advantage of COBRA, the 1985 law that allows employees and their families to continue in their former group plan for eighteen or thirty-six months, depending on the circumstances (Flynn 1992), probably because the cost of COBRA coverage is prohibitive for many. After all, when someone has just lost a job, the loss of income puts a considerable strain on one's budget. Most households choose to forgo insurance in order to pay for more essential living expenses.

MSAs would help alleviate this problem in two ways. First, Medisave accounts would provide a source of funds to purchase insurance during such a period. Second, the cost of continuation coverage would be much lower, because it would be catastrophic coverage. Thus, with MSAs, more persons would have the resources to purchase bridge-insurance between jobs.

MSAs might also encourage more Americans to save for future long-term care expenses. Current data on the savings and assets of the elderly suggest that many Americans cannot afford to pay for long-term care. At today's prices for nursing home care, for example, about 30 percent of the elderly would become totally impoverished by even a three-month stay in a typical nursing home (Health Insurance Association of America 1992). The roll-over/savings feature of MSAs might eventually make them an important source of resources for both long-term care services and long-term care insurance.

MSAs would also help alleviate the effective price distortion that currently exists between conventional and "alternative" medical care, such as chiropractic care and acupuncture. Because conventional services, such as physician visits, are insured more generously in most plans (Jensen et al., in 1998), consumers may seek physician care over alternative treatments, not because the former is more effective, but because it is probably cheaper for them (i.e., their out-of-pocket costs are lower) once insurance reimbursements are taken into account. With MSAs, however, both would be paid through a Medisave account. The relative price of alternatives to physician care would not be distorted, as it is now, and patients could make care choices based on value and the effectiveness of various treatments.

MSAs might also help alleviate medical price inflation if they stimulate greater price competition among providers. If more consumers were price conscious, as they would be if MSAs were more common, suppliers would find it harder to pass through price increases than they do currently.

The Present Tax Treatment of MSAs

MSA arrangements are uncommon in today's market largely because of their unfavorable tax treatment vis-à-vis standard health insurance. With the exception of two limited experiments, which are discussed below, workers who have employer-sponsored coverage receive no federal tax exemptions for deposits made to Medisave accounts or for the interest earnings on such accounts. Thus, both the employer and the worker must pay taxes on Medisave funds. The MSA's catastrophic insurance policy, on the other hand, receives the same tax treatment as do other types of health insurance. That is, an employer's premium contribution is considered tax-exempt compensation for the employee and a tax deduction for the employer.

In 1994, for a worker with an average household income (about $41,340), the tax subsidy for a typical employer-sponsored policy amounted to a savings of $1,477 if the worker elected family coverage, or 27 percent off the market price of such coverage. Of this amount, $1,075 was savings for the worker and $402 savings for the employer. By comparison, if the same total outlay were spent on an MSA, then the total tax exemptions (for the employee and employer) would be $951, only a 17 percent savings. The differential tax treatment effectively makes the price of MSA coverage about $382 more expensive than standard health insurance. The higher price is due solely to the current tax code.

An employer can still set up an MSA in today's tax environment (and indeed, some have), but if it does so, then the Medisave account must be funded with after-tax dollars. In other words, the employer and employee must both pay taxes on deposits, and interest on the account is also taxable.

Federal MSA Initiatives for Certain Subpopulations

In 1996 and 1997, Congress made tax-free MSAs available to a limited number of persons. Under the 1996 Health Insurance Portability and Accountability Act, Congress has allowed small employers (defined as those with fifty or fewer employees), self-employed workers, and uninsured persons to set up tax-free MSAs. Under the legislation, the number of tax-favored MSAs issued through small businesses and to self-employed workers will be limited to 750,000 nationwide on a first come, first serve basis. There are no restrictions on the number of dependents that can be covered under these policies, nor (initially) any limit on the number of uninsured who may apply for an MSA tax break. However, once 750,000 policies have been issued to workers in small businesses and the self-employed, no more uninsured will be eligible to set up a tax subsidized MSA. (Also, small businesses that set up MSAs for their workers may grow to 200 employees within the time period for the subsidy, without losing their tax-preferential status.)

The parameters for plan eligibility and the nature of the tax subsidy are as follows. The catastrophic policy to be coupled with the MSA must: (a) have an annual deductible of between $1,500 and $2,250 per individual or between $3,000 and $4,500 per family, and (b) limit maximum out-of-pocket expenses to no more than $3,000 per individual or $5,500 per family. If the policy meets these conditions, then tax deductible annual contributions to an MSA will be allowed up to 65 percent of the policy's deductible if the policy is for an individual, and up to seventy-five percent if the policy is for a family. Interest earned on MSA funds will be tax-free, and distributions will be allowed only for medical expenses. Funds withdrawn for nonmedical expenses will be considered taxable income, and additionally, a 15 percent penalty will be imposed, unless the withdrawal is made after age sixty-five or after the onset of a disability. Under the legislation there is no "sunset" provision for expiration of this federal tax subsidy. Rather, those who have set them up and filed with the Internal Revenue Service (IRS) will be able to keep them.

To be eligible for the tax break, eligible individuals were supposed to file Form 8851 with the Internal Revenue Service (IRS) by fall 1997. However, based on the number of forms the IRS had received up through spring 1997, it announced in summer 1997 that it was extending its cut-off date by a year—until fall 1998 (Patient Power Report 1997a). The IRS also reported that as of April 30, 1997, only 9,720 individuals had filed to establish an MSA under the legislation. Of these, 1,787 were persons who were previously uninsured, and another 550 were dependents of MSA primary-insureds, so 2,337 (1,787 + 550) were individuals who will not count toward the 750,000 cap on the number of policies to be issued (Patient Power Report 1997a).

Although the number of accounts actually filed with the IRS up through spring 1997 is lower than what some observers had expected, this slow take-up rate may be a result of consumer ignorance regarding MSAs. A 1997 consumer survey (conducted in the Chicago area) found that most persons still do not know what they are (National Center for Policy Analysis 1997). The good news in these numbers, however, is that among those who have signed up thus far, nearly a fifth (18 percent) are persons who were previously uninsured (Patient Power Report 1997a). This pattern suggests that MSAs have a real potential to help reduce the number of uninsured.

In 1997, Congress also enacted legislation (as part of the Budget Bill) which will allow a limited number of MSAs under Medicare beginning January 1, 1999. This legislation was actually part of a broader set of changes in the insurance options to be made available to beneficiaries. (Beginning January 1, 1998, beneficiaries were able to choose from a wide number of alternatives to basic Medicare— health maintenance organizations (HMOs), preferred provider organizations (PPOs), point-of-service (POS) plans, provider sponsored organizations (PSOs), and private fee-for-service (FFS) insurance plans in their area.)

Medicare MSA enrollment will be limited to 390,000 persons who sign up for such coverage before January 1, 2003. To qualify for a "Medicare Choice MSA," as they are called, the deductible under the catastrophic policy can be no more than $6,000 (in 1999). Medicare will set aside funds equal to the "Medicare capitation rate" to cover both the catastrophic plan premium for the beneficiary and his or her Medisave account. Medicare will pay the catastrophic premium first, and then deposit the remainder of its contribution (up to the Medicare capitation rate) automatically in the beneficiary's MSA (Patient Power Report 1997b).

Changing the Tax Code for All Americans

While these limited demonstrations are a step in the right direction, a major obstacle to the widespread emergence of MSAs is their unfavorable treatment under the general tax code when compared with standard employer plans. The tax code has effectively limited the demand for MSAs by workers and their employers, who instead now opt for generous FFS, PPO, HMO, and POS coverage, which is heavily tax-subsidized by the government. MSAs are not likely to become more widespread until they are granted a tax treatment equivalent to that provided to standard health insurance plans.

Virtually all proposed federal legislation to promote MSA arrangements would set new tax rules for these accounts. A discussion of several alternatives that have been proposed is presented below.

It should be noted that many state legislatures also either have enacted MSA tax legislation or are considering doing so. As of mid-1995, the total number of states that had enacted MSA laws was fifteen (Bordonaro 1995). However, because most state tax rates are quite low in relation to the federal tax rate (income tax plus FICA plus the Medicare tax), it is unlikely that legislation at this level will do much to stimulate the creation of MSAs. The main tax disadvantage of these accounts currently arises from their federal tax treatment.

Proposed Federal Reforms for MSA Tax Treatment

One common proposal is to broaden the federal tax-subsidy provided for MSAs, but leave intact entirely the present tax treatment of other types of health insurance. There are several proposals, which have at their heart, three basic reform components. First, employers, employees, and individuals would be allowed to make tax-free contributions to Medisave accounts, up to some specified limit, provided the account was coupled with a catastrophic insurance policy. Such contributions would be tax-exempt for employees or individuals and tax-deductible for employers. Second, withdrawals from such accounts would not be taxed if the funds were used for medical care. Withdrawals for nonmedical purposes would be counted in a person's taxable income and also subject to penalty (e.g., 10 percent), unless the account's balance had exceeded a certain level, in which case income taxes but no penalty would apply. Third, Medisave funds could be rolled over from one year to the next and could accumulate interest tax-free.

Senate Bill S121, which was sponsored by Phil Gramm in the 104th Congress, exemplifies this approach. Under this Bill, employer-sponsored MSAs as well as those set up by individuals would receive favorable tax treatment. The catastrophic policy would have to be a $3,000 deductible policy that covers physician services, hospital care, diagnostic tests, and other major medical expenses. The employer, employee, or individual could make contributions to the Medisave account, but the annual total would be limited to $3,000. Medisave contributions would be tax-deductible for the contributor. No minimum deposits would be required for the account, and any year-end balance could be rolled over. Funds withdrawn for uninsured medical expenses would not be taxed but, if used for other purposes, would be subject to a 10 percent penalty and taxed as ordinary income. However, once the account balance exceeded the $3,000 deductible, any excess could be withdrawn without penalty, although income taxes would apply.

A variant on this, which has also been proposed, would be specifically to limit tax-deductible Medisave contributions to the premium difference between the employer's old plan and the new catastrophic policy, or in other words, limit the total tax exemption (on insurance plus the Medisave contributions) to what it would have been had the employer stayed with its previous arrangement. While the Gramm proposal would not have done this directly, by stipulating a $3,000 limit on tax-exempt contributions, its effect should be roughly the same, because a catastrophic policy with a $3,000 annual deductible and full coverage above that costs about one-half to two-thirds as much as conventional coverage (Hammond 1993). Since employer premiums for family coverage are currently about $6,000, this suggests that a catastrophic policy costs somewhere between $3,000 and $4,000. Assume it costs $3,500. Then the total amount that would be tax-exempt under the Gramm plan would be, at most, $6,500 (=$3,500 + $3,000). In most cases, however, the actual exemption would probably be less. If MSAs either replace employers' current plans or are added as yet another option in the workers' menu of plans, MSA contributions are likely be set so that total outlays (catastrophic premium plus MSA deposits) are no more than what is being paid for standard coverage. In this case, the exemption would be the same as what is currently given.

On the surface, these proposals (and others similar to them) might appear to more or less equalize the tax treatment of standard employer-sponsored health plans and MSAs, because employer premiums for standard coverage are already fully tax-exempt, and the proposals allow roughly the same dollar outlay (insurance premium plus Medisave contributions) to be tax-deductible. Indeed, if demand for MSAs comes primarily from employers currently offering non-MSA plans, then these measures would likely be close to revenue-neutral. The premiums for these workers are already tax-exempt, and MSA allowances would simply substitute for them.

They do not equalize their tax treatment, however. As Mark Pauly (1994) has pointed out, these reforms would actually result in an expansion of our current tax subsidy. They essentially extend to anyone setting up an MSA a tax exclusion for all medical spending, whether insured or ñot, and whether paid by an employer or employee. As such, they represent a major departure from current tax policy, in which premiums for employer-sponsored health insurance are exempt from taxation, but out-of-pocket medical expenses and premiums paid directly by families are not. In addition, because medical spending from the accounts would not be taxed, while other (non-medical) purchases would be, these reforms would create a tax distortion favoring medical care, even if uninsured, over other goods and services. Medical purchases would be subsidized at a rate equal to the individual's marginal tax rate. In essence, they would extend the current tax break for one type of medical expense—employer-sponsored insurance premiums—to all types of medical spending.

The net result of this type of tax change would be that the individual would effectively face "discounted" prices for all medical care services—prices discounted by the amount of their marginal tax rate. Facing lower prices, an individual might well increase his or her overall demand for health care, which could end up increasing total medical care spending.

Could this in fact happen? A partial answer may be provided by looking at changes in health care spending which have occurred under so-called Flexible Spending Accounts (FSAs), which many large firms now sponsor for their workers. For nearly a decade now, as permitted under Section 125 of the Internal Revenue Code, employers and their workers who set up FSAs can set aside part of a worker's gross income each month, untaxed, and use it to pay out-of-pocket medical expenses incurred by their family. Unlike MSAs, the amount set aside for an FSA must be determined in advance; it cannot be changed during the year. If not spent by the end of the year, the employee forfeits whatever funds remain in his or her FSA.

In a recent study of the experience of workers at a large firm that offers an FSA, Davidoff (1997) found that (holding cost-sharing constant) total medical care spending increased by about 6 to 9 percent under an FSA. Although this would be an undesirable result for MSAs, it is a rather modest increase that might well be offset by the effect of the much larger deductible under an MSA arrangement. Unlike FSAs, an MSA would not merely extend additional tax subsidies for medical care spending. Rather, even if all Medisave deposits were tax-exempt, MSAs, in essence, would increase the effective point-of-purchase price for some services (those covered under the previous low-deductible insurance plan) while decreasing the price for other services (those previously paid out-of-pocket). Thus, the net effect on spending is unclear.

Also, as noted above, an FSA actually penalizes a worker for not spending his or her entire balance by year-end. The perverse incentive created by this may be to spend whatever is left in the account once year-end approaches, no matter how marginal or questionable the benefits of the services purchased. This feature may well account for part of the increase in expenditures observed by Davidoff, however, it would not be a factor with MSAs. On the other hand, consumers would probably deposit larger amounts of money into an MSA (knowing there is no chance they will lose it come year-end), and this factor might tend to increase their total medical care spending. On balance, we don't know which effect is stronger, but at least these recent experiences observed under FSAs suggest that it may not be much of an issue.

Nonetheless, in principle one can argue that allowing Medisave deposits to be tax-exempt would be, in fact, both inefficient and inequitable. It would be inefficient because it would further distort individuals' medical care spending. By newly subsidizing out-of-pocket medical purchases relative to spending on other goods, there is a small chance that it would encourage more spending on health care. Our existing tax subsidy is already inefficient in that, by reducing the effective price of insurance, it causes persons to allocate more of their total compensation to comprehensive health plans with little or no cost sharing, at the expense of other goods or savings. Creating new subsidies at the point of purchase might merely add more distortions.

It would be inequitable because, like the subsidy for health insurance, the implicit price reduction would rise with an individual's marginal tax rate. Higher income persons would receive a greater break than those with lower incomes. In addition, unless legislation were to equalize the existing tax subsidy for health insurance among persons with and without employer-sponsored coverage, MSAs not sponsored by employers would receive a lower tax break on the insurance part of those plans. Thus, this approach violates the principles of horizontal as well as vertical equity.

Tax Cap Proposals and MSAs

MSAs have also been proposed in the context of a tax cap on employment-based health insurance, that is, a maximum amount of the employer's contribution that could be treated as nontaxable income to the employee. If a plan with a higher premium than this level was offered, plan enrollees would be taxed on the difference.

One approach, which has been suggested, would be to extend a tax subsidy for MSAs while instituting a tax cap for all types of health insurance. Under this scenario, contributions to a Medisave account would be tax-deductible for the contributor—the employer, the employee, or an individual—provided the account was coupled with a catastrophic policy. The total deduction allowed for the MSA, i.e., for the policy plus account contributions, would be limited to the level of the tax cap. Contributions above this would be treated as taxable income to the employee.

With a tax cap the effective price of insurance for workers would rise by an amount equal to the extra taxes paid on their premium. More expensive plans would not be subsidized to the extent they are now, and workers would find them less attractive as a result. They would also have an incentive to include less insurance in their gross compensation package, that is, to choose less expensive plans.

MSAs might be particularly appealing in this environment. Obviously, their attractiveness over other insurance arrangements would depend on the level of the tax cap. The lower the cap, the more attractive MSAs would be. As noted earlier, catastrophic insurance is far less expensive than standard health coverage, so provided the cap was not too high, other plans' prices would rise relative to MSAs' catastrophic plans. Even if their tax-subsidized account contributions were limited to less than the deductible, many persons might still prefer MSAs. Persons for whom the financial risk involved would be small include those who anticipate having few medical expenses and those who have adequate personal savings.

Tax Credits and MSAs

An alternative proposed by Pauly and Goodman (1995) involves tax credits combined with MSAs. Under their proposal, all citizens, regardless of their employment status, would be eligible for a fixed-dollar tax credit contingent on obtaining an adequate combination of health insurance protection and an earmarked savings account. The credit would not be intended to encourage any particular form of insurance, rather it would be provided as long as the individual's insurance/savings package met a minimum standard set by the government. Defined in terms of a bundle of insurance and savings, the minimum would circumscribe an MSA arrangement, for example, a catastrophic policy with a $3,000 deductible coupled with a savings account containing at least $2,000. If a more generous insurance plan were selected, less savings would be required. Today's conventional and HMO plans would also qualify for the credit. MSAs would be established with after-tax dollars under their proposal, in contrast to the previous reforms discussed. Thus, the subsidy would not distort medical care purchases paid from such accounts. Both deposits and withdrawals would be independent of the credit.

The credit would not increase if an individual chose a more costly insurance plan or if medical care purchases were higher. This constancy contrasts sharply with the present tax subsidy, which increases as a function of both of these variables. It would also be refundable, meaning that if someone were eligible for the credit, but the tax liability (not counting the credit) was less than the credit, the IRS would refund the difference.

If designing tax policy from the start, Pauly and Goodman propose that the credit would be the only subsidy provided for health insurance and health care. However, given that massive change in the present tax code is not likely to be favored by politicians, they propose an alternative "incremental" version of their reform: Give groups and individuals a choice for how their health insurance is treated for tax purposes—let them retain the current system based on exclusions or, instead, take a refundable tax credit set at whatever the average tax subsidy is under the present system. To qualify for the credit, an individual would have to (1) obtain health insurance, at least a catastrophic policy with a deductible no less than the specified level, and (2) protect the deductible by establishing an MSA. Taking the credit would require giving up the previous system, for example, an employer's contributions toward the employee's health benefits would be newly subject to personal income and payroll taxes. Clearly, under this proposal, no one would be worse off than before, since maintaining the status quo is one of the choices. Still, many persons might desire a tax credit approach instead of the current system, and thus might choose to set up an MSA.

Unlike the tax treatment proposed in pending federal legislation and unlike a tax cap, a tax credit would not reward higher levels of insurance or earmarked savings with greater tax subsidies. Both of the other plans would, *albeit* up to some limit. Under Gramm's plan, for example, the subsidy increases until MSA contributions reach $3,000, while under a tax cap, it increases until the combined value of the catastrophic premium and MSA deposits reach the cap. This feature of the Gramm plan encourages purchases up to the subsidy limit, thus distorting the coverage individuals might otherwise choose. In particular, some persons who would otherwise obtain less insurance will purchase more, given a subsidized price of coverage.

A tax credit, however, differs from these other approaches in other fundamental ways. It extends an identical tax subsidy (measured in dollars) regardless of an individual's income. In contrast, both of the other approaches give a larger subsidy to higher-income persons, because the subsidy increases with marginal tax rates, at least until the limit is reached. Hence the benefits of the subsidy increase with income. On this basis, a tax cap would be much more equitable across individuals than either of the other proposals.

Still another suggestion has been to institute a tax credit for all Americans, instead of the current tax deduction, while permitting MSAs. The credit would apply for health insurance as well as unreimbursed medical expenses, but to be eligible, the insurance plan would have to meet certain federal qualifications. Unlike the fixed credit proposed by Pauly and Goodman, under this approach the credit would be structured so that it depends on both income and a person's total spending on insurance and medical care—specifically, it would be a function of the share of income a person spent on insurance and medical care. The credit would fall as income increases, but rise as the person's health and insurance expenditures increase. In addition, withdrawals for nonmedical purposes would be taxed as gross income and subject to a 10 percent penalty.

One criticism of this proposal is that, like our current system, the structure of the subsidy might encourage over-spending. Since the credit increases with both insurance and medical care expenditures, it could encourage excess spending. Another criticism is that it directly subsidizes greater out-of-pocket spending, both through its treatment of the MSA (because the tax break increases with contributions) and through the dependence of the credit on out-of-pocket spending. It does not at all resemble the Pauly/Goodman proposal. The credit is devised so that market distortions are bound to occur, leading to over-insurance among some persons and excessive out-of-pocket spending among others.

Other Issues Surrounding MSAs

One important issue regarding MSAs, if employers were to begin offering them, involves the possibility of "adverse selection." This could occur if MSAs were offered as one of several insurance options. It is not an issue if the only plan offered is an MSA. When faced with a choice of plans, individuals who foresee few medical needs during the year might be more likely to choose MSA coverage, because they do not expect to incur expenses. For them, Medisave deposits would be perceived as either pure savings or income to spend as they pleased. Persons electing MSA coverage would be more likely to have lower health care costs than persons electing more generous FFS plans and (possibly) HMOs. However, this difference would cause medical claims for more generous plans to be higher than they otherwise would be, and claims under the MSA's catastrophic plan to be lower. And once these differences began to reflect themselves in the premiums for different plans, adverse selection would hurt plans that compete with MSAs.

One obvious solution would be for an employer not to offer a choice of plans, in other words, to offer only an MSA. This precludes any adverse selection from occurring, and in some firms workers might consider such a change in benefits acceptable. If not acceptable, how-ever, a partial remedy might be to limit workers' opportunities for gaming their insurance choices as their medical needs change. Persons in MSAs, for example, who foresee an increase in their expenses, such as an anticipated pregnancy, clearly have a motive to switch into a generous plan to avoid drawing down MSA funds and then switch back to MSA/catastrophic coverage after those expenses have been paid by the more generous plan. To limit this source of adverse selec-tion, an employer could require prior notice of twelve months to switch from an MSA to a non-MSA plan, and then make such a choice irrevocable.

Another issue pertains to existing constraints in some parts of the country on insurers' ability to sell catastrophic group policies. In some states these plans must comply with a plethora of state-mandated benefit laws. These laws, which have evolved over the last two decades, let states prescribe the content of purchased group health insurance. If a mandate requires that group policies include what amounts to "front-end" coverage for a particular condition or service, then it limits insurers' from offering true catastrophic group plans. To prevent these laws from hindering the market for MSAs, state-mandated benefits need to be waived for catastrophic group plans.

As an illustration of the problem, in Wisconsin the Blue Cross Blue Shield Plan recently announced that it has stopped marketing MSAs due to conflict with that state's mental health mandate, which requires first-dollar coverage of mental health care (Patient Power Report 1997c). Although, technically, the plan could still be sold, if it were to satisfy the state mandate, it would no longer qualify for the federal tax advantage recently allowed for small businesses, the self-employed, and the uninsured. (Covering expenses below the deductible is not allowed under the 1996 law.) Without the tax break, however, the plan felt it would have too great a marketing disadvantage.

Summary

This chapter has examined the merits of recent proposals for Medical Savings Accounts as a way of paying for medical care. Based on the (albeit limited) experience of employers to date with these arrangements and on what we know from the research literature on the effects of cost-sharing on health care costs, we conclude that MSAs deserve a fair try. If more widespread, they would help fulfill several oft-stated goals of health reform. These include lowering health care costs, reducing the number of uninsured, and fostering increased personal savings for long-term care expenses.

The most useful step the government could take to develop a market for MSAs would be to restructure the tax treatment of health insurance in a way that does not penalize the choice of an MSA over other health insurance arrangements. Three alternative tax proposals have been put forth. The first would retain the existing tax treatment of non-MSA plans and create a new tax subsidy for individual savings accounts earmarked for out-of-pocket medical spending. The second, a tax cap plan, would place a limit on the amount of health insurance purchases that could be considered nontaxable income for a subscriber. The same deduction ceiling would apply to all types of plans, including MSAs. With the latter, the tax cap would apply to the catastrophic premium plus contributions to the MSA. The third, a tax credit plan, would give individuals a choice: stay with the current tax treatment or trade it for a fixed-dollar tax credit, which would apply equally to MSAs. If the credit were selected, then employer contributions toward health insurance would be included in a person's taxable income, but the employee would be given a fixed tax credit equal to the average value of the subsidy under the old system.

The first of these proposals, which is contained in most pending MSA legislation, would preserve the market distortions and inequities in our current tax system, adding new subsidies for the direct purchase of care paid for out of pocket. Rather than rectifying the reason that MSAs have failed to emerge on their own in present markets for health insurance and health care, this reform would simply add further price distortions on the demand side, now at the point of purchase for anyone electing an MSA. As Mark Pauly (1994) has aptly put it, "Do two wrongs make a right?" While the approach might indeed spur the development of MSAs, it would clearly weaken the potential for MSAs to contain health care costs. Instead of facing the actual price of care not reimbursed by their insurance plans, individuals with MSAs would effectively face a reduced price due to the method of tax treatment—a percentage price discount equal to their marginal tax rate. This approach also leaves intact the current tax inequities, providing a larger tax subsidy to persons with higher incomes.

The second and third approaches, a tax cap and a fixed-dollar tax credit, have more merit. Both would encourage less expensive insurance arrangements, in particular, MSAs. However, the efficiency and equity of these two tax treatments differ greatly. A tax cap would still distort the prices consumers face in the markets for health insurance and health care. As long as insurance outlays were under the level of the cap, the effective price of additional coverage would be reduced by a person's marginal tax rate, thus stimulating demand for further coverage. Likewise, purchases made from tax-subsidized MSAs under a tax cap proposal would also be, in effect, discounted. Given the tax savings that would accrue by using an MSA to purchase uninsured services, persons would have an incentive to over-consume through this channel. Also, like the first approach, a tax cap retains income inequities. Larger dollar subsidies would be provided to persons with higher incomes because, even with the same deduction, taxes saved rise with income.

In contrast, a fixed-dollar tax credit would be nondistortive and much more equitable. Since an individual's tax savings would not depend on level of coverage purchased (provided, of course, the insurance arrangement qualified), the effective price of insurance would be unaffected by the credit. Also, because MSAs would be funded with after-tax dollars, a credit would not create incentives to over- consume uninsured services. It would also be equitable, because the same dollar tax savings would be extended to all persons who acquire health insurance, regardless of their income or economic circumstances.

In sum, these three approaches to fostering MSAs through the tax code are very different. While all three would encourage MSAs, the first two do so in a way that either increases or preserves many of the distortions and inequities of our present system. The tax credit proposal, however, would be a step in the right direction. It would encourage MSAs while improving the efficiency of choices being made in insurance markets. It would also help to alleviate the lack of fairness in the current system. If allowed to evolve through the adoption of an incremental tax credit system, such as that proposed by Pauly and Goodman (1995), MSAs would be a potent force in the continuing battle against rising health care costs in America.

References

Barchet, Stephen. 1995. *Medical Savings Accounts: A Building Block for Sound Health Care*. Olympia, WA: Evergreen Freedom Foundation.

Bennett, Linda. 1993. "Want to Dramatically Lower Health Care Cost Increases? Link Benefits to Contributions to Company Success," *Compensation and Benefits Review*. (July/August): pp. 57-63.

Bordonaro, Molly Hering. 1995. "Medical Savings Accounts and the States: Growth From the Grassroots," NCPA Brief Analysis No. 170. (August). National Center for Policy Analysis, Dallas, TX.

Craig, Victoria C. 1994. "An Eight-Point Plan for Consumer-Oriented Reform." (February). Council for Affordable Health Insurance, Alexandria, VA.

Craig, Victoria C. 1995. "Medical Savings Account Legislation in the 104th U.S. Congress." (May). Council for Affordable Health Insurance, Alexandria, VA.

Davidoff, Amy J. 1997. "Medical Flexible Spending Accounts: Health Benefits Choice and the Demand for Insured Medical Care." (June 27-29). Paper presented at the Eighth Annual Health Economics Conference, Minneapolis, MN.

Eichner, Matthew J., David A. Wise, and Mark B. McClellan. 1996. "Insurance or Self-Insurance: Variation, Persistence, and Individual Health Accounts." NBER Working Paper 5640. (June). National Bureau of Economic Research, New York, NY.

Flynn, Patricia. 1992. "Employment-Based Health Insurance: Coverage Under COBRA Continuation Rules," in U.S. Department of Labor, *Health Benefits and the Workforce*, pp. 105-116. Washington, DC: U.S. Government Printing Office.

Goodman, John C., and Gerald L. Musgrave. 1994. *Patient Power: Solving America's Health Care Crisis*. Washington, DC: The Cato Institute.

Hammond, Tony. 1993. "Memorandum on Cost Estimates for High Deductible Health Plans." (March). Health Insurance Association of America, Washington, DC.

Health Insurance Association of America (HIAA). 1992. *Long Term Care: Needs, Costs, and Financing*. Washington, DC: HIAA.

Jensen, Gail A., and Robert J. Morlock. 1994. "Why Medical Savings Accounts Deserve a Closer Look." *Journal of American Health Policy*. (March/April): pp. 14-23.

Jensen, Gail A., Michael A. Morrisey, Shannon Gafney, and Derek Liston. 1997. "The New Dominance of Managed Care: Insurance Trends in the 1990s." *Health Affairs*. (January/February): pp. 125-136.

Jensen, Gail A., Canopy Roychoudhury, and Daniel C. Cherkin. "Employer-Sponsored Health Insurance for Chiropractic Care." *Medical Care*, 1998 vol 36, No 4: pp. 544-553

Johnson, Nancy P. 1993. "Not What the Doctor Ordered?" *Business Insurance*. (October 18): pp. 1, 76.

Matthews, Merrill Jr. 1996. "Medical Savings Account Legislation: The Good, the Bad, and the Ugly." NCPA Brief Analysis No. 211. (August 19). National Center for Policy Analysis, Dallas, TX.

Merline, John. "Employees as Health Reformers: Medical Savings Accounts Curbing Premium Costs." *Investors' Business Daily*. (March 18): p. 1.

National Center for Policy Analysis. 1997. Information about consumer awareness of MSAs based on a survey, which was posted on NCPA's web site, www.ncpa.org. (October 24).

Newhouse, Joseph P. and the Insurance Experiment Group. 1993. *Free for All?: Lessons from the Rand Health Insurance Experiment*. Cambridge, MA: Harvard University Press.

Patient Power Report. "IRS: No Cut Off in 1997 - 20% Previously Uninsured." August 1997a, p. 2.

Patient Power Report. "Medicare Reform in the Budget Bill." August 1997b, p. 1 and 4-13.

Patient Power Report. "Wisconsin Blues Drop MSAs." August 1997c, p. 2.

Pauly, Mark V. 1994. *An Analysis of Medical Savings Accounts: Do Two Wrongs Make a Right?* Washington, DC: American Enterprise Institute Press.

Pauly, Mark V., and John C. Goodman. 1995. "Tax Credits for Health Insurance and Medical Savings Accounts." *Health Affairs*. (spring): pp. 125-39.

Spencer, Peter L. 1993. "New Plan Cuts Health Care Costs in Half." *Consumers' Research*. (October): pp. 16-19.

Swartz, Katherine, and Timothy D. McBride. 1990. "Spells Without Health Insurance: Distributions of Durations and their Link to Point-in-Time Estimates." *Inquiry*, pp. 281-88.

Wildavsky, Rachel. 1993. "Here's Health-Care Reform That Works." *Reader's Digest*. (October).

4

Freedom of Contract: The Unexplored Path to Health Care Reform[1]

Clark C. Havighurst

During the televised vice-presidential debate in the 1992 election campaign, Ross Perot's running mate, Admiral James B. Stockdale, suggested that possible solutions to the problem of excessive health care spending might lie in the hands of "crafty people who know how to write contracts to change incentives or get . . . the incentives situation under control." Although Admiral Stockdale declared himself "out of ammunition" when asked a follow-up question, his initial observation contained an insight that has escaped most other analysts: Many of the problems of American health care can be attributed to the shortcomings of written contracts as vehicles for defining the legal rights of patients and the legal obligations of providers and payers. This chapter suggests the wisdom of enlisting drafters of health care contracts in the movement for fundamental health care reform—not as merely "crafty people," who might be inclined to deceive consumers, but as legal craftsmen seeking to give consumers better tools for choosing how to spend their health care dollars.

It might seem that the idea of relying on private contracts as instruments for defining patient rights and making health care choices received a setback when Admiral Stockdale's ticket failed to win the election of 1992. The successful presidential candidate, however, came to office with a mandate to launch a major health care reform initiative—and also, incidentally, with a running mate (in this case his

145

wife) ready to captain that initiative through political seas. In the fall of 1993, President and Mrs. Clinton presented to Congress and the American people a proposal for top-to-bottom reform of American health care. To be sure, the Clinton proposal would have made government rather than the private sector the main instrument for ensuring that the health care system serves the nation's needs, and its failure to survive in the political process was largely attributable to that fact. But the Clinton bill also purported to contemplate a significant role for consumer choice, and subsequent developments have reinforced the idea that market signals should guide the health care industry. Nevertheless, if consumer choice is to be a truly useful force in disciplining the American health care system, private contracts will have to play some role in defining competing health plans and in differentiating between them. Thus, it is not irrelevant to focus on private health care contracts as instruments by which consumers might exercise meaningful choice about their future health care.

The main objective of this chapter is to suggest that private contracts could be of substantial help in making efficient micro decisions about health care spending—that is, in making the myriad clinical choices concerning resource use that cumulatively determine how much of the nation's wealth is spent on health care. Contracts, it will be argued, have an unappreciated potential for transmitting signals from cost-conscious consumers on the demand side of the market, through health-plan middlemen, to health care providers on the supply side. Contracts can also simultaneously supply the legal authority that health plans and providers need before they can safely respond to economizing signals thus received. In general, private contracts, by offering consumers opportunities to dictate the legal entitlements they are willing to pay for, could greatly expand consumers' economizing options. Once consumers with appropriate public subsidies and economizing incentives have a full range of choices available in a well-constructed and carefully maintained marketplace, their decisions could finally and safely be trusted to guide health care spending in the United States.

This chapter first summarizes the evidence that contracts have been seriously underutilized as tools for ensuring efficient health care spending. It then outlines a basis for believing that, with the proper encouragement, innovative private contracts could complete the revolution in health care financing and delivery that commenced in the 1980s, when private health plans began seizing, and learning how to exercise, responsibility for controlling health care costs as agents for their subscribers.[2] The main theme is that contracts should be embraced precisely because they are capable of finally and fully empowering appropriately cost-conscious consumers, acting through appropriately instructed agents, to determine for themselves how much should be spent on their health care.

How Health Care Contracts Have Failed Consumers

The market failure that has put the cost of health care beyond effective control by its purchasers is, in the last analysis, a failure of private contract. The culprit most often blamed for the poor performance of the market for health services is, of course, the demand-liberating effect of health insurance—the effect that economists call "moral hazard," in reference to the behavioral changes that occur when people are put in a position to spend or risk the funds of others. Despite its cost-increasing effects, however, moral hazard is not something that consumers cannot or should not live with. A degree of moral hazard is a natural concomitant of virtually any arrangement, private or public, that gives people security about their future health care costs. Because such financial security is valuable to people, it is not irrational for them to incur some higher costs in order to obtain it.[3]

Thus, whether the health care market is performing well or poorly depends not on whether moral hazard is present but on whether competing health plans are doing all it pays to do to minimize its scope or counteract its influence. At present, poorly designed tax subsidies for the purchase of health benefits induce people to purchase coverage that is excessively tolerant of moral hazard.[4] But that is a remediable failure of government tax policy, not a market failure obviously calling for government intervention in the industry. Although the equilibrium that the market seeks is undoubtedly affected by tax subsidies, those subsidies are similar to other subsidies in the economy (such as for agriculture or residential housing) and do not in themselves invalidate reliance on the market finally to allocate scarce resources. The more critical issue is whether health plans possess and use all the tools they need to check the operation of moral hazard to whatever degree would most benefit subscribers. In fact, health care contracts have yet to be put to effective use in the battle against moral hazard and excessive spending.

Ordinarily, when purchasers contract for the future delivery of complex goods or services, the sales contract contains detailed specifications of the purchaser's requirements. Health care contracts, however, are not remotely of this kind. Thus, contracts between patients and the actual providers of care are usually unwritten and rarely say anything specific about the provider's obligations. Even more significantly, the subscriber contracts of private health plans employ only the most general terms in defining the services that subscribers are, in effect, purchasing on a prepaid, pre-need basis. Indeed, there appears to be a general assumption—detectable not only in health care contracts but in virtually all thinking about health care in America—that health care is not something that can or should be purchased in measured quantities of agreed-upon quality. Instead, "health care" is apparently viewed, within broad categories, as a familiar, fungible commodity that a purchaser identifies simply by pointing to the shelf on which the products he desires are stacked. Thus, health plan subscriber contracts generally define coverage by including (or excluding) services in blocks, which are variously defined by reference to the type of service (e.g., acute hospital services), particular diseases (e.g., temporomandibular joint syndrome), conditions (e.g., mental health care), procedures or therapies (e.g., autologous bone marrow transplants), treatment modalities (e.g., outpatient rehabilitation services), or types of provider (e.g., clinical psychologist services). Public policymakers are also accustomed to using such categorical terms in defining the coverage of public health plans—as if each category were self-explanatory.

Thus, under the health care contracts in use today, the nature, quality, and precise content of the services to be provided in the future are generally not defined to any appreciable degree in the contract itself. Such variables are left instead largely to the discretion of the providers of care and plan administrators, subject to whatever constraints the legal system imposes. Indeed, if one judges only from the terms of the contracts themselves, providers of care and private health plans enjoy wide discretion with respect to the quantity and quality of the services provided and the style and manner in which they are delivered. This lack of specificity concerning the quantity and quality of services to be provided in the future reflects, not an inevitable or unavoidable failure of contract as a practical tool, but a set of conventions that, although seldom examined, lie at the heart of the inability of purchasers to control the cost of the care they are buying. Under these conventions, health care providers, individually and collectively, exercise nearly exclusive responsibility for defining the entitlements of patients.

Of course, most health plan contracts are more in the nature of insurance policies than contracts for the future delivery of services.[5] As such, their actual function is not to prescribe the services that providers will eventually supply. Instead, it is to curb moral hazard—by limiting the services that insureds can purchase at plan expense. Today's health plan contracts, however, are crafted to counteract moral hazard only on the fringes of the problem. Thus, they impose few explicit limitations (other than categorical exclusions and limited cost-sharing requirements) on the obligation of the plan to pay for whatever services a physician prescribes. Under the test of "medical necessity," which serves almost universally as the contractual touchstone of plan coverage, the criteria used to check the spending discretion of providers are almost exclusively medical, not economic.[6] Omission of cost considerations from the coverage calculus obviously neglects a principal concern of consumers.

More ominously, the medical-necessity test perpetuates the values and preferences of health care providers whose imperative is to prescribe for patients everything that may be beneficial—and nothing but the best. Thus, today's health plan contracts are generally shaped in accordance with a convention, or paradigm, under which health care is not regarded, even at the margin, as a consumer good that people are free to purchase according to their preferences and economic circumstances.[7] Written primarily to create individual entitlements to whatever services providers competently and in good faith prescribe, health care contracts are simply never thought of as mutual undertakings by which individuals pool their funds to cover their future health needs and, in so doing, accept reciprocal limitations on their future right to make claims on the common fund.

The shortcomings of today's health care contracts are striking evidence of a failure of societal will to carry the war against inappropriate spending into the enemy's heartland. Indeed, there exists a "no man's land" in which economically inappropriate health care spending inspired by moral hazard is essentially immune from attack under the terms of health care contracts.[8] Sanctuary is thus provided, in the war against excessive spending, to many services that would be indefensible if their benefits had to be compared to their costs. Weapons designed only for a limited war cannot bring victory against a powerful enemy. Indeed, the contract failure described here is significant precisely because it reflects explicit or implicit acceptance of medical efficacy alone—what might be called an "any-benefit" test—as the sole criterion for deciding what care should be financed. Economic considerations enter in only in the form of a requirement that care be "cost-effective"—that is, no more costly than another equally effective mode of treatment. It should be noted that this test, too, embodies the any-benefit criterion.

Serious consequences have flowed from the ineffectiveness of health care contracts as instruments either for dictating terms to providers or for combating moral hazard in the benefit/cost no man's land. The inadequacy or absence of crucial terms in such contracts has meant that all concerned—patients, providers, plan administrators, and courts—have had to look elsewhere for rules and definitive decisions concerning the specific services to be provided in each case. Much of the content of the bundle of rights belonging to each consumer of health services is therefore ultimately established by judges, juries, and medical expert witnesses—arbiters unlikely to share, or implement, consumers' concerns about costs.[9] As so construed, patients' entitlements include the right to demand, at little or no direct cost to themselves, many health services that are of dubious benefit or marginal value. Also among the entitlements implicitly conferred on patients is the right—also of questionable value—to obtain a particular kind of legal redress for whatever the law (not the contract) defines as medical malpractice. Instead of serving as instruments of consumer choice and empowerment, health care contracts put consumers and their pocketbooks at the mercy of other actors with agendas of their own.

The adverse cost and legal consequences of inadequate health care contracts have become increasingly serious over time. With consumers and their agents poorly armed in the fight against overspending, the nation's physicians, technology suppliers, and hospitals have been free for nearly a generation (certainly since Medicare and Medicaid) to invent and sell ever more costly goods and services with little reference to cost considerations. The nation thus gradually came to incur health care costs that are now regarded as unbearable. At the same time, the courts, myopically mistaking where consumer welfare lies, picked up the costly professional standards and customary practices that evolved in the dysfunctional marketplace and used them to define the specific coverage obligations of health plans and to detect substandard care in malpractice suits.

The health care industry has thus operated for many years under a legal regime that threatens physicians, hospitals, and health plans with severe sanctions if they are caught violating standards that have increasingly lost touch with economic reality. By drawing its requirements from industry custom and professional practice, the legal system has exacerbated waste in a system that was already out of control. In addition to inducing risk-averse doctors to practice "defensive medicine" going beyond even what courts would probably require in fact, the law has served as a ratchet preventing standards that have gone up from ever coming down. Moreover, courts have also impeded reliance on private contracts as a means of escaping the tyranny of inefficient standards.[10]

Because it operates to a large extent under centrally prescribed rather than privately prescribed standards, the health care industry can usefully be thought of as a regulated industry. Whatever one thinks of government regulation in general, public regulators are at least accountable to elected officials and potentially capable of serving the overall public interest by balancing competing values such as benefits and costs. Unfortunately, the same cannot be said about the regulatory regime under which the health care industry operates. Neither the courts nor the professional sources from which they borrow standards are accountable to either voters or consumers. Moreover, they tend to focus on individual cases, not issues of public policy, and to consider only benefits to individuals, not costs to consumers or to the economy as a whole.

Although government regulation is often faulted for falling too much into the hands of the interests being regulated, actual industry capture of a regulatory program is presumably exceptional. The health care industry, on the other hand, has been effectively empowered to regulate itself. Under industry conventions strongly supported by the legal system, health care providers have broad powers, both individually and collectively, to decide without substantial cost constraints or effective oversight what services patients should receive at society's expense. Recent innovations in managed care and utilization management, although significant, do not invalidate these assertions. Without contracts that expressly authorize their cost-control efforts, health maintenance organizations (HMOs) and other managed-care plans can economize only *sub rosa* and not—because of legal constraints—to the full extent that cost-conscious consumers might approve.

For present purposes, the most important consequence of the defective regulatory regime under which the health care industry currently operates is that consumer choice is largely illusory in health care markets. Although the marketplace offers many apparent options, including a variety of managed-care plans, the real range of consumer choice is limited by the need for all plans to conform to ill-considered, often vague, but potentially demanding standards emanating from the same central source—the legal system, which borrows its standards wherever necessary from providers themselves. Consumers are thus denied, beyond a certain point, the freedom to benefit themselves by economizing choices. Specifically, they lack opportunities for prospective self-denial—that is, they are not free to contract voluntarily today to accept a degree of health care rationing tomorrow.[11]

Thus, the same consumers who are free to buy small, arguably less safe cars (or used cars or cars without air bags or antilock brakes) cannot make comparable economizing choices in purchasing health care. Unable to save money for other uses by assuming a small degree of risk (risks that, judging from the doubtful value of so much of today's health care spending, would almost certainly be near-negligible), purchasers of health coverage face essentially a Hobson's choice between different versions of the same health care Cadillac. Of course, American consumers have always had the option of going without health coverage altogether. The very large number of persons who have made that choice, however, is itself mute testimony to the need for intermediate alternatives.

In sum, the reason for the huge margin by which the United States leads other nations in per-capita health care spending is that its political and legal institutions have given it the worst of both worlds— regulation and the free market. On the one hand, the centrally prescribed, legally enforced standards that the nation has allowed to guide health care spending have never been evaluated as public policy or formally adopted as such. On the other hand, the private health plans to which the nation has entrusted great responsibilities have been either unwilling or unable to define private rights and obligations effectively by contract. Not only have the good intentions underlying the medical-legal system's insistence on high standards for everyone undercut the ability of market forces to determine the appropriate level of spending on health services, but they have tragically impeded efforts to guarantee universal access to health care. The same regulatory system that has priced so many individuals out of the health insurance market has also made prohibitive the cost of providing for them at public expense. Once again, the best has proved an enemy of the good.

The obvious implication of the analysis here is that the United States must finally come to terms with its schizophrenic nature and choose which way to go—whether to give more meaningful choices to consumers or to give to government all the powers it would need to give the people what it decides is good (enough) for them. Contract failure, even though it has long prevailed in the health care sector, is not necessarily a sufficient reason to introduce heavy-handed public regulation to prescribe or otherwise limit the health care that people can receive. Before adopting a government-dominated, choice-denying remedy for the problems of the health care industry, policymakers should consider whether contract failure might be overcome by a combination of private initiatives and legal change. In order to make this judgment, they must understand precisely why private contracts have not been used to maximum advantage in helping consumers of health care ensure that their money is well spent. To this subject, the discussion now turns.

Accounting for Contract Failure

The most obvious reason for the imprecision found in today's health care contracts is the great practical difficulty of writing contract language that would provide useful guidance in the myriad of different situations that can be expected to arise. It is manifestly impossible for a contract to specify the precise entitlements of subscribers, the precise payment obligations of the plan, or the precise duties of providers in all possible circumstances. It is not easy even to find contractual words that would effectively authorize the omission, in the interest of keeping premiums affordable, of a particular desired treatment on the ground that it had not been shown to be efficacious or had failed some kind of benefit/cost test.

The convention of deferring to professional norms and standards in health care contracts thus certainly reflects in large measure the high transaction costs of the alternative strategy of writing and administering highly specific and selective coverage. Indeed, it may have been entirely reasonable and efficient for the drafters of early health care contracts to rely upon professional standards as the "default rules" to which arbiters of disputes would turn whenever they found the contract silent on a particular issue. Whether that still makes sense today, however, is another question. Now that heavy spending is customary under a combination of misplaced incentives and misguided legal compulsions, contract drafters should reexamine their options. It should not be impossible, after all, to write explicit contracts that would serve subscribers better than continuing to rely on the medical profession and the courts to call all the tunes.

Circumstances besides drafting problems have also influenced health plans not to use their contracts to customize the entitlements of their subscribers.[12] One crucial factor has been the ways in which tax law and employer practices have hidden the true costs of health coverage from consumers. Unaware of total costs and even of the share of the burden they indirectly bear, workers not only have failed to demand aggressive economizing but also have come to view health care as an entitlement conferred on them at the expense of others. This entitlement mentality is fostered by the politics of the workplace, where employers and unions both use the health plan to signal their benevolence toward workers. In this context, no one has undertaken to educate workers about the full range of economizing possibilities. Employers and competing health plans alike have seen great danger in appearing concerned about anything besides the quality of care.

The diminished role of contracts in purchasing health care can also be traced to the dominance for many years of provider-controlled health insurers—particularly, the early Blue Cross and Blue Shield plans, which for a long time also set the standards for other (commercial) health insurers. In addition, the medical profession had great success in the early years of health insurance in using boycott threats and political influence to ensure that all health plans (eventually including even the federal Medicare program itself) operated only in profession-approved ways.[13] Finally, until almost the end of the 1970s, employers and private health plans must have seen little long-term advantage in pursuing potentially controversial innovations, because the federal government was apparently bent on controlling health care costs through regulation.

Not only did many circumstances thus combine to diminish the benefits and raise the risks and costs of contractual innovations, but health plans had little competitive incentive to incur such risks and costs. A specific problem was that their competitors could free-ride on their efforts, emulating their successes while letting them bear alone the costs of failures. A health insurer might shrink, for example, from incurring the costs of litigating an important legal issue concerning the validity of contracts when any favorable precedent that might be set would benefit its competitors as well. Moreover, health insurers may have been comfortable with the lucrative status quo and leery of stimulating competition in the highly uncertain business of controlling moral hazard. In any event, many years went by before the first olive got out of the bottle and competing health plans began to take substantial responsibility for the cost of care.

Many of the reasons for private health plans to adhere to conventional practices and defer to professional norms and standards weakened dramatically in the late 1970s and early 1980s. Not only did cost pressures become more palpable, but government suddenly ceased to promise that regulation would solve the problem. During this period, too, antitrust enforcement and other legal changes expanded opportunities for health plans to force providers to compete for their business. As a result, the 1980s saw health plans begin to make impressive progress in finding new ways to deal with providers and in designing more efficient kinds of coverage.[14] Indeed, policymakers should remember that the private sector has had only a relatively short time to master—in the teeth of provider resistance and consumer misunderstanding—the extraordinarily difficult art of protecting consumers against high costs while ensuring their access to appropriate care of good quality. They should in fact be heartened to discover a whole new kind of weaponry—private contracts—that has not yet been fully deployed in this fight.

Although private health plans have modified their subscriber contracts in significant ways in recent years, the contractual reforms undertaken so far have been relatively conservative. In particular, they have not yet challenged the conventional paradigm of health care under which only medical, not economic, criteria determine plan coverage. To be sure, the market of the 1980s did inspire substantial innovations in contracts between health plans and their participating providers. Indeed, during this period some health plans became quite aggressive in contracting selectively with physicians and hospitals, demanding both price concessions and cooperation in cost-containment efforts as *quid pro quo* for classification as a preferred provider. Not only did HMOs prosper, but substantial innovations occurred in the administration of benefits. Specifically, many health plans introduced methods of utilization management under which a plan and its agents could consult with treating physicians to establish the limits of the plan's coverage in advance of the provision of care. Despite the progress thus made in ensuring that services are appropriate, however, these new methods are of only limited utility in the absence of contracts expressly authorizing the rationing of care that is only arguably or only marginally beneficial.

A major reason why the 1980s produced only modest reforms in health plans' subscriber contracts was undoubtedly the performance of the courts in construing and enforcing restrictive terms in such contracts.[15] Contractual exclusions adopted by health plans to limit their obligations to pay for particular procedures or services—for example, new technologies not yet shown to be superior to existing modalities—were regularly viewed skeptically by judges reluctant to deny coverage to any patient with a sympathy-inspiring claim. Far from making allowances for the difficulty of writing clear contractual exclusions, some courts tended to look for any excuse—such as an arguable ambiguity or misrepresentation—to construe the contract against the plan responsible for its drafting. Partly because courts have become accustomed, under the medical-necessity and any-benefit criteria, to having the final say on health plan coverage, many of them do not shrink from adopting their own strained readings of contract language. Confronted with the likelihood that plan coverage would be "judge-made" in any event, contract drafters may not have seen much potential benefit in redrafting contracts to authorize controversial economizing.

The irony of this story is that, even though the health care industry has long operated under centrally prescribed rules and standards, its status as a regulated industry restricting consumer choice is more *de facto* than *de jure*. Adherence to professional standards or industry custom is rarely mandatory in the sense that the law specifically prohibits health plans from varying the law's own requirements by contract. Instead, the general uniformity that one finds in today's contracts is arguably more a product of convenience and convention than of positive law or of government regulation of the command-and-control variety. To be sure, health plans would certainly encounter some judicial resistance if they set out independently to define patient rights and provider obligations that differed appreciably from those that have become customary. But even though legal scholars have frequently mourned, applauded, or otherwise noted the "death of contract,"[16] well-drafted health care contracts that were fairly marketed and not manifestly unfair to consumers would stand a good chance of being enforced more or less according to their terms. Although the caution of lawyers in proposing such contracts is understandable, there is almost certainly more room for contractual innovation than they have sought to exploit.[17]

A window of opportunity exists today for using private contracts to assist in rationalizing health care spending in accordance with consumer preferences. Contract drafters are therefore invited to accept the challenge of writing economizing contracts that would be both fair and beneficial to consumers *ex ante* (that is, when they are entered into) and likely to be enforced by courts *ex post* (that is, when an individual patient desires to be released from his bargain). Even without new legislation expressly authorizing them, private contractual reforms that are introduced with candor and an eye to convincing courts of their validity could well prove capable of completing the revolution in the design and operation of private health plans that began in earnest in the 1980s. The new circumstances in which health plans are being purchased today—approximating in many cases the conditions contemplated by advocates of "managed competition"—should make courts willing to enforce health care contracts more or less according to their terms. In addition, the Employee Retirement Income Security Act (ERISA) protects employer-sponsored plans from many of the legal threats that might otherwise impede innovative contracting.[18]

Activating Contracts as Instruments of Consumer Choice

That health care contracts have served consumers poorly in the past does not prevent them from serving useful functions in the future. Indeed, the magnitude of their past shortcomings is itself a good measure of their potential value—if the constraints that have heretofore inhibited or precluded their use can be overcome. The message of this chapter is that there is a great deal of mileage left in this venerable but little used vehicle for advancing consumer interests. Although the chapter suggests some possible terms for economizing contracts,[19] its main purpose is to open minds to the potential of such private reforms, to encourage creative lawyering with a view to helping consumers get better value for their money, and to get courts and policymakers to respect and encourage rather than foreclose contractual innovations of all kinds.

Precisely because health care spending remains so far out of control, the potential gains from contractual innovation are greater today than ever before. Moreover, judging from the high administrative costs being incurred and the complaints being heard from providers and patient advocates, private health plans may have nearly exhausted the possibilities of their current cost-containment methods—cost-sharing, categorical limitations on coverage, utilization management, new methods of payment, and selective contracting with providers. They should therefore soon be searching for tools to authorize them to be more aggressive in economizing on the consumers' behalf. Even though consumers rightfully remain suspicious of low-cost offerings, an attractive price tag on a plan offered in the right circumstances might well induce them to modify their entitlement mentality and examine available options with an open mind. Despite the difficulty of marketing what may appear to be second-rate medicine, many things could be done—such as education concerning the minimal degree of risk—to prepare the way for responsible economizing. In any event, it is far from clear that today's contract failures could not be substantially ameliorated by a combination of private initiatives and public actions.

The most important objective of better health care contracts should be to authorize rational economizing in the provision of care.[20] Specifically, contract drafters should seek to free both health plans and providers from undue legal risks that currently inhibit even highly responsible efforts to economize in the spending of funds collected from subscribers. To be sure, innovative contracts to achieve this goal would be difficult to conceive, write, administer, and defend in court. Nevertheless, opportunities exist for restating the scope of plan coverage and clarifying the duties of providers. In particular, carefully conceived and well-validated clinical practice guidelines, incorporated by reference in health care contracts, have an immense potential for specifying the services that will (and will not) be provided at plan expense in particular cases.[21] In the long run, it is possible to imagine a marketplace in which health plans choose from an available variety of reliable guidelines those that best express the expectations of their subscribers with respect to the trade-off between probable benefit and cumulative cost. Even though a health plan contract should never (and could never) be a medical cookbook, the contract failure that has heretofore given providers wide *de facto* discretion in prescribing (or withholding) care could to a significant extent be responsibly overcome.

An important goal in writing innovative contracts must be to make them compatible with the reasonable concerns of physicians about their ability to care adequately for their patients with a minimum of bureaucratic interference.[22] With respect to the day-to-day administration of health plan coverage, contracts incorporating practice guidelines or other relatively specific standards governing resource use would have a great initial advantage over current methods of utilization management. Indeed, physicians have long demanded that health plans disclose the protocols and standards they employ in predetermining coverage. If competing health plans can be induced to include relatively clear and specific coverage provisions in their private contracts, there should be much less need for the kind of case-by-case bureaucratic oversight of medical practice that is widespread today. Moreover, wherever possible, participating physicians should themselves be given a major hand in designing and administering the contract. The plan should also be administered with due respect for the professionalism of individual practitioners. Indeed, in a properly run plan with well-qualified, cooperative, and committed doctors, it should rarely be necessary to refer to the letter of the contract rather than its spirit. Perhaps the main hurdle for physicians in accepting restrictions imposed by contracts would be to appreciate that those restrictions are legitimized by the patient's own choice in enrolling in the plan. Physicians should see their obligation to practice within contractual constraints as part and parcel of their professional obligation to the patient—their duty to do all that can be done within the limits of the patient's resources.

Another way in which physicians could benefit from innovative health care contracts is by obtaining real substantive relief from malpractice suits. The precise nature and extent of the relief to be given should of course be decided by the plan itself as an agent of its subscribers. In theory, however, nothing prevents any of the malpractice reforms that have been considered for legislative adoption from being implemented voluntarily by a single health plan in its contracts with its subscribers and providers.[23] The most obvious strategy would be to require aggrieved patients to bring their claims in a forum other than the public courts and under different, specified procedures and evidentiary rules.[24] (Similar methods of dispute resolution should also be employed for other grievances, including those related to interpretation of provisions governing plan coverage.)

Health care contracts might also restate the legal standard of care applicable in a malpractice suit,[25] so that a physician who acts reasonably and prudently under any resource constraints that the plan imposes will not be held to have negligently underserved the patient. One federal appeals court has entertained the possibility that "an employer and an HMO could agree that a quality of health care standard articulated in their contract would replace the standards that would otherwise be supplied by the applicable state law of tort."[26] If such contracts were accepted, adherence to practice guidelines specified in the contract would be an absolute defense in a negligence case. Thus, private contracts offer a valuable opportunity for a health plan to coordinate its own payment obligations with the duties of the physicians and hospitals providing covered care. Another way to achieve congruence in the respective duties of a plan and its providers would be to shift by contract to so-called "enterprise liability," under which the plan would assume full responsibility for the quality of care rendered under the contract.[27] (Not only would such an arrangement make malpractice risks less vexing, but it would make the health plan accountable for the quality of care, not merely for its cost, and would better align the plan's interests with the interests of its physicians.) It should not be difficult for a health plan to ameliorate the malpractice system's highly vexing interference in its physicians' professional lives without net injury, and probably with some gain, to plan subscribers.

Because economizing in the procurement of health care is a sensitive and sometimes risky undertaking, proponents of contracts as instruments of such economizing bear a heavy burden of persuasion. At a minimum, any health care economizing must be in the consumer's ultimate interest—not in the sense that all hardships are avoided but in the sense that any risks assumed are reasonable in relation to the savings derived. Moreover, if contracts are to be enforced by courts, it should probably appear that a plaintiff who regrets *ex post* having subscribed to an economical health plan *ex ante* was in a position to share, at least indirectly, in the savings. To be sure, there will be those who will hesitate to hold individuals to choices that were made for them by an agent or that they themselves made at an earlier time, perhaps unthinkingly or with inadequate information (particularly about their future needs) and possibly even with different preferences than they now profess.[28] Yet the market can hardly operate if the legal system regularly reverses consumers' *ex ante* choices. Moreover, even if it is doubtful that *ex ante* choices are reliably welfare-maximizing in every real-world case, the legal system should be concerned not with the justice of every rule it enforces but with the legitimacy of the legal regime that yielded the rules. In a democracy, choice legitimizes power, and it should suffice that the legal regime chosen—that is, the contract—was arrived at through a tolerable process of consumer choice and was not fraudulently induced.[29]

Egalitarian concerns would be less likely to distort the interpretation and enforcement of health care contracts if government were to ensure (perhaps by issuing vouchers convertible into health coverage) that everyone had enough purchasing power that they would not be forced to carry economizing to socially objectionable extremes.[30] Although a presidential commission on ethical issues in medicine opined in 1983 that society has some obligation to ensure that every American has access to adequate health care, it did not insist on equality, either actual or symbolic, as an ethical imperative in government health policy.[31]

Another prerequisite to the acceptance of private contracts as legitimate economizing tools is meaningful consumer choice. A patient whose care might be adversely affected by a health plan's contract must have had some choice about whether to subscribe to that contract or to receive care under conventional rules. A source of possible concern about encouraging innovative contracts is, of course, the seeming complexity of the comparisons that consumers must make between health plans with substantially different contracts. Consumers are certainly hard-pressed even today to compare plans with widely different benefit packages and cost-sharing requirements. For this reason, one of the cornerstones of the so-called "managed-competition" strategy for health care reform has been to standardize benefits so that consumers can better compare their options. Proponents of managed competition also assign a high priority to providing information from which consumers can judge the past performance of particular health plans and the participating providers. These strategies have much to recommend them and, if implemented even in a partial way, would go far toward validating the choices that consumers make.

It would be wrong, however, to leap from the desirability of requiring all health plans to cover the same conditions and impose identical cost-sharing requirements to the conclusion that all plans should have identical contracts. Uniformity in health plan contracts is no virtue if plans do or should differ in the balances they strike in deciding the specific services they will provide in particular circumstances. Significantly, the contracts of today's HMOs are glaringly deficient in disclosing their economizing strategies. Surprisingly, this deficiency does not prevent their being generally viewed, especially by advocates of managed competition, as legitimate vehicles for achieving cost containment. In any event, HMO contracts that reveal economizing intentions seem preferable to those that obscure them. Interestingly, one sees here the rationale behind calling an insurance contract a "policy." A health plan's subscriber contract should indeed be a statement of plan policy.

Thus, contracts have the potential merit of disclosing plan policies in advance of enrollment, making it easier for a court to presume that a subscriber to a contract voluntarily accepted the plan's limitations and thus to enforce the contract. On the other hand, there is good reason to regularize coverage by prohibiting exclusions of particular diseases or conditions and manipulations of deductibles and copayments that frustrate price comparisons. By insisting on uniformity in benefit packages and cost sharing, a sponsor of managed competition could ensure that price differences reflect real marginal differences in style and intensity—the things on which competition must focus if consumers are to have real options in the marketplace. With price a reasonable proxy for the depth of coverage being purchased, consumers' choices could more readily be deemed to reflect their preferences.

Although greater disclosure, openness, and comparability would facilitate more informed consumer choice, the prime objective of proposing more explicit health care contracts is not to ensure that individuals give "informed consent" to each economizing move that might be made in providing for their future needs. That goal is unattainable in the real world.[32] Moreover, analogizing the goal of contracts to the requirement of informed consent in medical care is a mistake. That requirement was developed, not to make every patient a truly informed, technically competent decision maker, but to protect important dignitary interests of patients and ethical values in doctor/patient relationships.[33] Perhaps the better analogy is to the emerging law of living wills and advance directives, under which less-than-fully informed prospective consent legitimizes what society otherwise regards as highly illegitimate.

Disclosure and consumer choice memorialized in an explicit contract would serve similar ethical objectives here. Indeed, the main advantage of explicit health care contracts, in addition to the flexibility, assurances, and accountability they provide, is that they can go very far toward legitimizing a health plan's economizing actions in the eyes of the community and the law. Thus, it would be wrong to object to the proposal to expand the role of private contracts on the ground that consumers cannot individually compare the options with which they are presented or know all the implications of their choice. While it is appropriate to call attention to the highly complex and technical character of the contracts being proposed, such an objection misses the main point of proposing their use—which is to legitimize and facilitate, in the most ethically satisfying way possible, the inevitable rationing of marginal health care in individual cases that the polity must somehow find a way to tolerate. One should not get hung up on a "supermarket" paradigm of consumer choice and thus fail to see the merits of contracts as instruments for creating alternative legal regimes under which consumers can obtain their health care.[34]

If health care contracts are drafted and administered with the care and in the manner contemplated here, the nation should be willing to accept contractual limitations on the availability of particular health services—even in cases where there is potential, arguable, or (inevitably) actual hardship. Not to enforce contracts that were reasonable *ex ante* would defeat the objective of allowing people, if they choose, to economize in procuring marginally beneficial health care. The only alternative policy, besides simply continuing to accept the squandering of resources on inappropriate health care, would be to turn the responsibility over to government, which would then either directly regulate medical practice itself or introduce resource constraints—perhaps in the form of "global budgets"—to force providers to ration health services without patient consent. Although some may value the symbolic egalitarianism of a nonconsensual scheme, most American consumer-voters would probably find objectionable the final socialization of decision making on a matter as critical and personal as the health care they can expect to receive.

Because some rationing must eventually be tolerated in the provision of health care, policy makers should seek to ensure that whatever economizing occurs is voluntary and warranted by the circumstances of the individuals affected. The ethical attractiveness of contracts as instruments for accommodating the difficult trade-offs that inevitably exist in a world of limited resources entitles them to a sympathetic hearing both in policy debates and in the courts.

Notes

1. This chapter is adapted, with permission, from chapter two of Clark C. Havighurst, *Health Care Choices: Private Contracts as Instruments of Health Reform*, Washington: AEI Press, 1995. That chapter, like this one, summarizes arguments and proposals made at greater length—with theoretical support, empirical evidence, and examples—in the rest of the book, which is cited herein as *Health Care Choices*.
2. For an early warning that the market-reform movement of the 1980s would fail to achieve its cost-control objectives if freedom of contract was not restored, see Clark C. Havighurst, "Decentralizing Decision Making: Private Contract versus Professional Norms," in Jack A. Meyer (ed.), *Market Reforms in Health Care: Current Issues, New Directions, Strategic Decisions*, Washington, DC: American Enterprise Institute for Public Policy Research, 1983, p. 22. For a more recent discussion of the questionable virtues of competition and consumer choice in the absence of effective freedom of contract, see Clark C. Havighurst, "Why Preserve Private Health Care Financing?" in Robert B. Helms (ed.), *American Health Policy: Critical Issues for Reform*, Washington, DC: AEI Press, 1993, p. 87.
3. See Paul Joskow, *Controlling Hospital Costs: The Role of Government Regulation*, Cambridge, MA: The MIT Press, 1981, p. 22.
4. See generally Mark Pauly, *Taxation, Health Insurance, and Market Failure in the Medical Economy*, 24 J. Econ. Lit. 629 (1986).
5. Even integrated health maintenance organizations (HMOs)—the only plans that assume any responsibility for actually providing care rather than merely financing it—make no special contractual commitments about the nature or content of the care they will deliver. Indeed, the subscriber contracts of such HMOs are even less informative with regard to plan policies and practices than the typical health insurance policy, which incorporates limitations designed to strengthen the hand of the plan in negotiating with physicians over proposed courses of treatment.
6. See generally Mark A. Hall and Gerard F. Anderson, *Health Insurers' Assessment of Medical Necessity*, 140 U. Pa. L. Rev. 1637 (1992).
7. See generally Clark C. Havighurst, *The Professional Paradigm of Medical Care: Obstacle to Decentralization*, 30 Jurimetrics J. 415 (1990).

8.   See Clark C. Havighurst, *Contract Failure in the Market for Health Services*, 29 Wake Forest L. Rev. 47, 51-54 (1994) (graphic illustration of "benefit-cost no man's land").

9.   On the legal standards employed in resolving disputes over the coverage of health care contracts, see generally Hall and Anderson, *supra* note 6. On the standard of care in malpractice law, Note, *Medical Malpractice Law and Health Care Cost Containment: Lessons for Reformers from the Clash of Cultures*, 103 Yale L.J. 1297 (1994); John Siciliano, *Wealth, Equity, and the Unitary Medical Malpractice Standard*, 77 Va. L. Rev. 439 (1991) (arguing that the legal standard of care should be modified to reflect patient's resources and ability to pay); Haavi Morreim, *Stratified Scarcity: Redefining the Standard of Care*, 17 Law, Med. & Health Care 356 (1989) (similar); Edward Hirshfeld, *Economic Considerations in Treatment Decisions and the Standard of Care in Medical Malpractice Litigation*, 264 J.A.M.A. 2004 (1990); Mark A. Hall, *The Malpractice Standard of Care Under Health Care Cost Containment*, *id.* at 347 (arguing that malpractice standards can evolve toward efficiency under the "responsible minority" principle); Haavi Morreim, *Cost Containment and the Standard of Medical Care*, 75 Cal. L. Rev. 1719 (1987) (arguing that third-party judgments on appropriateness should affect standard to which provider is held); Randall Bovbjerg, *The Medical Malpractice Standard of Care: HMOs and Customary Practice*, 1975 Duke L.J. 1375 (addressing the defenses available for economizing efforts by HMOs and their physicians).

10.   See generally Clark C. Havighurst, *Prospective Self-Denial: Can Consumers Contract Today to Accept Health Care Rationing Tomorrow?*, 140 U. Pa. L. Rev. 1755 (1992).

11.   See *id.*

12.   Health plans were inhibited in pursuing all forms of cost containment for many years and began to assume their responsibilities in this regard only in the 1980s. See generally Clark C. Havighurst, "The Questionable Cost-Containment Record of Commercial Health Insurers," in H. E. Frech III (ed.), *Health Care in America: The Political Economy of Hospitals and Health Insurance*, San Francisco: Pacific Research Institute for Public Policy, 1988, p. 221. The contractual strategies visualized in this article are apparently the most difficult to pursue and thus remain largely untried. Nevertheless, contractual reforms are the logical next (and final) step in completing the necessary reform of private health care financing. See Havighurst, *Why Preserve Private Health Care Financing?*, *supra* note 2.

13.   See Clark C. Havighurst, *Professional Restraints on Innovation in Health Care Financing*, 1978 Duke L.J. 303; Lawrence Goldberg & Warren Greenberg, *The Effects of Physician-Controlled Health Insurance: U.S. v. Oregon State Medical Society*, 2 J. Health Pol., Pol'y & Law 48 (1977).

14.   For surveys of developments, see Richard J. Arnould, Robert F. Rich, and William D. White (eds.), *Competitive Approaches to Health Care Reform*, Washington, DC: Urban Institute Press, 1993; Robert B. Helms (ed.), *American Health Policy: Critical Issues for Reform*, Washington, DC: AEI Press, 1993; *Private Sector Initiatives: Controlling Health Care Costs*, Washington, DC: New Directions for Policy, 1991; Clark C. Havighurst, *The Changing Locus of Decision Making in the Health Care Sector*, 11 J. Health Pol., Pol'y & Law 697 (1986).

15.   See generally Advisory Council on Social Security, The Influence of Current Judicial Doctrines on the Cost of Purchasing Health Care, Washington, 1991,

pp. 15-26; Hall and Anderson, *supra* note 6; Paul J. Molino, *Reimbursement Disputes Involving Experimental Medical Treatments*, 24 J. Health & Hosp. L. 329 (1990).

16. For example, P.S. Atiyah, *The Rise and Fall of Freedom of Contract*, New York: Oxford Univ. Press, 1979; Grant Gilmore, The Death of Contract, Columbus: Ohio State University Press, 1974.

17. For the most explicit attempt to bring contract theory to bear on health care contracts, see Maxwell J. Mehlman, *Fiduciary Contracting: Limitations on Bargaining Between Patients and Health Care Providers*, 51 U. Pitt. L. Rev. 365, 406-09 (1990) (arguing from principles of "informed consent" that health care contracts are unacceptable as sources of legal rights in part because they cannot be relied upon to express the preferences of the individual consumer on every point). These arguments, based on an unrealistic "supermarket" paradigm of consumer choice, are refuted in *Health Care Choices*, at 159-66.

18. See, for example., *Firestone Tire & Rubber Co. v. Bruch*, 489 U.S. 101 (1989) (holding, under ERISA, that contract language can make the plan administrator's interpretations of the contract presumptively binding if not in violation of its fiduciary obligations); *Corcoran v. United Healthcare, Inc.*, 965 F.2d 1321 (5th Cir. 1992) (under ERISA, no liability under state or federal law for denial of certification for hospitalization).

19. Explicit contractual clauses to accomplish objectives suggested here are proposed at various points in *Health Care Choices*.

20. On the prospects for "voluntary decisions by consumers to economize by accepting substantial restrictions on their freedom to draw upon a common fund for future medical needs," see Havighurst, *Prospective Self-Denial*, *supra* note 10.

21. See Clark C. Havighurst, *Practice Guidelines as Standards Governing Physician Liability*, Law & Contemp. Probs., spring 1991, p. 87; Clark C. Havighurst, *Practice Guidelines for Medical Care: The Policy Rationale*, 34 St. Louis U.L.J. 777 (1990).

22. See generally Robert A. Berenson, *Do Physicians Recognize Their Own Best Interests?*, Health Affs., spring 1994, p. 185 (discussing how conditions of medical practice under corporate health plans might be less onerous than physicians appear to believe).

23. See generally Richard A. Epstein, *Medical Malpractice: The Case for Contract*, 1 Am. Bar Found. Res. J. 87 (1976) (pathbreaking article suggesting contractual reforms in the era before market-based health reform became a recognized option); Clark C. Havighurst, *Private Reform of Tort-law Dogma: Market Opportunities and Legal Obstacles*, Law & Contemp. Probs., spring 1986 at 143; Glen O. Robinson, *Rethinking the Allocation of Medical Malpractice Risks Between Patients and Providers*, in *id.*, p. 173.

24. See, e.g., *Madden v. Kaiser Foundation Hospitals*, 17 Cal. 3d 699, 552 P.2d 1178 (1976) (enforcing term in HMO's subscriber contract requiring arbitration of malpractice claims).

25. See Clark C. Havighurst, *Altering the Applicable Standard of Care*, Law & Contemp. Probs., spring 1986, p. 265.

26. *Dukes v. U.S. Healthcare, Inc.*, 57 F.3d 350 (3d Cir. 1995).

27. See Clark C. Havighurst, *Making Health Plans Accountable for the Quality of Care*, 31 Ga. L. Rev. 587 (1997); Comment, *Tort Liability of Integrated Health Care Delivery Systems: Beyond Enterprise Liability*, 29 Wake Forest L. Rev. 305 (1994).

28. Welfare economists, in particular, have been troubled by the notion that individuals may make precommitments irrationally, with poor information, or without fully weighing alternatives and therefore send imperfect signals about their own welfare. See, e.g., Thomas C. Schelling, *Self-Command in Practice, in Policy, and in a Theory of Rational Choice*, Am. Econ. Rev., May 1984, p. 1; Amartya K. Sen, *Rational Fools: A Critique of the Behavioral Foundations of Economic Theory*, 6 Philos. & Pub. Affs. 317 (1977). For an example of similar thinking in the present context, see Henry J. Aaron, Serious and Unstable Condition: Financing America's Health Care 16-19 (1991). Aaron, an economist, deduces from the fact that living wills are revocable the existence of "an acute [societal] sensitivity to the possibility that preferences expressed by a healthy person about medical care in the event of illness should not bind that same person in any way if the reality of illness or anything else causes a change of heart." Id. at 17-18 n.21. Unfortunately, Aaron's analogy is misplaced, since no consideration was given for the initial declaration of willingness to accept less care. More pertinently, however, Aaron also observes that courts routinely treat insurance contracts as binding even when a patient later wishes for entitlements he did not pay for. Although professing an ethical concern about people who "gamble and lose," Aaron concludes by supporting essentially what is proposed here: an "opportunity for individuals to choose among certain optional insurance coverages . . .within a national or state plan." Id. at 19.

29. Legal authorities who quarrel with private contracts and consumer choice on the ground that consumers do not give "informed consent" to each element of the transaction frequently (and conveniently) forget the comparable (public-choice) imperfections in democratic theory, on which rests the legitimacy of governmental and judicial institutions (the only alternatives to markets). See *Health Care Choices*, pp. 159-66. ("Those who invoke the supermarket paradigm [of consumer choice] would apparently like to predicate the legitimacy of contracts on the consumer's actual consent to every contract term. Political legitimacy normally flows, however, from the process by which the consent of the governed is obtained and a particular legal regime is chosen over others.")

30. For cases invalidating on policy grounds contractual waivers of patients' tort rights even though they appeared to facilitate the provision of low-cost health care, see *Ash v. New York University Dental Center*, 164 A.2d 366, 564 N.Y.S.2d 308 (1st Dept. 1990); *Emory University v. Porubiansky*, 282 S.E.2d 903 (Ga. 1981).

31. President's Commission for the Study of Ethical Problems in Medicine and Biomedical and Behavioral Research, Securing Access to Health Care, Washington, 1983.

32. See note 16 *supra*.

33. See generally Peter H. Schuck, *Rethinking Informed Consent*, 103 Yale L.J. 899 (1994); Mark A. Hall, *Informed Consent to Rationing Decisions*, 71 Milbank Q. 645 (1993).

34. See note 16 *supra*.

Part II

Health Care Services

5

Hospital Regulation and Antitrust Paradoxical Policies

Barbara A. Ryan

Introduction

As the health care debate droned on earlier in the Clinton adminis-tration, market forces in the hospital industry quietly were beginning to achieve goals that had eluded years of government intervention.[1] Fundamental alterations were taking place in the structure and nature of competition in the hospital industry, due, to a large extent, to the increasing importance of managed care. Hospitals, which account for almost forty cents of every health care dollar spent in the U.S.,[2] have been forced to cope with this onslaught of market forces in addition to a complex web of government regulations and guidelines dictating in-vestment, pricing, planning, consolidation, and a myriad of other activi-ties. The hospital industry will be affected tremendously by any form of health care reform undertaken at the federal or state level. It is the thesis of this chapter that history can provide useful insight when evaluating the efficacy of government intervention in the hospital industry. In these pages I focus on two aspects of government intervention in the hospi-tal industry—regulation in the form of supply controls and rate-set-ting, and antitrust enforcement as it pertains to hospital mergers.

Hospital regulation in the U.S. resembles a patchwork quilt, and consensus does not exist with regard to its effectiveness. Currently, diverse federal and state laws govern virtually every aspect of hospital operations. Although the federal government has played a key role in expanding regulatory domination of hospital services over the past several decades, hands-on control is exercised predominately at the state level. Unanimity, however, is absent among states with respect to not only the type and extent of hospital regulation but also its appropriate direction. Regulation, re-regulation, and deregulation of hospital services are occurring simultaneously today in various areas of the country.[3]

Government regulation of the hospital industry stems from a fundamental distrust of market solutions in a health care context. Underlying this misgiving is a fear that unfettered competition will result in deterioration in quality of care and access, a deterioration that patients themselves may not appreciate until it is too late. Concerns about cost, quality of care, and access have led to the application of various forms of public utility regulation to the hospital industry even though virtually no one characterizes the industry as a natural monopoly. Regulation of hospital services exists largely in the form of supply controls and rate-setting, although regulations also govern virtually every area of hospital management.[4] States regulate hospital supply through certificate of need ("CON") legislation, which requires hospitals to obtain state approval before expanding services or offering new services. The federal government exerts control over the prices at which it procures services through Medicare, and state governments do so through Medicaid and other rate-setting mechanisms. The administrative costs associated with such governmental intervention are substantial.[5]

Federal and state governments also exert considerable influence over the hospital sector through antitrust enforcement. Federal antitrust enforcement in the hospital industry is a relatively recent phenomenon, compared to its regulation, and has been stimulated by the rapid changes taking place in the sector. The underlying distrust of competition in the hospital industry, which has engendered its regulation, however, is noticeably at odds with current antitrust policy towards the industry. While regulation of the hospital industry attempts to displace competitive market forces, antitrust policy is concerned with preserving competition among hospitals by maintaining hospital concentration levels in local communities. A tension, therefore, exists between regulation and antitrust enforcement in the hospital industry. Moreover, industry members perceive a conflict between antitrust enforcement and the goal of cost containment. For example, the American Hospital Association has noted that federal antitrust scrutiny may be having a chilling effect on industry cost reduction efforts.[6]

A retrospective discussion of federal regulatory and antitrust involvement in the hospital industry seems worthwhile, given recent interest in health care reform. I shall consider these topics within the context of economic theories of regulation and rent-seeking. I do not suggest that the hospital industry should be free of all government involvement, or that it should be immune from antitrust laws. My focus, rather, is on several specific issues. First, empirical studies show that various forms of hospital regulation that have been imposed on the industry over the years evidently have been less than successful at achieving a primary goal—cost containment. Second, hospital regulation and antitrust enforcement likely entail significant indirect, as well as direct, costs. Many of these indirect costs are related to opportunities that exist for strategic use of the regulatory process by private and public entities. Economic theories of regulation, including rent-seeking, are particularly helpful in understanding such costs. Third, as illustrated by the interplay of hospital supply controls and antitrust enforcement, paradoxical policy outcomes may result when government intervention in a particular industry is carried out by different agencies and entities, within different jurisdictions. Hospital regulation and antitrust enforcement have different goals regarding competition—one seeks to replace it and the other seeks to preserve and enhance it—and as such represent policies at war with each other. The problems that result from these conflicts are no less important than any of the other issues discussed here, and likely compound the costs associated with government intervention.

Theories of Regulation

The traditional public interest view of regulation is that government intervenes to eliminate externalities and market failures characterizing the consumption of public goods and production by monopolies. This view assumes that public officials and bureaucrats act in the public interest and that regulation enhances consumer welfare. It characterizes the political process as a "black box," the inner workings of which never seem to affect the outcome. Needless to say, few now believe that the public interest view adequately characterizes the regulatory process.

Today, most attempts to assess the outcome of regulatory activities have been consistent with at least one of the following economic theories of regulation: capture, competing-interest-group, and rent-seeking. These theories are based on the idea that the same economic influences underlying ordinary market behavior exist in the regulatory decision-making process and that government bureaucrats and policymakers act in their own interest, as opposed to the common good. The evolution of economic theories of regulation began with capture theory which asserts that regulated industries reap the pecuniary rewards of regulation by enlisting regulators in their causes, and predicts that industries will seek and successfully obtain regulation to acquire benefits that they are unable to obtain in the marketplace.[7] Ultimately, regulatory activity is conducted in the interest of the industry being regulated and at the expense of other groups, most notably consumers.

The capture theory was generalized by the competing-interest-group theory, the essence of which is that regulatory gains may, in fact, be shared by both winning and losing groups rather than simply captured by the regulated industry.[8] Regulatory benefits are bestowed by vote-maximizing politicians according to the political effectiveness of different interest groups competing for the benefits. Marginal changes in the political effectiveness of different interest groups induce politicians to shift regulatory benefits to groups with more clout; therefore, no one group is able to "capture" the regulators. The competing-interest-group theory predicts that regulation may be used to benefit either producer or consumer groups and that politicians may choose to bestow regulatory benefits on alternate groups at different times and in different amounts.

The political effectiveness of groups competing for regulatory benefits is a major determinant of the distribution of regulatory benefits, according to the competing-interest-group theory. In general, large groups, such as consumers, find it harder to coalesce effectively due to organizational costs and the free rider problem; thus, the political effectiveness of groups is influenced by group size.[9] A preponderance of benefits is likely to be bestowed upon smaller, well-organized interest groups, such as producer groups or subgroups, with the larger, more diffuse groups successful in obtaining regulatory benefits only to the extent that they are able to overcome free rider problems and other organizational costs.

One of the key observations of the competing-interest-group theory concerns the types of industries most likely to be regulated. The theory reveals that the political wealth generated by regulating a purely competitive or a purely monopolistic industry is greater than that generated from the regulation of oligopoly. Hence, the regulation of purely competitive industries and natural monopolies is more likely than the regulation of oligopolies.

To the extent that rewards accrue to groups that can effectively organize to obtain regulatory benefits, such groups will expend resources to obtain the rewards. The theory of rent-seeking helps explain how regulations create rewards and opportunities for the transfer of wealth to a variety of interested groups. Rent-seeking refers to efforts expended to capture wealth transfers that are created artificially by regulations and other government actions.[10] For example, government creation or enforcement of a group's right to earn monopoly rents through regulation increases that group's monopoly rents at the expense of other groups, such as customers. Rent-seeking also may include activities of government agents and bureaucrats in granting rents or of third parties to prevent artificial rents from being created or transferred.[11]

Rent-seeking associated with regulation has a number of direct and indirect costs. Rent-seeking regulation frequently eliminates competition, resulting in the inefficiencies associated with monopoly. Rent-seeking also creates waste because various interest groups may, in the process of competing for rents, actually dissipate the value of anticipated rewards, particularly when ongoing lobbying efforts must be made to maintain the regulatory advantages. In the process of competing for rents, costs are incurred by lobbyists, lawyers, bureaucrats, politicians, and others. These efforts are wasteful to the extent that they employ resources that could have been put to use in some alternative productive capacity.

The rent-seeking approach provides a useful view of regulation and has been examined empirically in a number of industries in which regulation is widely viewed as beneficial to the public, including safety, health, and environmental legislation.[12] Such studies reveal intra-industry differences in regulatory effect which, in certain cases, translate into competitive advantage for firms preferentially impacted by regulation. Regulatory competitive advantages provide industry members with incentives to use the regulatory process strategically. Bartel and Thomas, for example, note that indirect costs of regulations stem largely from two sources: compliance asymmetry, in which certain firms suffer a greater cost burden in complying with certain regulations, and enforcement asymmetry, in which regulations are more vigorously enforced on certain firms. In a related vein, Posner shows that regulations may be applied differentially within industries as a cross-subsidization mechanism in which excess profits are created in certain services to subsidize others.[13]

Despite widespread acceptance of the competing-interest-group and rent-seeking theories of regulation, until relatively recent times, antitrust was one of the last strongholds of the public interest view. While the goal of antitrust is to promote competition and enhance consumer welfare,[14] increasingly, examination of the ways in which antitrust actually is carried out reveals that interest groups can and probably do influence antitrust enforcement and outcomes. Numerous identifiable pressure groups are concerned with antitrust policy, including private firms that "invest" in antitrust in order to gain competitive advantages, enforcement officials, congressional overseers, and the antitrust bar.[15]

As in regulation, the rent-seeking model applies to antitrust when firms use the law strategically to gain competitive advantage over rivals or to obtain protection from vigorous competition. The idea has been stated succinctly by Baumol and Ordover:

> There is a specter that haunts our antitrust institutions. Its threat is that, far from serving as the bulwark of competition, these institutions will become the most powerful instruments in the hands of those who wish to subvert it. More than that, it threatens to draw great quantities of resources into the struggle to prevent effective competition, thereby more than offsetting the contributions to economic efficiency promised by antitrust activities.[16]

Baumol and Ordover cite as one example a complaint by a rival that a merger of its competitors is anticompetitive when it is expected to reduce costs for the merging firms and make it harder for rivals to compete effectively. Rivals may use the antitrust processes in numerous other ways to erect a protective shield about themselves. The direct and indirect costs of such activities likely are substantial.

In summary, economic theories of regulation reveal that government intervention tends to benefit certain groups that have lower organizational costs and greater political clout. These theories predict that government controls are likely to be asymmetrically enforced and that most regulatory rewards will accrue to the most politically influential producer subgroups, at the expense of less influential producer and consumer groups. There is no reason to suspect that the hospital industry is immune to these forces. Moreover, antitrust enforcement in the hospital industry probably is influenced by private interests as well. It is likely that resourceful producer/hospital concerns will search for ways to use the regulatory and antitrust processes strategically, and that such interferences with market forces will lead to substantial direct and indirect costs.

Regulation in the Hospital Industry

The case for hospital regulation has, over time, been given credence by the notion that the hospital industry does not conform to the competitive ideal. The traditional model of perfect competition describes an industry with many sellers and buyers, perfect information, free entry and exit, and a homogeneous product. Until fairly recently, it was commonly held that the hospital industry does not even approach this ideal, because of unique industry characteristics such as third-party payers, which shelter consumers from price effects, and the agency of physicians, which limits the flow of information to consumers. These and other factors diminish hospital price competition. Hospitals traditionally competed primarily on a non-price basis by adding amenities and increasing investments in expensive medical technology in order to attract physicians and patients. The result of such competition was hospital over-utilization, duplicative facilities, and high rates of investment, leading to escalating costs. Regulatory solutions to these alleged market imperfections were designed to limit the ability of hospitals to make such investments independently or alternatively to fund such investments by raising prices.

Although most hospital regulation is conducted at the state level, it has been significantly furthered by federal initiatives. A desire to have government involvement in health care planning initiated government intervention in the hospital sector with the passage of the Hill-Burton Act in 1946 which required states to develop plans for hospital construction.[17] State regulation was extended in the 1970s with the authorization of federal funds for hospital planning under the National Health Planning and Resources Development Act of 1974. In the 1970s and 1980s, regulation was enacted primarily for cost containment.

Today, the bloom is, or at least should be, off the rose with respect to certain forms of hospital regulation. First, hospitals increasingly are competing on the basis of price, due to the advancement of managed care, selective contracting, and the overall pressures of cost containment.[18]   Second, as discussed below, hospital regulation has substantial direct and indirect costs associated with rent-seeking. Finally, the ability of certain types of hospital regulation, particularly supply controls, to achieve cost containment goals is in doubt.

Hospital Supply Controls

Hospital supply has been regulated with CON laws, which shift major investment decisions from hospital managers to regulatory agencies. CON laws represent a classic form of public utility regulation that has most commonly been applied to industries thought to be natural monopolies. For example, in his industrial organization textbook, Scherer observes: "For industries *that are regarded as public utilities*, control by a regulatory authority often extends not only to prices, but also to entry and exit"[19] (emphasis added). The consequences of such policies are typically detrimental to consumers, particularly if the industry is not a natural monopoly. Competition benefits consumers; conversely, any restriction of competitive forces likely benefits suppliers. All else equal, most sellers would prefer to face fewer competitors in the marketplace and would be more comfortable selling in an environment without entrants hovering on the horizon. Another popular industrial organization textbook notes these costs and inequities. "By restricting entry into an industry, a government creates artificial scarcity and raises prices to consumers. The higher prices cause a transfer of wealth from consumers to firms in the industry. That is, the government creates property rights—the rights to operate a firm in the industry—and transfers these rights to a few, lucky individuals."[20] Thus, it is not surprising that in the early 1970s Posner derided entry controls in the hospital industry: "the general proposal to treat health care providers as public utilities is unsound because it ignores both the failure of public utility regulation in its traditional setting and the differences between those settings and the health care field that make such regulation even less likely to succeed in the latter setting."[21]

CON laws require hospitals to obtain state approval before adding new services or making capital investments that exceed specified amounts. CON approval commonly requires a review of the proposed project that considers state criteria and an assessment of community need. The comprehensiveness of current CON laws, however, varies significantly by state, with some states restricting purchases by physicians, ambulatory care centers, and other health care providers, as well as hospitals. State CON laws also differ in the cost threshold that leads to state review.[22] Moreover, states have applied a variety of criteria and varying standards of review in the CON process, which is marked by a large degree of discretion.[23]

Although twenty-six states had passed some form of CON legislation by 1974, several federal laws enacted during the 1970s hastened CON adoption.[24] Beginning in 1972, under the federal Section 1122 program, hospitals were required to obtain state approval for expansion investments in order to secure Medicare/Medicaid payment for capital expenses. Many states passed CON laws in order to participate in the Section 1122 program. In 1974, the National Health Planning and Resources Development Act, P.L. 93-641, required all states to adopt a CON program by 1980 and created a system of health service areas and agencies to allocate health resources within states. By 1983, CON laws had been implemented in every state in the U.S.[25]

During the 1980s, the federal government ended financial support for CON laws, which led to elimination or relaxation of CON laws in a number of states. However, the vast majority of states still have some form of CON restriction. Some states recently have strengthened their CON laws and a number of states imposed moratoriums on CON approvals or extended CON approval requirements to outpatient settings during the 1980s.[26]

The traditional view holds that CON laws were enacted to correct market failures in the hospital industry. According to the theory, unfettered competition among hospitals would result in excessive entry and excess capacity in the industry. In addition, physicians may be more likely to send borderline patients to hospitals when hospital beds are expected to be available.[27] Increased demand for hospital services ultimately leads hospitals to make investments in medical equipment and facilities. CON laws were supposed to prevent excessive expansion of facilities and equipment. They were a favored form of regulation because it was thought that they could control costs, improve quality and accessibility, and involve the community in the health planning process, all at the same time.

Even if one subscribes to the discredited public-interest view of regulation, CON laws make sense only if the benefits of government-sanctioned barriers to entry outweigh their costs. Yet, as discussed below, empirical studies reveal that the costs of CON laws, although unquantified, are likely substantial while the benefits are empirically unproven. True to theory, government-created entry restrictions such as CONs create monopoly rents that regulators may bestow upon some fortunate party. The creation of rents by the government through CON legislation may lead to rent-seeking and anticompetitive behavior with substantial direct and indirect costs to society. Quite separate from the rent-seeking aspects, the construction controls likely distort firms' incentives and lead to inefficient behavior.

Opportunities for anticompetitive use and abuse of the CON process are built into the system in a variety of ways. First, as a result of the mandatory involvement of existing providers and community members in the CON approval process and the determination of "need," numerous interested groups participate in the decision process. For example, in a landmark study of hospital CON laws, Salkever and Bice identify consumers, providers, and other interest groups as active participants in the setting of standards and CON review process.[28] As a result, incumbent hospitals are provided plenty of opportunity to protect their self-interest. This participation, akin to letting the fox guard the henhouse, is consistent with the competing-interest-group theory of regulation in which the most influential groups obtain regulatory benefits on the margin, at the expense of less influential groups such as excluded potential entrants and consumers, who may benefit from such competition. Salkever and Bice, for example, note the following:

> Large, politically powerful institutions willing to devote considerable resources to defending their proposals through appeals, legal action, or legislative attempts to override agency decisions threaten to deplete agency resources and, if successful, to tarnish the agency's public image as a fair and effective regulatory body. This would suggest that certificate-of-need controls will be applied selectively among existing providers, favoring those with access to economic or political power.[29]

The authors also note that existing providers are granted preferential CON treatment and that CON agencies adopt a more lenient posture toward expansions in equipment and services compared to bed expansions. The implication of these enforcement asymmetries is that under CON restrictions the unit cost of providing hospital services

may increase, due to the bias toward granting technological and service expansions, while the overall level of hospital services provided,
as measured by number of beds or patient admissions, may remain
stable or even fall.[30]

Enforcement biases are also observed by Simpson, who notes that
under California CON laws, existing hospitals could undertake any
investment while surgical centers were required to obtain a CON for
investments in excess of $1 million. Asymmetrical treatment with
respect to new hospitals and outpatient facilities led to his conclusion
that the law is intended to protect incumbents from new competition
or alternative forms of service that might be in the interest of consumers.[31]   Campbell and Fournier show that in Florida the amendment of
CON laws to exempt certain hospital services in 1987 was followed
by a noticeable increase in for-profit hospital and hospital substitute
entry.[32] Miller observes that, due to the participation of incumbent
providers in the approval process, "the statute actually enhances the
potential for regulatory capture."[33]

Second, CON laws may foster cartelization in the hospital industry.[34] CON controls on hospital beds fix-market shares based on capacity and limit the ability of individual hospitals to cheat on cartel
agreements by expanding output.[35] The laws limit the actions that
competitors can take to increase market share by removing from their
control the power to expand output, if they have no excess capacity.
CON restrictions on capital investments and service additions also
may restrict the ability of hospitals to cheat on cartel agreements by
improving the quality or level of care offered. Finally, CON laws may
provide hospitals with a cartel enforcement mechanism by releasing
into the public domain information submitted by existing providers
and potential competitors to planning agencies when they apply for
CONs, when such information may otherwise be confidential.

Third, CON laws discourage entry by raising its costs and risks.
The CON application process entails substantial resources to persuade
the authorities to grant the application and to fight challenges in the
courts of law. The regulations invite litigation, often adding years to
the time required to obtain final approval for construction. By discouraging entry, CON laws limit the number of competitors offering health
care services in a given area and may increase the profitability and
success of collusion.[36] Certainly, the laws limit the number of choices
available to health care consumers.

Fourth, CON laws create opportunities for strategic use of the regulatory process. For example, hospitals may expand to preempt competitors from doing so, secure in the knowledge that certain types of CONs are limited by health planning authorities. Hospitals may apply for a CON to be the first hospital in an area to offer a service and thus gain advantages over competitors. Competitors may use the CON process strategically to raise the costs of their rivals, by challenging a competitor's CON application and delaying its approval for years at tremendous legal expense to the hospital trying to expand. Such challenges by competitors to CON decisions are common.

Economic theories of regulation predict that incumbent hospitals are the likely beneficiaries of CON laws. Indeed, consistent with the notion that the regulated industries will be in favor of regulation and will, in fact, strongly support it and lobby on its behalf, there is ample evidence that CON laws have been supported by hospital groups. The adoption of CON programs at the state level was supported by state hospital associations[37] and by the American Hospital Association.[38] Wendling and Werner present empirical evidence that CON laws were more likely to be enacted in states where the hospital industry faced strong competitive pressures and industry organization costs were low due to high levels of industry concentration.[39]

On an empirical basis, CON laws have been discredited as cost containment vehicles. In an early study, Hellinger found that hospitals did not reduce their investments as a result of CON laws, and instead anticipated the effect of CON restrictions and engaged in compensatory investment in the period preceding legislative enactment.[40] Salkever and Bice found that CON regulations had no net impact on total hospital investment, since reduced hospital bed expansion was offset by increases in other forms of hospital capital investment. They conclude that CON programs failed to achieve cost containment.[41]

More recent studies add credence to these findings.[42] Sloan and Steinwald (1980a and 1980b) document anticipatory increases in hospital bed growth prior to CON enactment, with no post-regulatory offset. Sloan (1983) finds that CON programs had no effect on hospital costs. Ashby concludes that CON programs have failed in containing costs. Lanning, Morrisey, and Ohsfeldt conclude that there appears to be little economic justification for continuing CON regulation. Campbell and Fournier suggest that CON restrictions had as a primary goal the cross-subsidization of hospital indigent care rather than cost containment and that, in Florida, providers of indigent hospital care received preferential CON treatment. They also find that CON regulators consciously protected the interests of existing hospitals, particularly those that provided indigent care.[43]

Taken as a whole, the evidence overwhelmingly supports the conclusion that CON laws likely result in substantial direct and indirect costs and have not succeeded in achieving cost containment goals. The entry of possibly more efficient competitors and less expensive patient alternatives to inpatient care, including ambulatory care and surgery in other outpatient settings, has probably been prevented or delayed countless times. The rent-seeking view of regulation, although not empirically tested in this application, seems to have been the case. CON laws tend to benefit incumbent hospitals, which have tended to support their enactment. In addition, they entail the establishment of bureaucracy and the involvement of community members and other interested parties in what was once a private investment decision.

Hospital Rate-Setting

Another form of public utility regulation applied to hospitals is rate-setting. Hospital rate-setting is problematic because, unlike most public utilities, hospitals offer heterogeneous services and bundles of products to diverse groups of patients. Establishment of appropriate rates for such a diverse group of services and products can lead to an administrative nightmare. Not all hospital rate-setting has been sponsored by the government. Historically, Blue Cross has played a significant role in hospital rate setting. In addition, rate-setting has not always been mandatory. A number of states adopted voluntary, rather than mandatory, price controls for hospitals.

At the federal level, hospital rate-setting has occurred under Medicare's Prospective Payment System ("PPS"), which since 1983 has established diagnosis-based price ceilings for hospital admissions. PPS attempts to contain Medicare spending by creating incentives for hospitals to be more efficient. While PPS appears to have restrained the growth of Medicare spending, it has not had a proven restraining effect on overall hospital costs.[44] Hospitals have responded to PPS by shifting unreimbursed Medicare costs to other types of patients, exacerbating the rate of cost growth for those groups. Moreover, asymmetrical treatment of hospitals under Medicare suggests that certain types of hospitals have benefited under PPS. PPS reimbursement rates differ by hospital location, local labor costs, and Medicare mix. Medicare payments are higher to urban hospitals than to rural hospitals. Hospitals with teaching facilities, graduate medical education programs, and a disproportionate share of low-income patients also receive higher reimbursement rates under PPS.[45]

States began experimenting with hospital rate-setting during the 1970s, using various methods, but the difficulty of effective price regulation of hospitals at the state level is indicated by the low number of states with rate-setting programs. Only eleven states operated mandatory hospital rate-setting programs during the 1980s. Of the eleven, only four—Maryland, Massachusetts, New Jersey, and New York—operated systems under which the state set rates for all payer groups. Of those four, all but Maryland have since abandoned their programs.[46]

Despite the small percentage of states that engage in mandatory rate-setting, a large amount of research has been conducted on its cost containment efficacy. The earliest empirical results for the effectiveness of rate-setting were inconclusive.[47] Most subsequent studies have concluded that certain forms of rate-setting may have been effective in lowering hospital expenditures,[48] but that the effectiveness of rate-setting at the state level is dependent on the particular attributes of the system. On the whole, it is difficult to draw conclusions from the empirical research on state rate-setting, because the cases are so varied and because each state that sets rates faces different institutional factors that may influence outcomes. These factors may be impossible to completely account for in a study.[49] In addition, at least one study has shown that estimates of the effectiveness of state hospital rate-setting laws may be significantly biased.[50]

Cone and Dranove provide a competing-interest-group theory to explain why certain states enacted rate-setting laws while others did not, and why they adopted them when they did.[51] States that adopted rate-setting programs tended to be politically liberal, with generous Medicaid programs. The authors find that rate-setting programs were adopted in these states to reduce Medicaid transfers to recipients and to mitigate anticipated cost shifting of unreimbursed Medicaid expenses to other patient populations. The rate-setting programs were adopted within a few years of the federal Medicaid programs. Thus, it appears as though hospital price controls are also subject to interest group pressure.

The larger issue with respect to rate-setting is whether market forces can provide a more equitable solution to hospital cost inflation. In addition to the cost shifting and other inequities inherent in all but an all-payer system, hospital rate-setting entails tremendous bureaucratic costs. Rate regulation also has been associated with reductions in quality of care and access.[52]

Antitrust and Hospitals

Until the mid-1970s, the hospital industry was virtually immune from federal antitrust scrutiny due largely to special competitive characteristics of the health care industries.[53] During the past decade, however, hospitals have been consolidating, downsizing, and closing in record numbers due to cost containment pressures and declining hospital utilization, both accentuated by the explosive growth of managed care. These developments have led to increases in the importance of price to consumers of health care, and to stronger price competition among hospitals.[54] The increase in hospital merger activity, along with the increasing importance of price competition in the industry, has led to increased antitrust scrutiny.[55]

Government enforcement of antitrust laws in the hospital industry is carried out by the Department of Justice's Antitrust Division ("Division") and the Federal Trade Commission's Bureau of Competition ("FTC"). In enforcing antitrust laws, these agencies apply the Horizontal Merger Guidelines ("Guidelines"),[56] which establish the methods and principles used by the government to review the competitive consequences of horizontal mergers. The primary purpose of the Guidelines is to prevent mergers that would create or enhance market power through collusion or monopolization. Product and geographic markets are defined, and within those markets concentration statistics are computed.[57] The Guidelines call for examination of the competitive effects of mergers, the likelihood and profitability of entry, efficiencies generated as a result of the merger, and the possibility of firm exit in the absence of the merger. Any of these factors may overcome a presumption based on concentration levels that the merger is anticompetitive. It is important to note that the Guidelines are based on a traditional microeconomic model that assumes that consumers are price sensitive and firms have the incentive, and the ability, to operate efficiently. The Guidelines do not make allowances for special characteristics of the hospital industry. Although the Division and the FTC issued special merger guidelines for the health care sectors in 1993,[58] in practice, the agencies apply virtually the same Guideline standards to the hospital industry that apply to other industries.

Certain conflicts arise whenever a heavily regulated industry undergoes intense antitrust scrutiny because fundamental differences exist in the goals of the two forms of policy. As mentioned previously, regulation typically involves displacement of competitive market forces, while antitrust seeks to preserve competition. In the hospital industry, the uncoordinated interplay of antitrust and regulation has a particularly paradoxical result. In an antitrust context, CON laws represent a classic barrier to entry. The existence of CON laws, therefore, is of interest to antitrust enforcers in their analyses of the competitive effects of proposed hospital mergers. All else equal, hospital mergers in states with CON laws are more likely to be challenged than mergers in states with no limitations on hospital entry. Most courts, in deciding whether to allow hospital mergers challenged by the government to proceed, have viewed the presence of CON laws in the hospital industry as a factor increasing the likelihood of collusion. Thus, the perverted outcome of the interplay of CON regulation and antitrust enforcement in the hospital industry is that CON laws, enacted to contain costs and prevent duplication of facilities, tend to limit the ability of hospitals (in states where such laws exist) to consolidate in order to achieve the same underlying purpose—reduce costs and eliminate duplicative capital investments. Of course, this conclusion assumes that hospital mergers are driven by cost containment considerations. In the current circumstances, such an assumption is not outlandish.[59]

To date, the Division and the FTC have challenged in court well over ten mergers of acute care hospitals, others being challenged and settled with consent orders or abandoned by the parties.[60] As reflected by the court decisions in the challenged mergers, the issues debated in hospital merger litigation have evolved over the past decade. In the early challenged cases, arguments revolved around several general issues, including whether hospitals engage in meaningful competition, and whether the enforcement agencies have jurisdiction over nonprofit hospital mergers. Most of the recent challenges have focused increasingly on market definition issues.

While the competitive consequences of each hospital merger clearly are influenced by the unique facts underlying each, various hospital markets share certain fundamental competitive characteristics. Despite these commonalities, conflicting court decisions have been reached concerning market definition, competitive effects of mergers, efficiencies likely to be generated as a result of a merger, and other factors.[61] In addition, as discussed below, noneconomic factors appear to have been major influences in a number of challenged hospital mergers. These issues and conflicts raise questions about the antitrust enforcement process as it has been applied to hospital mergers.

In recent years, antitrust authorities have typically defined relatively narrow product and geographic hospital markets.[62] The agencies have argued that the relevant product market within which market shares of merging acute care hospitals should be measured is limited to inpatient acute care services, while merging hospitals have argued that outpatient facilities compete with hospitals and should somehow be taken into account, due to evidence of ongoing conversion of inpatient procedures to outpatient services.[63] While a narrow product market definition might be warranted for certain highly complex procedures that are not conducted on an outpatient basis and are not likely to be carried out in outpatient facilities in the future, hospitals may face competition from outpatient facilities for many simpler procedures, and for such procedures, a broader market definition might be more appropriate. By excluding all forms of outpatient services, the narrow product market definition does not give full consideration to all available substitutes for inpatient hospital services. This narrows the number of providers in given market areas within which concentration measures are calculated, leading to higher concentration statistics and an increased probability of a challenge.

The assumption that hospitals compete in local and narrow geographic markets also may lead to prohibitively high concentration measures, frequently reflecting as few as three competing hospitals. Such high concentration can be, and has been, cited by the government as evidence that a proposed hospital merger is presumptively illegal. Certainly, competition among hospitals is relatively local compared to other industries that may compete in broad regional or even national geographic markets. This rigid devotion to an extremely narrow geographic market principle for hospitals is not inviolable, however. To support the narrow geographic market positions, reliance is typically placed on rudimentary analyses of patient origin data, information contained in contemporaneous business documents of merging hospitals, geopolitical boundaries, and the views of other hospitals or organizations. These are static indicia, which do not fully reflect the dynamic nature of hospital competition. In addition, business documents cannot be expected to embody the insight required to define economically meaningful relevant geographic markets, and the views of other hospitals or customers may be influenced by separate agendas.[64]

Dynamic forces affecting the hospital industry support broader geographic markets, particularly for highly complex procedures that cannot be performed in outpatient facilities or in less specialized hospitals.[65] Underlying the narrow geographic market hypothesis are the assumptions that patients are rigidly loyal to their doctors and doctors do not make changes in their hospital affiliations. Managed care has broken down these loyalties, however. Patients switch doctors when their employer changes or their insurance plan changes its group of participating providers. Doctors alter their affiliations with hospitals. As a result, managed care organizations can and do bypass local hospitals to contract with more distant hospitals in order to reduce costs and patients willingly change their doctors and travel to more distant hospitals.[66] Moreover, hospitals with underutilized beds must extend their geographic reach to compete for patients. The result of these forces is that hospitals have been forced to broaden the geographic areas in which they compete, and to compete more intensively within those areas.

Despite the widespread acknowledgment that the hospital industry is underutilized, antitrust enforcers generally do not place much weight on the competitive consequences of excess hospital capacity in their competitive effects analyses. This affects the outcome in several ways. First, excess hospital capacity nearby the merging hospitals, but outside of the narrow geographic market, may be significant in both geographic market definition and competitive effects analysis. Many proposed (and challenged) hospital mergers occur in smaller towns and cities where substantial excess capacity exists. In some cases, the merging hospitals are located within reasonable distance of larger, more sophisticated hospitals. It may be the case that low utilization of merging hospitals is due, in part, to their inability to compete effectively with the larger, more sophisticated hospitals located nearby. Patients may be willing to travel to more heavily populated areas to receive medical care that they perceive to be of higher quality than that available in their own areas.[67] In this case, the ability of the merging hospitals to engage in post-merger anticompetitive behavior may be adversely affected by the presence of the larger, nearby hospitals. Thus, the supply elasticity of hospitals located outside the immediate vicinity of merging hospitals may be an important competitive and market definition issue.

Second, the presence of post-merger excess capacity may act as a deterrent to collusion among hospitals since competitive pressure brought about by the existence of excess capacity can be particularly intense. When beds are underutilized, hospitals must compete vigorously for marginal patients. Thus, the existence of extreme excess capacity in the industry is very likely a key element of competition.

Finally, despite the cost reducing motivation driving most hospital mergers, efficiencies defenses to hospital merger challenges generally have not been successful due to an impossible set of qualifying criteria.[68] This is unfortunate, given the apparent need for the industry to rationalize to increase technical efficiency and position itself for the competitive nature of managed care. According to the Guidelines and previously cited court decisions, in order for efficiencies to quality as a defense, they must not be achievable by any other less anticompetitive method, must represent substantial "real" cost savings, and must generate benefits that flow directly to consumers rather than to the bottom line of the merging parties. Efficiencies also must be the motivation for the merger. Merging hospitals typically have found these requirements impossible to satisfy since they are rarely in a position to adequately document and quantify all expected cost savings prior to actual merger and antitrust laws preclude potential merging partners from exchanging detailed cost and operating information.[69] Ironically, hospitals in close proximity are most likely to achieve cost efficiencies through merger. These are the mergers in which very narrow geographic markets are most likely to be defined, making consummation of such mergers uncertain.

A close review of the history of hospital merger enforcement also suggests that antitrust laws may be applied asymmetrically. Mergers of hospitals located outside of urban areas appear more likely to be challenged than those in densely populated areas. This, of course, is related to the structural conditions in such areas and, under the rules established by the antitrust enforcement agencies, is a matter of pure mathematics. Small communities support only a small number of hospitals, and mergers in such areas can easily generate prohibitively high concentration under the Guidelines, if markets are defined narrowly. Merging hospitals in such areas must defend a merger that, based on concentration statistics, the antitrust authorities may argue is presumptively illegal under the Guidelines.

However, it is not always the case that hospital mergers in small communities are challenged by the government, and there is no clear way to predict which hospital mergers are likely to be challenged. In 1994, the government halted mergers in small towns in Iowa[70] and in Colorado.[71] Numerous hospital mergers in small communities, however, have been permitted to proceed in recent years, to the bewilderment of industry members. In 1994, the government permitted a merger in a small town in New Hampshire to proceed[72] and media reports at least eleven hospital consolidations in small towns permitted by the government as of 1993.[73] Such apparent disparate decisions send mixed messages to the industry about the consequences of consolidation. Industry observers assert that merger enforcement inconsistency increases the unpredictability of the hospital merger review process and creates confusion and uncertainty among hospitals contemplating consolidation.[74]

Based on case histories, one factor that appears to affect the probability of a challenge to a merger is the potential for community and competitor involvement in the merger review process. Although such involvement does not always take place, it appears more likely to occur in smaller towns than in more densely populated areas. Unlike mergers of obscure corporations or huge conglomerates, hospital mergers in smaller locales tend to invite community involvement. The loss of control when an out-of-town entity acquires a community hospital or two local hospitals merge and try to achieve efficiencies through elimination of duplicative hospital functions may incite community action because it is likely to reduce local employment and choice of facilities. Private interests have less incentive to aid a government challenge to a merger in more densely populated areas, where individuals are less likely to be concerned about hospital consolidation.

The government has at times embraced community involvement and has encouraged the participation of individuals in the hospital merger litigation process via affidavit and testimony.[75] The involvement of community members benefits the antitrust enforcers, providing effective information conduits and useful allies. Despite the good intentions of the citizenry, this involvement points to special interest policymaking, as the opposition of local citizens to a particular hospital merger may not be based on the competitive consequences or likely efficiencies of the merger but, rather, may reflect personal interests.

Competitors also have played key roles in a number of the hospital mergers that were challenged and prevented by the federal antitrust enforcement agencies, by complaining that the proposed hospital mergers were anticompetitive.[76] Complaining competitors aid the agencies investigating or challenging a merger because they provide key information that may otherwise be unavailable to the government. Assuming a competitor is rational, however, if a merger increases the likelihood of collusion, that competitor, as well as other hospitals in the market, should be looking forward to gains from collusion following the merger. A complaining competitor, therefore, is likely concerned about tougher competition due to lower costs or increased services resulting from the merger, outcomes that are in the public interest.

A "raising rivals' cost" theory has also been put forth in several challenged hospital mergers either by or on behalf of key competitors opposed to the merger.[77]   For example, in one case, the FTC argued that the acquisition of a nonprofit by a for-profit hospital corporation would increase the indigent burden at the nearest competitor, a nonprofit hospital, resulting in significant adverse financial pressure and an inability to compete effectively.[78] The economic incentives underlying such a complaint, as well as the merits of the complaint, should be examined closely by the government before a competitor's concerns are accepted at face value. Moreover, social policy issues, including the care of the indigent, do not fall comfortably within the domain of antitrust policy. "[A]rguments about care of the indigent, although important, are probably handled better in another forum. The indigent problem should not be used to prevent competition."[79] Just as the regulatory process is used by self-interested parties in their rent-seeking endeavors, antitrust authorities may be subverted by less efficient competitors who seek to prevent efficiency-enhancing mergers, with consequent significant social waste. The goals of antitrust, to protect competition and enhance consumer welfare, should be paramount, not the interests of private entities.[80]

It is difficult to avoid the conclusion that the rules established by the government in hospital merger review benefit it by providing maximum discretion and flexibility in determining which mergers to challenge. Preferred methods of defining product and geographic markets result in a bias towards highly concentrated markets, leading to presumption of anticompetitive conduct. In addition, the Guidelines may be asymmetrically enforced, with the likelihood of challenge enhanced in instances in which mergers incite community involvement. Asymmetrical enforcement thus appears to benefit certain hospitals and community groups that have an interest in preventing mergers, as well as the special interest group referred to as the "antitrust bureaucracy."[81] Outraged community members and complaining competitors, serving as allies of the government and information conduits, may well increase the likelihood of a successful challenge to a hospital merger.

Another factor that adds to asymmetrical enforcement in hospital mergers is dual conduct of the hospital merger review process. Since 1948, duplication of effort between the Division and the Bureau has been controlled under the FTC-Antitrust Division case allocation system in which one agency is granted "clearance" by the other to pursue an investigation. The division has been according to industry of respondent and type of complaint, with each agency "specializing" in certain industries. The hospital industry is unique in this regard, however, in that the Division and the Bureau both actively review hospital mergers. While the effects of dual enforcement are not fully resolved[82] it is clear that, at a minimum, it increases the uncertainty of merger review. In addition to possible differences in standards of review regarding hospital mergers and differences in how each agency perceives the nature of competition in the hospital industry, the two agencies operate under different administrative and judicial processes. Such differences increase the uncertainty and risk hospitals face when contemplating merger.[83]

In summary, antitrust enforcement with respect to hospital mergers presents a number of concerns. The interaction of antitrust enforcement and hospital regulation reveals the problems that can result when government intervention is multifaceted and uncoordinated. In addition, hospital merger challenges, and the resulting legal records, reflect conflicts and asymmetries in the merger enforcement process, and a strong indication that the rules established by the government may provide it with advantages that increase its discretion in decision-making. Moreover, the involvement of community members and complaining competitors in merger review activities introduces noneconomic factors and special interests into the antitrust decision-making process.

Conclusions

The notion that government intervention tends to benefit certain groups at the expense of others and that interferences with market forces may entail substantial direct and indirect costs is well established. This exploration of hospital regulation and antitrust enforcement reveals that hospital regulations have not been particularly successful in achieving their intended benefit—cost containment—and likely have resulted in substantial direct and indirect costs to consumers or in benefits to certain consumer groups at the expense of others. In addition, the interplay of hospital regulation and antitrust enforcement policy with respect to hospital consolidations may have further hindered cost containment objectives by preventing cost-reducing hospital mergers and consolidations. The cost to taxpayers of the bureaucracy that supports hospital regulation and antitrust enforcement must also be considered in any analysis of the pros and cons of further government intervention. Regulatory interventions involve direct and indirect costs that must be anticipated, assessed, and given adequate weight along with any anticipated benefits of nonmarket controls. History reveals that government intervention tends to benefit certain groups at the expense of others and presents plenty of opportunities for strategic use and abuse of the regulatory process. The hospital industry is not unique in this respect.

Notes

1.   As reported in the *Wall Street Journal*, "Health reform, which a year ago appeared certain to be shaped by a single, sweeping piece of legislation, now is likely to be forged in a market place tussle between cost-minded purchasers and rapidly merging providers." See "With Congress Stalled, Health Care is Shaped by the Private Sector," *Wall Street Journal*, August 26, 1994.

2.   Prospective Payment Assessment Commission, *Medicare and the American Health Care System, Report to the Congress* (June 1994).

3.   In recent years, Minnesota, Florida, Vermont, and North Dakota have increased regulation while Washington, Massachusetts, New Jersey, and New York have relaxed regulation. "Market Forces or Force the Market," *Modern Healthcare*, December 21/28, 1992, and "State Health Reform," *Hospitals*, October 5, 1992. In addition, comprehensive health care reforms, which affect the entire health care delivery system and address both cost containment and universal coverage goals, have been passed recently in Florida, Hawaii, Massachusetts, Minnesota, Oregon, Vermont, and Washington (Prospective Payment Assessment Commission [1994]).

4.   See, for example, "The Private Hospital is Being Threatened with Over Regulation," *Modern Healthcare*, January 1977, in which a hospital administrator

complains that "[a]lmost every area of hospital management today is influenced in some measure by government regulations pending or in effect. Our practice of hiring personnel, paying them, dismissing them and pensioning them are controlled. Permits and licenses cover everything from our nurses to narcotics, from our facilities to alcohol. Our premises are subject to inspection from agencies that govern the ways we dispose of waste, the ways we protect against fire, the ways we maintain sanitary conditions. Stringent controls govern our participation in Medicare and Medicaid. Other coming regulations seek to restrict us on the patients we can and we cannot accept, the rates we can charge, the facilities we can add."

5.   See, for example, "One Hospital Tells the Cost of Regulation," *Wall Street Journal*, June 26, 1990, in which a hospital reports that it required 140 full-time employees to comply with regulations and government audits and estimated its annual costs of complying with regulations at $7.8 million. Also see "Hospital Administrative Costs Surge as Regulatory Requirements Increase," *Wall Street Journal*, July 1, 1993.

6.   For a discussion of the views of the hospital industry on federal antitrust enforcement, see *Hospital Collaboration: The Need for an Appropriate Antitrust Policy*, American Hospital Association, 1992.

7.   George J. Stigler, "The Theory of Economic Regulation," *The Bell Journal of Economics and Management Science* 7 (spring 1971).

8.   Sam Peltzman, "Toward a More General Theory of Regulation," *Journal of Law and Economics* 19 (August 1976).

9.   Mancur Olsen, *The Logic of Collective Action*, Cambridge: Harvard University Press, 1965.

10.   For more extensive discussions of rent-seeking, see Gordon Tullock, "The Welfare Costs of Tariffs, Monopolies, and Theft," *Western Economic Journal* 5 (June 1967); Richard A. Posner, "The Social Costs of Monopoly and Regulation," *Journal of Political Economy* 83 (August 1975); Robert D. Tollison, "Rent Seeking: A Survey," *Kyklos* 35 (1982); and Charles K. Rowley, Robert D. Tollison, and Gordon Tullock (eds.), *The Political Economy of Rent Seeking*, Boston: Kluwer Academic Publishers, 1988.

11.   Fred S. McChesney, "Rent Extraction and Interest-Group Organization in a Coasean Model of Regulation," *Journal of Legal Studies* 20 (January 1991). According to McChesney, rather than performing a simple transfer function, politicians choose between transferring and threatening a groups' surplus bestowed by regulation, a choice that is influenced by the relative net gains to the politicians.

12.   Some examples of the empirical examination of rent-seeking in industries widely viewed as beneficial to the public interest include Ann P. Bartel and Lacy Glenn Thomas, "Predation Through Regulation," *Journal of Law and Economics* 30 (October 1987); B. Peter Pashigian, "Environmental Regulation: Whose Self-Interests are Being Protected?" in *Chicago Studies in Political Economy*, George J. Stigler (ed.), Chicago and London: The University of Chicago Press, 1988; and Michael Maloney and Robert McCormick, "A Positive Theory of Environmental Quality Regulation," *Journal of Law and Economics* 25 (1982).

13.   Richard A. Posner, "Taxation by Regulation," *The Bell Journal of Economics and Management Science* 2 (1971).

14.   Robert H. Bork, *The Antitrust Paradox, A Policy at War With Itself*, New York: Basic Books, Inc., 1978.

15.   For a discussion of rent-seeking in antitrust, see William F. Shughart II, *Antitrust Policy and Interest-Group Politics*, New York: Quorum Books, 1990, and

Roger L. Faith, Donald R. Leavens, and Robert D. Tollison, "Antitrust Pork Barrel," *Journal of Law and Economics* 25 (October 1982).

16. William J. Baumol and Janusz A. Ordover, "Use of Antitrust to Subvert Competition," *Journal of Law and Economics* 28 (May 1985), p. 247.

17. The objective of the Hill-Burton Act was expansionary, not restrictive, and it did lead to significant increases in hospital capital. The act, however, also added substantially to regulation by imposing numerous requirements on hospitals.

18. See, for example, Jack Zwanziger and Glenn A. Melnick, "The Effects of Hospital Competition and the Medicare PPS Program on Hospital Cost Behavior in California," *Journal of Health Economics* 7 (December 1988); Glenn A. Melnick, Jack Zwanziger, Anil Bamezai, and Robert Pattison, "The Effects of Market Structure and Bargaining Position on Hospital Prices," *Journal of Health Economics* 11 (October 1992); and David Dranove, Mark Shanley, and William D. White, "Price and Concentration in Hospital Markets: The Switch from Patient-Driven to Payer-Driven Competition," *Journal of Law and Economics* 36 (April 1993).

19. F. M. Scherer, *Industrial Market Structure and Economic Performance*, 2nd ed., Houghton Mifflin and Company, 1980, p. 481.

20. Dennis W. Carlton and Jeffrey M. Perloff, *Modern Industrial Organization*, Scott Foresman and Company (1989), p. 814.

21. Richard A. Posner, "Certificates of Need for Health Facilities: A Dissenting View," in *Regulating Health Facilities Construction*, Clark Havighurst (ed.), American Enterprise Institute, 1974, pp. 130 and 113.

22. Prospective Payment Assessment Commission, *Medicare and the American Health Care System, Report to the Congress* (June 1993).

23. The use of discretion, rather than rules, in policy making and statute interpretation has been associated with abuse of the regulatory process. See, for example, James C. Miller III, *The Economist as Reformer, Revamping the FTC, 1981-1985*, Washington, DC: American Enterprise Institute, 1989, in which Miller describes how vague statutory language in parts of the enabling statute for the Federal Trade Commission led to redefinitions and reinterpretations of the law by various commissioners on an "ad hoc" basis, leading to "major abuses of FTC statutory authority" (p. 19).

24. James B. Simpson, "State Certificate-of-Need Programs: The Current Status," *American Journal of Public Health* 75 (October 1985).

25. Prospective Payment Assessment Commission (1993); Simpson, "State Certificate-of-Need Programs."

26. Prospective Payment Assessment Commission (1993). As stated on p. 147 of the report, "[c]ertificate of need has reemerged recently as states attempt to contain health care costs by limiting the supply of expensive technology and health care services. Some states have reinstituted CON programs, others have delayed sunset provisions in their programs, and still others have strengthened their existing programs. For example, Virginia essentially repealed its CON law in 1989 but recently reinstituted it. Delaware, Georgia, Iowa, and Pennsylvania have expanded their programs. Currently, 38 states and the District of Columbia have some form of CON program in place."

27. The notion that hospital supply may fuel demand for hospital services, coined the "availability effect," is discussed in Joseph P. Newhouse and Charles E. Phelps, "New Estimates of Price and Income Elasticities of Medicare Services," *The Role of Health Insurance in the Health Care Sector*, R. N. Rossett (ed.), 1976.

28. David S. Salkever and Thomas W. Bice, *Hospital Certificate-of-Need Controls: Impact on Investment, Costs, and Use,* Washington, DC: American Enterprise Institute, 1979. On p. 7, the authors note that "[t]ypically, certificate-of-need programs relied on a participatory process in which consumers, providers, and other interest groups set standards and carried out reviews."

29. Salkever and Bice, *Hospital Certificate-of-Need Controls*, pp. 18-19.

30. *Id.*

31. Simpson, "State Certificate of Need Programs," p. 1227.

32. Ellen S. Campbell and Gary M. Fournier, "Certificate-of-Need Deregulation and Indigent Hospital Care," *Journal of Health Politics, Policy and Law* 18 (winter 1993).

33. Francis H. Miller, "Antitrust and Certificate of Need: Health Systems Agencies, the Planning Act, and Regulatory Capture," *The Georgetown Law Journal* 68 (1980), pp. 878-79.

34. The use of CON laws as cartel facilitators is discussed in Posner, "Certificate-of-Need for Health Facilities" and William J. Lynk, "Antitrust Analysis and Hospital Certificate-of-Need Policy," *Antitrust Bulletin* 32 (spring 1987).

35. This is mitigated to the extent that excess hospital capacity exists.

36. All else equal, the likelihood of collusion increases as the number of competitors declines. See, George J. Stigler, "A Theory of Oligopoly," chapter 5 from *The Organization of Industry*, Richard D. Irwin, 1968.

37. Salkever and Bice, *Hospital Certificate-of-Need Controls*, pp. 18-19.

38. See Posner, "Certificate-of-Need for Health Facilities"; Frank A. Sloan and Bruce Steinwald, "Effects of Regulation on Hospital Costs and Input Use," *Journal of Law and Economics* 23 (April 1980a); and Frank A. Sloan and Bruce Steinwald, *Insurance, Regulation, and Hospital Costs*, Lexington, MA: Lexington Books, 1980b.

39. Wayne Wendling and Jack Werner, "Nonprofit Firms and the Economic Theory of Regulation," *Quarterly Review of Economics and Business* 20 (Autumn 1980).

40. Fred F. Hellinger, "The Effect of Certificate-of-Need Legislation on Hospital Investment," *Inquiry* 13 (June 1976).

41. In *Hospital Certificate-of-Need Controls*, Salkever and Bice state that "[s]avings from the lower admissions rates and total hospital days resulting from control over bed growth were approximately offset by higher average per diem costs stemming from the upgrading of styles of care. Indeed, the results suggest the possibility that investment controls may actually have exacerbated the cost inflation problem during the 1968-1972 period" (p. 75).

42. See, for example, Sloan and Steinwald, "Effects of Regulation;" Sloan and Steinwald, *Insurance, Regulation, and Hospital Costs*; Frank A. Sloan, "Regulation and The Rising Cost of Health Care," *Review of Economics and Statistics* 63 (November 1981); Frank A. Sloan, "Rate Regulation as a Strategy for Hospital Cost Control: Evidence From the Last Decade," *Milbank Memorial Fund Quarterly* 61 (1983); Paul L. Joskow, *Controlling Hospital Costs*, Cambridge, MA, and London, England: The MIT Press, 1981; John L. Ashby Jr., "The Impact of Hospital Regulatory Programs on Per Capita Costs, Utilization, and Capital Investment," *Inquiry* 21 (summer 1984); and Joyce A. Lanning, Michael A. Morrisey, and Robert L. Ohsfeldt, "Endogenous Hospital Regulation and Its Effects on Hospital and Non-hospital Expenditures," *Journal of Regulatory Economics* 3 (1991).

43. Campbell and Fournier, "Certificate-of-Need Regulation."

44. Prospective Payment Assessment Commission (1993).

45. *Id.*

46. Prospective Payment Assessment Commission (1993) and "Market Forces or Force the Market," *Modern Healthcare.*

47. See, for example, Sloan and Steinwald, "Effects of Regulation."

48. See, for example, Sloan, "Regulation and the Rising Cost;" Craig Coelen and Daniel Sullivan, "An Analysis of the Effects of Prospective Reimbursement Programs on Hospital Expenditures," *Health Care Financing Review* (winter 1981); Sloan, "Rate Regulation as a Strategy"; and Lanning, Morrisey, and Ohsfeldt, "Endogenous Hospital Regulation."

49. For example, despite empirical studies suggesting that favorable results were obtained in New Jersey, the New Jersey rate-setting system also has been criticized for its inability to achieve savings and ultimately was abandoned. See Jeffrey Wasserman, "The New Jersey Experience With DRGs: A Lesson in the Limits of Hospital Rate Regulation," *Journal of Health and Human Resources Administration* (summer 1985) and "Market Forces or Force the Market," *Modern Healthcare.*

50. See, for example, David Dranove and Kenneth Cone, "Do State Rate Setting Regulations Really Lower Hospital Expenses?" *Journal of Health Economics* 4 (1985).

51. Kenneth R. Cone and David Dranove, "Why Did States Enact Hospital Rate-Setting Laws," *Journal of Law and Economics* 29 (October 1986).

52. See, for example, Michael A. Morrisey, Douglas A. Conrad, Stephen M. Shortell, and Karen S. Cook, "Hospital Rate Review, A Theory and an Empirical Review," *Journal of Health Economics* 3 (April 1984).

53. For a discussion of the history of federal antitrust activities in the health care field, see Arthur N. Lerner, "Federal Trade Commission Antitrust Activities in the Health Care Services Field," *Antitrust Bulletin* 29 (summer 1984), and John J. Miles, "Hospital Mergers and the Antitrust Laws: an Overview," *Antitrust Bulletin* 29 (summer 1984).

54. Recent studies examining the extent to which hospitals compete on the basis of price include Zwanziger and Melnick, "The Effects of Hospital Competition"; Melnick et al., "The Effects of Market Structure"; and Dranove, Shanley, and White, "Price and Concentration."

55. For a discussion of the antitrust policy implications of recent empirical studies documenting the existence of price competition in the hospital industry, see Robin Allen, "Policy Implications of Recent Hospital Competition Studies," *Journal of Health Economics* 11 (October 1992).

56. U.S. Department of Justice and Federal Trade Commission, *Department of Justice and Federal Trade Commission Merger Guidelines*, April 1992.

57. Following market definition, the agencies measure concentration within the market, including the production or sales of all current participants in the market and uncommitted entrants. Concentration is measured with the Herfindahl-Hirschman Index ("HHI") which is calculated by summing the squares of the shares of all of the market participants. The HHI ranges from zero in an atomistic market to 10,000 in a monopoly. In assessing the concentration levels resulting from a proposed merger, the agencies consider both the level of the HHI and the change in the HHI post-merger. The Guidelines identify three HHI ranges characterizing the degree of concentration in the market and whether the concentration level indicates that the market is a) unconcentrated and the merger is unlikely to have anticompetitive effects; b)

the market is moderately concentrated and the merger thus raises potentially significant anticompetitive concerns; or c) the market is highly concentrated and the merger is presumed likely to create, enhance, or facilitate the exercise of market power.

58. U.S. Department of Justice, *Statement of Antitrust Enforcement Policy in the Healthcare Area*, September 1993, and subsequently updated.

59. The existence of excess capacity in the hospital industry, and its need to rationalize to survive in a managed care environment, is not in dispute. During the 1980s, cost containment led to increased pressure on hospitals to become cost effective and to compete on the basis of price, which they did in part, and continue to do, by converting services traditionally performed on an inpatient basis to outpatient basis. These efforts have contributed to excess capacity in the industry, which has led to intensified competition and hospital consolidation.

60. These include *United States v. National Medical Enterprises, Inc. and NME Hospitals, Inc.*, Civil Action No. F-83-481-EDP, *In re American Medical International, Inc.*, 104 FTC 1 (1984)(No. 9158), *Hospital Corporation of America v. FTC*, 807 F.2d 1381 (7th Cir. 1986), *cert. denied*, 481 U.S. 1038 (1987); *In re Hospital Corporation of America*, 106 F.T.C. 455 (1985), *United States v. Carilion Health System and Community Hospital of Roanoke*, 707 F. Supp. 840 (W.D. Va. 1989), *affirmed*, 1989-2 Trade Cas. (CCH) ?68,859 (4th Cir. 1989) (Unpublished Opinion), *United States v. Rockford Memorial Corporation and Swedish American Corporation*, 717 F. Supp. 1251 (N.D. Ill. 1989), 898 F. 2d. 1278 (7th Cir.), *cert denied*, 111 S. Ct. 295 (1990), *In re Adventist Health System/West and Ukiah Adventist Hospital*, FTC Docket No. 9234, *FTC v. University Health, Inc.*, 938 F.2d 1206 (11th Cir. 1991), *vacating* 1991-1 Trade Cas. (CCH) ?69,400 (S.D. Ga. 1991), *FTC v. Columbia Hospital Corporation*, DC MFla, No. 93-30-CIV-FTM-23D, *FTC v. Freeman Hospital*, DCWMo, No. 95-5015-CV-SW-1, *U.S. v. Mercy Health Center*, DC NIowa, No. 94-1023, and *FTC v. Butterworth Health Corp.*, DCWMich, No. 1:96-CV-49.

61. For example, courts have found that acute care hospitals compete in the following product markets: 1) the cluster of services offered by acute care hospitals, including outpatient care, patient acute care hospitals and outpatient clinics that patients might have turned to; 2) services offered only by acute care hospitals; and 3) inpatient acute care hospital services. In addition, courts have identified both narrow and broad hospital geographic markets. The most egregious example of this conflict occurred in the nearly simultaneous release of directly contradictory opinions in *U.S. v. Rockford* and *U.S. vs. Carilion Health System*, in which the former reflected a three hospital market and the latter reflected a market including twenty hospitals plus outpatient facilities. Needless to say, the latter merger was allowed to proceed and the former was not.

62. For example, a Division official stated "[h]aving done a number of hospital merger investigations involving middle to large sized cities...we have become receptive to the possibility that, at least in some instances, the relevant geographic market may be just a portion of a metropolitan area," Remarks of Robert E. Bloch before the Fourteenth Annual National Health Lawyers Association, titled *Antitrust Enforcement in the Health Care Field: A Report from the Department of Justice*, February 1991. In addition, in every hospital merger challenged except its first, the Bureau has argued that hospitals compete in very local, narrow geographic markets.

63. A plethora of evidence exists showing that hospitals are continuously converting services previously available only on an inpatient basis to outpatient services and that outpatient services compete with inpatient services. See, for example, Suzanne W. Letsch, Helen C. Lazenby, Katherine R. Levit, and Cathy A. Cowan, "National Health Expenditures, 1991," *Health Care Financing Review* (winter 1992), and Prospective Payment Assessment Commission (1993).

64. For example, a hospital that opposes a cost-reducing merger of its competitors may have an interest in signing an affidavit for the government stating that it does not compete with the merging hospitals in order to support a narrow market definition that may help prevent the merger from occurring.

65. Moreover, the increased geographic scope of competition may partially or fully offset the reduced substitution between inpatient and outpatient services for highly complex procedures.

66. In *U.S. v. Mercy Health Center*, DC NIowa, No. 94-1023 and *FTC v. Freeman Hospital*, DCWMo, No. 95-5015-CV-SW-1, the courts recognized these dynamic forces affecting the geographic scope of hospital competition and rejected the government's narrow geographic market definitions.

67. See, for example, Harold S. Luft, Deborah W. Garnick, David H. Mark, Deborah J. Peltzman, Ciarnan S. Phibbs, Erik Lichtenberg, and Stephen J. McPhee, "Does Quality Influence Choice of Hospital?" *Journal of the American Medical Association* 263 (June 1990) and Emmett B. Keeler, Lisa V. Rubenstein, Katherine L. Kahn, David Draper, Ellen R. Harrison, Michael J. McGinty, William H. Rogers, and Robert H. Brook, "Hospital Characteristics and Quality of Case," *Journal of the American Medical Association* 268 (October 1992), which discuss the role of quality in patient choice of hospital.

68. For the first time in 1996 the court found that consumer cost savings were sufficient to overcome the FTC's evidence of increased market power following the merger of the two hospitals and in 1997 the decision was affirmed by the U.S. Court of Appeals for the Sixth District (*FTC v. Butterworth Health Corp.*, DCWMich, No. 1:96-CV-49 and *FTC v. Butterworth Health Corp.*, CA 6, No. 96-2440).

69. In 1995, former FTC Commissioner Christine A. Varney acknowledged that previous enforcement attitudes toward efficiencies flowing from hospital mergers had been overzealous. "Sometimes in the past antitrust enforcers have been too dismissive of the efficiency defense in hospital merger investigations. Indeed, in the past, some have attached what I can only call 'killer qualifications' to any defense based on asserted efficiencies. My view is that, when a merger does not impose a severe threat to competition, efficiencies should be presumed to flow to the benefit of consumers." Remarks of Christine A. Varney before the SMS Health Executives Forum, titled *The Health Care and Antitrust Interface in an Era of Fundamental Industry-Wide Realignments*, October 23, 1995.

70. See "Division Opposes Merger of Two Hospitals in Dubuque," *Antitrust & Trade Regulation Report*, The Bureau of National Affairs, Washington, D.C., June 16, 1994.

71. See "FTC Nixes Merger in 2-Hospital Town," *Modern Healthcare*, February 7, 1994.

72. See "Feds Approve Merger in 2-Hospital Town; Colo. Deal Awaits Decision," *Modern Healthcare*, January 31, 1994.

73. See "Mergers: Two Hospital Towns Try Togetherness," *Modern Healthcare*, December 6, 1993.

74. See, for example, American Hospital Association, *Hospital Collaboration*.
75. For example, in *FTC v. Columbia Hospital Corporation*, numerous community members submitted affidavits to the court on behalf of the FTC and, as FTC witnesses, provided testimony opposing the merger.
76. See Thomas Campbell and James W. Teevans, "Mixed Signals: Recent Cases Make the Legality of Future Hospital Mergers Less Predictable," *Antitrust Law Journal* 3 (1991), which discusses the role of complaining competitors in hospital mergers. In addition, in *FTC v Columbia Hospital Corporation*, the president of a competitor was one of the FTC's witnesses and the FTC submitted to the court numerous affidavits from other hospitals in the area.
77. See Steven C. Salop and David T. Scheffman, "Raising Rivals' Costs," *American Economic Review* 73 (May 1987).
78. This occurred in *FTC V. Columbia Hospital Corporation*.
79. Erwin A. Blackstone and Joseph P. Fuhr, Jr., "Hospital Mergers and Antitrust: An Economic Analysis," *Journal of Health Politics, Policy and Law* 14 (Summer 1989), p. 401.
80. As noted by Baker, the raising rivals cost theory as a justification for a complaining competitor permits the government to "avoid its responsibility to decide the case on the evidence because it substitutes a third party's judgement as to competitive consequences for the decision maker's own analysis." See Jonathan B. Baker, "The Antitrust Analysis of Hospital Mergers and the Transformation of the Hospital Industry," *Law and Contemporary Problems* 51 (spring 1988), p. 159.
81. Shughart, *Antitrust Policy and Interest-Group Politics*, p. 82.
82. See Richard S. Higgins, William F. Shughart II, and Robert D. Tollison, "Dual Enforcement of the Antitrust Laws," in *Public Choice and Regulation: A View From Inside the Federal Trade Commission*, Mackay, Miller, and Yandle, eds., Stanford, California: Hoover Institution Press, 1987.
83. Shughart, *Antitrust Policy and Interest-Group Politics*. On p. 97, Shughart notes that "[s]ome critics have argued that the potential for wasted resources is less serious than the uncertain legal standards that businesses face because of dual enforcement: Dual antitrust policies force 'the business community to risk being caught between two conflicting federal agencies'. This matters because if the alleged violator 'happens to draw the Justice Department, he will be accorded a federal court trial and due process, but if he draws the FTC, he will be relegated to a quasi-judicial procedure, where his rights are not so great.'"

6

The Antidiscrimination Principle in Health Care: Community Rating and Preexisting Conditions

Richard A. Epstein

The single most important political question of our time concerns the delineation of the respective spheres of influence for government and private action. Those who believe in a system of limited government instinctively gravitate to a system of private property and freedom of contract, and recognize that the first and most important application of that principle rests not in the terms of individual contracts, but in the right to choose one's trading partners. In modern times that principle has come under assault for a wide range of reasons, one of which is a universal antidiscrimination principle that seeks to specify the grounds under which people are, or are not, allowed to determine their trading partners. The principle of free association is replaced by a rule that limits the grounds on which refusals to deal may take place. And since these interactions are now coerced, the antidiscrimination principle must go a step further and indicate the terms and conditions under which certain transactions are allowed to take place.

The antidiscrimination norm has achieved its most powerful application in the field of employment law, where a full range of civil rights statutes prohibit discrimination on the grounds of race, sex, age, religion, disability, and perhaps sexual orientation. But the attack on private discrimination also proceeds apace in the area of insurance, as it relates to such lines as home, auto, and health. In this chapter, which addresses discrimination in this last area, I hope to show that government intervention in this area, as in so many others, leads to counterproductive and destructive outcomes. I shall focus my attention on two types of prohibition against discrimination that loomed large in the debates over the ill-fated Clinton Heath Security Act, and which continue to attract attention and support even after the bill's grandiose ambitions have been squelched. I will thus address the difficulties that arise in dealing first with systems of community rating, and then with the more focused question of whether health insurers should be prohibited by regulation from taking into account the preexisting medical conditions of their insured. Both forms of regulation have impressive levels of support today, but both should be condemned as unwarranted interferences with contractual freedom.

Risk Classifications

It is an odd commentary on the temper of times that one of the most common criticisms of unregulated private insurance markets is that they all uniformly seek to match the premium charged with the risk assumed by the carrier. That result can only be achieved if potential insureds are separated into categories that roughly mirror their anticipated costs to the carrier. The insurance carriers that voluntarily lump disparate individuals into a single risk classification allow high-risk individuals to mingle with low-risk persons, and to obtain a subsidy which, if large enough, will either drive low-risk persons out of the pool or, if uniform rates are too low, plunge the entire pool into bankruptcy.

Almost evidently, no insurance company possesses the knowledge or resources to measure precisely the risk for each individual person. So in the end the equilibrium is reached when an additional dollar spent on better risk classifications only yields an additional dollar in benefits obtainable from the more accurate determination of premiums. The unregulated system thus contains some wobble and tolerates some redistribution, but only as the inevitable concession to imperfect information, not as its primary object. Individuals can obtain protection against a high variation in outcome, but they cannot get a rate that ignores their very high expected losses. If there is a 50 percent chance of incurring $2,000 in medical costs and 50 percent chance of incurring none, the premium cannot fall below $1,000, before allowing for administrative costs. And for these purposes it does not matter who else is in the pool. Thus let someone else have a 5 percent risk of the same $2,000 and his premium should be $100 before allowing for administrative costs. Market insurance tends to set each person's premium at the same level, regardless of the composition of the remainder of the pool, for only that approach precludes any substantial and deliberate redistribution between individuals that leads to the dissolution of the pool. Persons who have high risks before insurance will always be asked to pay high premiums to private insurers, if they can get any coverage all. By the same token those who face low risks will be able to get a far better rate than they could without that risk categorization.

The constant political attacks on the insurance mechanism in the end stand or fall solely on its failure to redistribute: a necessary feature (or failing) of all markets. Yet by the same token, no one can trot out that other hardy argument for market regulation, that insurance carriers and their insureds systematically misperceive or misprice their risk. The familiar villains of asymmetrical or imperfect information are not the source of public unease. Rather, the complaint is directed to the converse result: the available information is too accurate, and therefore requires those with the greatest need for health insurance to pay the most for it. The social argument against private insurance is only that it is better for healthier people to pay for the health insurance premiums of sicker ones. Making the insurance industry more efficient pushes hard in the opposite direction. Efficiency means more accurate risk classification at lower administrative cost. Efficient markets bleed out redistribution; they do not foster it. Only regulation can do that.

Whatever the proper response to this discrimination question, the issue is not about irrationality; nor is it about economic efficiency. While a constant chorus of complaints alleges that insurance companies have concentrated market power to exploit isolated individuals, the true business risks run in the opposite direction. Large insurance firms, like small firms everywhere, are constrained in the prices that they can charge by the number of competitors and by the constant demand of customers to economize on costs. Insurance carriers cannot exploit unless they have a degree of monopoly power not obtainable in the highly competitive health industry.

On the other side, a potential insured in the high-risk category has something far more valuable than any fleeting claim of market power: private knowledge of the medical risks that he presents. If allowed to keep that information private, he will be in a position to purchase insurance at bargain rates relative to the risks in question. The low-risk person has no comparable advantage, and is anxious to confirm to skeptical insurers that he falls into the preferred class. The common law of insurance has long recognized the different incentives of various insureds and has sought to counter the devious behavior of high-risk insureds by a requirement of full disclosure of all material information. As early as 1828, Judge Bayley wrote, "I think that in all cases of insurance, whether on ships, house or lives, the underwriter should be informed of every material circumstance within the knowledge of the assured; and that the proper question is, whether any particular circumstance was in fact material, not whether the party believed it to be so."[1] The duty, as codified by statute, is stated with especial strictness for marine insurance: "the assured must disclose to the insurer, before the contract is concluded, every material circumstance which is known to the assured, and the assured is deemed to know every circumstance which, in the ordinary course of business, ought to be known by him. If the assured fails to make such disclosure, the insurer may avoid the contract."[2]

It is very clear that the traditional view regarded the mischief-maker as the potential insured, not the insurer. The effort to redistribute wealth through the insurance mechanism marks therefore a major change in worldview about the fundamental role of insurance. This clash between efficiency and redistribution in insurance markets comes to a head over two issues, one grand and abstract and the other of narrower focus but enormous practical importance. The larger issue is that of community rating, and the smaller one is that of preexisting medical conditions, that is, known disabilities of an individual who has sought health insurance, either individually or as part of some group plan. It is useful to take up these issues in sequence.

Community Rating

"Community rating" limits the grounds on which an insurance carrier can classify the risks that it assumes. Systems of this sort are already in effect with respect to other forms of insurance. It is now commonplace for state insurance codes, for example, to limit the grounds on which insurance carriers can classify drivers for the purpose of automobile insurance. Programs of this sort have been enacted in many large states, including New Jersey and California. But the longest running program of this sort has operated in Massachusetts, where the distaste for discrimination led to a radical revision of automobile rate structures starting in the mid-1970s.

B. Glenn Blackmon, Jr., and Richard Zeckhauser offer an excellent account of the resulting distortions.[3] They note first that the Massachusetts system works to undercut systematic ratings in two ways: insurance carriers can take no account of certain variables such as sex and age; and while they may take account of other variables, such as territory, the permissible rate range is "tempered," that is, variations in the rates are kept systematically below the expected variation in payout levels. One consequence of this program has been to force large numbers of drivers into assigned risk pools to exploit these differences.[4] As one might expect these operate at healthy deficits, and the surcharge is imposed on those hardy drivers that remain in the voluntary market. Blackmon and Zeckhauser calculate that the deficit for the assigned risk pool amounted to about $519 million, which translates into a surcharge of about $239 per covered vehicle. Their estimate of the deadweight losses from the program was about 40 percent of total subsidy, or $217 million. Losses of that sort cannot be accounted for by risk aversion. Indeed Blackmon and Zeckhauser calculate that to justify the allocative losses, "an individual's marginal utility of income drops by an implausible factor of 295 as his income increases from $15,000 to $30,000."[5] Assume that they are wrong by a factor of 100, and the results are still dramatic. The shrinkage in the size of the pie is too large to account for any affection for equal shares. Worse still, Massachusetts's peculiar system of subsidies at best may, for all we know, be only weakly correlated with income. The automobile precedent then gives no reason to be optimistic about the consequences of a similar foray into health.

But that foray is what we have. It is easy to think that each person has a right to drive a car and a right to health care. It is harder to be systematic about the content of the correlative duties. The upshot is that pressure for uniform policy coverage migrates from automobile to health: age and sex are more frequently regarded as irrelevant characteristics, notwithstanding their predictive value. Territory may be taken into account in setting community rates, but the variable of claims experience, regarded as so critical to automobile insurance, is generally deemed irrelevant as well.

At bottom, however, the community rating systems in both automobile and health insurance are adopted to negate the traditional risk classifications that private insurers use to combat any redistributive effects. An extreme version of this effort is found in early drafts of the ill-fated Clinton Health Security Act, which championed a community rating system that allowed risk classification only by family size and geographical area.[6] The present New York Law is narrower in scope, but applies the same general principle. That statute requires community rating only for the sale of policies to individuals or to groups of between three and fifty individuals.[7] For that group, it is illegal to take into account age, sex, health status, or occupation. In addition, open enrollment is a staple of these plans: any individual, group member, or dependent "must be accepted at all times throughout the year for any hospital and/or medical coverage offered by the insurer to individuals or small groups. . . ."[8] Other statutes of equally recent vintage follow the same line.[9] Still others have adopted modified versions of community rating plans that allow some, but not all factors on the list to influence the rate set. The New Jersey code disregards age, sex, occupation, and geographical location, but allows health status to be taken into account.[10] Florida's modified community rating system permits insurers to rely on the "eligible employee's and eligible dependents gender, age, family composition, tobacco use, or geographical area."[11]

It is clear that pure forms of community rating lead to far more powerful interferences with ordinary underwriting practices than modified community rating statutes, and that any complete assessment of these statutes would require a detailed examination of how each variation works out in practice. For my purposes, however, it is most instructive to look to the purest form of the system in order to assess its effects. The New York statute was passed in 1993, and the early evidence on its impact is consistent with established economic theory.[12] The first and most obvious consequence of this state mandate is the creation of massive cross subsidies. The American Academy of Actuaries in its report details the basic shifts in fortunes as follows: "the young would subsidize the old, males would subsidize females at most ages, the healthy would subsidize the sick and the poor may subsidize the wealthy, since young people generally earn less income than older people."[13]

The evidence bears out this assessment. Before the passage of the statute, rates for twenty- and sixty-four-year-old persons could vary between four- to sixfold.[14] Once the program became law, the premiums compressed: nine percent of the groups and 18 percent of the individuals enjoyed premium reductions in excess of 20 percent.[15] At the other end, 21 percent of the groups and 30 percent of the individuals were hit with rate increases of up to 20 percent, with five percent of both individuals and groups suffering increases in excess of 100 percent. Some fraction of the previously insured pool dropped out of the system altogether. Reviews of the program were mixed: the New York State Commissioner of Insurance Salvatore R. Curiale pronounced the program a success, given its stability for individuals and groups with bad experience but still seeking renewals.[16] But those who were made to foot the bill were less pleased with facing a choice between a cost squeeze or exiting the system altogether.

Individual testimonials are of limited value because they appear in all subsidy situations; the relevant inquiry is to compare the size of gains and losses. On this point, the implications of the standard theory are ominous. First, the New York subsidy plan undercuts the prior rate distinction between employed and unemployed workers. It thus reduces the incentives of firms to keep their workers in fighting trim: the benefits of lower claim experience will be shared by other firms that did not help implement these health measures.[17] To be sure, these recalcitrant firms have other strong incentives to retain programs that improve worker productivity, but at the margin the effects of community rating are likely to be negative. The sheer magnitude of the overall subsidy—estimated at $44 billion per year nationally—should both reduce the profitability of the regulated firms and increase the level of unemployment.[18] The implicit subsidy for not working should reduce workforce participation, imposing a still greater burden on those who do.

Second, community rating has already driven large numbers of younger workers out of the insurance system. Within a year of its operation, the median age of policy holders under one insurance plan (Mutual of Omaha) rose by 3.5 years from 41.5 to 45 years old, which indicates a substantial withdrawal of coverage from the plan by low-risk younger workers.[19]

Third, community rating cannot survive if all insurers must depend solely on premiums collected from their individual insurance programs. Whether by design or by chance, individuals with disabilities, or of greater age, will more heavily subscribe to some plans than others. These preferred firms will all go bankrupt if they fail to receive side-payments from other firms with superior books of business, or from the public treasury. Stated otherwise, the traditional forms of rating have to be preserved as between insurance carriers in order to keep all the players on an even keel.[20] A parallel dynamic in the automobile insurance industry requires the assigned-risk pool business to be distributed by formula among all carriers. The program would collapse if individual drivers could all pick the carrier of their choice.[21] That lesson at least has been learned with the community rating programs. For example, the New York statute contains provisions that allow the Commissioner of Insurance "to promulgate regulations to assure an orderly implementation and ongoing operation of the open enrollment and community rating" systems established under the statute.[23] But it offers no guidance on how these laudable objectives are to be achieved, and the legislative command adds substantial administrative costs to the system, funded out of general revenues.

Fourth, it is unlikely that community rating will be able to operate within its previous budget constraints. Its compliance costs are not trivial, and the composition of the insurable pool should deteriorate under the pressure of the system of cross-subsidies. The shift in the composition of the health plans, and the reductions in incentives for care should increase the frequency and severity of claims. In addition, it is quite inconceivable to accurately calibrate any proposed transfer payments in a political setting when low-risk individuals are exiting the pool and high-risk individuals are entering it. The projected long-term equilibrium is for system-wide instability, even if the renewal prospects for certain high-risk individuals under the plan are more stable in the short run than they were before.

The New York experience indicates the difficulties of grafting systematic subsidies onto a market system that preserves exit rights for low-risk insureds. The law can try to stop exit from the system by subjecting competing institutions to a similar norm, and one of the primary features of all Clintonesque health plans is that they do not permit any individuals to exit the system if they think it is in their interest to do so.[23] Universal health coverage is as much a duty as it is a right. On the other side, some states, like New Jersey, have passed laws that make it exceedingly difficult for insurers to exit the market (and utterly improbable for new insurers to enter it). But as the New

York experience suggests coercion against recalcitrant parties does not return the system to the pink of competitive health. The individuals and firms who are net payers work hard to reduce their exposures. Established insurance companies seek to reduce their market share; local individuals seek to reduce the scope of insurance plan coverage. Since they are not allowed to exit, the imperatives of self-interest make it more likely that they will fight, where they will meet a worthy and determined adversary in the AARP (whose eligibility for membership begins at fifty). In the end therefore some (modest) form of exit may well take place: if people cannot leave plans while staying put, they may decide to leave the state or nation in order to avoid its regulatory burdens. That effect has surely taken place with estate and income taxes. In principle it could happen here, although likely at lower rates.

Fifth, since others now are required to bear some portion of their risk, the pooled system will induce some individuals at the margin to engage in riskier activities, thereby increasing the total demands inside the system but simultaneously reducing the subsidy extracted from those individuals by their forced membership in the pool. The anticipated reduction in the health conservation actions of firms, noted above, is likely to be one such consequence, difficult to measure, but impossible to ignore. A second is the decision of individuals, faced with fixed rates, to engage in riskier activities now subsidized by others. A third is the likely deterioration in quality of care across the pool, given the enormous demands placed on existing resources. The antidiscrimination norms thus have powerful negative effects even when, and precisely because, legislation foreclosures the exit option.

Preexisting Conditions

Conditions Covered

Community rating requires as a backstop a concerted legislative attack on the contractual provisions of the standard insurance policy that exempt from coverage preexisting conditions, or require waiting periods before policy coverage goes into effect. Thus, consistent with its basic design, the Health Security Act proposed to make it illegal to exclude preexisting conditions or to impose waiting periods of coverage, the two basics of the standard contract clause.[24] This regulatory program was put forward both as matter of distributional fairness among individuals, and as a justification for coerced membership in a national health system. The former purports to rest on the unassailable proposition that like contributions deserve like benefits. But the purported equality is only skin deep: dollar contributions and formal coverage may be the same, but the expected payouts under some of these policies will be far greater than others. With a variegated risk pool, formal equality in insurance coverage necessarily has disparate impacts: the expected payouts for some exceed their contributions, and for others it falls far short. The mandated participation comes from the sentiment that any person who is not content with formal equality in effect shirks on his duties to others, and thus should be forced to remain in the plan, if not for his own good, then for theirs. Quite simply, without regulation, the losers would exit the system until the entire program unraveled. People must be roped into the system to provide the additional cash needed to subsidize the poorer risks.

These health conditions covered by the proposed statutory language can arise in all sorts of ways. Some of them are simply matters of previous accidents or illnesses that may manifest themselves again in the future, with greater probability than for the population at large. Many of these conditions are genetically triggered, such that the refusal to extend coverage for various forms of preexisting conditions is now condemned as genetic discrimination, typically defined as "discrimination directed against an individual or family based solely on an apparent or perceived genetic variation from the 'normal' human genotype."[25] Genetic discrimination is important in dealing with such matters as marriage, reproduction and adoption, and it also raises issues of preexisting conditions in two related ways.[26] First, because these characteristics are inherited, they are less likely to be influenced by behavior and more likely to form part of background conditions. Second, now that testing is possible to identify these conditions, both individuals and insurers may obtain advance knowledge about these conditions that is far more reliable than that which could be inferred simply by knowing something of the genetic history of parents or other relatives. As might be expected, the dominant view condemns as stigmatizing insurer efforts to peg insurance rates to the severity of genetic conditions. Only base and irrational prejudices against these individuals sustain the market practices.[27]

Genetic discrimination meets the same hostile response as other forms of risk classifications.

Contractual and Behavioral Responses

To see the magnitude of the proposed policy shift, it is instructive to ask what would happen if the common law norm in insurance—one that called for full disclosure of all material risks—applied today in these medical settings. Today routine tests allow for reliable identification of the AIDS virus or the gene for Huntington's disease.[28] Without the norm of disclosure, rational individuals would privately test for these diseases, and not disclose the results. If they test negative, they can breathe a sigh of relief. If they test positive, they can purchase large amounts of insurance at standard rates, and thus reap an enormous windfall at the expense of the general population. The stakes are large and the potential for selection bias is great. In an unregulated market, insurers will be alert to that possibility and will insist on full disclosure of all conditions that materially affect risk, just as the common law rule routinely required.

No sensible business, however, would rely solely on the general law of nondisclosure and misrepresentation to protect its vital financial interests. It would also use other contract devices to prevent exploitation from its potential customers. Insurers alert to the costs of preexisting conditions actively guard against advantage-taking, both for the benefit of the firm, and by indirection of its better customers. One strategy is to administer through its own physicians the medical tests used to identify these conditions, which may lead to the exclusion from coverage of individuals with AIDS and Huntington's disease. A second strategy is to stipulate by contract that no health insurance coverage is supplied for preexisting conditions, at least until the person has been enrolled in the plan for a certain minimum period of time. A typical clause of this sort reads:

> No benefits are payable for a condition, sickness, or injury for which you or your dependent were seen, treated, diagnosed, or incurred medical expenses in the six-month period just before insurance starts until the earlier of: . . . for you or your dependent, the end of a period of twelve consecutive months after insurance starts.[29]

This provision guards against obvious risks: the person who enrolls in a plan on day one and then schedules major surgery on day two.

But it also covers any identification of any dangerous condition before the onset of the period for which treatment is sought within twelve months after the policy goes into effect. Clauses of this sort are generally held to apply when symptoms are evident before the coverage begins even though the diagnosis is only made afterward.[30] Only where the policy language is not tightly drafted does insurance law limit the scope of the exclusion.[31] Yet by the same token none of the standard clauses deny coverage for conditions that were asymptomatic and otherwise unknown when coverage took effect: in those cases the moral hazard is not present and the insurer in an open market can profit by extending the coverage at fair rates. The basic function of these clauses is to preserve the minimum conditions for stable contracting: namely that all parties are better off on signing the contract than they were before; otherwise voluntary markets will surely unravel.

This contractual exclusion of preexisting conditions is attacked on a number of grounds. It is often said to operate as an ill-concealed effort to cut out business, in order to "cherry pick" the best risks.[32] But in fact it is clear that regulation and not markets drives cherry-picking by insurance firms that maximize profits subject to their external constraints.[33] No company has made a dime from the insurance policies that it does not write. It only makes money from sales whose costs are less than the premium received. The true form of exclusion would deny any coverage to a person with a preexisting condition, rather than deny coverage only for the condition itself. A person with the AIDS virus or Huntington's disease could still receive health insurance for an automobile accident or an appendicitis. Providing this partial coverage of persons with preexisting conditions is not an effort to reduce the size of the market; it is rather an effort to expand the market by offering some protection to persons who would be wholly uninsurable unless some limits and conditions were attached to their coverage. A company will only cherry pick the best risks if it is forced under regulation to charge a uniform price for all comers: it will then seek to exclude high-risk persons from the plan. But if it can reduce its assumed risk and adjust its premium levels, it will seek to reach all market segments, so long as it knows that at the end of the day its contractual limitations will be fully respected and enforced. It is only when the contractual limitations are themselves subject to judicial invalidation, that there is a greater willingness to restrict offerings or to exit the market altogether.

The issues here range far wider. The standard criticisms of the present contractual regime do not take into account the behavioral adjustments that will occur if parties are no longer allowed to restrict coverage for preexisting conditions. In order to understand what is at stake consider what happens when the law denies to private insurers the right to exclude coverage for preexisting conditions. One obvious consideration is the time that individuals in voluntary markets will choose to first purchase comprehensive health care coverage. If preexisting conditions can be excluded, prudence dictates taking constructive steps at an early age, whether or not health insurance coverage is locked in at that time. For individuals without disability, one path is to stay healthy as long as possible while going bare: the plan is to save on premiums while young and purchase the insurance with a clean record later on. A second path is to buy insurance while healthy in order to secure coverage for a not-yet-existing condition, thereby mooting the preexisting condition limitation. It is very difficult in the abstract to state which path is superior, but state mandates will, at least in some cases, undercut the incentive to make an early response to the problem.

More generally, any change in the coverage rules falsely assumes that the frequency and severity of preexisting conditions are independent of the insurance mechanisms used to deal with them. But that conclusion is no more appropriate here than it is in other contexts. The mere fact that insurance is always available for these conditions raises the familiar moral hazard problem: lax coverage rules will increase over time the number of preexisting conditions in any fixed population. An individual will willingly bear his very small fraction of the increased costs of insurance protection instead of his far larger fraction (close to one) of the costs of prevention that would otherwise fall his way. Since prevention costs are not limited medical services, they cannot be similarly socialized without tolerating state domination of all aspects of human life. We should expect some higher level of utilization of medical services when preexisting conditions are covered than when they are not. It is hard to make a guess exactly what the levels of increase are, but if conditions associated with drugs and alcohol abuse are included on the list, as they were in the abortive Clinton plan,[34] the effects are likely to be huge, not small. So once again the conflict between redistribution and production is not eliminated. It is just obscured.

Nor can it be said that these incentive and moral hazard arguments are irrelevant to genetic defects, given by birth and capable of being triggered at any time. In some cases, even here individual behavior may heavily influence the chances that a latent condition will turn active. One need only think of the relationship between diet and diabetes or between exercise and heart disease. Some portion of most genetic risks remains under individual control, at least as to the timing of onset and the severity of the condition. Even for those risks that are not, why should individuals have legal claims against others who are in no sense responsible for their conditions? What did the fellow workers of a given employee do that requires them to provide the needed subsidy? And how should the size of any such subsidy be determined? Is there any moral argument for increasing subsidies from healthy individuals, no matter what the wealth or the conduct of the person who receives that subsidy? Any claim for assistance should be lodged against society at large, not particular coworkers. If tax revenues become the source of the subsidy, then perhaps it would be better to tax those goods for which demand is more inelastic than health insurance, or to tax the complements to risky behavior, as the theory of optimal taxation generally indicates.[35] As a last resort, general tax revenues could make up the difference between the market rates that an insurer must charge to supply coverage and the lesser amount that the political system wants a certain class of preferred insureds to pay.

There are, then, good reasons to predict substantial allocative losses if the usual insurance practice of excluding coverage for preexisting conditions is reversed by law. But it is sometimes said that the coverage for preexisting conditions will increase the efficiency of the overall job market in ways that fragmented competitive firms cannot.[36] The problem—and it is a problem—arises when unemployed persons with known conditions cannot obtain jobs because of their medical risks. It also arises when the employer's insurance coverage changes for workers who keep their old jobs. Finally, it arises when employed persons must forfeit existing coverage by leaving their present employer and signing up for a better job by a contract that contains the usual exclusion for preexisting conditions.

The ideal scenarios are not hard to state. In the first case it would be better for people to be on the payroll than not. In the second case it would be better if the new company took on exactly the same risks as the prior carrier. In the third case it would be better for the worker to take the new job. In all, the optimal set of legal rules should encourage the free mobility of labor, or the free substitution of insurance carriers, goals which are frustrated by any contract based system of health insurance that ties people to their present work. The reluctance of workers to lose existing coverage clearly retards the levels of mobility relative to some social ideal.

Yet we should be aware of drawing an overhasty inference that the current forms of job rigidity are attributable to the contractual approaches to preexisting conditions. In the first case, the exclusion of preexisting conditions from insurance coverage does not prevent people from entering the workforce. It allows them to enter, but without one portion of insurance coverage. To the extent that they are better off with a job and some insurance than no job and no insurance, then the traditional contractual provision exerts no negative influence on their behavior. The difficulties only arise when unemployed individuals lose the coverage that they receive under Medicaid, but that is an incentive difficulty that should be laid at the doorstep of Medicaid (which could extend its coverage into the initial job period), not of the contractual system. Any system of welfare payments creates a disincentive to work, and this one is no exception to that rule.

The situation is more complicated when one insurance carrier takes over the business from another. But even here, it should be possible for voluntary markets to organize a solution. Here are two possibilities, the efficiencies of which are hard to compare in the abstract. Under the first coverage attaches to the date that the underlying condition is contracted, not to the date in which the condition manifests itself. This keeps the first carrier on the risk even after the expiration of its contractual period. My guess is that this solution would prove unworkable. Timing the underlying cause of medical conditions is always dicey business, and the division of responsibility between current and past carriers could create real management problems. If a person has two conditions, one old and one new, what should be the division of responsibility between the two carriers? At a guess, therefore, it seems that some clean break is preferred. In dealing with large-number problems, the second insurer could be paid to accept a "relation-back" clause whereby it assumes the liability of the first firm, perhaps in exchange for an additional premium from the insured, or, better, a payment from the current carrier now spared liabilities for preexisting conditions by the timely arrival of a new carrier. The experience of the existing firm should afford the basis on which these financial calculations could be made.

The third situation—in which workers shift jobs—is perhaps the most frequent. The initial reaction should be one of puzzlement as to why there is a problem at all. The limitations on insuring preexisting conditions are commonplace in insurance contracts, but these would not survive if the inefficiency is as pronounced as critics urge. Presumably the losses to these employees would be so great that they would be prepared to pay for extended health benefits that allowed job mobility even if it meant taking a lower current wage to preserve a future employment opportunity. There are no obvious externalities or informational barriers to revising existing contracts, so why then do the contractual practices continue to create this well understood and wholly unwelcome problem? One possible answer is that the change of employers only makes sense for the second firm if it does not have to bear the costs of the treatment for earlier ills. Thus if the new job promises additional social gains of $5,000, but will cost the new employer $10,000 to cover the preexisting condition, then it will have to bear a private loss in order to achieve a social gain, something that it will not do in the absence of coercion. Socially, however, the $10,000 loss to the second firm is offset by the $10,000 gain to the first firm from the release, so that all that is left if the improvement in production obtainable by having the more efficient match between worker and firm. Why don't these renegotiations take place?

The puzzle seems all the greater because it seems to be eminently possible to deal with this inefficiency by contract. Thus suppose that a worker with a preexisting condition is more valuable to a prospective employer than the current employer, but the new employer (and its insurance carrier) will not cover preexisting conditions. In principle it should be possible to arrange for a three-cornered deal in which the present employer (or its insurer) agrees to pay the prospective employer (or its insurer) a fixed sum of money for that second firm to assume the potential liabilities of the existing insurer. That transaction is not costless, and will require both firms to make some estimate of the anticipated costs of the future service under the existing policy. But cost calculations of that sort are not normally insuperable, and if so, then a market response will allow the job shift without incurring all the costs of state regulation.

It is, of course, quite possible that this technique will not work in all cases. It is not likely that anyone will assume the liabilities for an existing illness covered by the present policy when the financial liabilities are as yet undetermined because the patient has not yet settled on a course of treatment, especially without any one-to-one connection between a given condition and its appropriate treatment. But it might prove to be of use when the risks of injury are still latent, yet frequent enough to allow prices to emerge in some orderly fashion. These are, moreover, likely to be an important subset of cases. Individuals who are undergoing active chemotherapy are not likely to assume the added burdens of a new job. But a worker whose latent condition has a 10 percent chance of flaring up might be a good candidate for the shift.

In those situations (latent conditions, with low probability of future harm) where buyouts are possible in the spot market, it should be feasible to design an insurance contract that builds in the cost of coverage for the subsequent buyout at the front end.[37] The basic plan is for the initial purchase of insurance to charge a premium that covers two contingencies, the cost of care for the initial period, and an additional sum—call it a severance payment—sufficient to fund the purchase of the more expensive second insurance policy for the next period in the event that some dangerous condition is detected during the first policy period. That severance payment can then be spent to renew the policy at the higher rate of insurance or to purchase a new policy from some other carrier. It is not even necessary that the original carrier specialize in certain high-risk markets, but it is necessary for some organized market to set risk classifications appropriate for persons with identifiable conditions: there must be a secondary market for persons, for example, who are HIV positive, or at risk for the onset of diabetes within the next period. That market also must be an unregulated market, for if its recontracting prices are kept below their true cost, then the severance payment will no longer be sufficient to cover the risk, so that all potential takers of the insured with a known condition will flee coverage, fearing an anticipated loss. Government intervention in pricing therefore is likely to undo the effort to build in cash payments at the front end.

This long-term market has not yet emerged, even though it is a common practice in other commercial insurance markets for buyouts between different insurers of a given risk to pay money for some other carrier to assume their fraction of the risk. For example, an excess carrier may receive a substantial payment from the primary carrier to assume the risk of environmental or product liability. One possible culprit for its nonappearance may well be regulatory risk. Insurers could well fear that government will then alter the terms of severance or renewal so as to lock them into long-term losses by regulating the renewal prices; hence they avoid this market altogether.

A second possibility, of course, is that these contracts will fail because of high transaction costs. But even if that is the case, it hardly follows that these contractual responses to preexisting conditions should be overridden by regulation. The behavioral responses to a change in rule must be considered as well. Not only will the worker have at the margin less of an incentive to avoid potential risks, say from toxic exposures, but the first employer will have a reduced incentive to take care: after all it will bear fewer costs if it knows that the insurance cost will be picked up by some other entity if the worker changes jobs. The second firm will also be alert to the possibility of hiring a high-risk case, and will in turn try to take suitable defensive precautions. In the first place it may well conclude, sensibly, that any preexisting condition may well impair productivity, and would therefore decline to hire that person, even if it did not have to pick up the additional health insurance costs. Once those costs are imposed by law, the second firm has a still greater incentive to hire cautiously. Word-of-mouth hiring will tend to displace general advertising, because more is known about backgrounds and conditions.

Statutory Interventions

State Law. The future course of developments for preexisting conditions is likely to take place subject to heavy government regulation. Recently a number of states have enacted statutes that, parallel to the mandate for community rating, have restricted the capacity of insurers to limit coverage for preexisting conditions. For example, in 1993 New York included in its recent insurance reforms a provision designed to allow insureds to transfer their coverage for a preexisting condition to a new insurance carrier. The statute provides that the waiting period for coverage under any new policy for a preexisting condition shall not exceed twelve months from the date that the new policy has gone into effect.[38] It then says that so long as the individual in question has been insured under another policy within sixty days of obtaining the new coverage, then the period of previous coverage should be credited against the statutory waiting period, even if (as it appears) the insured was receiving medical attention under the last policy.[39] For any person then who has been continuously insured for twelve of the previous fourteen months the coverage is continuous, not interrupted.

It should be noted, however, that this statutory solution does not work in the same fashion as the three-cornered contracts mentioned above because it supplies no compensation to the second carrier for conditions that initiated under the previous coverage. The problem here is of especial importance because of the possibilities for game-playing. Thus an earlier version of the New York statute provided that coverage was available under the second policy so long as it dove-tailed with the first. It did not take into account the possibility that the coverage provisions of that second policy could be far more generous than those of the policy it replaced, a clear invitation to shift in order to accrue net benefits. A statutory revision cured this particular problem by requiring that the second policy be issued on terms that were substantially similar to those of the policy that it replaced.[40] Yet even here the opportunities for strategic shifts in coverage (coverage which, it appears, cannot be refused) have not been fully blunted, for the statute does not state whether the exhaustion of the limits of the prior policy counts as a reason to deny or limit coverage under the second policy. Nor does the statute exclude coverage for the very conditions that exhausted the limits on the first policy. So an insured group or plan could have to furnish fresh limits for old illnesses. In light of this risk, the break in coverage of sixty days could be of critical importance, yet it is uncertain whether the second carrier, given its obligations to serve, can delay the inception of its policy long enough to prevent the continuation of coverage for prior illnesses. But once again for each and every strategy there is a counterstrategy: the covered insureds can apply early and often for alternative coverage before their existing policies expire. Under these circumstances it is an open question as to how effective these preexisting conditions limitations can be, and whether the insurers doing business within the state will be able to remain.

Federal Law. The failure of the Clinton health plan did not end the federal efforts to reform health care. The post-1994 approach to health care reform has proceeded incrementally to allay social fears of the creation of any vast new federal bureaucracy with power to collect taxes and dispense favors. In 1996, these efforts bore fruit with the passage of the Health Insurance Portability and Accountability Act (HIPAA) which makes it illegal under federal law for any health insurance to refuse to supply coverage because of the health status, medical condition, claims history, medical history, or evidence of insurability of any insured.[41] This statute raises no issue of principle not canvassed with similar state programs, so I shall not consider it further here, notwithstanding its obvious national importance.

The question of preexisting conditions also crops up in other employment contexts closely tied into health insurance, most notably under the Americans with Disability Act,[42] which contains complex provisions that are squarely directed at the identification of preexisting conditions.[43] The statutory tightrope stipulates generally that an employer "shall not conduct a medical examination or make inquiries of a job applicant as to whether such applicant is an individual with a disability or as to the nature and severity of such disability,"[44] but then allows "preemployment inquiries into the ability of the applicant to perform job-related functions,"[45] without explaining how the second task can be done without violating the basic prohibition. Surely some employers will find it wise to make no inquiries at all, lest they run afoul of the law. But if all sources of information dry up, then the cost of hiring all workers increases, to the detriment of sick and healthy alike.

There is also a serious question of whether the prohibitions in place are sufficient to wall off the prospective employer from the information about disabilities. In particular, the ADA does not appear to address squarely the possibility that a healthy worker may volunteer information about his medical history precisely because he knows that his impaired rival cannot follow suit. If that becomes common practice, then the interpretive question is whether the employer has made an "implied inquiry" because of evident unwillingness to hire persons that do not make such declarations. Should the practice continue, pressures will build to amend the legal regime to prohibit any *truthful* disclosures of good health as well. The circle of prohibition thus grows to suppress truthful statements for the benefit of both the speaker and listener in order to protect a subsidy given to a third party.

The situation is still more complex for an employee who wants both to reveal and conceal information about medical history, albeit for different purposes. The ADA thus partitions the use of information, so that it is unavailable for the initial hiring decision but available for diagnosis and treatment. While no medical examination can be made before an offer of employment, one may be required thereafter, but only if two conditions are satisfied. First, the examination has to be conducted on all employees, if it is to be conducted on any—nondiscrimination again.[46] It is as though one must drill for oil even when it is known to be absent in order to drill where it might be present. This ADA provision thus chases after the legal but not the economic form of discrimination: an equal formal incidence with disparate economic returns. Second, the ADA now provides that the information gleaned from the examination must be placed in a confidential file where it is used only for limited purposes: to allow managers to learn of necessary restrictions on employment, and to give them information necessary for first aid and safety functions.[47] Otherwise the information cannot be used at all, especially on matters of job assignment, promotion, and transfer. Once again the ADA seeks to separate the efficiency from the distributional uses of the information, by allowing the former and excluding the latter. Yet this law can only have partial success. Clearly, the information cannot be kept quiet where the handicap is visible for the world to see: it is perfectly evident who is in a wheelchair and who is deaf.

For latent disabilities, the problem may not arise with initial hiring because the employer is allowed to collect that information only after the candidate has been hired. But that strict sequence of business first, health second, cannot be maintained on decisions relating to promotion or transfer. I suspect that few workers want to reveal information about latent defects notwithstanding the assurances of the ADA, given the questions of practical enforcement that surely remain.

This system of partial disclosure will also induce employers to adopt other strategies to cut their losses in a world that regards concealment as an employee birthright and not an employer peril. First, we should expect to see a trend to higher wage and salaried workers. When workers have better health and higher productivity, the employer wins both ways. Furthermore, there will be an increased tendency for plants to continue to locate away from the inner city, where these risks (like others) are perceived as greater. We should also see an intensification of the shift in labor markets from employees to independent contractors. The independent contractor works on a short-term basis for so many different employers that it is difficult for any one employer to bear the full burdens of the welfare state. Social security gives the necessary clue: the independent contractor pays his own, and the same legal regime applies for insurance and medical benefits as well. People who should be able to participate in employee insurance pools will no longer be employees, even if they do constitute good insurance risks. But no hard-pressed employer can be asked to take those consequences into account. Workers will be shed at the cost of some organizational efficiency in order to deflect a greater regulatory burden.

For those workers who do remain on the payroll, we should likewise expect to see employers work with their insurers to downsize the set of "neutral" insurance packages that are offered. Since employers cannot exclude certain diseases and disabilities by name, they will have to cut back coverage across the board in order to keep their costs under control. It is also likely that workers will have to bear some reduction in wages (or smaller increases) to offset the mandated costs. The great risk with disability is that a small fraction of individuals will impose enormous costs on the rest of the system. Plans will therefore be tailored to increase copayments and deductibles, and most importantly, to place sharper limits on the amount of catastrophic coverage that is available. Once again the costs of these shifts are borne in part by an employer (who cannot make the most efficient offer), in part by other workers who would have received greater benefits if employers could have excluded persons with latent conditions or diseases from the pool, and in part by insurers who have to learn to make do in a shrinking market with diminished contractual options. Finally, we should expect to see some shift from investments in human capital to investments in plant, equipment and other machinery, as the price of labor increases relative to that of equipment. At this point, the ADA's prohibition against discrimination should be seen for what it is—an elaborate set of cross-subsidies that reduces the total level of social wealth as it transfers it between parties.

It still remains to be asked how the refusal to take preexisting conditions into account will influence the operation of a possible national health system that is not entirely employment-based, such as the provisions found in the defunct Clinton Health Security Act. At one level the consequences depend on whether the movement is toward a single payer system, or to some hybrid system that allows multiple choices under the rubric of managed competition. In dealing with the former, much depends on the mode for establishing premiums. If these are done on a per capita basis, wholly independent of the level of individual risk, then the individual employer has less of an incentive to worry about the system-wide costs, which is not to say that he will be indifferent to the health of his workforce, given the costs of absenteeism, retraining, and the like. The long-term pressures therefore will come to bear on the definition of the package of benefits. The build up of additional costs will require either an increase in the total budget for health care beyond those projected in models that assume that refinancing of medical benefits does not alter the patterns of use, or it will require some painful exclusion of benefits that are quickly seen as entitlements by their recipients. The struggle here is likely to be tumultuous, with the outcome uncertain. The centralized political decision will be made across the board, and may come in times of financial stress. It is likely to bring in its wake some sharp discontinuities in the level or types of coverage. It is not a political posture in which intelligent determinations are likely to be made.

Under a managed competition system, the same choice between reduced coverage and increased appropriation will still loom large, but a third choice will not be added. Where the plan permits large employer groups to be formed, as the Clinton plan did, then all the questions about concealing information and monitoring hiring will be part of the overall picture, as before. Yet in addition, the various purchasing plans will each seek to exclude through means fair or foul individuals whose health records promise increased costs for the other members of that local plan, which, in turn, will generate the kinds of responses now endemic under the ADA. Nor is there any reason to think that insurers for the unemployed will be indifferent to the composition of their risk pool, so that the process of dissembling and delay will continue apace by programs which will face enormous cost pressure from the outset. Once again, there is no clean solution once individuals are forced to enter into losing contracts against their will.

The question then arises: is there any way to accommodate people with preexisting conditions, apart from forcing employers and insurers to offer them health protection against their institutional will? One possibility is to do nothing at all, and trust that private cost reduction and overall increases in productivity will in the long run redound to the benefit of persons with preexisting conditions. Limited insurance coverage and steady work may emerge from the overall picture, and the dislocations in other aspects of economic growth may be avoided.

A second possibility is to reshape the public subsidy. Today these costs are hidden from public view by forcing private employers and insurers to bear risks for which they receive insufficient compensation. But suppose the shortfall in compensation were now made explicit by forcing its payment from the public purse? Eligible individuals could receive an annual subsidy, calibrated by the severity of their condition, which they could then spend on health care as they choose. The public would know the size of the subsidy, which it can compare with other claims for public support, perhaps tying the size of its payments to the wealth of the recipients if such were desired. If, after deliberation, the government subsidy still leaves persons with preexisting conditions short of their perceived needs, it is just too bad: the claims for redistribution always exceed available resources, so that some disappointment has to be tolerated so long as resources are scarce, which they always are. Insurance markets need no longer be hobbled with the distortions and inefficiencies that arise when concealment of information and evasion of potential liability are the only winning strategies available to market participants. The quirks of geography or choice of plan or insurer will no longer influence the incidence of the burdens needed to fund the subsidy. It will be borne from general revenues.

Yet even this revised program will work only if the public payments are fixed in advance, leaving individual recipients to seek out their best market opportunities. The public system must create some barrier against providing additional resources when individual cases turn out poorly, for otherwise the lump sum payment will come to be regarded as a down payment on an open line of credit. Even here, deciding who gets what subsidy for what conditions will prompt anxious and inconclusive public debate. Are all genetic disabilities covered? All workplace injuries? The system could easily evolve into a grand version of the black lung disease program in which disputes over eligibility have laid low everything in their path. We already have Medicare and Medicaid disability programs whose mushrooming costs should counsel caution on the usefulness of lump sum subsidies contingent on proof of special medical need. In the end, one despairs of doing anything sensible through the political process. Of all the alternatives, market solutions seem socially most desirable, and politically least feasible.

Notes

1. Lindenau v. Desborough, 8 B. & C. 586, 108 *Eng. Rep.* 1160 (1828). For other sentiments of the same view, see Lord Mansfield's earlier opinion in Carter v. Boehm, 3 Burr. 1005, 97 Eng. Rep. 1162 (1766); London Assurance v. Mansel, 11 Ch.D. 363 (1879), holding that an insured must disclose all that is known to him, even if he does not understand that the information is material to the evaluation of the risk.

2. Marine Insurance Act, 1906, s. 18(1).

3. B. Glenn Blackmon, Jr., and Richard Zeckhauser, "Mispriced Equity: Regulated Rates for Auto Insurance in Massachusetts," 81 *Am. Econ. Rev.* 65 (Pap. & Proc., May, 1991).

4. Richard A. Epstein, "A Clash of Two Cultures: Will the Tort System Survive Automobile Insurance Reform?," 25 *Valparaiso L. Rev.* 173, 183-89 (1991).

5. Blackmon and Zeckhauser, supra note 3, at 67-68.

6. See, for example, HSA § 1384. "(a) Application of Community-Rated Premiums.—The premiums charged by a corporate alliance for enrollment in a corporate alliance health plan shall . . . vary only by class of family enrollment . . . and by premium area."

7. 27 McKinney's (N.Y.) § 3231. N.Y. L. 1992, c. 501. "For the purposes of this section, 'community rated' means a rating methodology in which the premium for all persons covered by a policy or contract form is the same based on the experience of the entire pool of risks covered by that policy or contract form without regard to age, sex, health status or occupation." It appears that the phrase "policy or contract form" does not refer to the policy or contract issued to a given insured, but to all insureds who receive insurance under the same basic type of policy or contract.

8. Id.

9. See, for example, Maine R.S. § 5011A, "Rates for policies subject to this subsection may not vary based on age, gender, health status, claims experience, policy duration, industry or occupation." This section replaces an earlier statute, Maine R.S. § 6059, which allowed age, sex, and geographical location to be taken into account, but limited the variation in organizational rates to 150 percent of a standard rate.
See also Mass. Ann. Laws Ch. 495. Same restrictions as New York, with additional provision, excluding "any other factor which the commissioner may specify by regulation."

10. N.J. § 17B :27A-2 (1993).

11. Fla. Stat. § 627.6699(6)(b)(1).

12. See, for example, Mark V. Pauly, "The Welfare Economics of Community Rating," 37 J. of Risk and Insurance 407 (1970); Roger L. Pupp, "Community Rating and Cross Subsidies in Health Insurance," 48 *J. of Risk and Insurance* 610 (1981).

13. American Academy of Actuaries, quoted in Robert Pear, "Pooling Risks and Sharing Costs in Effort to Gain Stable Insurance Rates," *New York Times*, May 22, 1994, p 14.

14. Pear, "Pooling Risks."

15. Ibid.

16. Ibid.

17. Pear, "Pooling Risks," at 14. "If their health insurance is community rated, businesses say, they will not get the benefit of savings they achieve through

efficient management of their health plans and through programs promoting healthy behavior by employees." The word "full" should be inserted before "benefit."

18. Ibid., p. 14, col. 5.
19. Pear at 14, col. 5. Cecil D. Bykerk, Mutual of Omaha, Chief Actuary.
20. Pear at 14, at cols. 3 and 4. Statement of Alice Rosenblatt, actuary at Coopers & Lybrand.
21. Epstein, "Clash," supra at note 4.
22. 27 McKinney's (N.Y.) §3233.
23. Elizabeth McCaughey, "No Exit: What the Clinton Plan Will Do for You," *New Republic*, vol. 210, no 6, p.21 (February 7, 1994).
24. HSA § 1402 (b) "No Limits on Coverage; No preexisting-Conditions Limits.— A health plan may not—(3) exclude coverage of an alliance eligible individual because of existing medical conditions; (4) impose waiting periods before coverage begins."
25. Paul R. Billings, Mel A. Kohn, Margaret de Cuevas, Jonathan Beckwith, "Discrimination as a Consequence of Genetic Testing, 50 *American J. of Hum. Genetics* 476, 476 (1992). The use of "solely" in this context is probably too restrictive, if the parallel definitions of discrimination in employment and other areas are used as precedents. The use of "normal" in quotation marks is yet another effort to avoid the issues presented by discrimination by writing as though the stated grounds for distinction are themselves suspect.
26. For my general views on these issues, see Richard A. Epstein, "The Legal Regulation of Genetic Discrimination: Old Responses to New Technology," 74 *Boston U. L. Rev.* 1 (1994).
27. In addition to the Billings article supra, see Joseph S. Alper and Marvin R. Natowicz, "Discrimination as a Consequence of Genetic Testing," 50 *American J. Hum. Genet.* 465 (1992); and Larry Gostin, "Genetic Discrimination: The Use of Genetically Based Diagnostic and Prognostic Tests by Employers and Insurers," 17 *American J. of Law & Med.* 109 (1991).
28. Huntington's disease is fatal condition that sets in after reproductive years that is carried by a single dominant gene, which can now be identified by genetic testing. For discussions of the various legal and ethical issues about the gene, see Gwen Terrenoire, "Huntington's Disease, and the Ethics of Genetic Prediction," 18 *J. Med. Ethics* 79 (1992); Natalie Angier, "Researchers Locate Gene That Triggers Huntington's Illness," *New York Times*, March 24, 1993, at T1, reporting on the discovery of the gene.
29. Clause from New England Mutual Life Insurance Co., as reproduced in Bullwinkel v. New England Mut. Life Ins. Co., 18 F.3d 429 (7th Cir. 1993).
30. Kirk v. Provident Life and Acc. Ins. Co., 942 F.2d 504 (8th Cir. 1991) (symptoms of bacterial endocarditis before period, diagnosis made afterward).
31. Mannino v. Agway Inc. Group Trust, 600 N.Y.S.2d 723 (A.D. 2 Dept. 1993). That clause provided "You have to wait 11 months * * * before we will cover services for preexisting conditions. A preexisting condition is one for which medical advice was given, treatment was recommended by or received from a health care provider . . . . within 12 months before you were covered by this contract." The alleged ambiguity was the absence of an "or" before treatment. It could have been that the exclusion applied only if both advice and treatment were given. The exclusion was denied for a patient in need of a bone marrow transport for leukemia who had a first visit with a specialist the day before the policy took effect. The clause in Bullwinkel would clearly cover the case.

32. See, for example., Paul Starr, "The Framework of Health Care Reform," 329 *New Eng. J. Med.* 1666, 1670. "Without [regional health alliances], or if they are only voluntary, insurers will continue to be able to cherry-pick the healthy and shun the sick."

33. See, for a formal demonstration, Mark V. Pauly, "Is Cream-Skimming A Problem for the Competitive Medical Market," 3 *J. Health Econ.* 88 (1984).

34. HSA, § 1115, which makes benefits available to any person who has in the previous year "a diagnosable mental or substance abuse disorder," and who is "experiencing, or is at significant risk of experiencing, functional impairment in family, work, school, or community activities." Id. 1115(b)(1). That just about covers the waterfront.

35. Roger Feldman and Bryan E. Dowd, "Biased Selection—Fairness and Efficiency in Health Insurance Markets," *American Health Policy: Critical Issues for Reform* 64 (R.B. Helms ed. 1993).

36. Paul Starr "Framework," supra note 32.

37. See John H. Cochrane, "Time-Consistent Health Insurance," 103 J. *Pol. Econ.* 445 (1995).

38. 27 McKinney's N.Y. §3232(b). The section also gives a somewhat narrower definition of a preexisting condition, which covers only those conditions that would lead "an ordinary prudent person to seek medical advice, diagnosis, care or treatment," or one for which these were, in fact, received in the previous six months.

39. 27 McKinney's N.Y. § 3232: "In determining whether a preexisting condition provision applies to an eligible person, the group or blanket accident and health insurance policy or individual health insurance policy shall credit the time the person was previously covered under a previous health insurance plan or policy or employer-provided health benefit arrangement, if the previous coverage was continuous to a date not more than sixty days prior to the date of the new coverage."

40. The statute does not allow the credit in all cases, but provides: "Such credit shall apply to the extent that the previous coverage was substantially similar to the new coverage." Ibid. at § 3232(a). It does not talk about the exhaustion of the older limits.

41. HIPAA, Pub. L. 104-191, codified as part 7 of The Employee Retirement Security Act of 1974, 29 U.S.C. § 702(a). The reference to portability is not quite accurate because the basic statute requires the new employer to supply its own coverage to the insured, not to carry over the insurance supplied by some previous carrier.

42. Pub L Law No. 101-336, 104 Stat. 327, 42 U.S.C. 12101-12213, 47 U.S.C. § 225 and § 611.

43. 42 U.S.C. § 12112(d), covering both inquiries and examinations.

44. 42 U.S.C. § 12112(d)(2)(A).

45. 42 U.S.C. § 12112(d)(2)(B).

46. 42 U.S.C. § 12112(d)(2)(B)(3)(A).

47. 42 U.S.C. § 12112(d)(2)(B)(3)(B).

7

State Health Care Reform: Protecting the Provider

Michael A. Morrisey

"I predict that before this decade is out, American physicians will be on their knees, at the state and federal level, begging for protection."
—Uwe Reinhardt

Given the failure of the Clinton administration health care reform proposal and the results of the 1994 mid-term elections, it has become the conventional wisdom to suggest that health care reform is dead. The conventional wisdom is wrong. Health care reform at the state level will emerge as the regulation of health care markets to the benefit of providers. I expect to see three major forms of regulation develop. First, certificate of need (CON) will reemerge as a vehicle to control costs and its effect will be to protect hospital providers from the cost containing forces of the market. Second, the states will enact any-willing-provider laws in the name of a level playing field for all providers, but these laws will actually serve to protect physicians and other providers, and undermine attempts to cut prices to consumers. Finally, in the name of expanded insurance coverage for the uninsured, states will push for waivers or the elimination of the ERISA (Employee Retirement Income Security Act of 1974) exemption for self-insured employers which will expand the health benefit package, increase the number of newly insured, and thereby increase the demand for provider services.

The paper proceeds in four sections. Section I reviews the empirical literature on the growth and effects of price competition in health care. This work indicates remarkable price sensitivity both on the part of consumers for insurance coverage and on the part of insurers for provider services. Hence, managed care has significant potential to reduce health care prices.

Section II argues that state regulation of health care is the result of the demand and supply of regulation. Legislatures supply laws. Providers of services demand laws that limit the entry of competitors and expand the demand for their services. Opponents seek to convince the legislature not to enact the law. The economic theory in this regard is well articulated. The rigorous empirical literature on this topic in health care, while still limited supports the theory.

Section III discusses the three principal forms of regulation that I expect to see promoted: CON, any-willing-provider, and ERISA exemptions. It presents some background on the nature of the laws, the findings of the existing regression-based literature, and a summary of current legislative efforts. The empirical literature on CON is extensive. Its conclusions are virtually unanimous with respect to cost containment: CON has neither controlled hospital costs nor restrained service diffusion. The laws, however, have prevented entry of new providers into the markets and made life more comfortable for existing providers.

The evidence on any-willing-provider laws comes from California. It suggests that hospital price competition is markedly enhanced when laws encouraging selective contracting are enacted.

Since the enactment of ERISA the states have enacted enormous numbers of laws regulating health insurance. By 1990 there were 854 state laws mandating insurance coverage for specific illnesses and conditions, specific categories of providers, and specific categories of beneficiaries (Jensen, Cotter, Morrisey 1995). Following this trend has been the growth in the number of self-insured firms, which are exempt from state insurance laws under ERISA. The empirical research suggests that these two trends are related.

Finally, Section IV briefly summarizes the themes of the chapter.

Competition in Health Care Markets

To begin an examination of health care competition, consider the nature of the health insurance market. In 1992, 182.4 million nonelderly Americans—nearly 83 percent of these under age sixty-five—had health insurance coverage. Of these, almost 90 percent (88.6) obtained their insurance through the workplace (Snider and Boyce 1994).

Some have argued that the reliance on employer-sponsored health insurance has inhibited price competition. The opposite is closer to the truth. Indeed, that so many people purchase their insurance through their employer reflects their sensitivity to price. Health insurance tends to be cheaper when purchased through an employer because of the tax treatment of employer sponsored health insurance; because of favorable selection, whereby workers as a rule are healthier than nonworkers; and because of lower administrative costs, as employer personnel offices already do much of the administrative work that an insurer would otherwise have to do.

Employers also have a greater incentive to search for lower cost health insurance than do individuals. An individual will continue searching for an insurance plan of higher net value until the expected benefits of additional search just equal the expected costs. An employer follows the same decision rule, but because she may have many employees, she has an incentive to search longer and harder. The potential benefits are greater. Unfortunately, to my knowledge there is no empirical evidence on either the extent or effect of employer search on health care costs or prices.

However, employers have been offering their workers more health insurance options. As long ago as 1985, 34.5 percent of medium and large employers offered more than one health insurance option (Jensen et al. 1987). Workers have been shown to be enormously sensitive to differences in the out-of-pocket premium of plans offered to them. Morrisey (1991) presents for a full review of this literature, but three studies will make the point.

Welch (1986) used the Bureau of Labor Statistics Employee Benefits Survey data to investigate the extent to which the choice of fee-for-service versus HMO enrollment was a function of price differences between the plans offered. He found that a 10 percent increase in the monthly out-of-pocket premium for the HMO led to a 2 percent reduction in the HMO's share of subscribers in one year and a 6 percent decline after workers had fully adjusted. Increases in the fee-for-service premium led workers to shift from that plan to the HMO plan.

Long et al. (1988) found larger responses to changes in the out-of-pocket premiums paid by workers. Using data on over 1,500 subscribers in three Minneapolis-St. Paul HMOs during 1984, they found that a $5 per month increase in an HMO's out of pocket premium relative to premiums offered by other plans resulted in a 66.7 percent increase in disenrollment. The larger price elasticity reflects this study's ability to better control for substitutes. The extent of disenrollment depends upon the number of alternative plans available. With three choices, the five-dollar increase implied 58 disenrollments per 1,000 subscribers; with eight options the same premium increase implied a disenrollment of 100 per 1,000 subscribers.

These studies still underestimate the extent of worker willingness to change plans because of higher prices. They were unable to take into account all the actual alternatives. A worker with an employed spouse, for example, often has a much wider range of insurance options than does a married worker whose spouse is not in the labor force. Failure to take these insurance options into account leads to an understatement of the price sensitivity of workers.

Feldman et al. (1989) did much to overcome this difficulty by using 1984 data from seventeen firms in Minneapolis and St. Paul. They examined the plan choices made by nearly 1,000 single workers who had no dependents and over 2,000 single parent families and married workers whose spouse was not covered elsewhere. They found that workers were much more willing to switch between plans of the same type than across types. That is, an increase in an HMO's premium led to greater switching to another HMO than to a fee-for-service plan, and vice versa. Also, the presence of more plans led to more plan switching. They found, for example, that if an HMO enrolled 40 percent of the single workers in a firm, and if all of the HMOs offered by that firm enrolled 80 percent of the single workers, then a $5 increase in the HMO's out-of-pocket premium would result in the HMO losing nearly half (45 percent) of its single subscribers. With fewer HMO substitutes, this HMO would lose fewer subscribers.

One can conclude from these studies, and others, that workers are very sensitive to the prices they have to pay for insurance. They will switch plans if premiums increase. Since workers—and by extension, their employers—are so price-sensitive, managed care firms and insurance companies must be concerned about their costs.

There is growing evidence that managed care firms are paying much greater attention to the prices they pay providers. They can negotiate lower hospital prices based upon local market conditions. They have not been affiliating with hospitals based upon price, but once an affiliation is established, the number of patients admitted to an affiliated hospital by the managed care firm depends, to a significant extent, on the prices that have been negotiated. Price appears to determine volume even if it does not determine affiliation status.

Hospitals have generally been viewed as competing for patients or physicians or both. Typically one might expect hospitals to behave as other providers of complex services, distinguishing themselves on the basis of the bundle of services, quality, and amenities that they offer and the price that they charge. It has been argued, however, that the hospital market is very different from that of other services. Widespread health insurance allows individual consumers and their physician-agents to be much less concerned about the price of care. (While the price of insurance matters, once the insurance is purchased, the out-of-pocket price of doctor and hospital services is low.) They have an incentive to use every service and amenity available as long as the perceived value is greater than the out-of-pocket cost. Intensive use of services, of course, will drive up the price of insurance, but the "prisoner's dilemma" aspect of the problem makes this consequence largely irrelevant. Thus, in competing for physicians and their patients, hospitals have historically put much more emphasis on the services and amenities they offer than on the prices they charge.

If hospitals have been competing on the basis of services and quality to the exclusion of price, then in communities with more hospitals one should see higher costs. Using 1982 hospital data, Robinson and Luft showed that hospitals in communities with more hospitals did have higher costs per admission. Hospitals with eleven or more competitors had costs 26 percent higher than those with no competitors, given the same hospital characteristics, case mix, population characteristics, and local wage rate (Robinson and Luft 1985).

More recent empirical work shows that the nature of the hospital market, at least in some communities, has changed substantially. See Morrisey (1994) for a more complete discussion of this literature. In 1983, the State of California allowed insurers to selectively contract with providers. It also implemented a selective contracting program that allowed the state Medicaid program to enter into contracts only with hospitals willing to provide inpatient services through a competitive bidding process. These contracts were based, in part, on the prices the hospitals were willing to accept. Zwanziger and Melnick (1988) examined the rate of increase in hospital costs in the periods before and after the Medicaid and selective contracting legislation took effect. The results are summarized in Figure 7.1. In the earlier period, hospital costs behaved as the service competition model suggested. Hospitals in communities with more competition had more rapid rates of cost increase than hospitals with fewer competitors. In the PPO period, however, the hospitals in the more competitive markets had lower rates of increase. Indeed, their real costs actually declined slightly. In contrast, the hospitals in less competitive markets had a more rapid rate of cost increase in the "after" period. These results remain when one controls for hospital output, case mix, input prices, teaching, ownership and related hospital characteristics, as well as the Medicare prospective payment system that was being phased-in during this period.

FIGURE 7.1
Effects of California Selective Contracting Laws

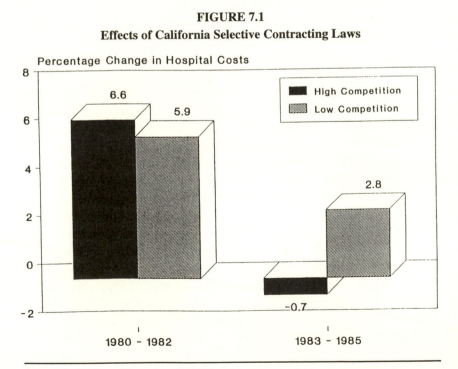

Source: Melnick and Zwanziger (1988)

Hospital average costs in the more competitive markets continued to decline throughout the last half of the 1980s, relative to those of hospitals in less competitive markets. In 1980-82, hospital costs in more competitive California markets were 12 percent higher than in others. By mid-1988 the costs were equal, and, in 1989 and 1990, hospitals in more competitive markets had average costs below those of less competitive markets (Zwanziger et al. 1993).

These researchers also explored the "black box" of how competition worked (Melnick et al. 1992). Blue Cross of California provided them with a hospital specific index of the actual prices that its preferred provider organization (PPO) had negotiated with 190 hospitals in California in 1987. The index was the price per day negotiated with each hospital in the PPO network, divided by the average price per day paid by the PPO. Thus, a high-priced hospital had an index value greater than one and therefore greater than average. They used these data to examine the effects of local hospital competition and bargaining strength on the prices negotiated. Their regression work controlled for hospital and market characteristics and focused on the market determinates of the negotiated price.

Four findings emerged from the analysis. First, controlling for other factors, the PPO paid a lower price to hospitals located in more competitive markets. Thus, the presence of more local hospitals allowed the PPO to negotiate a lower price. Presumably the PPO was able to raise a credible threat that it would move its patients to another provider. Second, the larger the percentage of a hospital's total patient days accounted for by the PPO, the greater the leverage the PPO had with the hospital and the lower the price the PPO obtained. Volume of business matters. Third, the larger the share of the PPO's admissions concentrated in a single hospital, the higher the price the PPO paid. This effect was magnified as the number of other hospitals in the community declined. Thus, the more dependent the PPO was on a hospital, the weaker was the PPO's bargaining position. The results relate to the strength of the conflicting loyalties of patients. Patient loyalty to the PPO (and perhaps to its doctors) means that the hospital has to worry that intransigence over price on its part will lead the PPO to channel patients elsewhere. Patient loyalty to the hospital (and perhaps to its doctors) means that, for its part, the PPO must fear that it will lose subscribers if it tries to sever patients' relationships with established providers. Finally, the study found that high occupancy affects the negotiated price in a straightforward way. Hospitals with high occupancy located in markets with high average occupancy successfully charge higher prices to the PPO. Hospitals with high occupancy in other markets do not. Presumably the fear that the PPO will channel its patients to other hospitals in the local market keeps the price down.

This research is important because it demonstrates that hospitals do compete on a price basis and that the prices actually negotiated are consistent with a rather standard model of firm behavior. This and supporting work by Gruber (1992) provide strong evidence that hospital pricing in California changed dramatically with the enactment of state laws encouraging selective contracting by private insurers—an important fact when we come to consider any-will-provider legislation. If this interpretation of the California experience is correct, one should see analogous pricing behavior elsewhere in the country. The magnitude of the effects will depend, in part, on the extent of hospital competition and the freedom of PPOs to contract.

One non-California study does suggest that insurers are sensitive to the actual prices charged by hospitals and that they channel their patients to preferred hospitals. Feldman et al. (1990) examined the price sensitivity of six HMOs in four large metropolitan cities in 1986. The four unnamed communities included two immature HMO markets, one of which had only 6 percent of the population enrolled in any of the five operating HMOs. Only one site constituted a well-established HMO market. The six HMOs had enrollments ranging from 42,000 to 216,000. Two were staff-model HMOs, two were network models, and two were independent practice associations (IPAs). None of these HMOs affiliated with all of the hospitals in their market areas. See Table 7.1. The HMOs affiliated with between 10 and 47 percent of the hospitals in their respective market areas. The study sought to determine why some hospitals obtained HMO affiliations and whether the prices negotiated with the hospitals affected hospital affiliation or use.

The study found that staff and network model HMOs were more likely to affiliate with hospitals that had a reputation for high quality. Teaching and *nongovernmental* ownership were the available measures of quality. The model did not do a good job of predicting hospital choice by IPAs (independent practice associations), in part because IPAs, by their very nature, include physicians from throughout the

TABLE 7.1
Hospitals Used by HMOs

City	HMO	HMO Type	Hospitals in Area	Percent of Hospitals Used
1	A	Staff	71	10
	B	IPA	107	43
2	C	Staff	36	22
3	D	Network	32	47
	E	Network	33	25
4	F	IPA	53	34

SOURCE: Feldman et al. (1990)

community. They undoubtedly have privileges at a diverse set of hospitals. Only higher occupancy had a statistically significant effect in predicting IPA-hospital affiliations. It is important to note that the average cost per admission had only a small effect and lacked statistical significance for all types of HMOs. If anything, the HMOs appeared to choose hospitals with reputations for high quality regardless of cost.

From each HMO the researchers obtained the price per admission and the number of admissions at each affiliated hospital. The effect of price on the use of hospitals was quite dramatic. A 1 percent increase in the price of an admission led to a 3 percent reduction in the number of admissions for staff and network model HMOs. For the IPAs a similar 1 percent increase led to a 1 percent reduction in admissions at the hospital with the higher price.

These findings have three implications. First, HMOs are responsive to hospital prices within the set of hospitals with which they affiliate. HMOs apparently will channel patients to hospitals that provide better prices. Second, staff and network HMOs are much more price sensitive, undoubtedly because they are able to contract with a relatively small number of physician groups and to more easily direct patients to preferred hospitals. IPAs have much greater difficulty directing patients to specific hospitals. Finally, note that this study was not carried out in "hotbeds" of HMO competition. Only one site was a mature HMO market, and the regression results did not suggest that it dominated the results in any way. Thus, even relatively small HMOs (and PPOs) in communities that have only a tradition of conventional insurance coverage appear to be able to channel patients among hospital providers and negotiate hospital prices with the promise of more volume.

This evidence is limited to a few studies, but they are very well done. Taken as a whole they suggest that managed care firms have to be careful of the premiums they charge because individuals are willing to switch plans for very small differences in prices. Further, managed care firms can, at least in some markets, negotiate with providers on the basis of price and reward lower prices with increases in volume.

Providers and insurers are concerned about the emergence of price competition in their markets, because it can lower prices, shift patient flows, and reduce profits and surpluses. So providers seek government barriers to entry in their markets.

The Demand for State Regulation

In one view, state laws and regulations spring from a widespread desire to correct inefficient or inequitable market practices. This so called "public interest" view holds that state health care regulation such as certificate of need or any-willing-provider legislation is designed to correct problems in the health care market. Certification of need is viewed as an attempt to reduce hospital costs by limiting duplicative resources used in hospitals. Any-willing-provider legislation might be viewed as an attempt to level the playing field so that all hospitals or physicians willing to accept a given payment structure would be allowed to participate in a managed care plan.

An alternative view of regulation is that state laws and regulations stem from an attempt by self-interested parties to further their private interests. See Posner (1974) for a discussion. In this view, CON laws are attempts by hospitals to limit the entry of new hospitals or to restrict the extent of service competition, and any-willing-provider legislation an attempt to keep rivals from offering lower prices.

The economic theory of regulation stems from work by Stigler (1971) and Peltzman (1976), among others. The idea is straightforward. Legislators seek election and reelection. To that end they provide services to their constituents. Individuals and groups seek legislative services, i.e., laws. They trade political support—votes, publicity, campaign assistance, and contributions—for those laws. In general, individuals have a position on virtually every issue; they perceive themselves as gaining or losing in each instance. However, they are also economically rational. For most issues the expected gain or loss is smaller than the costs of political activity. Hence they do nothing. Thus, one of the strong predictions of this theory is that benefits will accrue to relatively small groups who are deeply committed to a particular issue. Costs tend to be imposed on the diffuse majority.

Individuals consume thousands of different commodities annually. Producers specialize in very few. Thus, the proponents and opponents of legislation tend to be producers, whose gains or losses are large enough to warrant the costs of political action. Further, because producers are fewer than consumers, it is less costly for the few producers to organize to support or oppose a bill.

Government is not captured by a single producer group. In general, a group gets less than it wants because other groups of producers are harmed by the proposed action. The legislature seeks a compromise of the opposing interests (Peltzman 1976). In the political vernacular this might be phrased as, "Some of my friends support the bill. Some of my friends oppose it. I support my friends." For a discussion of the theory and applications in several areas, see Stigler (1988).

There have been a number of case studies of the enactment of health legislation. Feldstein (1977, 1988) presents excellent applications of the economics of regulation to the health care industry. However, he does not develop and test an empirical model of legislative or regulatory action. Mueller (1986) has analyzed congressional voting on nine health policy issues over the course of the 1970s. Controlling for political ideology and party affiliation, Muller concluded that the influence of physicians, as measured by AMA membership, and the size of the Medicaid program in the states played major roles. One can interpret the Medicaid variable as the voice of other state constituencies seeking to limit the use of state funds for this purpose. (Mueller appears to interpret it as a measure of public interest.) Feldstein and Melnick (1990) examined congressional voting on the Gephardt amendment to President Carter's hospital cost containment legislation. The amendment effectively gutted the Carter effort to place mandatory limits on hospital revenues. Feldstein and Melnick concluded that the hospital interest group variable had the largest impact on the probability that a member of Congress would reject the revenue limits. Congressional members in states with higher shares of the state budget going to Medicaid supported the limits. These results are consistent with the interest group view of health regulation.

Three sets of studies apply the interest group model to state health care issues. These deal with certificate-of-need laws, state regulation of hospital charges, and insurance mandates for mental health and psychologist series.

Wendling and Werner (1980) examined state enactment of certificate-of-need laws between 1964 and 1973, prior to federal health planning legislation that increased the incentives for states to enact the laws. They argued that the demand for legislation depended on the expected benefits, the cost of "buying off" the opposition and the costs of organizing. Empirically, hospitals demanded CON to restrict entry of new competitors. The potential gain from regulation was measured by the change in occupancy rates in the state over the period. As occupancy fell, demand for legislation increased. The higher the costs of organizing, the less likely favorable legislation was to pass. The extent of hospital concentration in the state served as a proxy variable for organizational costs. As the price of legislation increased, less legislation was demanded. Wendling and Werner measured the price of legislation as the percent of the legislature in the governor's political party. As the percent increased, the price of enactment increased, because the party could act more like a monopolist if it controlled both the legislature and the executive. Monopolists, of course, provide less of a good and sell it at a higher price. Wendling and Werner also included a variable intended to measure consumer benefits from the CON enactment measured by the change in hospital costs per day over the period leading up to enactment. The argument was that more rapidly increasing costs would lead to greater consumer demand for regulation to contain costs.

Their results were consistent with the theory. CON was enacted in states where occupancy rates were falling and hospitals easy to organize. As the proportion of the legislature with the same political affiliation as the governor increased, the probability of enactment declined. All of these results were statistically significant at the conventional levels. The increase in hospital costs, the measure of consumer benefits for regulation, was of the correct sign but lacked statistical significance.

In rate-setting a state regulatory agency determines the prices that hospitals will be paid for some or all of their patients. Cone and Dranove (1986) examined which states had enacted these laws by the early 1970s. They considered two views of why states regulate hospital prices. The first is a public interest view in which rate-setting is enacted to limit hospital expenditures. The second is that the laws are enacted to reduce "politically inefficient" transfers to Medicaid recipients. By reducing Medicaid expenditures via the price controls, the legislature will have more state revenues available for other public purposes. In their state level analysis, hospital expenditures were measured alternatively as expenditures per admission and per capita. Medicaid was measured as per capita Medicaid hospital expenditures. The model controlled for the extent of any deficit in the state budget and the degree of liberality in the state, as measured by the Americans for Democratic Action voting score of the state's congressional delegation. Cone and Dranove's model correctly predicted thirty-nine of the forty states that did not adopt rate-setting and nine of the ten states that did. They find no support for the public interest view. Rather, "Liberal states with budget deficits and large Medicaid hospital expenses were most likely to enact rate-setting laws" (p.298).

These results are consistent with work by Fanara and Greenberg (1985). They used a less well-developed public-choice model, but also found that state rate-setting was associated with a higher proportion of the state budget allocated to Medicaid. This result they attribute to opponents who would prefer to see state money spent on other projects. The investigators also found that a higher proportion of for-profit hospital beds in the state was associated with a smaller probability of enactment. In contrast to Cone and Dranove, Fanara and Greenberg found that a higher rate of increase in hospital costs per admission was associated with a greater probability of enactment. They viewed this variable as a measure of employer/consumer concern over cost increases.

All states have enacted legislation mandating that health insurance sold in the state include coverage for particular illnesses, types of providers, or categories of beneficiaries. However, only one study has attempted to investigate empirically the enactment of these statutes. Lambert and McGuire (1990) used a public choice model to examine the determinants of insurance mandates for minimum coverage for psychotherapy (mental health services) and psychologists' services.

Using state data from the mid-1970s, they attempted to explain whether each of these mandates was enacted by 1983. Two measures of mandates were used. The first related to whether the law was enacted; the second considered "mandated option" laws, in which an insurer is required to *offer* the coverage to its clients, who may refuse it. Their general model makes regulation a function of: proponent strength, opponent strength, the political environment, and state demographics. They found that somewhat different measures explained the enactment of mental health and psychologist mandates and that the results were sensitive to the precise sets of variables examined. They concluded, however, that "a number of groups influence whether or not mental health mandates and FOC (freedom of choice to choose a psychologist) laws are passed. Most groups act in their own interest, and some groups act in the public interest....The political activity of psychologists, the need of community mental health centers for additional revenues, and the history of a state in passing insurance mandates in other areas had estimated effects bordering on or close to the conventional level of significance" (Lambert and McGuire 1990, p. 183).

In short, while the empirical evidence is limited, the general conclusion is that provider support has been critical in the enactment of certificate-of-need and state insurance mandates, and providers have been important opponents of limits on hospital revenues. Proponents of other uses of state revenues, typically proxied as the proportion of the state budget going to Medicaid, stand out empirically as countervailing forces.

State Regulatory Actions

It is now widely acknowledged that major reform of the U.S. health care industry by means of federal legislation will not occur soon. It is also widely believed that market forces in the form of managed care are themselves rapidly reforming the industry. More and more people are enrolled in HMOs. Nearly 49 million Americans, 19.4 percent of the population, were enrolled in HMOs in 1993, for an increase of 30 percent from just 1990 (Marion Merrell Dow 1994). An estimated 121 million individuals were eligible to use a PPO in 1992, up 48.7 percent from 1991. Some 2,500 separate PPO networks of physicians and hospitals operate in the U.S. (Marion Merrell Dow 1993).

We have established that managed care organizations of these sorts have the potential to introduce considerable price competition into health care. Some PPOs have negotiated lower prices from hospitals, and some HMOs have apparently channeled patients to hospitals in their networks offering lower prices. Comparable evidence for physicians and other health care providers is not available. Hospitals and other providers have already been to the legislative door seeking protection, and such demands will surely increase.

Certificate of Need Laws

Background. Certification of need is a process of state approval required of hospitals and nursing homes prior to the construction or renovation of a facility or the addition of major new programs or equipment. Steinwald and Sloan (1981) and Simpson (1985) provided good historical overviews. New York State was the first to develop a CON process in 1964. New beds or major capital purchases could be licensed only if they were approved by the state health planning agency. By 1975 some twenty-six states had enacted CON legislation. The federal government enacted health planning legislation in 1976 requiring that hospitals and nursing homes have prior approval for new facilities and major equipment if the care rendered using the facilities and equipment was to be eligible for reimbursement under Medicare and Medicaid. If a state did not adopt a CON program to consider such requests for expansions, a federal process would be used. All states except Louisiana enacted health planning laws.

The public interest rationale for the CON laws revolved around the effects of insurance in the health services sector. It was argued that the presence of widespread health insurance meant that many people did not bear the true cost of service utilization. As a result, consumers had an incentive to demand, and physicians as good agents of their patients had strong incentives to provide, everything of potential benefit to the patient. As a result, hospitals competed for physicians and their patients by providing more services, giving rise to allegations of unnecessary duplication of services (Roemer and Shain 1959). Alternatively, it was argued that the competition for patients led hospitals to expand services and beds. These beds and services may not be fully used, but the nature of cost-based reimbursement meant that both public and private insurers paid the costs of these unneeded services.

In the early 1980s, the federal government largely eliminated funding for health planning, and, in 1987, the federal health planning statute was repealed, in part because it was ineffective in controlling costs. Between 1983 and 1990, seventeen states dropped their CON laws as they applied to hospitals (AHA 1992, Sherman 1988). Fewer states, ten, repealed them as they applied to nursing homes (Morrisey et al 1992). However, the majority of states continue to have CON regulations in place. The provisions of the regulations vary significantly by state. Burda (1991) reports, for example, that Indiana and Oregon require any capital expenditure by a hospital to obtain a CON approval. Vermont has a threshold of $300,000, Massachusetts of $7.5 million. Five states require approval for any hospital purchase of medical equipment; Alabama has an equipment threshold of just below $275,000. Eighteen states require hospitals to obtain a CON approval for any new services. As I note below, however, since 1990 CON has been reintroduced and its scope expanded in many states.

The continued existence of CON and, indeed, its reintroduction and expansion despite overwhelming evidence of its ineffectiveness as a cost control device suggest that something other than the public interest is being sought. The provider self-interest view is worthy of examination.

Suppose that hospitals, at least in many markets, enjoy some degree of market power. If they are profit maximizing entities, one would expect them to set prices that allow them to extract all available profits. With no unique hospital resources and no artificial barriers to entry into hospital markets, one would expect new providers to enter these markets, offer their services, and eventually drive prices down to the level of marginal costs. In this simple world, certificate of need serves as an artificial barrier to entry, keeping new entrants out and profits up.

One could argue that because 90 percent of the hospital industry is organized on a nonprofit basis, this model is inapplicable. However, the principal difference between for-profit and nonprofit organization is how the profits are spent. For-profit enterprises spend them on shareholders. Nonprofit entities are prevented by law from explicitly doing so. However, they may spend the profits on charity care, medical education, the provision of unremunerative services, or they may spend them by prices set below the profit maximizing level. As I have argued elsewhere (Morrisey 1994), if the hospital's mission is anything other than providing reduced-price care to paying customers, it will act like a profit maximizing facility. And the entry of new providers into the market will reduce the ability of the existing providers to achieve their missions.

Thus, if hospital markets become more competitive with the spread of managed care firms, hospitals of various organizational stripes are likely to seek protection from entry into their markets. CON provides such protection. The empirical research suggests that CON has been effective in this regard.

Empirical Evidence. Certificate of need has attracted many empirical studies. They find virtually no cost containment effects. However, they do show higher profits and restricted entry by for-profit hospitals, hospital systems, and contract management firms. Steinwald and Sloan (1981), and Sloan (1988) provide detailed reviews of the early literature.

Consider first the cost containment issues. In a pair of studies, Sloan (1981, 1983) used a pooled time series of cross sections of state data to examine the effects of CON and other factors on hospital costs and the change in hospital costs per day and per admission. He examined the periods 1963-78 and 1963-80, respectively, looking for anticipatory effects of hospitals trying to "beat" CON implementation, and studied both programs in their early years of development and mature programs. He found that CON had no statistically significant effect on costs or changes in costs. These findings are borne out by other state-level analyses (Salkever and Bice 1976, 1979), (Melnick et al. 1981), (Joskow 1981), (Misek and Reynolds 1982) and (Ashby 1984). Morrisey, Sloan and Mitchell (1983) used metropolitan-area data over the period 1967-81 and found no effect of CON on hospital costs. Sloan and Steinwald (1980a, 1980b) used hospital-level data over the period 1970-75 and found no statistically significant effect of CON on hospital costs. Coelen and Sullivan (1980) used hospital data over the 1969-78 period and also found no economically meaningful effects of CON on hospital costs.

More recent investigations have examined the potential effects of CON over a longer period of time. They have evaluated the effects of CON repeal and considered the interaction of CON with other regulatory programs. These studies suggest that rather than controlling costs, if anything, CON programs tended to increase costs. Sloan, Morrisey and Valvona (1988) and Sherman (1988) found that the repeal of

CON had no effect on hospital costs per capita. Antel, Ohsfeldt, and Becker (1995) use 1968-90 state data on hospital costs per day, per admission and per capita. They allowed for interaction effects between CON programs and other state and federal regulatory programs, thereby allaying the concern of some proponents that one must look at regulatory programs in the milieu of regulatory constraint in the state. They found that CON had no statistically significant effects in any of the empirical specifications. In any event, their estimates imply that, if anything, CON raised hospital costs. Lanning, Morrisey and Ohsfeldt (1991) considered the enactment of CON laws to depend upon the efforts of proponents and opponents of the program in the states. After taking this into account, they found that hospitals in states with CON had costs 20.6 percent higher. CON has not contained hospital costs.

There is some early evidence that CON reduced the number of hospital beds, but this savings appears to be lost in expansions of assets per bed. See Salkever and Bice (1976, 1979), Joskow (1980), Misek and Reynolds (1982), and Ashby (1984). More recent work by Sloan, Morrisey and Valvona (1988) examined the effect of CON repeal. Using 1972-1985 state data, they found that dropping CON had no statistically significant effect on hospital investment but did increase nonlabor costs per adjusted hospital admission.

The empirical literature also suggests that CON has not been effective in restricting the diffusion of new technologies. Russell (1979) found evidence that CON resulted in less diffusion of open-heart surgery programs in 1975, a finding challenged by later work by Sloan et al. (1986). Russell found no effect of CON on the diffusion of hospital renal dialysis programs. Joskow (1981) found no effect of CON on the diffusion of CT scanners. Case studies by Policy Analysis-Urban Systems (1980) suggest why. Hospitals could avoid the CON process by leasing CT units, by the purchase of scanners by physicians, purchase of units just below the CON regulatory threshold, and purchase of mobile and component units exempt from CON review. These results are consistent with Cromwell and Kanak's (1982) findings that CON had no effect on hospital offerings of "complex," "quality enhancing," and "community" services. The only study to systematically find an effect of CON on service diffusion is recent work by Ford and Kaserman (1993). However, their study did not deal with hospitals. Instead, they determined whether the state CON regulation applied to independent for-profit renal dialysis clinics in each year from 1982 through 1989. This application could be interpreted as regulation of potential hospital competitors. They found that the presence of an applicable CON law reduced the growth in dialysis clinics by 1.5 clinics per year per state and the number of dialysis units by 3.4 per year per state.

While CON did not control costs it does appear to have had advantages for existing hospitals. Noether (1988) used Medicare price and cost data from 1977 and 1978. She found that costs were higher the longer CON had been in effect in the state, a finding consistent with some of the other work on CON. However, she also found that prices were higher and that, overall, the longer CON was in effect, prices were higher relative to costs and therefore profits were higher. This finding also suggests that CON served to restrict entry into hospital markets. The higher costs imply that some of the gains from restricted entry were dissipated by quality, service, and amenity competition.

Several early studies examined whether CON laws restricted the entry of investor-owned hospitals. See Havighurst (1982) and Frech (1976) for a discussion of why CON agencies may oppose for-profit ownership. Sloan and Steinwald (1980b) found no differential effect of CON based on hospital ownership. Similarly, Mullner and Hadley (1984) found no effect of CON on the growth of investor-owned multihospital system beds.

However, McCarthy and Kass (1983) have challenged studies of this sort. They argue that if the adoption of CON is an attempt to restrict entry, this condition must be taken into account in examining the effects of CON on the growth of investor-owned hospitals. They replicate the results of the early studies. Then they predict the toughness of the CON program in the state based upon the sort of political variables discussed above and reestimate the effect of CON on the share of investor owned hospital beds in the state. The results indicate that a 1 percent increase in CON "toughness" is associated with a .43 percent reduction in for-profit market share. They then show that this effect was driven by effects in states in which for-profit hospitals had less than the median share of hospital beds (given they had any). In these states, a 1 percent increase in CON toughness led to a 1.3 percent reduction in the for-profit market share. They interpret these results as indicating that CON laws were used to restrict entry of investor-owned hospitals in states in which nonprofit hospitals had comparatively more political strength. (They similarly argue that CON would be disproportionately used against nonprofit hospitals in states where investor-owned hospitals have a more dominant position. However, they did not have data to test this hypothesis.)

Alexander and Morrisey (1988) examined the growth of multihospital systems during the period 1980-83. They found that the longer the state had had a CON program in effect, the less likely the hospital was to join a multihospital system. They concluded, "It appears that the certificate of need 'franchise' to operate in the area conveys some market power which increases the value of the hospital to its current owners and decreases the net gain to a potential acquirer." It may be that the probability that the CON agency would approve the sale was low.

Alexander and Morrisey (1989) used a similar methodology to examine the likelihood that a hospital would be managed under contract by an external organization. They found that the longer a CON program had been in existence in a state, the less likely a hospital was to be managed by a for-profit management firm. The effects for nonprofit management firms were much weaker. They concluded, "Our findings with regard to regulation support the view that CON may act to inhibit market forces and protect weaker hospitals from environmental resource constraints."

Finally, Campbell and Fourier (1993) used Florida CON applications and found that hospitals with greater indigent care loads were more likely to have their application approved even controlling for indigent care loads applications from investor-owned hospitals were less likely to be approved.

Thus, a reasonably large body of evidence suggests that CON has been used to the benefit of existing hospitals. Prices and costs were higher in the presence of CON, investor-owned hospitals were less likely to enter the market, multihospital systems were less likely to be formed, and hospitals were less likely to be managed under for-profit contract.

Current Actions. Although evidence of CON effectiveness in controlling costs is all but nonexistent since 1990 a number of states have taken action to reinstate, continue, or expand their CON programs. See Table 7.2. Minnesota and Wisconsin have reinstated their CON programs for hospitals. Five states did not allow their CON sunset provisions to go into effect. More than a dozen states have expanded their CON programs. These expansions relate to three types of activities. First, the programs have been expanded to cover ambulatory facilities such as surgical centers, birthing centers and the like regardless of ownership.

Second, CON review of specific types of equipment has been expanded to include newly acquired equipment in physicians' offices. Finally, two states have enacted legislation applying CON to HMOs.

TABLE 7.2

Status of Hospital Certificate of Need, 1992

State	Repealed CON	Reinstated CON	Did Not Implement Sunset Provisions	Expanded CON
AZ	1985			
AR	1990			
CA	1987			
CO	1987			
DE				yes (a)
FL				yes (b)
GA				yes (c)
ID	1983			
IN	1987			
IA				yes (d)
KS	1985			
LA	1988			
MD				yes (b)
MA				yes (e)
MN	1984	1992		
MT	1989			
NM	1983			
OH			1991	
OK	1989			
OR			1991	yes (f)
PA				yes (c)
SC				yes (g)
SD	1988			
TN			1991	yes (g)
TX	1985			
UT	1984			
VT				yes (c)
VA			1991	yes (c)
WV			1991	yes (c)
WI	1987	1992		
WY	1987			

SOURCES: AHA (1992), IHPP (1991), Jee (1993), Lewin/ICF (1991), Sherman (1988).

(a)   Applied to freestanding facilities (IHPP 1991).
(b)   Applies to HMOs (IHPP 1991), (AHA 1992).
(c)   Applied to all health care providers (Jee 1993).
(d)   Applies to new equipment in physician's offices (AHA 1992).
(e)   Approval formally linked to the provision of charity care (AHA 1992).
(f)   Applies leased equipment (AHA 1992).
(g)   Applies to freestanding facilities (AHA 1992).

One explanation for this continued and expanded interest has to do with the increased competition between hospitals and other hospitals and freestanding facilities. The expanded scope of CON activities suggests an attempt to limit new forms of competition.

The health care trade press provides anecdotal evidence that the CON process is being used to inhibit competition among existing hospitals. See Greene (1994), Margolis (1992), and Sussman (1992). Burda (1991) describes five cases throughout the country that, in his view, constitute attempts by one provider or set of providers to thwart competition through the CON process.

● In Lincoln, Nebraska, a national hospital chain sought approval to build a freestanding psychiatric facility. The existing inpatient provider submitted its own CON application for a freestanding facility. In the words of a Nebraska Hospital Association official: "We're beginning to see the use of CON laws against competitors in the hospital arena."

● In Lebanon, Tennessee, a hospital sought to rebuild its facility five miles away from its existing, flood-prone site. The other hospital in the community, located two miles from the new site, opposed the CON authorization on the grounds that the community was already overbedded. After more than three years of hearings and appeals, the legislature passed a law allowing the renovation.

● In Flint, Michigan, a major hospital sought to rebuild an office tower with no change in beds, but a conversion of some beds from general medical/surgical to specialty use. Other hospitals in the community opposed the application, arguing that the community was overbedded, with occupancy rates ranging from 57 to 74 percent. They said other hospitals could handle the patient volume that would arise from the closure of the unrenovated units. The hospital's application indicated that its current (1990) occupancy was 71.8 percent and was expected to rise to 89.5 percent after the renovation. The hospital's application was approved after six months. Said the hospital's CEO, "When you're doing well when others are not, you'll breed some resentment."

● In Alpharatta, Georgia, three hospital systems sought approval to build a new hospital in the affluent suburbs forty miles north of Atlanta. Said an official of the state planning agency, "You're going to have a CON fight over anything that potentially will make big bucks for a hospital."

● In Olympia, Washington, a national chain sought to build a 44-bed rehabilitation hospital. One month later a local hospital submitted a similar CON request. Three other hospitals formally opposed the applications because they already provided an adequate supply of rehabilitation beds. A representative of the state health department observed, "Things have gotten competitive for hospitals. It's not unusual for a hospital to oppose another hospital's CON application."

The certificate of need mechanism serves to prevent or delay the entry of new sources of supply. The empirical evidence suggests that as a result of CON, hospital costs are no lower and may be higher. Prices are higher. The nature of the industry is different. There are fewer investor-owned facilities, and fewer hospitals are in systems or are managed by investor owned chains. In an increasingly price-competitive environment it is difficult to justify such restrictions. Additional capacity means that prices will fall or at least not rise as rapidly. Increasing competition will lead to greater demands by hospitals for the reintroduction of certificate of need and its expansion to nonhospital providers.

Any-Willing-Provider Laws

Background. While there is no available summary of the state legislative history for any-willing-provider laws, it appears that they have come into being in the last five to ten years. The laws first applied to pharmacies; more recently they have been applied to all providers. The advocates of the legislation tend to characterize them as attempts to assure individuals freedom of choice in their selection of providers. They have also been advocated as a mechanism to assure that rural residents will have convenient access to pharmacies or other providers.

The laws are straightforward. An any-willing-provider law is designed to prevent a managed care organization or insurer from excluding providers who are willing to abide by the terms and conditions of the contract. Suppose an insurer or managed care firm enters into a contract with, say, Michael's Pharmacy. The contract specifies that the pharmacy will be the preferred provider of prescription drugs to subscribers of the managed care firm. If a subscriber went to another drugstore, the prescription drugs would not be covered by the insurance plan (or perhaps would be covered only at a higher copayment). The law, however, requires that any pharmacy willing to accept the terms and conditions of the contract must be included as a preferred provider. Thus, the managed care firm can't exclude Elaine's Drug, if it agrees to all the contractual terms.

The rationales for the law appear to be several. First, there is a concern (at least on the part of Elaine's Drug) that consumers' freedom of choice will be restricted. Second, it has been argued that the managed care firm may contract only with large drugstore chains. Rural subscribers of the managed care firm may find that the drugstore in their small town is not a preferred provider, and they will have to travel long distances to obtain medications. Third, it is argued that the managed care firms will, indeed, contract with large drugstore chains and drive the family-owned local pharmacy out of business.

All of these arguments, of course, are designed to protect the Elaine's Drugs of the world from price competition. The key question is why a managed care firm would wish to extend a preferred provider contract to a drugstore. The answer is that the preferred stores offer some acceptable combination of quality, location, and price. The empirical literature examined earlier with respect to HMO contracts with hospitals indicated that HMOs affiliated with hospitals that had "badges of quality," but that patients were directed disproportionately to the affiliated hospitals with the lowest prices.

One would expect the managed care firm to affiliate with pharmacies that, given acceptable quality and location, offered the lowest prices on prescription drugs. The drugstore has an incentive to offer low prices in exchange for a greater volume of business. The preferred status or exclusive contract offers an assurance of increased volume of drug sales. Those that win the contract sell to the managed care firms subscribers. Those that don't, don't.

Any-willing-provider legislation removes the incentive to compete aggressively on a price basis. If Michael's Pharmacy offers a low price, it can no longer be assured of a greater volume. Instead of getting some prescription customers who would have gone to Elaine's and other drugstores, those stores must be included in the network if they are willing to accept the price list to which Michael's agreed. Given this, no one has an incentive to offer much of a discount since discounts will result only in lower prices with little or no expanded volume.

Empirical Evidence. To date, the only studies of any-willing-provider laws pertain to California. Earlier we reviewed the work of Melnick and Zwanziger in the California hospital market. These studies found that after the enactment of state law encouraging managed care firms to exclusively contract, the rate of increase in hospital costs was reduced and was reduced more in communities with more hospitals (Zwanziger and Melnick 1988, Melnick et al. 1992).

Gruber (1992) also examined this hospital market. He examined the 1982-84 and 1984-88 period, extending the time period of the original work by Melnick et al. He studied the change in the percentage discount given to all nongovernmental payers and the change in the net revenues from nongovernmental payers per hospital day. The analysis controlled for hospital ownership, teaching status, the Medicare and Medicaid programs, urban-suburban-rural location, and region of the state. He found that, in the period after the enactment of the selective contracting law, hospitals located in more competitive markets had greater increases in the size of the discounts they provided. The average hospital in Los Angeles County, for example, increased its discount by more than 7 percent more than did the average hospital in less-competitive northern California. Also, average transaction prices rose more slowly in markets with greater hospital competition. Thus, the results were not simply an artifact of hospital strategies to boost list prices in order to grant "discounts" but reflect true price moderation. These studies suggest that any-willing-provider legislation will thwart price competition.

Unfortunately, no other markets have been studied and, therefore, one may question whether these results reflect the true and full effects of price competition spurred by the absence of any-willing-provider legislation or something unique to California. Morrisey (1994), which examines national hospital discounting data, suggests that the effect is more than a California effect. This study, however, is by no means definitive.

Current Actions. As of June 1994, some fourteen states had any-willing-provider laws that applied to pharmacies. See Table 7.3. An additional eight states have enacted laws that apply to all providers. Illinois has enacted an any-willing-provider law that applies only to physicians and chiropractors, and Minnesota has enacted one that applies only to allied health practitioners.

Any-willing-provider laws have taken a variety of forms. Those we have described relate to a willingness to accept all the terms and conditions of the contract. Others, which Loss et al. (1994) refer to as "freedom of choice" laws, restrict or eliminate the right of insurers to narrow a subscriber's selection of providers in return for a discount.

The Alabama law passed in the closing moments of the 1994 legislature exemplifies a freedom of choice law. It stipulates that nonpar-

TABLE 7.3

Status of Any-Willing-Provider Legislation, 1994

State	Any-Willing-Provider Law	Freedom of Choice Law
AL	yes - _	yes - _
AR	yes - _	
CT	yes - _	yes - _
DE	yes - _	
FL	yes - _	
GA		yes - _
ID	yes – all	
IL	yes - m,c	
IN	yes – all	
IA		yes - _
KS	yes - _	
KY	yes – all	
LA	yes - _	yes - _
MD		yes - _
MN	yes – allied	
MS	yes - _	yes - _
NH	yes – all	
NJ	yes - _	yes - _
NC	yes - _	
ND	yes - _	yes - _
OK		yes - _
RI		yes - _
SC	yes - _	
SD	yes - _	
TN		yes - _
TX		yes - _
UT	yes – all	
VA	yes – all	yes - _
WA	yes – all	
WI	yes - _	
WY	yes – all	

SOURCE: Blue Cross and Blue Shield Association (Loss et al. 1994).

_	Applies to pharmacy only.
all	Applies to all providers.
m	Applies to physicians only.
c	Applies to chiropractors only.
allied	Applies to allied practitioners only.

ticipating providers who choose not to contract with insurers can be assured of the same payment rates as the participating providers who have signed contracts. What's more, noncontract providers are reserved the right to bill the patient for the difference between their usual charge and the contract price (Capilouto and Morrisey 1994). Under these conditions, who would ever contract?

As part of the 1994 health care reform efforts at the federal level, there were proposals to guarantee the inclusion of specific types of hospitals. These can be viewed as prototypes of legislation that will be proposed at the state level. Efforts to include "essential community providers," academic health centers, children's hospitals, rural health facilities, or county health departments are the equivalent of selective any-willing-provider statutes. Such laws will potentially preclude managed care firms from negotiating with these providers on the basis of price. Also, to the extent that subscribers use these facilities, they deny volume to other providers who, arguably, would have offered lower prices for the higher volumes.

The move to protect providers from potential price competition continued during 1994. Loss et al. (1994) report that seven states defeated all-provider any-willing-provider laws and another nine had bills under consideration. Eleven states had "freedom of choice" bills defeated or pending. Given the rise of managed care and the spread of price competition in health care, these defeated laws almost certainly will be back, with even greater support from provider groups.

State Mandated Benefits Laws

Background. Another form of state regulation likely to be expanded relates to state insurance mandates. All states regulate the sale of insurance. Historically, these laws related to minimum reserve requirements, sales practices and the like and were designed to assure that consumers were not mislead and that sufficient assets would be available to pay claims. In some states, the insurance commissioner also must be notified of premium changes or approve them. The states also tax policies sold in the state, many assessing higher taxes on insurance firms headquartered outside the state.

In the health insurance market all states have passed laws defining the coverages that must be included in policies sold within the state. These are state-mandated-benefit laws. They fall into three general categories. First are mandates for coverage of specific illnesses, conditions, and services, including pregnancy, alcohol abuse, mammography screening, and *in vitro* fertilization. Second are mandates that require coverage for specific types of providers, including chiropractors and psychologists. Third are mandates for coverages for specific categories of enrollees, for example, adopted children. Restrictions on preexisting conditions and continuation coverage also fit in this category. In addition to mandated benefits are mandated option laws. These require only that the insurer offer to include the benefit in the insurance package. The client, however, may decline to accept it.

The effects of these provisions depend upon the precise nature of the legislation. All policies sold in the state must provide the coverage. Once covered, *in vitro* services, for example, are subject to a copay, which lowers their effective price; more people use the care or use it longer. Coverage of psychologists' or podiatrists' services lowers the out-of-pocket prices of their care as well as their prices relative to psychiatrists and orthopedic surgeons. A continuation-of-coverage mandate provides for insurance when someone changes jobs. It keeps

FIGURE 7.2

Growth in State Mandated Benefit Laws

Number of Mandates

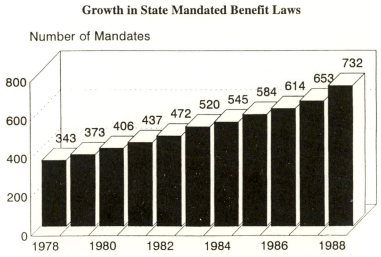

Source: Gabel and Jensen [1989]

the out-of-pocket prices for medical care low at a time when an unemployed worker may have more time to seek care. Figure 7.2 demonstrates the growth of state insurance mandates between 1978 and 1988.

The states have also used insurance regulation to attempt to provide health insurance coverage to the uninsured and the uninsurable. Typically, the state creates an insurance fund or pool from which the uninsured or uninsurable can buy coverage at a reduced rate. Since the rates are below those existing in the private market for equivalent coverage and risk, the insurance funds almost certainly will lose money. If these loses are not covered by the state general fund (directly or indirectly through state tax credits to insurers incurring risk pool loses), they are paid for by premium taxes (GAO 1988).

Employers have avoided many of these states' laws, however, by self-insuring. The Employee Retirement Income Security Act of 1974 (ERISA) exempts self-insured firms from state insurance regulation. Thus, if a firm is self-insured it is not subject to state minimum reserve requirements, state premium taxes, or state insurance mandates. Many large, medium, and small sized firms have adopted self-insurance.

Ironically, ERISA may have caused the proliferation of state insurance mandates. One of the most effective forces opposing providers in state politics is likely to be large employers. To the extent that the workers in a firm do not particularly value a proposed mandated benefit, the firm would exert some political effort to defeat that law. ERISA, however, gives the firm a low-cost alternative to fighting proposed mandates. As more firms self insure, they take themselves out of the political market on mandated benefits. As provider groups have fewer organized opponents, more mandates are passed, and smaller firms increasingly seek to avoid the mandates by self-insuring.

This process is important because recent efforts at state reform have called for either the repeal of the ERISA exemption or a waiver for the state to experiment with various reforms. Given the large number of existing state benefit mandates, the enactment of a waiver or the elimination of the ERISA exemption will increase the demand for services of providers.

Empirical Evidence. The research on state insurance mandates is rather sparse. It has established that the mandated benefits tend to be expensive and raise insurance premiums. There is some evidence that the decision to offer individual coverages is affected by the existence of state benefit mandates and that firms have self-insured to avoid the mandates.

Recent research demonstrates that mandated benefits add substantially to the cost of employer-sponsored health insurance costs (Dyckman and Anderson-Johnson 1989, Jensen and Morrisey 1990, and Frank et al. 1991). Jensen and Morrisey looked at the group insurance premiums per worker paid through medium and large firms from 1981 through 1984. Substance abuse coverage increased family premiums by 8.8 percent, psychiatric hospital coverage by 12.8 percent, and psychologist coverage by 11.8 percent, controlling for other factors.

There is little evidence that state insurance mandates have led firms not to offer or to drop health insurance coverage. Initial work by Jensen and Gabel (1992) suggested substantial effects in the small-employer market. However, these effects were an artifact of erroneous state mandate data. When estimated with better data, the effects lose statistical significance (Jensen, personal communication). Gruber's (1994) analysis of state-mandated maternity coverage also failed to find effects on the overall decision to offer coverage. Instead, he finds that wages fall to reflect the full cost of the state laws.

There is some evidence that individual mandates affect the provision of individual coverages offered by employers. Morrisey and Jensen (1993) examined substance abuse and mental health mandates. The results indicated that state mandates reduced the probability that a firm provided outpatient mental health coverage. No statistically significant effects were found with respect to alcohol, drug abuse, or inpatient mental health mandates, however. Further, there appeared to be spillover effects. As the total number of mandates in a state increased, a firm was less likely to offer specific coverages. The mechanism generating these results was asserted to be self-insurance. A self-insured firm may or may not offer a mandated benefit. However, as the number of mandates increase, the firm is alleged to become self-insured and use its new discretion to not offer the coverage. The relationship between self-insurance and the offering of a specific coverage was the strongest finding. Controlling for other factors, including firm size, a self insured firm was nearly 30 percent less likely to offer alcohol (or drug abuse or inpatient mental health) coverage and over 44 percent less likely to offer outpatient mental health coverage.

Firms have increasingly turned to self-insurance. Jensen et al. (1988) estimated that only 15 percent of workers with basic hospital coverage were covered through a self-insured plan. Piacentini and Foley (1992) report that in 1986, 46 percent of employers had self-insured plans; by 1991, 65 percent.

Jensen, Cotter and Morrisey (1995) found that the decision to self-insure is tied to the extent of state mandated benefits and state premium taxes. We examined the periods 1981-1984/5 and 1984-87, using two different sets of employers. We sought to determine whether the decision to switch from conventional coverage to self-insured coverage depended upon state insurance regulations. We found that in the earlier period two-thirds of new conversions could be attributed to state insurance regulations. There was no statistically significant effect in the later period. This was attributed to compositional changes. Legislative enactment of large numbers of mandates began in the late

1970s. In response, firms that had the most to gain from avoiding state regulations converted to self-insurance. As mandates and premium taxes grew, firms that were less well-suited to self-insurance, nonetheless, converted. By the later 1980s additional mandates had little or no effect on conversions. By 1991, 81 percent of firms with 40,000 or more workers self-insured. Amazingly, 41 percent of firms with less than 500 did too (Piacentini and Foley 1992).

Current Action. The existing research suggests that additional state benefit mandates will have a negligible effect on the decision to self-insure and a limited effect on the costs of providing insurance coverage to workers. But this reading of the evidence would be a myopic. If employers switched early to avoid state insurance regulation, they expected significant cost advantages from doing so. If *these firms* are now subjected to either all of these mandates or to new state mandates designed to expand insurance coverage to the uninsured, their costs will increase significantly, and wages paid to currently employed workers will fall.

The states are currently seeking either outright repeal of the ERISA waivers or waivers to allow experimentation. Such waivers would allow experimentation with new options to expand insurance coverage to the uninsured.

● The Employee Benefit Research Institute (1994) reported (before the election) that the "battle lines are being drawn between multistate and other employers that self-insure and individual states that will seek exemptions from the ERISA. For example, Sen. Patty Murray (D-WA) on October 5th introduced a bill to obtain an ERISA waiver for the state of Washington. In an attempt to fend off moves by lawmakers to push for state flexibility in health reform, (outgoing) Sen. Dave Durenberger (R-MN) has distributed a 'Dear Colleague' letter that warns against ERISA peremption exemptions."

● "State policymakers attending a conference sponsored jointly by the Henry J. Kaiser Family Foundation and the IHPP (Intergovernmental Health Policy Project) on September 27 and 28 singled out the ERISA as the make-or-break factor in their efforts to forge ahead with health care reform. At the meeting...attendees warned that without a change in the federal ERISA statute, state initiatives will fall flat, as a growing number of businesses leave the regulated insurance market and opt to self-insure their employees" (IHPP 1994).

● Six states are covered by ERISA waiver legislation proposed by Bob Graham (D-FL) and Mark Hatfield (R-OR). Maryland, Hawaii, New York, Oregon, Washington, and Connecticut would be given permission to continue or to launch alternative health care reform systems. The bill would set a ninety-day limit on Department of Health and Human Services and Department of Labor review of ERISA waiver applications (Medicine and Health 1994).

The turnover in state governorships and legislatures in 1994 elections may slow the push for ERISA waivers. However, the underlying demands have not changed. The push of managed care and the desire to experiment at the state level with mechanisms to provide coverage for the uninsured will continue to lead providers to seek waivers allowing state employer mandates.

Summary and Conclusions

The last decade has witnessed remarkable change in the health care industry. Health maintenance and preferred provider organizations have quietly grown. These plans now enroll substantial proportions of the population in many communities. Together with this growth has come much greater emphasis on the price of health care services as well as their availability and quality, shifting the focus of competition from services, quality, and amenities to services, quality, amenities, and price. Hospitals, physicians, pharmacists and others are discovering that managed care firms are affiliating with only selected providers and then channeling patient volume based upon price. Consequently, some providers see fewer patients, some have empty waiting rooms, and some close entire units of their facilities.

I have reviewed the empirical literature on the emergence of price competition in health care. This research finds that the introduction of price competition has reduced both the rate of increase in hospital costs in more competitive markets and, more recently, the level of hospital costs. It has also demonstrated that the usual industrial organization models of markets apply. With more providers in the market, negotiated prices are lower; with excess capacity in the markets, lower still. The price elasticity of managed care firms, at least with respect to hospital admissions, is remarkably high. A 5 percent increase in price is associated with a 15 percent reduction in admissions by a staff or network model HMO.

Providers have turned to the government to protect their markets or expand the demand for their services. State governments have responded. Hence, the reemergence of certificate-of-need programs, the enactment of any-willing-provider laws, and the attempts to remove the ERISA exemption for self-insured firms.

The rather exhaustive literature on CON yields virtually no evidence that it has controlled health care costs. However, it has kept hospital "profits" high and restricted the entry of new hospitals, hospital systems, and contract management firms. Since the mid-1980s, when a number of states eliminated CON laws, two states have reintroduced the program. Several others have delayed or eliminated the sunset provision of their CON programs, and others have expanded their scope. In an era of price competition, these laws are hard to justify; they are simply barriers to the restructuring of the market.

The most recent development in state health care regulation has been the development of any-willing-provider laws, which limit the ability of insurance companies or managed care firms to enter into contracts with selected providers. They require that the firm accept any provider willing to abide by the terms of the contract. This innocuous-sounding provision seriously damages price competition in health care. A provider is willing to offer a price concession to a managed care firm in exchange for the assurance of a greater volume of patients. Given an any-willing-provider law, greater volume cannot be expected. Other providers simply match the price. Thus, price cuts only reduce revenue, and therefore no one has an incentive to make them. Thirty-one states have enacted some form of any-willing-provider law, most relating only to pharmacies. However, nine cover all providers. Many state legislatures received proposals for such laws in their last session, and undoubtedly more will appear.

Many states require that health insurance plans include coverage for specified illnesses and treatments, types of providers, and categories of subscribers. Employers have avoided many of these laws by self-insuring under the provisions of ERISA. However, by taking themselves out of the state political process on these issues they have allowed provider interests to dominate. By one count, there were 854 such mandates in the states by 1990. Many states are now calling for an end to the ERISA exemption or at least a waiver to allow them to expand health insurance coverage to the uninsured or the uninsurable. A waiver or a repeal would allow states to tax self-insured health insurance plans to expand coverage to the uninsured. It would potentially also expose self-insured employers and their workers to all of the mandated benefits they have avoided under ERISA.

A cloud surrounds every silver lining. The growth of managed care promises to create more price competition in health care, but state regulatory efforts cloud the prospect.

References

Alexander, Jeffrey A., and Michael A. Morrisey. 1988. "Hospital Selection in Multihospital Systems." *Medical Care* 26(2):159-176 (February).

Alexander, Jeffrey A., and Michael A. Morrisey. 1989. "A Resource-Dependence Model of Hospital Contract Management." *Health Services Research* 24(2):259-284 (June).

Antel, John J., Robert L. Ohsfeldt, and Edmund R. Becker. 1995. "State Regulation and Hospital Costs." *Review of Economics and Statistics.*

Ashby, John L. 1984. "The Impact of Hospital Regulatory Programs on Per Capital Costs, Utilization, and Capital Investment." *Inquiry* 21:45-59 (spring).

American Hospital Association. 1992. "Certificate of Need (CON): Back to the Future?" *State Issues Forum* no. 8, (October).

Burda, David. 1991. "CONspiracies to Crush Competition." *Modern Healthcare* 21(27):28-30, 32-4, 36 (July 8).

Campbell, Ellen S., and Gary M. Fournier. 1993. "Certificate-of-Need Deregulation and Indigent Hospital Care." *Journal of Health Politics, Policy and Law* 18(4):905-926 (winter).

Capilouto, Eli and Michael A. Morrisey. 1994. "Here's How to Keep Health Care Expensive." *Birmingham News* (May 29): B1.

Coelen, Craig, and D. Sullivan. 1980. "An Analysis of the Effects of Prospective Reimbursement Programs on Hospital Expenditures." *Health Care Financing Review* 2:1-40.

Cone, Kenneth R., and David Dranove. 1986. "Why Did State Enact Hospital Rate-Setting Laws?" *Journal of Law and Economics* 29(2):287-302 (October).

Cromwell, Jerry, and J. Kanak. 1982. "The Effects of Prospective Reimbursement Programs on Hospital Adoption and Service Sharing." *Health Care Financing Review* 4(2):67-88.

Dyckman, Zachary, and Judy Anderson-Johnson. 1989. "The Cost of Mandated Health Insurance Benefits: The Maryland Experience." American Public Health Association convention (October).

Employee Benefit Research Institute. 1994. "Health Reform." *EBRI's Washington Bulletin* 6(20):1 (October 7).

Fanara, Philip, and Warren Greenberg. 1985. "Factors Affecting the Adoption of Prospective Reimbursement Programs by State Governments," in Jack A. Meyer, ed. *Incentives vs. Controls in Health Policy*. Washington, DC: American Enterprise Institute, pp. 144-56.

Feldman, Roger, Michael Finch, Byron Dowd, and S. Cassou. 1989. "The Demand for Employment-Based Health Insurance Plans." *Journal of Human Resources* 24:115-42.

Feldman, Roger, Hung-Ching Chan, John Kralewski, Byron Dowd, and Janet Shapiro. 1990. "Effects of HMOs on the Creation of Competitive Markets for Hospital Services." *Journal of Health Economics* 9(3): 207-22 (September).

Feldstein, Paul. 1977. *Health Associations and the Demand for Legislation*. Cambridge, MA: Ballinger Publishing Co.

Feldstein, Paul. 1988. *The Politics of Health Legislation*. Ann Arbor, MI: Health Administration Press.

Feldstein, Paul, and Glenn Melnick. 1984. "Congressional Voting Behavior on Hospital Legislation: An Exploratory Study." *Journal of Health Politics, Policy and Law* 8(4):686-701 (winter).

Ford, Jon M., and David L. Kaserman. 1993. "Certificate-of-Need Regulation and Entry: Evidence from the Dialysis Industry." *Southern Economic Journal* 59:783-91 (April 1).

Frank, Richard G., David S. Salkever, and Stephen S. Sharfstein. 1991. "A Look at Rising Mental Health Insurance Costs." *Health Affairs* 10:116-123.

Frech III, H. E. 1976. "The Property Rights Theory of the Firm: Empirical Results from a Natural Experiment." *Journal of Political Economy* 84:143-152 (February).

Gabel, Jon, and Gail A. Jensen. 1989. "The Price of State Mandated Benefits." *Inquiry* 26:419-31.

General Accounting Office. 1988. *Risk Pools for the Medically Uninsurable.* GAO/HRD-88-66BR (April).

Greene, Jay. 1994. "Miss. Links CON, Community Benefit." *Modern Healthcare* 24(13):22 (March 23).

Gruber, Jonathan. 1992 "The Effect of Price Shopping in Medical Markets: Hospital Responses to PPOs in California." National Bureau of Economic Research, working paper 4190 (New York, October).

Gruber, Jonathan. 1994. "The Incidence of Mandated Maternity Benefits." *American Economic Review* 84(3):622-41.

Havighurst, Clark C. 1980. *Deregulating the Health Care Industry: Planning for Competition.* Cambridge, MA: Ballinger Publishing.

Intergovernmental Health Policy Project. 1991. "Certificate of Need: Taking a New Look at an Old Program." *State Health Notes* 114:1-2, 6 (June).

Intergovernmental Health Policy Project. 1994. "ERISA Still a Sticking Point; State Officials Lament Its Impact." *State Health Notes* 15(190):2 (October 17).

Jee, Melissa. "Certificate of Need Laws Back in Style Again." *Journal of American Health Policy* 3(2):59-60.

Jensen, Gail A., Kevin D. Cotter, and Michael A. Morrisey. 1995. "State Insurance Regulation and the Decision to Self Insure." *Journal of Risk and Insurance.*

Jensen, Gail A., and Jon R. Gabel. 1992. "State Mandated Benefits and the Small Firm's Decision to Offer Health Insurance." *Journal of Regulatory Economics* 4(4):379-404.

Jensen, Gail A., and Michael A. Morrisey. 1990. "Group Health Insurance: An Hedonic Approach." *Review of Economics and Statistics* 72(1):38-44.

Jensen, Gail A., Michael A. Morrisey, and John W. Marcus. 1987. "Cost Sharing and the Changing Pattern of Employer Sponsored Health Insurance." *Milbank Quarterly* 65:521-50.

Joskow, Paul L. 1981. *Controlling Hospital Costs: The Role of Government Regulation.* Cambridge, MA: The MIT Press.

Joskow, Paul L. 1980. "The Effects of Competition and Regulation on Hospital Bed Supply and the Reservation Quality of the Hospital." *Bell Journal of Economics* 11(2):421-47.

Lambert, David A., and Thomas G. McGuire. 1990. "Political and Economic Determinants of Insurance Regulation in Mental Health." *Journal of Health Politics, Policy and Law* 15(1):169-89 (spring).

Lanning, Joyce A., Michael A. Morrisey, and Robert L. Ohsfeldt. 1991. "Endogenous Regulation and Its Effects on Hospital and Non-hospital Expenditures." *Journal of Regulatory Economics* 3(2):137-54.

Lewin/ICF and Alpha Center. 1991. *Evaluation of the Ohio Certificate of Need Program.* Washington, DC: Lewin/ICF (June 28).

Long, Stephen, Russ F. Settle, and C. W. Wrightson. 1988. "Employee Premiums, Availability of Alternative Plans, and HMO Disenrollment." *Medical Care* 26:927-38.

Loss, Ira S., Laura E. Miller, and Kelly M. Baldrate. 1994. "HMOs and the Threat of 'Any Willing Provider' Statutes." *Health Care* (June 28).

Margolis, Robin Elizabeth. 1992. "Competitors Can Take Advantage of Certificate of Need Proceedings, Rules 9th Circuit." *HealthSpan* 9(4):22-23 (April).

Marion Merrell Dow. 1993. *Managed Care Digest.* Kansas City, MO.

Marion Merrell Dow. 1994. *Managed Care Digest: HMO Edition.* Kansas City, MO.

McCarthy, Thomas R., and David I. Kass. 1983. "The Effect of Certificate of Need Regulation on Investor-Owned Hospital Market Share." Paper presented at the American Economic Association annual convention, San Francisco, CA (December).

Medicine and Health. "Lawmakers Offer Six ERISA Waivers," vol. 48, no. 38, p. 2 (September).

Melnick, Glenn A., John R. C. Wheeler, and Paul J. Feldstein. 1981. "Effects of Rate Regulation on Selected Components of Hospital Expenses." *Inquiry* 18:240-46 (fall).

Melnick, Glenn, and Jacl Zwanziger. 1988. "Hospital Behavior Under Competition and Cost Containment Policies." *Journal of the American Medical Association* 260(18):2669-75 (November 11).

Melnick, Glenn A., Jack Zwanziger, Anil Bamezai, and Robert Pattison. 1992. "The Effects of Market Structure and Bargaining Position on Hospital Prices." *Journal of Health Economics* 11(3):217-33 (October).

Misek, Glen I., and Roger A. Reynolds. 1982. "Effects of Regulation on the Hospital Industry." *Quarterly Review of Economics and Business* 22(3):66-80 (Autumn).

Morrisey, Michael A. 1994. *Cost Shifting in Health Care: Separating Evidence from Rhetoric.* Washington, DC: AEI Press.

Morrisey, Michael A. 1991. *Price Sensitivity in Health Care: Implications for Health Care Policy.* Washington, DC: National Federation of Independent Business Foundation.

Morrisey, Michael A., and Gail A. Jensen. 1993. "State Mandates, Self-Insurance, and Employer Demand for Substance Abuse and Mental Health Insurance Coverage." *Advances in Health Economics and Health Services Research* 14:209-224.

Morrisey, Michael A., Robert L. Ohsfeldt, and Elaine Asper. 1992. *The Effects of CON Repeal on Medicaid Nursing Home Expenditures* final report to the Alabama Medicaid Agency, Montgomery, AL (August 31).

Morrisey, Michael A., Frank A. Sloan, and Samuel A. Mitchell. 1983. "State Rate Setting: An Analysis of Some Unresolved Issues." *Health Affairs* 2(2):36-47 (July).

Mueller, Keith J. 1986. "An Analysis of Congressional Health Policy Voting in the 1970s." *Journal of Health Politics, Policy and Law* 11(1):117-136 (spring).

Mullner, Ross, and Jack Hadley. 1984. "Interstate Variations in the Growth of Chain-Owned Proprietary Hospitals, 1973-1982." *Inquiry* 21:144-51.

Noether, Monica. 1988. "Competition Among Hospitals." *Journal of Health Economics* 7(3):259-84 (September).

Peltzman, Sam. 1976. "Toward a More General Theory of Regulation." *Journal of Law and Economics* 19(2):211-40 (October).

Piacentini, Joseph S., and Jill D. Foley. 1992. *Source Book of Health Insurance Data – 1992.* Washington, DC.

Policy Analysis, Inc -Urban Systems Research and Engineering, Inc. 1974. *Evaluating the Effects of Certificate of Need Programs, Final Report.* Washington, DC (August).

Posner, Richard A. 1974. "Theories of Economic Regulation." *Bell Journal of Economics and Management Science* 5(2):335-58 (Autumn).

Robinson, James C., and Harold S. Luft. 1985. "The Impact of Hospital Market Structure on Patient Volume, Average Length of Stay and the Cost of Care." *Journal of Health Economics* 4(4):333-57 (December).

Roemer, Milton I., and Michael Shain. 1959. *Hospital Utilization Under Insurance.* Chicago: American Hospital Association.

Russell, Louise B. 1979. *Technology in Hospitals: Medical Advances and Their Diffusion.* Washington, DC: Brookings Institution.

Salkever, David S., and Thomas W. Bice. 1979. *Hospital Certificate of Need Controls: Impact on Investment, Costs, and Use.* Washington: American Enterprise Institute.

Salkever, David S., and Thomas W. Bice. 1979. "The Impact of Certificate of Need Controls on Hospital Investment." *Milbank Memorial Fund Quarterly* 54 (spring): pp. 185-214.

Sherman, Daniel. 1988. *The Effect of State Certificate-of-Need Laws On Hospital Costs: An Economic Policy Analysis.* Washington: Federal Trade Commission Staff Report (January).

Simpson, James B. 1985. "State Certificate-of-Need programs: The Current Status." *American Journal of Public Health* 75(10):1225-1229 (October).

Sloan, Frank A. 1988. "Containing Health Expenditures: Lessons Learned from Certificate-of-Need Programs," in Frank A. Sloan, James F. Blumstein, and James M. Perrin, eds. *Cost, Quality and Access in Health Care: New Roles for Health Planning in a Competitive Environment,* pp. 44-70. San Francisco: Jossey-Bass Publishers.

Sloan, Frank A. 1983. "Rate Regulation as a Strategy for Hospital Cost Control: Evidence from the Last Decade." *Milbank Memorial Fund Quarterly* 61(2):195-2321.

Sloan, Frank A. 1981. "Regulation and the Rising Cost of Hospital Care," *Review of Economics and Statistics* 63(4):479-87 (November).

Sloan, Frank A., Michael A. Morrisey, and Joseph Valvona. 1988. "Effects of the Medicare Prospective Payment System on Hospital Cost Containment: An Early Appraisal." *Milbank Quarterly* 66(2):191-220.

Sloan, Frank A., James M. Perrin, Joseph Valvona, and Killard Adamache. 1986. "Diffusion of Surgical Technology: An Exploratory Study." *Journal of Health Economics* 5(1):31-61 (1986).

Sloan, Frank A., and Bruce Steinwald. 1980a. "Effects of Regulation on Hospital Costs and Input Use." *Journal of Law and Economics* 23: 81-109 (April).

Sloan, Frank A., and Bruce Steinwald. 1980b. *Insurance, Regulation and Hospital Costs.* Lexington, MA: Lexington Books.

Snider, Sarah, and Sarah Boyce. 1994. "Sources of Health Insurance and Characteristics of the Uninsured." *EBRI Special Report and Issue Brief,* no. 145. Washington, DC: Employee Benefit Research Institute (January).

Steinwald, Bruce, and Frank A. Sloan. 1981. "Regulatory Approaches to Hospital Cost Containment," in Mancur Olsen, ed., *A New Approach to the Economics of Health Care,* pp. 274-308. Washington: American Enterprise Institute.

Stigler, George J. 1988. *Chicago Studies in Political Economy.* Chicago: University of Chicago Press.

Stigler, George J. 1971. "The Theory of Economic Regulation." *Bell Journal of Economics and Management Science,* 2(1):1-21 (spring).

Sussman, David. 1989. "Humana Group Division May Leave Kentucky in Spat Over CON Law." *Managed HealthCare* (November):19.

Welch, W. Peter. 1986. "The Elasticity of Demand for Health Maintenance Organizations." *Journal of Human Resources* 21:252-66.

Wendling, Wayne, and Jack Werner. 1980. "Nonprofit Firms and the Economic Theory of Regulation." *Quarterly Review of Economics and Business* 20(3):6-18 (autumn).

Zwanziger, Jack, and Glenn A. Melnick. 1988. "The Effects of Hospital Competition and the Medicare PPS Program on Hospital Cost Behavior in California." *Journal of Health Economics* 7(4):301-20 (December).

Zwanziger, Jack, Glenn A. Melnick, and Anil Bamezai. 1993. "California Providers Adjust to Increasing Price Competition," in Robert B. Helms, ed. *Health Policy Reform: Competition and Controls,* pp. 241-58. Washington, DC: AEI Press.

Part III

Drugs and Medication

8

Regulation of the Pharmaceutical Industry

Ronald W. Hansen

In the recent debates over health reform, the pharmaceutical industry has been the subject of much criticism. Although pharmaceuticals represent only 8 percent of total health care expenditures, pharmaceutical firms represent some of the largest individual suppliers of health products. Official reports indicating that pharmaceutical prices rose faster than most other health care prices during the 1980s and recent introductions of new products at prices that seem high by historical standards have drawn additional attention to prices and profits in the industry. Despite the growth of HMOs and other comprehensive health plans, outpatient pharmaceuticals remain one of the major health care services that are paid directly by patients. Even though pharmaceuticals are a relatively minor part of the total expenditures on health services, they often represent the single largest direct expenditure for individuals. It is not surprising therefore that the pharmaceutical sector has been singled out as a potential source for cost savings either through price controls or formulary restrictions.

Even without major health care reform legislation from Congress, the pharmaceutical marketplace like many other segments of the health care sector is undergoing major changes. Despite the best efforts of some groups to hold back the tides, these marketplace changes will continue to have a major impact on the conduct and performance of the pharmaceutical industry. The locus of decision-making in pharmaceutical markets has changed. While physicians continue to play a key role in selecting pharmaceuticals for their patients, pharmaceutical utilization decisions are increasingly being influenced by health care administrators. HMOs and other plans with pharmaceutical reimbursements often employ formularies that restrict the choice of pharmaceuticals or have provisions that encourage the utilization of less expensive or generic products. Several firms have faced the choice of either giving an HMO deep discounts or dealing with the prospect of being excluded from the formulary. These changes have shifted the focus of pharmaceutical marketing from an almost exclusive focus on medical effectiveness to more consideration of cost-effectiveness. Thus the existing and projected changes in the health care marketplace will exert considerable influence on the research and development investment decisions by pharmaceutical firms.

In the midst of all the changes in the pharmaceutical marketplace, firms must also be concerned about the regulatory environment that affects their ability to generate new products for the evolving marketplace. Pharmaceutical research and development remains one of the most heavily regulated industrial activities. All pharmaceuticals must be approved by the Food and Drug Administration (FDA) prior to marketing. The FDA's influence extends to the research and development process leading up to a marketing approval as well as to the manufacturing of the product and the marketing claims which the firms can make. The FDA policies determine which potential technologies are available, affect the cost of developing those technologies, and at least indirectly influence the research areas pursued by the pharmaceutical industry.

Regulation of Pharmaceutical Products

The federal government's role in regulating the pharmaceutical industry began with the 1906 Pure Food and Drugs Act. Adulteration of food was the primary focus of the bill and the Department of Agriculture was responsible for enforcing the provisions of the Act. Of the first 1,000 notices of judgment issued by the Department's Bureau of Chemistry prior to August 1911, over three-quarters were for food violations (Wardell and Lasagna 1975). The Act focused on proper labeling, not advertising. In 1911, the Supreme Court ruled that therapeutic claims were not covered by the provisions prohibiting false and misleading claims. False and fraudulent claims in patent medicine were banned by the tougher Sherley amendment in 1912. Even with this act the court subsequently ruled that if the seller believed his therapeutic claims, then there was no case of fraud, thus greatly limiting the government control of drugs.

Prior to the 1930s, most of the drugs were derived from plant materials. The Agriculture Department's concern was primarily with the quality of the derived product and its labeling. The 1930s witnessed the development of the sulfa drugs. After the Elixir Sulfanilamide tragedy in 1937, the Food, Drug, and Cosmetics Act of 1938 was passed which required that firms demonstrate to the FDA that their products were safe prior to market.

The wonder drugs of the early post World War II period sparked the growth of the modern pharmaceutical industry, complete with an emphasis on research, development, and promotion of new products. This resulted in concern about controlling the promotion and usage of these more powerful drugs. The Humphrey-Durham amendment in 1951 codified the distinction between prescription-only and non-prescription drugs.

As the modern pharmaceutical industry continued to expand, so did the criticism of the industry. In December 1959, Senator Estes Kefauver, chair of the Subcommittee on Antitrust and Monopoly, opened hearings on the drug industry that extended over twenty-six months. In the course of these hearings, critics claimed which firms engaged in excessive and unsubstantiated promotion, earned excessive profits, and spent too much on "me-too" innovation. The massive legislation that grew out of these hearings nearly died in Congress. However, the occurrence of the thalidomide tragedy focused attention on the potential for harm from the new pharmaceuticals and revived interest in strengthening the regulation of the pharmaceutical industry. Although many of Kefauver's proposals were shelved, the Congress unanimously passed the revised Kefauver-Harris bill in 1962 (Lasagna, 1989).

The legislation, which is referred to as the 1962 Amendments to the Food, Drug, and Cosmetics Act, is a major milestone in the history of pharmaceutical regulation. One principal feature of the act was to require firms to wait for FDA approval prior to marketing. (The previous law required them to submit evidence of safety to the FDA and then they could begin marketing if the FDA did not object.) Another central feature was the efficacy requirement, which required firms to demonstrate that their product was efficacious for all the claimed indications. Although we often use the language that a product is approved for marketing, in fact it is only approved for sale for specific claims. If firms wish to broaden their claimed indications, they must file a supplemental new drug application (NDA) and submit evidence to support these claims.

Simultaneously with the new amendments, the FDA began regulating clinical trials. Prior to testing new drug candidates in humans, firms must file an IND (Investigational New Drug Exemption). To obtain approval of an IND, firms must submit evidence of the drug candidate's safety. Since most new drug candidates are new chemical entities (NCEs) which have not been used by humans, this evidence consists largely of data from animal trials. The firm must also submit its clinical testing protocols including evidence that only human subjects who give informed consent will be test subjects.

Through this mechanism which is designed to protect human subjects and its GLP (Good Laboratory Practices) regulations, the FDA exerts considerable control over the conduct of clinical trials. This is in sharp contrast to the pre-1962 period in which FDA involvement usually began when the firm submitted its application to market a product.

The clinical trial stage is usually described as occurring in three phases, progressing from relatively short term trials in Phase I, which are usually designed to show safety in healthy volunteers, to initial trials in patients in Phase II, and finally to the large-scale clinical trials in Phase III, which are designed to demonstrate efficacy as well as to provide further evidence of safety. When the firm gathers evidence it deems to be sufficient to demonstrate safety and efficacy, it files a new drug application (NDA) with the FDA. On average this occurs approximately six years after the beginning of clinical trials. The FDA reviews the NDA. Approval of an NDA typically requires thirty months. Depending on the nature of the drug candidate, the clinical trials may extend into the NDA review phase.

Regulation does not end with the approval of an NDA. The GMP (Good Manufacturing Practices) regulations provide standards for the manufacture of products. The FDA also monitors the promotional efforts of pharmaceutical firms. Firms can only make claims about their product which have been approved by the FDA and they are also required to supply information on possible adverse effects. In some cases, the pharmaceutical firm and the FDA spend a lot of effort negotiating the language, which can be used in promotional efforts.

The 1984 Drug Price Competition and Patent Term Restoration Act clarified the requirements for firms to obtain generic versions of products whose patents expired while simultaneously providing for some extension of patents based on regulatory review times. Although this act had little effect on the manner in which new pharmaceuticals were regulated, it has had a major impact on the pharmaceutical marketplace and on the FDA's workload. Applications for generic approvals virtually overwhelmed the FDA staff and resulted in serious questions about the FDA's ability to conduct its other functions. This was in part responsible for the initiation of a NDA filing fee that is supposed to provide supplemental funding for FDA's review of NCE NDAs.

Lately, there has been considerable concern about unapproved uses of pharmaceuticals and the possible role of firms in promoting these uses. As noted earlier, when the FDA approves a new pharmaceutical, it specifies the claims or uses that are approved. Often a pharmaceutical product may have other potential uses. In some cases the firm may have been aware of the potential uses during the clinical trial stage, but either chose not to invest the additional resources necessary to demonstrate those uses or was unable to obtain FDA approval for those claims. Other times these uses are discovered only after the product has been approved. Firms may choose to conduct additional clinical trials and file a supplemental NDA to broaden the claimed uses. If the patent has expired, or is about to expire, the firm may have little incentive to finance these additional tests. (It does receive three years exclusivity for marketing these claims, but often it is hard to monitor or enforce.) Physicians often become aware of these unapproved uses either through articles in medical journals or through less formal sources. The FDA cannot prevent physicians from prescribing drugs for unapproved uses, however, liability concerns or managed health care oversight may prevent physicians from doing so. At the FDA, concern has arisen about the role of the pharmaceutical firms in sponsoring clinical trials on additional uses (but not filing a supplemental NDA) or in disseminating the published articles.

Although the statutory authority has remained relatively unchanged, there is a constant evolution of FDA initiated regulation of the development, manufacturing, and distribution of drugs and medical devices. Some of these changes are codified in specific regulations, others are more subtle changes in interpretations. Since many changes occur gradually, it is often hard to measure their impact.

Costs and Benefits of Regulations in an Ideal Environment

In the best of all worlds there are several benefits and costs which might result from the regulation of the pharmaceutical industry by the FDA. The principal benefit claimed is the elimination of unsafe and ineffective drugs thereby reducing the harmful effects to patients either directly from unsafe drugs or from delaying proper therapy as the result of using an ineffective drug. Control over the claims that companies can make for their products reduces the need of physicians to verify independently the claims made for products which they prescribed, thus reducing information costs. To the extent that the administration of the regulations discouraged me-too research, research would be directed to more innovative projects.

Against these benefits, even strong proponents of regulation recognize that there are some additional costs. Achieving the desired proof of safety and effectiveness may require more testing than the firms would voluntarily conduct and hence increase development costs. How great this effect might be depends not only on the stringency of the FDA regulations but also on the nature of liability laws and importance of reputation effects in the marketing of products.

One source of a measured increase in the average cost of developing approved new drugs is the elimination of unsafe or ineffective drugs from the list of approved drugs used to calculate the average. If this were the only source of increased average cost, then there should not be much concern about increased average development cost. To the extent that FDA regulations truly increased the cost of developing safe and effective drugs, then the regulations will reduce R&D efforts. In particular, these increased costs will endanger the development of drugs for small therapeutic markets. The market may be small because the underlying disease is rare or because only a small number of people do not respond satisfactorily to the existing therapies. This gave rise to concern over the so-called orphan drugs, drug candidates that could not find a sponsor willing to conduct the clinical trials necessary to obtain FDA approval. The 1984 Orphan Drug Act provided special tax relief and/or exclusive marketing rights to companies that developed orphan drugs.

To the extent that the regulations have discouraged the development of me-too products there are costs which are often overlooked by those who view such research as wasteful. First, a relatively minor change in a drug's composition may provide a major improvement in therapy or a reduction in side effects. It may also provide an alternative therapy for those patients who do not respond to or cannot tolerate the first drug in the class. The me-too products also provide market competition for the initial innovator. Many firms are discovering that the pharmaceutical marketplace is increasingly being influenced by price-sensitive managed health care providers and the existence of me-too products has had a depressing effect on their prices and sales. Those who argue for less me-too research should not simultaneously deplore the lack of competition in the pharmaceutical marketplace.

Critics of FDA Regulations

There have been a large number of critics of the FDA's regulation of the pharmaceutical industry. The principal criticisms fall into three main categories: excessively long approval times, excessive costs, and improper decisions.

Dr. William Wardell (1973) published a study that compared availability of new pharmaceuticals in Great Britain and the U.S. for the decade ending in 1971. The study revealed that not only were more drugs exclusively available in Great Britain, but for products introduced in both countries, drug approval averaged two years later in the U.S. This phenomenon, which became known as the "drug lag," has been studied by other researchers using different time periods and countries for comparisons. A study by Kaitin et al. (1989), for the period 1977 through 1987, demonstrated that the drug lag continues to average about two years. These drug lag studies have been used as benchmarks for measuring performance of regulatory agencies.

The significance of a drug lag extends beyond its measurement on regulatory performance. On average, therapies are not available to patients in the United States until two years after they are in use in Great Britain. The significance of this unavailability depends on the particular drug therapy as well as the therapeutic alternatives available in each country. Kaitin et al. note that of drugs classified by the FDA as representing important therapeutic gains (class 1-A), four times as many were first introduced in the United Kingdom. However, as they note, determining the overall therapeutic significance is very difficult.

Several studies have investigated the time required to obtain approval to market pharmaceuticals. For studies of the drug approval process in the U.S., typically three milestones are used: the date of IND approval (or alternatively the date of the start of clinical trials), the date of NDA filing, and the date of NDA approval by the FDA. The period from IND approval to NDA filing is often referred to as the clinical development or IND phase, the time from NDA filing to NDA approval as the regulatory review or NDA phase, and the total time from IND approval to NDA approval as the total regulatory phase. The Center for the Study of Drug Development has published a series of papers tracking the drug development process (DiMasi et al. 1991a; Kaitin et al. 1994; Mattison et al. 1988). The most frequently used data series involves self-originated new chemical entities (NCEs) of U.S. owned companies. Their studies demonstrate that there has been a rather steady increase in overall development times. Even if the decade of the sixties is ignored (due to start up effects in the data series), published studies reveal a significant increase in time required to obtain marketing approval from around six years in the early 1970s to over eight years currently. There has been an increase in both the IND and the NDA phases.

One unintended consequence of the lengthening regulatory period was the reduction of effective patent life (defined as the time between approval to market and the expiration of the product patent). Eisman and Wardell (1987) demonstrated that for new drugs approved in the early 1980s, the effective patent life had declined to less than ten years. Concern about this effect of the lengthening regulatory process resulted in legislation to provide extensions of pharmaceutical patents for up to five extra years, provided that the total effective patent life shall not exceed fourteen years. While these provisions in the Price Competition and Patent Term Extension Act of 1989 provide some relief to pharmaceutical firms for the longer regulatory period, as Grabowski and others have pointed out, a one-year reduction in regulatory time is of much more value then a one-year extension of patent.

In addition to these general studies, some critics focus on particular drugs or drug categories. The most dramatic recent examples are provided by those concerned with the development of AIDS therapies. Their vocal criticisms of the FDA have led to a variety of policy changes. In October 1988, the FDA issued its Interim Rule on Procedures for Drugs Intended to Treat Life-Threatening and Severely Debilitating Illness, designed to speed the development and approval of new therapies to treat AIDS and other life-threatening diseases. In particular, it contains provisions designed to provide for greater preapproval use of therapies through treatment INDs and reduced premarketing studies in exchange for expanded post-marketing studies. These procedures are similar to those which the FDA followed on a more ad hoc basis in approving AZT for AIDS treatment and L-Dopa for Parkinson's disease (Kaitin, 1991).

The rising cost of developing new pharmaceuticals has been blamed in part on excessive FDA regulations. When I conducted my first study of the cost of developing new chemical entities as pharmaceuticals based on a sample of NCEs that were first tested in humans between 1963 and 1975, my estimate that the average cost was $54 million (1977 $) contrasted sharply with the previously generally accepted number ($20 million) and pre-1962 estimates of $6 million (Hansen, 1979). In a study of a more recent period (drug candidates who entered clinical trials between 1970 and 1982), Joe DiMasi, Henry Grabowski, Lou Lasagna, and I estimated the average cost to be $231 million (1987 $) (DiMasi et al. 1991b). The Congressional Office of Technology Assessment estimated the development cost using the DiMasi et al. data but applying a higher cost of capital which ranged from 14 percent for early development periods to 10 percent for the later stages (U.S. Congress 1993). Their estimate of R&D costs was $359 million (1990 $). The Hansen, DiMasi et al., and OTA studies are all capitalized pretax estimates.

Part of the increase between the Hansen study and the later studies is due to inflation (in 1987 $ the earlier estimate would be $114 million), the use of an 8 percent rather than the 9 percent cost of capital in DiMasi et al., and the sliding scale used in the OTA study. Correcting for these differences in parameters, the studies indicate that real development costs have doubled in roughly ten years. The DiMasi et al. study further revealed that the cost escalation is likely to continue. The average cost of testing for the drugs in the latter half of the sample was roughly double that for those in the first half.

These studies measure the cost of developing new pharmaceuticals but do not try to separately identify sources of cost increases. Changes in acceptable standards of evidence, differences in therapeutic areas (more for chronic conditions which require more testing), and extra studies for marketing purposes are all offered as explanations. However, the rising cost and other evidence, some of which is anecdotal, points to regulation as one of the major causes of increased development cost. Critics also note that despite large increases in the funds spent on R&D, the number of drugs approved annually dropped after 1962 and has remained relatively stable in the low twenties.

Wrong Decisions

One of the problems for the FDA is that the decisions that they make based on the evidence from clinical trials may later prove to be incorrect. In part this is due to the occurrence of rare effects which may not appear in the clinical trial data or of effects which become apparent only after prolonged exposure or the passage of time. Should the FDA approve a drug that later is shown to have serious side effects, the FDA can be assured of criticism. Moreover, with hindsight some may be able to point to clues in the clinical data that should have indicated the presence of this negative effect.

Less visible are the effects of delaying or failing to approve a useful new drug. Individuals who may benefit from the new therapies are denied access to products that may extend or improve their lives. Some people travel abroad to obtain new therapies, but most are unaware of improved therapies prior to FDA approval. Even if the drug is ultimately approved, some users are effectively denied access.

What is the optimum error rate? Attempts to reduce errors of the first type may involve increases in the numbers of test subjects, longer testing times and increased data collection per subject. All these will add to the cost of developing drugs and hence may result in decisions not to pursue drug candidates, some of which may have very beneficial properties. Moreover to the extent that these measures add to the total length of time required to develop a drug, they add to the second type of error, effectively denying some patients access to a useful therapy. With consideration to the relative costs of type one and type two errors (which will vary by product) one would recommend different standards be applied across drugs. At present there are differences in testing protocols, many of which do vary across drug classes. An interesting question, but one which requires medical expertise, is how well these requirements correlate with minimizing the cost of type one and two errors.

Inherent Problems in Regulating the Safety of Medical Technologies

One fundamental problem in regulating the safety of medical technologies is to define safety. Pharmaceuticals and many other medical technologies are designed to treat conditions that are "unsafe." One needs to be concerned not only with the inherent safety of the medical technology, but also with the risk of the underlying disease. In an ideal setting, one should try to reduce total risk by balancing off the disease and medical technology risks.

Balancing technology and disease risks is difficult to do in a one-size-fits-all system. Individuals differ in their willingness to accept treatment risks versus disease risks. One individual may find the disease so intolerable that he/she would accept a 50-50 chance of cure versus death, whereas others with identical disease conditions would submit to the therapy only if the potential for an adverse outcome were less than 2 percent. In theory, we could have the FDA act as an information-certifying agency and allow doctors and patients to decide whether the risk of the drug was preferable to the risk of the disease. In practice, we recognize that the risk information can be difficult to interpret and that the FDA eliminates some of the choices by not approving them for market. Implicitly we have a lower level of product risk below which the FDA will not allow the product to be marketed. This eliminates products which some segments of the market might find useful. Empirically it is an open question as to whether the cost of these lost uses exceeds the additional cost from the extra decision making and potentially wrong choices.

There are institutional biases in the safety assessment process. As noted earlier, the errors that can be made are (1) to approve what turns out to be a bad drug, and (2) the denial or delay in approving a useful drug. It has often been noted that the system does not reward speedy approvals of useful new drugs nor does it punish the second errors. However, it does punish approvals of drugs that turn out to be undesirable. Thus, institutionally, there is a bias in favor of slow decision and high thresholds of safety. This bias is not due to bad regulators. Rather it is a product of the incentive system facing the regulatory agency.

Inherent in the institutional problem are problems of information and risk perception. On the information side, the public at large, and even many physicians, are basically unaware of what is in the system. Only after the drug is approved or nears approval is there likely to be widespread awareness of the activity of the drug. Thus there is little cost to delay in the approval. The other problem is rooted in risk perception. Consider a drug that is an improvement in an area where there are already some therapies. Even if the new drug reduces mortality from 30 percent to 20 percent, usually one can't identify the 10 percent who would not have survived with the existing therapy. But if the drug is shown to be responsible for killing a specific individual, then that loss becomes much more identifiable than all the survivors. The public and Congress will respond to the identifiable risks, which will take a disproportionate role. Even if the regulators were to attempt to incorporate both the observed and unobserved risks, the public and congressional pressures would be immense to force a behavior biased toward the observed. In the case of pharmaceutical regulation, the effect will be biased against new introductions.

As noted earlier, pharmaceuticals also must be shown to be effective. The proof of efficacy poses a different problem. Ultimately we are interested in the health of individuals. In predicting the future health status we often use surrogate measures such as blood pressure and cholesterol levels. High levels of either of these markers are associated with a higher risk of coronary disease. For drugs designed to reduce high blood pressure or lower cholesterol, is it sufficient to demonstrate that they do lower these levels, or is it necessary to further demonstrate that this will result in a lower risk of heart disease? Some independent studies indicate that lowering these levels may not be sufficient to reduce heart disease. Should we then require that firms do longer-term studies, say an additional five to fifteen years, to demonstrate that their drug indeed reduces mortality and morbidity or are the surrogate markers sufficient? Obviously the answer to questions such as these have major implications for the cost of developing drugs and for the timing of new therapeutic introductions.

Regulatory Reforms

There are several suggestions for regulatory reforms, which will, if approved, encourage the development of new medical technologies.

Regulatory reforms were addressed by Vice President Dan Quayle's Competitiveness Council and the Lasagna Committee. The Competitiveness Council, in focusing on ways to make the U.S. pharmaceutical industry more competitive in world markets, suggested several reforms in the FDA regulatory process. Chief among the recommendations was to reduce the premarketing tests and substitute more postmarketing studies, holding the FDA responsible for faster review times and harmonization of U.S. regulations and data requirements with foreign, particularly European, regulatory authorities.

Eliminating Phase III and relying on expanded postmarketing surveillance is a particularly attractive option for pharmaceuticals designed to treat life-threatening illnesses for which there are no suitable therapies. As noted earlier, the FDA has already taken steps in this direction. Applying the same procedure to other pharmaceutical products also has the potential for an earlier introduction of improved therapies. The procedure may also lower the expected development cost and further enhance pharmaceutical innovation. There is the possibility that the expected savings may be eroded by Phase II creep, i.e., the Phase II trials may be expanded and partially offset the savings resulting from the elimination of Phase III.

A more serious danger to this proposed reform lies in the possibility that a drug marketed under this procedure is found to have serious adverse effects after being marketed. Depending on the seriousness of the adverse effects, this may cause the whole system to collapse back to its current structure. It should be noted that several years ago many AIDS activists were strong proponents of eliminating Phase III trails in order to obtain speedier access to promising AIDS therapies. As noted earlier, the FDA did enact procedures to provide early release of AIDS drugs. Now some of these activists are concerned about the side effects of drugs released early and have proposed a return to earlier approval standards.

The proposal to harmonize our drug regulations with those of the European community seems particularly attractive on the surface. It certainly should make the life of the regulatory affairs staff in a pharmaceutical company much easier. They potentially could file the same application in all their major markets, rather than tailor each to the requirements of individual agencies. There is a danger lurking in this proposal which may in the longer term make it much harder or more costly to obtain marketing approval.

As noted earlier, one event that focused attention on the performance of the FDA was the publication of the drug lag studies. These studies effectively benchmarked U.S. approval times to those in the United Kingdom. If the major regulatory agencies harmonize the regulatory process, particularly if the systems effectively collapse into a single agency, there will be no benchmark for comparison. Should the super agency prove to be slower in decision making or more conservative in the approval process, it will be harder to determine what innovative technologies are delayed or lost. Although the work harmonization puts a very positive cast on this proposal, perhaps we had better think of it as regulatory monopoly.

The FDA in the New Health Care Market

This paper began with the observation that the pharmaceutical marketplace is in the process of major changes. In particular many of the industry's customers are interested in cost-effectiveness as well as medical effectiveness. How do FDA regulations fit in this new environment?

The FDA has long regarded itself as focused on safety and medical effectiveness, not price. To be acceptable, a new pharmaceutical must be at least as safe and effective as existing products and hopefully superior in one dimension. To a large extent its criteria for acceptability have evolved into relative safety and relative effectiveness. There does not appear to be room for a product that is almost as safe as or almost as effective as existing products but cheaper. If there are Cadillacs on the market, then Chevrolets are not approvable.

The FDA's criteria fit relatively well with the firm's objectives when the marketplace focused on improved medical effectiveness. However, the emerging concern with cost effectiveness is potentially at odds with FDA's approval criteria. The purchasers of pharmaceuticals may be willing to trade away some medical effectiveness to obtain cost savings. In markets where the existing technologies are relatively expensive, market forces would encourage firms to devote R&D to developing less expensive technology even if it were slightly inferior in terms of safety or efficacy. However, these technologies may not be approvable by the FDA using past criteria.

This poses a major dilemma for regulatory policy. Should cost-effectiveness be part of the criteria? I suspect that if you polled pharmaceutical industry leaders and FDA officials, the answer would be a resounding "no." There are major unresolved methodological issues in cost effectiveness analysis in health care. In particular there is no consensus on how one should value changes in health. Defining cost-effectiveness has some of the same characteristics as defining safety noted above. A product may be cost-effective in some situations but not in others. This may depend on the patient's other medical conditions, his preference or parameters such as age, income, etc. Should we try to define cost-effectiveness sans specifying the context or would FDA need to specify conditions in which the product is approvable?

R&D managers are right to be concerned that a cost-effectiveness mandate would add one more degree of uncertainty to the approval process. The FDA has not had to develop expertise in this area. Adding this as a criterion would require a significant change in personnel and the decision process.

It may be difficult to find individuals willing to advocate that R&D be invested in developing medical technologies that are therapeutically inferior to existing technologies. But if cost limits access to the first-line technologies, then a compelling case could be made for developing somewhat inferior technologies if this broadens access. If this view is accepted, then the next challenge will be to make the FDA process consistent with accepting less effective or less safe technologies. It's a view that runs counter to the prevailing practice.

References

DiMasi, J. A., Bryant, N. R., and Lasagna, L. "New Drug Development in the United States from 1963 to 1990." *Clinical Pharmacology and Therapeutics*, 50(5):471-486. 1991a.

DiMasi, J. A., Hansen, R. W., Grabowski, H. G., and Lasagna, L. "Cost of Innovation in the Pharmaceutical Industry." *Journal of Health Economics*, 10:107-142, 1991b.

Eisman, M. M., and Wardell, W. M. "The Decline in Effective Patent Life of New Drugs." *Research Management,* 24:18-21, 1987.

Grabowski, H. G., Vernon, J. M., and Thomas, L G. "Estimating the Effects of Regulation on Innovation: An International Comparative Analysis of the Pharmaceutical Industry." *Journal of Law and Economics,* 21(1):133-63, 1978.

Hansen, R. W. "Effects of Incremental Costs on Pharmaceutical Innovation." *Economic Costs of FDA Regulations.* Pharmaceutical Manufacturers Association (ed.). Washington, DC: Pharmaceutical Manufacturers Association, 1981.

Hansen, R. W. "The Pharmaceutical Development Process: Estimates of Development Costs and Times and the Effects of Proposed Regulatory Changes" in R I. Chien, ed. *Issues in Pharmaceutical Economics.* Lexington, MA: Heath, 1979.

Kaitin, K. "Case Studies of Expedited Review: AZT and L-Dopa." *Law, Medicine and Health Care* 19(3-4):242-46. 1991.

Kaitin, K. I., Manocchia, M., Seibring, M., and Lasagna, L. "The New Drug Approvals of 1990, 1991, and 1992: Trends in Drug Development. *Journal of Clinical Pharmacology,* 34(2):120-27. 1994.

Kaitin, K. I., Mattison, N., Northington, F. K., et al. "The Drug Lag: An Update of New Drug Introductions in the U.S. and UK, 1977 Through 1987." *Clinical Pharmacology and Therapeutics,* 4:121-38. 1989.

Lasagna, L. "Congress, the FDA, and New Drug Development: Before and After 1962." *Perspectives in Biology and Medicine,* 32(3):322-43. 1989.

Mattison, N., Trimble, A. G., and Lasagna, L. "New Drug Development in the United States, 1963 Through 1984." *Clinical Pharmacology and Therapeutics*, 43:290-301. 1988.

Merrill, R. A. "Regulation of Drugs and Devices: An Evolution." *Health Affairs*, 13(3):47-69. 1994.

Salbu, S. R. "Regulation of Drug Treatments for HIV and AIDS: A Contractarian Model of Access." *Yale Journal of Regulation*, 11(2):401-453. 1994.

U.S. Congress, Office of Technology Assessment. *Pharmaceutical R&D: Costs, Risks and Rewards,* OTA-H-522. Washington, DC: U.S. Government Printing Office, February 1993.

Wardell, W. M. "The Drug Lag Revisited: Comparisons by Therapeutic Area of Patterns of Drugs Marketed in the U.S. and Great Britain from 1972 Through 1976. *Clinical Pharmacology and Therapeutics*, 24:499-524. 1978.

9

Ignorance is Death:
The FDA's Advertising Restrictions

Paul H. Rubin

The Story of Aspirin

Every morning I take an aspirin. The form is a product made by
Bayer, "Adult Low Strength Enteric Safety Coated, for Aspirin Regimen Users." The packaging of this product is remarkable. The box
indicates that the product is "For the temporary relief of minor aches
and pains" but the package insert indicates that "Because of its delayed action, BAYER® Enteric Aspirin will not provide fast relief of
headaches, fever or other symptoms needing immediate relief." The
package also suggests that consumers should "Ask your doctor about
new uses for BAYER® ENTERIC Aspirin." *But nowhere in any of
the materials (the box, the insert, or the bottle itself) is there any
indication of the purpose of this product, or of what these "new uses"
might be.*

In fact, this product is made for heart attack prevention. There is
substantial medical evidence that taking a daily dose of aspirin can
reduce the risk of heart attack in middle-aged males (a category to
which I now belong) by almost 50 percent.[1] Indeed, the results are so
well known that there exists a pamphlet, *Amazing Aspirin,* available
for 89¢ at the checkout stand of grocery stores, which discusses this
benefit at great length.[2] What is surprising is that neither the package

for the aspirin itself nor any advertising for it indicates this valuable use. Why does Bayer largely forgo the possibility of the increased sales from providing this information to consumers?

On March 2, 1988, at a meeting in the offices of FDA Commissioner Frank Young, all companies making aspirin were told that they could not advertise the benefits of the product in reducing risks for first heart attacks. If they did, the FDA would bring legal action. All of the companies agreed to comply; as of today, no one advertises or promotes aspirin for heart attack prevention.[3] The publishers of the 89¢ pamphlet can provide the information because the First Amendment protects them. The FDA does not believe that this Constitutional protection of free speech applies to the pharmaceutical industry.[4]

This episode is important in its own right: the ban on aspirin advertising undoubtedly causes tens of thousands of needless deaths per year. Elimination of this ban would probably be one of the simplest measures to reduce death rates available. In addition to its direct significance, this ban also illustrates several important points about the FDA's general policies with respect to advertising and promotion.[5]

These points are:

- Much of the FDA's power is extra-legal.

- FDA regulation denies consumers and others valuable information.

- The FDA focuses on the risks of advertising and promotion, and neglects the benefits.

- The result of the FDA's policies is that consumers are made less healthy.

I will first discuss these points with respect to aspirin advertising. I will then discuss the two main areas of FDA advertising regulation: advertising of prescription drugs to physicians and to consumers. We will see that the policies are extremely harmful, and that the policy with respect to aspirin is, indeed, typical of the FDA's general behavior. On the other hand, one recent change in FDA policy with respect to direct-to-consumer advertising has been a real improvement.

Aspirin: The Details

I will now consider in detail each of the points made above with respect to the aspirin advertising ban.

Much of the FDA's Power is Extra-Legal. In the case of aspirin, there was no formal procedure for imposing the ban. At a meeting in the Commissioner's office, the aspirin manufacturers were simply told that they should not advertise aspirin as a heart attack preventative. The manufacturers complied. Had they not, then the FDA would have been forced to take various administrative actions to enforce its policy. Ultimately, if any manufacturer had wanted to pursue the issue far enough, it would have been litigated in court. The firms would then have been able to assert various rights, including a First Amendment right to free speech.

Commercial speech receives less protection from the courts than other forms of speech. Thus, had the matter been litigated it is possible that the FDA would have succeeded in imposing the ban. It is also possible that the agency would have lost. After all, many authorities believe that the FDA commonly violates the First Amendment to the Constitution when it regulates speech.[6] While the courts have held that false commercial speech does not receive full First Amendment protection, in this case (as in many others involving the FDA) there was no issue of falsity: No one argued that the claims were untrue or that there was any deception. Thus, had the matter gone to the courts, it is at least possible that the FDA would have lost its case.

Why did no firm choose to litigate the issue? Firms are deathly afraid of the FDA, and with good reason. The agency does not merely control advertising of pharmaceutical producers. It controls every aspect of the behavior of such firms. It controls approval of new products. It also inspects firms to make sure they comply with FDA rules regarding the manufacturing process. Thus, firms are generally afraid of antagonizing the FDA, and will commonly agree with regulatory actions rather than litigate. As David Kessler, the former Commissioner of the FDA, has put it, "Companies interested in maintaining positive relationships with the FDA usually agree to the FDA's remedy."[7] Thus, the FDA uses its general powers to punish firms to coerce them into actions even when the agency might lack the power to enforce these actions in a legal forum.

FDA Regulation Denies Consumers and Others Valuable Information. This point is quite clear in the case of aspirin. When the reports of the benefits of aspirin were first released, there were stories in newspapers and on TV regarding the findings. Any consumers who happened to read the paper or watch TV on that day would have learned this information. However, a news story itself is a poor way of learning about a procedure aimed at causing an actual modification of life-style, such as taking a pill every morning. After the story was first released, the fact that aspirin prevents heart attacks is no longer newsworthy, and so is not generally discussed in the press. Consumers may read books or magazine articles with this information; I mentioned a pamphlet available at the grocery checkout above. Such methods may be useful for some consumers, and particularly for more educated higher income consumers. Other consumers can learn about the benefits of aspirin from physicians. However, this is possible only for those who are in regular contact with a physician—again, usually higher income consumers—and for whom the physician thinks to mention aspirin, and, although there is no legal risk to the physician from doing so, most do not.[8] For the mass of consumers who get most of their information from TV and commercials, the FDA's ban essentially means that they do not learn that their lives could be lengthened by taking aspirin.[9] Moreover, a news story cannot report on new forms and dosages of aspirin, such as the low dose pill I take daily.

Beginning in 1995, Bayer did use advertising in an attempt to link pain control and heart attack prevention to aspirin. They began advertising, "powerful pain relief, and so much more." This ad campaign has been successful, raising Bayer's market share in the pain relief market from 4.5 percent to 5.2 percent, in spite of the introduction of Aleve.[10] This advertising would be useful to those who already have some idea about the meaning of "so much more," but again, those who do not know would have no mechanism for learning. The success of this clandestine advertising for the heart attack prevention function of aspirin indicates the potential for a major campaign, if it were allowed.

The FDA Focuses on the Risks of Advertising and Promotion, and Neglects the Benefits. Why does the FDA have this policy with respect to aspirin advertising? One semi-official statement is from David Adams, Associate Chief Counsel for Drugs for the FDA.[11]

In another interesting case, a group of aspirin makers suggested the possibility of press conferences to present to the public new evidence on the beneficial effects of a daily aspirin regimen in preventing heart attacks in individuals who had not previously had a heart attack. Although this information was important, the agency was concerned that, for some individuals, the risk of having a heart attack might be less than the risk of other, harmful effects posed by the aspirin regimen. The agency impressed on the drug companies that this sort of education should come from physicians rather than from a press conference by an aspirin manufacturer (p. 56-57).

The risks mentioned are a slightly increased risk of a certain type of stroke for some individuals if aspirin is used. However, the level of increase in this risk is small; indeed, the risks were not even statistically significant.[12] The reduction in risk of heart attack from taking aspirin for the middle aged tremendously outweighs the slightly increased risk of stroke. Moreover, advertising and promotion could easily indicate that aspirin was not a suitable drug for young females and any other group for whom the risks might outweigh the benefits.

This behavior is typical of the FDA. It invariably places a much greater weight on any potential harm from a pharmaceutical than on any benefit from the product. This explains the tremendous delays in FDA approval of new drugs: the agency is much more fearful of approving a harmful drug than of delaying or blocking a beneficial drug. The result is excess deaths. The FDA's timidity in allowing advertising and promotion of drugs is based on the same fear.[13]

It is also true that the FDA has not approved aspirin for heart attack prevention. Part of the reason is that no manufacturer has applied for such approval. The FDA's approval process is costly, and it would cost some tens or hundreds of millions of dollars to obtain approval for aspirin as a heart attack preventative.[14] Indeed, because the benefits of aspirin are so well documented, it might be impossible for ethical reasons to undertake such a study at all; researchers would probably be unwilling to deny any patients the benefits of aspirin, as is required in such a study. The one study cited above was terminated early because of the overwhelming evidence of the benefits of aspirin. But even if the study were possible, no manufacturer would be willing to finance it. This is because aspirin is no longer covered by a patent, so that any manufacturer could use the results of a study in selling its product. In other words, any firm undertaking this research would be unable to reap the benefits. This is often the case for drugs available in generic versions as well. However, the case is worse for aspirin: not only is the product not covered by a patent, but even the name ("Aspirin") has lost its trademark protection.

The Result of the FDA's Policies Is That Consumers Are Made Less Healthy. By now, this point should be obvious. It is possible that a small number of consumers have benefited from the FDA's policies because otherwise they might have inappropriately taken aspirin and suffered strokes. However, many more consumers have been harmed than benefited. In particular, middle-aged males (and many females) who would have learned of the benefits of aspirin from a vigorous advertising campaign have been denied this benefit. Indeed, Bayer tried to market enteric coated aspirin (the sort most useful for heart attack prevention) in a "blister" pack, designed for daily use, but the FDA even forbade this form of packaging.

Advertising of Prescription Drugs to Physicians

The FDA regulation of advertising and promotion of prescription drugs can best be understood if we consider promotion to physicians and to consumers separately. In this section, I will consider advertising to physicians; in the next section, I will consider consumers.

Benefits of Promotion. One sometimes sees criticisms of the amount the pharmaceutical industry spends on promotion. A typical complaint will be that the industry spends as much or more on promotion as on research and development.[15] Such complaints are fundamentally misguided and demonstrate a lack of understanding of the industry and of the purpose of promotional expenditures.

In one sense, promotional expenditures are not different from expenditures on research. Begin with some chemical of unknown properties. Research is a way of determining what these properties are and what, if any, uses the chemical has as a drug. That is, research expenditures are a way of obtaining information about the drug. The culmination of this spending is the approval by the FDA of the drug for marketing.

But at this point the drug has no economic value. Moreover, no matter how useful the drug may be, it has little value as a medicine. This is because the information in the research already conducted is valueless until physicians who will prescribe the drug are aware of the information. The way physicians obtain this information is through advertising and promotion. Without this spending, the drug will not be prescribed and will not be available to cure patients. Research and advertising are both information generating activities.

A recent study found that spending by pharmaceutical companies increased the sales of their products.[16] Physicians were more likely to request the addition of products to hospital formularies (lists of acceptable drugs for use in the hospital) if they had been involved with the promotional activities of the pharmaceutical company. This result is, of course, not surprising. After all, the purpose of promotion is to promote. However, the interpretation of these results is important. Some might interpret the findings as indicating that pharmaceutical companies unduly influence behavior of physicians through promotional expenditures. At least one of the authors, Mary-Margaret Chren, has been a critic of pharmaceutical promotional expenditures, as mentioned above. However, this interpretation should be resisted.

Rather, the article documents the social benefit of information provision by pharmaceutical companies. The article indicates that all of the fifty-five requests to add new drugs to the formulary were made by physicians, often after interactions with drug companies. Thirteen of the requests were for drugs that represented a major therapeutic advance over existing drugs, and thirteen for drugs with a modest therapeutic advantage. Thus, the study indicates that pharmaceutical promotion was responsible for the addition of these drugs to the hospital formulary. Without such promotion, it is less likely that the drugs would have been made available to patients.

Twenty-nine of the recommended additions to the formulary had no clinical advantages over existing drugs; twenty-three of these drugs were approved for addition. Price information regarding the drugs is not given in the article. It is possible that some of the twenty-nine drugs that were reported as having little or no therapeutic advantage were lower priced than existing drugs; this is particularly likely for the twenty-three that were actually added to the formulary. It is competition from drugs with similar clinical profiles that is the most powerful force restraining drug prices. Thus, this study indicates some of the benefits of promotional expenditures.

There is further evidence of the value of additional pharmaceutical promotion. A well- known study examined behavior of "expert" physicians, those writing medical textbooks and review articles in medical journals.[17] This study found that experts writing about myocardial infarction (heart attacks) in many cases recommended treatments that were "several years" behind the best data available. Thus, the evidence indicates that physicians do not receive enough information about new drugs. If more resources were spent on promotion, patient health would improve.

There are some additional examples of the benefits of promotion.[18] First, the National Cholesterol Education Program increased the awareness of the danger of high cholesterol among physicians from 39 percent to 64 percent within two years. The number of adults who had had their cholesterol checked increased from 35 percent in 1983 to 66 percent in 1989. Second, Smith Kline Beacham publicized the benefits of its hepatitis B vaccine, and this campaign was associated with a significant decline in the incidence of hepatitis B.

Regulation of Promotion. Excessive regulation of promotion and advertising by the FDA reduces expenditure on drug promotion. The FDA has always taken a very expansive view of its authority to regulate advertising and promotion. As the former Commissioner of the FDA indicates,

> The [Food, Drug and Cosmetic] Act does not define what constitutes an advertisement, but the FDA generally views anything, other than labeling, that promotes a drug product and that is sponsored by a manufacturer as advertising....The definitions of labeling and advertising taken together cover—at least in the FDA's opinion—virtually all information disseminating activities by or on behalf of a prescription drug manufacturer.[19]

While regulation of pharmaceutical advertising to physicians has always been excessive, in recent years this regulation has greatly increased and become more harmful. In order to fully understand this increase in regulation, we must first define the concepts of "approved" and "unapproved" uses of a drug. When a pharmaceutical firm obtains approval for a drug, the drug is approved only for certain uses, listed in the application filed with the FDA and on the drug label. (Approved uses are also called "on label" uses.) Other potential uses of the drug are "unapproved" (or "off label") uses. For example, in the discussion above of aspirin, the use of aspirin as a first heart attack preventative would be an off label use.

There Is Nothing Wrong with Using a Drug for an Unapproved or Off Label Use. Any physician is free to prescribe a drug for any purpose he feels desirable. Often, as in the case of aspirin, substantial medical evidence will be published in journals attesting to the efficacy of a drug for an off label use. One-third of drugs given to cancer patients are for unapproved uses, and an estimated one-fourth of all U.S. prescriptions are for such uses.[20] Of particular importance are drugs for pediatric cancer, since the low incidence of cancer in children means that manufacturers will seldom seek approval for such uses. Instead, physicians will commonly use drugs approved for adults in treating children. Off label uses for drugs may also be listed in various medical compendia (lists of uses of drugs).[21]

There are various reasons why a use may be off label. A firm may be in the process of obtaining FDA approval for the new use. It can take a long time for such approval to be granted. Requests for "supplementary" approval are often given lower priority by the FDA than initial requests. One study has found that requests for original approval take an average of 23.5 months, and for supplemental uses, which ought to be quicker since the drug has already been found to be safe, take an average of 21.5 months. The difference in approval times is not statistically significant.[22] Moreover, a firm may never obtain such approval. As mentioned in the case of aspirin, if a patent has expired then it will not pay for a firm to spend the money required to obtain such approval. Even if the patent has not yet expired, as a drug gets older, the length of time until the patent will expire becomes shorter. Thus, it may not pay for a firm to spend the money to obtain supplementary approval when the time to benefit from this approval will be shorter than for the initial use.

The FDA forbids advertising of off label uses. Since these uses are important, this policy is harmful. There is evidence, for example, that sales of drugs for newly approved uses increase dramatically after approval, because of promotion, even though the drug was available for this use before approval.[23] But the FDA has recently greatly increased its regulation of such advertising and promotion. In recent years, the FDA has begun to restrict non-advertising efforts of pharmaceutical companies to inform physicians of unapproved uses. For example, it is now often illegal for pharmaceutical companies to send reprints of scientific articles reporting research on this class of use to physicians. A drug company can send reprints, if "there is an unsolicited request for the information. If the detail man has suggested to the physician that he request such information from the company, the agency [FDA] will regard the activity as promotional."[24] It is also difficult for these companies to sponsor symposia and seminars for physicians to inform them of such uses. Moreover, for FDA regulation, truth of a claim is not a defense: "Such promotion is prohibited even if these uses are supported by studies in the medical literature."[25]

Thus, since about 1991, the agency has increased regulation and virtually prohibited promotion of off label uses. Moreover, the basis for this change in policy was a "Draft Concept Paper" that the FDA never officially adopted; this is another example of use of extra legal authority by the agency.[26]   This policy means that it will take longer for the medical community to learn about some uses of drugs and, since firms never seek approval for some uses, it will be impossible for manufacturers to ever promote many uses of drugs. This policy has been extremely harmful.[27]

As suggested above, pharmaceutical companies have been unwilling to challenge this policy. The Washington Legal Foundation (WLF), a public interest law firm in Washington, has protested the FDA policy. The foundation first filed a Citizen Petition. Interestingly, although eight groups (one of which is an umbrella for nine additional organizations) filed comments in support of the WLF, none of these groups represented pharmaceutical manufacturers. More recently, the WLF has filed a suit against the FDA regarding promotion of off label uses.

Benefits of Regulation: Are Ads Deceptive?[28] The benefits of regulation and restriction of pharmaceutical advertising may be measured in terms of reduction of deception. This raises the issue of the amount of deception in pharmaceutical ads. For several reasons, we would not expect much deception. The reputations of large firms are valuable assets, so such firms would avoid deception wherever possible.[29] This should be even more true for pharmaceutical firms than for others. Not only are pharmaceutical firms large, but their customers, physicians, are skilled buyers and also repeat customers. If such customers learn that a company is deceptive with respect to one product, they are more likely than most customers to discount all advertising by that company. There is also evidence that firms engaging in deception lose substantial amounts of value when deception in advertising is detected.[30] Thus, we would not expect much deception in pharmaceutical advertising.

Contrary to these expectations, some claim that there is evidence of such deception. A major article in the *Annals of Internal Medicine* examined advertisements for pharmaceuticals in medical journals.[31] The popular press reported the results of this study widely, and interpreted it as finding that ads were "Often Misleading" (*New York Times).*[32] Partially as a result of this study, proposals were made to require preapproval of ads by an independent review group or by the FDA, and one congressman proposed a bill that would have denied tax deductibility to prescription drug advertisements not approved by an independent review board. This policy would have led to examination of all ads by such a board. It is unfortunate that this paper was potentially so influential because there are serious problems with the analysis.

The study was a survey of physicians and pharmacists regarding their views of a sample of pharmaceutical advertisements. All ads of at least one page from the first issue of 1990 from ten medical journals were sampled. After elimination of duplicates, there were 109 such ads. Each ad was sent to three reviewers, two physicians with experience in the area of medicine relevant for the ad and an academic clinical pharmacist. Reviewers were asked a total of thirty-six questions about each ad. Of these, twenty-eight questions were based on FDA regulations and eight were more general questions. Ads were only evaluated with respect to a particular issue if two or more of the reviewers felt that the issue was relevant. For example, in fifty-three of the 109 cases, two or more reviewers believed that the drug was promoted as "the drug of choice" for some condition. Questions regarding the appropriateness of that claim were only evaluated for those fifty-three drugs.

The key findings of the analysis were: Reviewers concluded that 92 percent of the ads were not in full compliance with FDA criteria in one or more of the twenty-eight categories examined. Twenty percent of ads were judged to have no educational value; 37 percent had little; 33 percent had some; and 4 percent had a great deal. With respect to prescribing behavior, "Only 44 percent of reviewers felt that the advertisement would lead to proper prescribing if a physician had no other information about the medicine other than that presented in the advertisement."

The final question was "If this advertisement were subject to the same review criteria as a scientific article, would your overall suggestion to a journal editor be to accept in present form, accept contingent on minor revisions, accept contingent on major revisions, or reject the advertisement?" In seventy-six cases, two or more reviewers agreed on the appropriateness of publication. On this basis, 28 percent of the ads would have been rejected, 34 percent would have required major revision, 35 percent minor revision, and 4 percent would have been accepted without change.

Thus, as reported, the results of the study imply that there are serious problems with pharmaceutical advertising. However, flaws in the study mean that these results have little if any relevance to policy.

First, at no time did the authors of the study attempt to determine if the respondents themselves were deceived, or if anyone else was actually misled. Rather, the questions asked if the respondents *believed* that others would be deceived by the ads. But the respondents were not experts in deception or in psychology. Thus, the fundamental research paradigm on which the article was based was misspecified. For example, as a professional economist, I may be able to evaluate the economic content of newspaper articles reporting on economics, but I cannot evaluate the impact of these articles on readers of newspapers. Such evaluation requires market research techniques that were not included in the study. I do not use such techniques here, but they provide an alternative method of evaluating the study.[33]

The analysis which follows is based on the article itself. In performing this analysis, I did not have access to the actual data generated by the authors. An analysis that did have access to that data also finds flaws in the study. For example, this analysis concludes that "Because of numerous methodological flaws in constructing the survey instrument and conducting the study, no conclusion can be drawn that the advertisements reviewed misled physicians....What little can be gleaned from the article suggests that advertising is performing its function of delivering information, which in the vast majority of cases is unlikely to mislead physicians."[34]

I analyze the study from the perspective of the economics of information. This approach begins with the observation that information is both valuable and costly. Thus, an economist asks about incentives of relevant parties to provide and absorb information. While this approach recognizes that deception is possible, the method of analysis also pays particular attention to the information that would be lost if the ads were eliminated or restricted. The approach also pays attention to consumers of information. Time of consumers of advertising (whether direct consumers or their agents, such as physicians) is also valuable, and information must be provided in a manner that will reduce costs of absorbing the information. Producers of goods are often in the best position to provide such information in a way that will be cost-effective. Consumers also come to market with information of their own, so an important issue is the interaction of new information with the information already in existence.[35]

I consider each of the major points in the article. These points are: the extent to which the ads meet FDA standards; the amount of educational value in the ads; the effect of ads on prescribing behavior; the extent to which the ads would meet the criteria required for articles to be accepted for publication in a refereed journal; and the article's policy recommendations.

FDA Standards. Although the reviewers believed that many ads violated at least one FDA standard,[36] they were not trained in the use of FDA standards by FDA officials, and did not necessarily evaluate the ads as would these officials. Many of the rules require judgment: they are full of terms like "appropriate," "likely to mislead," and "adequate." These terms do not have objective meanings; they are regulatory terms of art, and can be defined only in the context of normal enforcement strategies. Some authorities believe that almost any ad could be found "deceptive" under some readings.[37]

This is not meant as a critique of the FDA. Any legal standard will require elaboration, either through administrative clarification or through a common law process. The point is simply that the unguided intuition of a physician or pharmacist is not likely to derive the most useful meaning of such legalistic terms. The FTC, which also regulates "deception," has spent thousands of internal staff hours debating the meaning of such points, and no doubt the FDA has as well.

Moreover, FDA bureaucrats, like all law enforcement officials, use "prosecutorial discretion" in deciding which matters are worth attention. The FDA regulations are so broad that it is almost impossible to write an ad that does not technically violate some rule, which may be why the study purports to find that 92 percent of the ads did violate FDA standards. But FDA officials wisely ignore many purely technical violations, even in a climate where enforcement efforts have greatly increased in recent years. Reviewers who do not use a similar degree of tolerance will be likely to focus on trivial "violations" of FDA rules.

Finally, in evaluating compliance with FDA standards, it is important to note that the ads contained the FDA mandated brief summary, as described above. A plausible scenario for a physician reading an ad is to first read the ad itself. If the medicine appears promising, the physician might then turn to the brief summary for further data. Under this scenario, most physicians would ignore the brief summary because they would have no interest in the product, but those actually considering prescribing the medicine would not.

Educational Value. Although the authors report that the reviewers believed the ads had relatively little educational value, they never defined "educational value." If educational value is defined as the information provided in a lecture or in a journal article, then the measure is meaningless. For example, many ads are reminders, which do not purport to have any educational value. These ads are aimed at keeping the name of the drug before the physician who already prescribes the drug. Other ads indicate that an existing medicine is available in a new dosage or new form. To criticize these ads for lacking educational value is inappropriate.

A more useful question would be to ask if the ads provide any information. Here the answer would of necessity be different. In one sense, any ad provides information. First, the ad indicates that the manufacturer has enough confidence in the product to spend resources advertising it; this is itself valuable information to prospective purchasers. Of course, this information is not definitive, but it is nonetheless valuable. If advertisers believed that a physician would prescribe a product only once or a few times and then cease using it, they would not find the product worth advertising.[38] Second, even if the ad only mentions a drug and a condition, the physician is alerted that this may be a product worth further examination. Indeed, this appears to be the major message conveyed by almost all pharmaceutical ads.[39]

Prescribing Behavior. The study also claims that many of the ads would lead to improper prescribing behavior *if the physician had no other information than that found in the ad.* It is impossible to evaluate the ability of ads to deceive in a vacuum. Readers always have some prior information. By making alternative assumptions about the amount of this information, it is possible to conclude that any ad is deceptive. This is why marketing research techniques (that measure the effects of ads on actual consumers with actual prior sets of information) are necessary to truly measure deception.

The hypothesis that the physician has no other information is clearly incorrect. Physicians have ten or more years of training and access to journal articles, medical texts, and other sources of information. A more reasonable question would have asked if the ad would lead to improper prescribing behavior *if the physician had the amount of information we would expect a normal, practicing physician to possess.* Even then, the authors would have been relying on one set of physicians and pharmacists to guess what another set of physicians will learn from some ads. They provide no evidence that any ad actually deceived anyone. Indeed, the methodology of their study made in impossible to determine if there was actual deception.

Moreover, consider the ads themselves. For an ad to lead to improper prescribing behavior there must be some more appropriate drug that doctors should prescribe. If so, physicians would also have access to ads for this more appropriate remedy, and to assume that the physician has no other information ignores information from ads for a competing product that was itself part of the study. While these additional ads might not provide all the information a physician needs to properly prescribe, it is nonetheless improper to ignore them totally, as does the phrasing of the question ("no other information").

The set of ads examined in the study apparently does provide exactly this sort of competitive and balancing information. The reviewers found sixty-six ads (for sixty-two drugs) that they believed deserved rejection or major revision. Of these ads, only eleven were for drugs from a class with less than four competing drugs in the sample itself. For antibiotics, there were twenty-four competing ads in the sample (of which the report criticized seventeen). While not all of these drugs would compete with each other, there are probably few, if any, conditions for which only one drug would be advertised. In other words, in most cases, drugs competed against other advertised drugs in the sample itself. Undoubtedly, many other drugs that did not advertise in the sample month or in the sample journals compete and provide information useful to physicians for comparing those drugs that did advertise.

Many of the ads themselves provide names of competing products, so that a physician would know exactly which products to consider in comparing the advertised product with alternatives. Thus, it is improper to argue that the ads exist in a vacuum. In the same way that aspirin, ibuprofen, and acetaminophen ads provide competing information to consumers of over-the-counter headache remedies, so advertising of prescription drugs to physicians also provides competing information. To claim that ads would lead to improper prescribing behavior if the physician had no other information is contradicted by the ads themselves, which provide other information.

In a "Reply" to various critics, Wilkes et al. claim that "advertisements profoundly influence the way prescription drugs are used in our society...all too often, they are the decisive source of information about new pharmaceutical products."[40] But this skirts the issue: An ad may be influential in leading to prescribing behavior if the ad only directs attention to a new product and if the physician then seeks additional information about the product. By implying in their response that ads do more than this, the authors are themselves being somewhat deceptive.

Peer Review. The last question asked reviewers was, "If this advertisement were subject to the same review criteria as a scientific article, would your overall suggestion to a journal editor be to accept in present form, accept contingent on minor revisions, accept contingent on major revisions, or reject the advertisement?" Many of the reviewers would have rejected the ads or required major revisions. However, this information is not useful.

It is inappropriate to expect ads to meet the same standards as refereed journal articles, or to evaluate ads using the criteria relevant for such articles. Nothing meets these standards except these articles. For example, no newspaper article (including those reporting the results of the study) would meet these standards. But this misses the point. Readers know what they are reading. A physician knows that an ad does not serve the same purpose as a refereed article and does not meet the same standards. Readers of newspapers, for example, do not place the same faith in the ads as in the text. Many of the ads contain only a few lines of text. Obviously, such an ad would not meet standards for publication as an article; just as obviously, no reader would expect the ad to meet these standards.

If we sent 100 medical journal articles to advertising directors, they would find all 100 overly long, poorly written, and incoherent. This could lead to a headline, "Study finds medical research uninformative and ill presented." The result from such a study would tell us nothing about articles in medical journals because the study would be based on the use of inappropriate criteria.

Peer review is not itself legally required for any purpose. Medical and other academic journals have decided that this method of screening articles is worthwhile because it increases the credibility of the articles and therefore the value of the journal to readers. If medical editors felt that peer review of ads would make their journals more valuable, or if drug manufacturers felt this, then either party could voluntarily engage in such review and publicize this practice. There is no need for an outside party to mandate such scrutiny, just as no one has mandated this process for current journals.

Policy Suggestions. For a criticism to be helpful, it should contain suggestions for improvement. This is where the study shows its greatest weaknesses. The authors suggest that "One approach would be to ban pharmaceutical advertising from journals." This would be useful only if the net effect of the existing ads was to reduce the information available to physicians, a claim that the study never makes or even considers. The authors reject this proposal only because they claim that other methods of promotion are even more difficult to regulate, not because they understand that the effect would be to reduce available information. The authors of the study are primarily academics, not practicing physicians, and one gets the feeling that they believe physicians should obtain all information from articles in medical journals. This would greatly reduce the time available for practice and increase the costs of medical care, but the authors are apparently indifferent to costs borne by consumers.

Another suggestion is for increased FDA enforcement of existing regulations. The authors realize that any program would impose additional costs, but they believe that the costs should be "borne by the manufacturers." Economic analysis clearly indicates that any increased cost will result in higher prices paid by consumers.

Based on this article, some have suggested an independent review board be created to review all pharmaceutical ads. A requirement for preapproval of advertisements for pharmaceuticals would lead to delays in drug advertising, to fewer ads, and to reduced information in each ad. There is no doubt that such a review process would greatly reduce the number of advertisements. It would also increase the cost of advertising, and would mean that ads would take longer to reach their audience. During the delay, physicians would be denied valuable information, particularly about new products or new uses of existing products.

Moreover, it is likely that ads approved by a board would provide less information than ads written by the companies because such a board would be innately conservative. Consider the decision process of a company in drafting an ad under the current regulatory regime. The company wants to make expansive claims in order to increase sales. However, there are risks from claims that are too expansive. If a claim is made with insufficient support, there may be regulatory penalties. In addition, physicians who learn that a particular company makes unreliable claims for its products will discount future claims for all products made by this company. Thus, the company has incentives to try to sell the product, but to avoid any costs of making insufficiently based claims.

Now consider the decision process of a review board. A review board is subject to only one side of this equation. The board would have an incentive to disallow any claim that is at all doubtful because the board gains nothing from additional sales, but will be subject to criticism if any claim turns out to be unreliable. Thus, there would be incentives for the board to be excessively cautious in approving claims. The result would likely be reduced information to physicians about useful drugs and thus reduced health of consumers. Indeed, the results of the Wilkes study itself demonstrate this. Here, a group of outside "experts" found almost all ads subject to criticism, even though all pharmaceutical companies have intense internal reviews of ads.[41] We would expect that most of the ads submitted to an external review board, if one were mandated, would need to be rewritten at least once, adding to delay and denying physicians the information in the ads.

We may conclude that there is no evidence that pharmaceutical ads are deceptive. Since any benefits of regulation would be in terms of reduced deception, there is no evidence of a need for increased regulation. Moreover, since we saw earlier that physicians have too little information, an attempt to increase regulation of pharmaceutical ads would clearly be misguided.

Direct Advertising to Consumers[42]

In this area, the FDA has actually recently improved its policies so as to allow pharmaceutical firms to provide more information to consumers. This is one of the few bright spots in FDA information regulation, and it is important to note this progress. To understand the changes, it is necessary to understand the previous set of regulations.

It is impossible to understand regulation of drug advertising to consumers without understanding the "brief summary of prescribing information." This document is a distillation of the package insert, required in all pharmaceuticals. It is a technical summary of the uses, side effects, and contraindications for a drug. (A "contraindication" is a condition making the use of a particular drug undesirable. For example, for some drugs pregnancy may be a contraindication. Some drugs should not be taken together, so use of one drug may be a contraindication for another drug.) Until the recent changes, this brief summary (brief only in bureaucratic terms) was required with (almost) all advertising of the drug. It is a technical document, written for physicians and other professionals, and virtually incomprehensible to consumers. It is the one page of small unreadable type that always follows an ad for a drug.

The regulations regarding the document were bizarre and could only have been produced by a bureaucracy. They can best be understood by defining those ads that did not require the brief summary. If an ad mentions only the name of a drug but not its use or purpose, then the brief summary is not required. (For example, an ad saying that "Seldane is now on sale" without mentioning allergy loss would not require the brief summary.) Similarly, if an ad mentions that some treatment is available for some condition from a physician but does not mention that the treatment is a drug, then again the brief summary is not needed. An example is Glaxo's discussion of heartburn, ultimately aimed at selling Zantac® which, however, is not mentioned in the ad. If the ad mentions a drug and a condition, then a brief summary is required, even if the ad does not mention the name of the drug or the producer.

Although the rules make only bureaucratic sense, the FDA enforces them with nit-picking zeal. In one case, an advertiser was required to change the wording of a message in an ad from "Now there's an effective treatment your doctor can prescribe" to "Your doctor can prescribe an effective treatment program."[43] In another case, an actor was prohibited from scratching his head during a Rogaine® commercial because the FDA believed that this indicated that the product was related to hair.

Although these policies seem ludicrous, they, in fact, had substantial detrimental effects. The requirement of a brief summary adds greatly to the cost of print ads. The brief summary will often be as long as or longer than the ad itself; thus, on average, this requirement probably doubles the cost of print advertising, and therefore reduces the quantity. More importantly, the requirement for a brief summary made it virtually impossible to advertise prescription medicines on TV; indeed, this may be one purpose of the requirement.[44] This reduced greatly the amount of information available to consumers. Moreover, it is less educated consumers who are most likely to get information from TV, and so who were most likely to be harmed by this policy.

The change in policy, effective August 8, 1997, allows prescription drug advertising on TV without the brief summary.[45] This is a major improvement in policy, and will enable producers to provide useful information to consumers. (The policy will also provide additional revenue for TV, and the media were a major force in favor of the new rule. For example, at a FDA hearing in October 1995, at which I testified, many paid representatives of the media and the advertising industry also participated.)[46] To understand the benefits of this policy, it will be useful to analyze the benefits of direct-to-consumer advertising of prescription drugs.

Benefits of Direct Advertising

Health Benefits. Analysis of direct-to-consumer advertising has identified several health benefits. These benefits accrue because consumers will have some information about themselves that is not readily accessible to a physician. The information known only to individual consumers about their own health status can sometimes be combined with information in pharmaceutical ads to better match patients and drugs. Of course, the physician also has information about pharmaceuticals. However, direct-to-consumer advertising will provide greatest benefits in those circumstances where the consumer would not otherwise consult a physician. We may identify the following benefits from direct advertising:

1. Advertising can inform a consumer that a treatment exists for some condition. Without the advertising, the consumer might not know of the existence of the treatment, and so would not consult a physician. An example is Lamisil®, Sandoz' medicine for toenail fungus. A consumer might know that he has the condition but not know that there is a treatment. Advertising can indicate that there is an effective treatment for this condition. Similarly, Imitrex® advertising tells those who suffer from migraine that there is a new treatment.

2. A consumer may suffer some symptoms (e.g., thirst) without realizing that these are symptoms of a disease (e.g., diabetes). A consumer who does not realize that symptoms indicate a disease will not consult a physician and therefore cannot learn in this way that he has a treatable disease. Recent ads for Merck's Proscar® indicate that urinary problems may be symptomatic of prostate enlargement, and that there is a non-surgical treatment for this condition. Lamisil® ads indicate that discolored or misshapen toenails may be a symptom of toenail fungus. Ads for Prozac® discuss the symptoms of depression.

3. A consumer may have been previously diagnosed with some then-untreatable disease for which a new treatment has since become available. Because the consumer believes that the disease is not treatable, or because previous remedies have been ineffective, he will not contact a physician and will not learn about the new therapy. Advertisements can inform him and lead to treatment. A similar analysis applies to the creation of a new vaccine or preventative for a condition to which some consumers may know themselves to be susceptible. An example is a vaccine for hepatitis B, a disease to which homosexuals are particularly susceptible. Ads for Wyeth-Ayerst's Premarin® and Ciba-Geigy's Estraderm® indicate that these post-menopausal medicines can reduce the chance for osteoporosis, and some of the ads provide information about susceptibility to this condition.

4. A new remedy with reduced side effects may become available. Advertising can provide benefits in two cases. Consumers who do not know that symptoms they are experiencing are side effects, and so would not ask a physician about them, may learn from ads that there are alternatives without these side effects. Consumers who have ceased treatment because of side effects, and so are not seeing a physician, may begin treatment again if they learn of therapies that do not impose the same side effects.

An example is impotence caused by some antihypertensives. Some consumers may not know that the condition is drug related; others may have stopped therapy because of the condition. Either class of consumers can benefit from ads indicating that a treatment with reduced side effects is available. Other examples include the Marion Merrill Dow campaign for Seldane-D® and the Janssen Pharmaceutica campaign for Hismanal® as allergy medicines less likely to cause drowsiness.

5. A medication may simply be available that is more convenient than existing medications. For example, Searle advertises Daypro® as an arthritis medicine that can be taken only once a day. Depo-Provera® is advertised as a method of birth control that does not require daily medication. A physician might not be aware that the less convenient form is a problem for a particular consumer. Alternatively, a consumer might have stopped using the medication because of the inconvenience, and so not be in contact with a physician. Thus, direct advertising in this instance can be quite useful.

For all of these cases, it is important to remember that a physician must approve the purchase of all of the medicines under consideration.

Thus, if an ad misleads a consumer, there is an immediate check. The only cost to the consumer is the cost of a (perhaps) superfluous visit to a physician. On the other hand, the cost of not allowing the advertising is that some consumers may needlessly suffer the symptoms of disease, when treatments are available. This health cost will generally outweigh the money cost of the visit to the physician.

Price Reductions. Direct-to-consumer advertising will also lead to price reductions for pharmaceuticals. There is evidence from many markets that increased advertising leads to lower prices.[47] The Supreme Court cited this evidence in decisions overturning state bans on advertising of attorney services and of eyeglasses. Price is currently less effective as a competitive tool in pharmaceuticals than in many other lines of commerce because the physician chooses the product but the consumer has to pay for it. Therefore, providing information to consumers enabling them to compare prices more easily would have a larger than average effect on price because this advertising would provide information to the party actually paying for the product.

There are several mechanisms through which advertising can lead to lower prices. Advertising can inform consumers that two versions of the same drug (a branded version and a generic) are, in fact, equivalent. Consumers can also learn that two different drugs are effectively equivalent and that one is cheaper, and thus ask physicians to prescribe the lower priced product. For example, an ad campaign for Ciba-Geigy's Lotensin® indicates that it is cheaper than Capoten® or Vasotec®, competing blood pressure medicines. Increased competition brought about by increased advertising can lead manufacturers to reduce prices for drugs. If one ad can simultaneously list the use of a drug, the price, and the name, then price competition between retail pharmacies can be increased.[48] As of today, an ad cannot provide all of this information without including the "brief summary."

Summary

When we think of the FDA and overregulation, we tend to think of the inexcusable delays in approval of new drugs. Scholars have long been aware that the agency causes unnecessary deaths and suffering by this policy. Nothing in this paper is to be interpreted as minimizing this cause of needless suffering.

But this is only part of the problem with the FDA. Once the FDA approves a drug, users must learn of it. This can occur either through advertising and promotion to physicians or directly to consumers. In both cases, the FDA's policies greatly retard the spread of such information. This set of policies also has substantial detrimental effects on health. One single policy, the banning of advertising of aspirin for first heart attack prevention, may be the single most harmful regulatory policy currently pursued by any agency of the U.S. government. On the other hand, the FDA's recent change in policy for direct-to-consumer advertising on television has been a real improvement.

What other policies might correct this problem?[49] The best reform would be to give regulatory power over pharmaceutical advertising and promotion to another agency, such as the Federal Trade Commission (FTC).[50] The FTC had this jurisdiction until 1962, so the reform would not be a radical departure. This shift in power would be appropriate not because the FTC is a more enlightened agency, but because it has less power over pharmaceutical companies and therefore could not regulate in as arbitrary and capricious a manner as does the FDA. If the FTC tried to enforce counterproductive regulations, companies would be more likely to challenge it in court, and would sometimes win.

Several intermediate steps are also available. The FDA should immediately cancel all its recent initiatives reducing promotion of off label uses and return to the pre-Kessler world. The FDA should allow manufacturers to advertise any claim for which reliable scientific evidence exists, whether or not this claim has been approved for the label, and this advertising should be allowed for both consumers and physicians. No policy requiring prior approval of advertisements should be mandated, by Congress or by the FDA. With respect to ads to consumers, the requirement of the "brief summary" should be abolished for print as well as TV advertising. The FDA should allow free and unrestricted advertising of pharmaceuticals on TV and in print, subject only to regulation for "falsity," but not for "deception" as currently defined. The results will be greatly improved health of consumers, and also reduced prices of pharmaceuticals.

Notes

1.   Steering Committee of the Physicians' Health Study Group, "Final Report on the Aspirin Component of the Ongoing Physicians' Health Study," *The New England Journal of Medicine*, V. 321, No. 3, July 20, 1989, p. 129-35.

2.   This publication is by no means a scientific gem. For example, it has an ad for horoscopes on the inside front cover. Nonetheless, the consumer information about aspirin seems accurate.

3.   This meeting is described in detail in Charles C. Mann and Mark L. Plummer, *The Aspirin Wars*, Harvard Business School Press, Boston, MA, 1991. Aspirin can be advertised as a preventative for a second heart attack, and some Bayer advertising does make this point.

4.   Discussed at length in Richard T. Kaplar, ed., *Bad Prescription for the First Amendment: FDA Censorship of Drug Advertising and Promotion*, The Media Institute, Washington, 1993.

5.   The regulation of aspirin advertising is atypical in one sense. Generally, the FDA regulates advertising of prescription drugs, and the Federal Trade Commission (FTC) regulates advertising of over-the-counter (OTC) drugs. Regulation of an OTC drug by the FDA is thus anomalous. However, other aspects of this regulation are typical.

6.   See the discussion in Kaplar, Bad *Prescription for the First Amendment*.

7.   David A. Kessler and Wayne L. Pines, "The federal regulation of prescription drug advertising and promotion," 264 *Journal of the American Medical Association* 2409-2415 (1990) at 2410. This article was written before Kessler became Commissioner of the FDA, but it appears to express his views as commissioner as well.

8.   Alison Keith, "Regulating Information About Aspirin and the Prevention of Heart Attack," *American Economic Review* 85, May 1995, 96-99.

9.   This point has been documented in detail for fiber in diets. When cereal-makers began advertising that fiber was healthy, the main beneficiaries were relatively less educated, lower income consumers. See Pauline M. Ippolito and Alan D. Mathios, "Information, Advertising and Health Choices: A Study of the Cereal Market," *The Rand Journal of Economics*, V. 21, No. 3, autumn 1990, pp. 459-80.

10. Discussed in Milt Freudenheim, "Aspirin's Heart Benefits Help Bayer's Bottom Line," *New York Times*, August 9, 1997.

11. David Adams, "Pharmaceutical Advertising: Education versus Promotion," in Dev S. Pathak, Alan Excovitz, and Suzan Kucukarslan, eds., *Promotion of Pharmaceuticals: Issues, Trends, Options*, Pharmaceutical Products Press, Binghamton, NY, 1992, pp. 53-66.

12. Steering Committee of the Physicians' Health Study Group, "Final Report on the Aspirin Component of the Ongoing Physicians' Health Study," *The New England Journal of Medicine*, V. 321, No. 3, July 20, 1989, p. 129-35.

13. The original research showing excessive delays was by Sam Peltzman, "An Evaluation of Consumer Protection Legislation: The 1962 Drug Amendments," *Journal of Political Economy*, V. 81, September 1973, pp. 1049-1091. A summary of the literature appears in William S. Comanor, "The Political Economy of the Pharmaceutical Industry," *Journal of Economic Literature*, V. 24, 1986, pp. 1178-1217. Recent discussions are available in Sam Kazman, "Deadly Overcaution: FDA's Drug Approval Process," *Journal of Regulation and Social Costs*, V. 1, No. 1, September 1990, pp. 35-54, and Michael R. Ward, "Drug Approval Overregulation," *Regulation*, fall 1992, 47-53. A legal analysis is in C. Frederick Breckner, III, "The FDA's War on Drugs," *Georgetown Law Journal*, V. 82, No. 2, December 1993, pp. 529-62.

14. On average, it costs $359 million to develop a new drug. Pharmaceutical Manufacturers Association, *The Case for the Pharmaceutical Industry*, Washington, DC, 1993, p. 9.1. Since most of this cost is for clinical testing, the costs of seeking approval for a new use for aspirin would be in this range.

15.   For example, see Mary-Margaret Chren, "The Need for Guidelines about Pharmaceutical Promotions to Physicians," in Pathak, et al. *Promotion of Pharmaceuticals.*

16.   Mary-Margaret Chren and C. Seth Landefeld, "Physicians' Behavior and Their Interactions With Drug Companies," *Journal of the American Medical Association*, V. 271, No. 9, March 2, 1994, 684-89.

17.   Elliott M. Antman, Joseph Lau, Bruce Kupelnick, Frederick Mosteller, and Thomas C. Chalmers, "A Comparison of Results of Meta-analyses of Randomized Control Trials and Recommendations of Clinical Experts," *Journal of the American Medical Association*, V. 268, no. 2, July 8, 1992, 240-48.

18.   These are from Pharmaceutical Research and Manufacturers of America, *The Case for America's Pharmaceutical Research Companies*, Washington, DC, 1994, Section 12, which also contains additional examples.

19.   Kessler and Pines, "The federal regulation of prescription drug advertising and promotion," at 2410, footnotes omitted.

20.   J. Howard Beales, III, "Economic Analysis and the Regulation of Pharmaceutical Advertising," *Seton Hall Law Review*, V. 24, No. 3, 1994, at 1386.

21.   The major compendia are the *American Hospital Formulary Drug Service Information;* the *American Medical Association Drug Evaluations;* and the *U.S. Pharmacopoeia Drug Information.*

22.   Cited in *The Case for the Pharmaceutical Industry,* at 23.2.

23.   Beales, "Economic Analysis and the Regulation of Pharmaceutical Advertising," p. 1391.

24.   David Adams, "Pharmaceutical Advertising," p. 63.

25.   Kessler and Pines, at 2411.

26.   Discussed in Arthur N. Levine, "The FDA's Expanding Control over Drug Promotion," in Kaplar, *Bad Prescription*, pp. 23-39.

27.   See John E. Calfee, "FDA Regulation: Moving Toward a Black Market in Information," *The American Enterprise*, V. 3, No. 2, March/April 1992, 34-41.

28.   This section is based on Paul H. Rubin, "Are Pharmaceutical Ads Deceptive,*"* *Food and Drug Law Journal*, 1994. That paper has a more detailed analysis and provides some additional criticisms of the article. Some of the arguments made here were briefly raised in Paul H. Rubin, "New Study on Drug Ads Misleads," *Wall Street Journal*, June 4, 1992, A8.

29.   Discussed, for example, in Paul H. Rubin, *Managing Business Transactions*, Free Press, New York, 1990.

30.   Sam Peltzman, "The Effects of FTC Advertising Regulation,*"* *Journal of Law and Economics,* V. 24 (December 1981): pp. 403-48; Alan Mathios and Mark Plummer, "The Regulation of Advertising by the Federal Trade Commission: Capital Market Effects," in Richard O. Zerbe, ed., *Research In Law and Economics*, V. 12, 1989, pp. 77-93.

31.   Michael S. Wilkes, Bruce H. Doblin, and Martin F. Shapiro, "Pharmaceutical Advertisements in Leading Medical Journals: Experts Assessments," *Annals of Internal Medicine*, V. 116, No. 11, June 1, 1992, 912-19.

32.   June 1, 1992, p. 1.

33.   These points are elaborated on in Jacob Jacoby, "Misleading Research on the Subject of Misleading Advertising," *Food And Drug Law Journal*, 1994, which does apply marketing research techniques to the study.

34.   J. Howard Beales III and William C. MacCleod, "Assessments of Pharmaceutical Advertisements: A Critical Analysis of the Criticisms," 50 *Food and Drug Law Journal* 415 (1995).

35.   To students of the FDA, this approach may seem novel. This is because the FDA regulates promotion and advertising from a perspective that does not generally include these considerations. However, the Federal Trade Commission, the major body charged with regulating advertising, does consider exactly these questions in its decisions regarding regulation of advertising. I was Director of the Division of Consumer Protection in the Bureau of Economics at the FTC, 1983-85, and my research on the advertising policies of the FDA began at that time; see Alison Masson and Paul H. Rubin, "Matching Prescription Drugs and Consumers: The Benefits of Direct Advertising," *New England Journal of Medicine* 313 (August 22) 1985, 513-15. Some published materials detailing the economic approach are: Howard Beales, Richard Craswell, and Steven C. Salop, "The Efficient Regulation of Consumer Information," *Journal of Law and Economics* 24 (1981), 491-539; Richard Craswell, "Interpreting Deceptive Advertising," *Boston University Law Review* 65 (1985), 658-732; Jack Calfee, *Health Information in Advertising*, American Enterprise Institute, 1997 and Paul H. Rubin, "The Economics of Regulating Deception," *Cato Journal* 10 (winter 1991), pp. 667-90. All of these authors spent time at the FTC. The last study has an extensive bibliography on the economics of information and deception, and applies the analysis to many FDA policies.

36.   While some of these standards were important, others are more doubtful. For example, thirty-one ads were faulted for "headlines or subheadlines," which were not "Adequately referenced" (Table 3).

37.   Richard Craswell, "Interpreting Deceptive Advertising," *Boston University Law Review* 65 (1985), 658-732.

38.   This is a standard economic point in analyzing advertising. It was first made by Philip Nelson, "Advertising as Information," *Journal of Political Economy*, V. 82, July 1974, pp. 729-54. Applications to deception are in Paul H. Rubin, "The Economics of Regulating Deception."

39.   "Short, punchy claims are the most effective way to attract their [prescribing physicians] to the limited number of products about which they will be willing to spend some effort to absorb and evaluate details." Richard M. Cooper, "Marketing 'Violations,'" *Food and Drug Law Journal* 47, 1992, pp. 155-62, at p. 156.

40.   Wilkes, Doblin, and Shapiro, "In Response," *Annals of Internal Medicine*, V. 117, No. 7, 1 October 1992, pp. 618-19.

41.   Discussed in Cooper, "Marketing 'Violations'," p. 157.

42.   For discussions, see Alison Masson and Paul H. Rubin, "Matching Prescription Drugs and Consumers;" Paul H. Rubin, "The FDA's Prescription for Consumer Ignorance," *Journal of Regulation and Social Costs*, 1991, pp. 5-24; Paul H. Rubin, "From Bad to Worse: Recent FDA Initiatives and Consumer Health," in Richard T. Kaplar, ed., *Bad Prescription for the First Amendment;* and Allision Keith, "The Benefits of Pharmaceutical Promotion: An Economic and Health Perspective, in Pathak et al., *Promotion of Pharmaceuticals*.

43.   Cited in Kessler and Pines, at 2413.

44.   Kessler and Pines at 2413.

45.   News Release, Food and Drug Administration, "FDA to Review Standards for All Direct-to-consumer Rx Drug Promotion," August, 8, 1997; Bruce Ingersoll and Yumiko Ono, "FDA to Clear the Way for Blitz of TV Drug Ads," *Wall Street Journal*, August 8, 1997.

46.   I was not one.

47.   Lee Benham, "The Effect of Advertising on the Price of Eyeglasses," *Journal of Law and Economics*, V. 15, 1972, p. 337; Robert Steiner, "Does Advertising

Lower Consumer Prices?" *Journal of Marketing,* V. 37, 1973, p. 19; Howard Marvel, "The Economics of Information and Retail Gasoline Price Behavior," *Journal of Political Economy,* V. 84, October 1976, p. 1033; John Kwoka, "Advertising and the Price and Quality of Optometric Services," *American Economic Review,* V. 74, 1984, p. 211; Deborah Haas-Wilson, "The Effect of Commercial Practice Restrictions: The Case of Optometry," *Journal of Law and Economics,* V. 29, April 1986, p. 165; Paul Farris and Mark Albion, "The Impact of Advertising on the Price of Consumer Products," *Journal of Marketing,* V. 44, summer 1980, p. 17; Mark Albion and Paul W. Farris, *The Advertising Controversy: Evidence on the Economic Effects of Advertising,* Boston, Auburn House, 1981.

48. Only 36.4 percent of consumers "Never" use the price of a prescription product as a basis for choosing a pharmacy; see Alan P. Wolfgang and Matthew Perri, III, "Consumer Price Sensitivity Towards Prescriptions," *Journal of Research in Pharmaceutical Economics,* V. 1, No. 4, 1989, pp. 51-60. Greater provision of information would facilitate such price shopping between pharmacies, and more information would also allow price shopping between brands and drugs.

49. Based on the discussion in Rubin, "From Bad to Worse."

50. Also suggested by Calfee, "Moving Towards a Black Market in Information."

10

Exploring Free Market Certification of Medical Devices[1]

Noel D. Campbell

Introduction

No manufacturer can market a medical device, alter manufacturing processes for a device, or propose a new use for an existing device without the prior approval of the Food and Drug Administration (FDA). The FDA monopoly over market access is a bottleneck, delaying the introduction of new medical devices for up to three years and restricting the flow of information from manufacturer to user about approved devices. These actions not only interfere with the rights of device manufacturers and consumers to trade with one another; they have resulted in thousands of deaths.

The solution to the problems caused by the FDA's monopoly over market access and dissemination of information is to turn over the certification of medical devices to certification agencies competing in a free market. The best known of the privately funded institutions that certify safety and performance in other markets is Underwriters Laboratories, Inc. UL's and similar organizations' product safety certification provides valuable information to consumers, increases the market for manufacturers and leaves manufacturers and consumers free to trade with one another.

Unlike reforms that leave the FDA's monopoly intact, the market solution ensures that consumers will be able to choose in a market well-stocked with safe, effective devices, guided by qualified experts with superior information. Certifying organizations, anxious to maintain their reputations as guardians of safety and efficacy and, hence, their commercial viability will protect consumers from a "race to the bottom" and from "fly-by-night" manufacturers. When, as sometimes happens even currently with the FDA certification, unsafe or ineffective products mistakenly reach the market, the court system provides a mechanism for redress. The incentives for certifiers in a free market are far more effective for generating good results than the incentives for bureaucrats with monopoly powers.

The Nature of the Problem

The basic problem with the FDA can be stated with a simple example from statistical theory. When the FDA makes decisions about whether or not devices are safe and effective, two types of errors are possible. A Type I error occurs when a true hypothesis is rejected. For example, if the FDA's null hypothesis is that a given device is unsafe and ineffective, and this hypothesis is incorrectly rejected, then a Type I error has occurred. It results in an unsafe or ineffective device being marketed. A Type II error occurs when a false hypothesis is accepted as true. A Type II error occurs when the FDA mistakenly believes that a product is unsafe and ineffective when, in fact, it is safe and effective. A Type II error prevents or delays the entry of a safe and effective device into the market.

The FDA spends too much time and too many resources trying to prevent the introduction of devices that may later prove to be unsafe or ineffective (preventing Type I errors). Consequently, the FDA does not spend enough time and resources ensuring that safe and effective devices are not locked out of the market (preventing Type II errors). The result is that safe devices are subject to long, costly delays before they can be marketed.

The FDA behaves this way because it is a public agency answering to politicians, and Congress and the President pass on the political pressure they feel to the agencies under them. Ironically, the pressure Congress feels comes from the public who is harmed by the FDA's subsequent behavior. The death and suffering resulting from an unsafe device is very visible, while the death and suffering attributable to the lack of safe and effective devices is much more difficult to detect. Thus, Congress' actions have been described as follows:

From FDA commissioner to the bureau heads to the individual NDA [New Drug Application] reviewers, the message is clear: if you approve a drug with unanticipated side effects, both you and the agency will face the heat of newspaper headlines, television coverage and congressional hearings. On the other hand, if FDA insists on more and more data from a manufacturer, and finally approves a drug, which should have been on the market months or years before, there is no such price to pay. Drug lag's victims and their families will hardly be complaining, because they won't know what hit them....They only know that there is nothing their doctors can do for them. From the standpoint of...politics, they are invisible.[2]

Though stated in terms of drugs, the analysis still holds true when discussing medical devices.

The Perils of Delaying Medical Devices

All regulatory agencies are human institutions: they make mistakes and produce delays. When the FDA makes a Type I mistake and allows unsafe and harmful products on the market, people suffer or die. But what is not so clearly seen is that people also suffer and die when the FDA fails to act or acts too slowly in allowing devices on the market.

One can seldom specify the deaths that occurred because the FDA was slow to allow a device on the market. There are, however, some well-known examples:

● Seven thousand Americans die every year because the AmbuCardioPump, a CPR device used in emergency rooms and available in most industrialized nations, is not available in the United States.[3]

● In 1993, the FDA disallowed the use of a specialized infant ventilator, a machine that helps very sick infants to breathe. The FDA's action cost the lives of ten to several hundred infants.[4]

● FDA action in 1992 halted production of Physio-Control's cardiac defibrillators for more than two years, before allowing production to resume. A defibrillation authority, Dr. Richard Cummins, estimates "that FDA's shutdown of Physio-Control might have caused a thousand deaths."[5]

● "Balloon implants used to plug life-threatening holes in brain arteries were rejected by the FDA because the developers did not properly document their benefits. Some neurosurgeons call the balloons `the world's standard of care.'"[6]

● Annually, 40,000 men undergo surgery to correct benign prostate swelling. An American-designed, safe, painless, permanent alternative—a tiny implantable wire coil—was still not available in the United States six months after its introduction in Europe.[7]

- Despite the clearly demonstrated safety and accuracy of the home HIV test, FDA delayed its marketing for five years. As a result, an estimated 10,000 people were infected with HIV because people who would have used the test to find out that they were carriers of the virus could not do so.[8]

These numbers reflect only some of the fatalities and suffering that can be laid at the FDA's door. Quality of life suffers when the FDA refuses to allow drugs and medical devices to be sold until its exhausting, circuitous approval procedures are completed.

Taxpayers also bear a large, direct burden because of the FDA. The FDA is a monumental, costly enterprise funded almost entirely by tax dollars. The FDA budget has hovered just below $1 billion annually since 1994.[9]

The FDA and Medical Devices

Developing a medical device is a lengthy process that usually goes through three steps after prototypes are first manufactured: pre-clinical testing on animals, clinical testing involving human beings, and FDA review for approval. The FDA review process imposes significant delays upon the marketing of new devices.

A Brief History of Medical Device Regulation

The fundamental sanctioning law of the FDA, the Federal Food, Drug, and Cosmetic Act of 1938 (FDC Act), clearly separated medical devices from pharmaceuticals and gave the FDA power of premarket approval over pharmaceuticals, but gave it no corresponding power over medical devices. "Pharmaceuticals" are products that produce an effect through chemical or metabolic action. "Biologics" are products of biological origin that have pharmaceutical properties. A "medical device," according to the General Accounting Office (GAO), "can be any product used to cure, prevent, diagnose, or treat illness, provided that its principal intended purposes are not achieved primarily by chemical or metabolic action."[10] Devices range from Band-Aids and tongue depressors to kidney dialysis units to MRI units and artificial hearts.

Under the 1938 law, the FDA's options for regulating devices were limited to asking the courts for the authority to block new devices or to remove existing devices from the market. Within that limited sphere, the FDA blocked or removed dozens of fraudulent medical devices during the next quarter century. Following passage of the 1962 amendments to the FDC Act, which expanded the FDA's mandate to require proof of effectiveness as well as safety for drugs and which increased the FDA's enforcement powers, the FDA struggled to secure the same authority over medical devices that it already had over drugs.[11]

The Medical Device Amendments of 1976 enjoined the FDA to "provide reasonable assurance of the safety and effectiveness of the device." The most significant aspect of the 1976 amendments was the establishment of the FDA as the gatekeeper over market access for medical devices. Power had clearly shifted to the FDA. Instead of being required to demonstrate its case to the satisfaction of a court, the FDA could now ban devices on its own legal authority, and it was left to the injured party to seek a judicial review.

The next significant event in medical device regulation was the November 1990 passage of the Safe Medical Devices Act (SMDA). The pattern repeated itself. The FDA garnered more power, added more layers of costly reporting and bureaucratic requirements, and gained more powers of interference in the market. The SMDA instituted a massive system of postmarket surveillance and a reporting scheme wherein medical device users, of any sort, were required to file reports anytime a device could be implicated in a patient's injury or illness.[12] In addition, the FDA received new authority to impose civil penalties for violations of the Act, or not to impose the penalties, at the FDA's discretion. Finally, some of the more egregious reporting burdens of SMDA were rolled back by the FDA Modernization Act of 1997.

Classes and Tiers of Medical Devices

The 1976 amendments established three classes of medical devices (Classes I, II, and III), corresponding to devices of low, medium, and high risk. In 1994, the FDA implemented a three-tier system that ranks devices according to the intensity of required review. Tier I devices require the least review. With the combination of the class and tier systems, the FDA can categorize medical devices in nine different ways (for example, Class I, Tier I; Class II, Tier I; Class I, Tier II, etc.). Some devices are novel, and some devices are similar, or nearly equivalent, to existing devices. For high-risk novel devices, the

FDA requires a full premarket approval (PMA) review before allowing the marketing of the device. Low-risk novel devices similar to other approved devices are evaluated under a provision called "510(k)" (after a section of the 1976 law). The 510(k) process initially required only that the manufacturers notify the FDA about the device and convince the agency that it was equivalent to an existing device. The FDA does not require full PMAs before considering approval for new uses of approved devices. Those are evaluated as "PMA supplementals" and require only an abbreviated approval process.

These neat distinctions, if they ever existed, have been battered down by the FDA's constantly expanding requirements. The 510(k) process, through arbitrary and baffling FDA requests for more information, ballooned from a simple notification process into a system often tantamount to a full PMA.[13] In an apparent acceptance of reality, the SMDA of 1990 formally altered the 510(k) process from notification to an approval process and augmented the types and quantities of required data.

Approval Rates for Medical Devices

Table 10.1 shows the number of submissions for FDA approval of medical devices and the number of approvals each year from 1989 through mid-1995.[14] As can be seen, the number of submissions was highest in 1989, probably because of manufacturers' desires to avoid the new requirements expected with the passage of the SMDA in 1990. Since then the number of 510(k) submissions remained steady, though trending down in the late 1990s. PMA submissions fell in the early 1990s, but climbed again in 1997 and 1998. PMA Supplemental submissions have fallen from about 600 to about 400.

Approvals per year of 510(k)s remained nearly constant through much of the 1990s, and approvals of PMAs and PMA Supplementals fell, rose, then fell again through the late 1990s. According to a 1995 GAO report, the FDA has approved 73 percent of the 40,950 510(k) applications received during 1989 through May 1995 and disapproved 2 percent. As of May 1995, 4 percent of the 1989 PMAs were unresolved, and 81 percent of the 1994 PMAs were still in review. The FDA is far short of reaching its 1976 Medical Device Amendments-mandated requirements to complete reviews of 510(k)s in 90 days and PMAs in 180 days, despite increases in funding and personnel.

TABLE 10.1
Submissions and Approvals for Medical Devices

Year	510(k)s Total/ Approved	PMAs Total/ Approved	PMA Supplementals Total/ Approved
1989	7,023/ 5,258	84/ 45	804/ 640
1990	5,835/ 4,633	77/ 36	660/ 557
1991	5,835/ 4,513	72/ 21	595/ 493
1992	6,533/ 4,888	66/ 21	605/ 474
1993	6,306/ 4,654	40/ 7	394/ 311
1994	6,446/ 4,342	43/ 3	372/ 269
1995	3,033/ 1,429	19/ 0	210/ 78

Source: "Medical Devices: FDA Review Time," GAO/PEMD-96-2, October 1995, p.27.

How Long Does FDA Review Take?

The 1976 law requires the FDA to complete review of 510(k) devices within 90 days and review of PMAs within 180 days. Those requirements have proved unreachable for the FDA. In 1995, at the request of Representative Joe Barton (R-Tex.), the GAO examined the FDA review times for medical devices from fiscal year 1989 to May 18, 1995.[15] In its October 1995 report, the GAO found that FDA had failed to meet the review deadlines.

For 510(k)s:

● The median approval time for 510(k) applications was 222 days for applications submitted in 1993.

● The average for all 510(k)s was even greater, 269 days, and will continue to grow as the remaining open cases (3 percent) are gradually closed.

For PMA Supplementals:

● For PMA Supplementals submitted in fiscal year 1991, the median review time was 154 days, the mean was 261 days, and 3 percent of the submissions remained open.

● The mean time for review of all PMA Supplementals was 238 days.

For PMAs:

● The median review time for PMAs completed in 1993 was 804 days. The mean was 591 days for all PMAs over the 1989 through 1993 time period.

The GAO analysis showed that the time used by manufacturers to gather new information had held steady during 1989-1993.[16] The increases in review times resulted almost entirely from FDA actions.[17]

Drawing heavily on government sources, the Competitive Enterprise Institute found that for fiscal year 1997 the FDA improved on its 1996 average of 786 days by approving 48 PMAs in an average of 497 days, still more than twice the statutory limit.[18] For premarket notifications (510(k)), the FDA reviewed 5,155 premarket notifications, 408 fewer than in 1996, in an average of 130 days, or roughly 44 percent longer than the statutory limit. This number is expected to fall, as the FDA Modernization Act of 1997 exempted many devices and changes from the 510(k) process.[19]

The final results are long delays between the development of a device and the time it becomes available to consumers who need it. In addition, the FDA's more stringent gatekeeping over which applications it will consent to review may be leading to the rejection of useful devices in order to reduce review times.

Reform Is Not the Solution

Responding to the delays and inefficiencies in FDA review, Congress has considered a number of FDA reforms, culminating in the FDA Modernization Act of 1997 (FDAMA 97). These reforms have changed the FDA's marching orders but left its monopoly over market access largely intact. In addition, the FDA is experimenting with "reform" of medical device review. That experiment is no more than an outsourcing of the FDA's work to be paid for by device manufacturers. It, too, leaves the FDA's monopoly intact. In any case, it has not accomplished much.

Perhaps the FDA's claims to have significantly reduced review times and boosted market access through the late 1990s are completely accurate and truthful. Even so, none of the sweeping reforms enacted, internal and external to the Agency, seriously impair the FDA's tight control over market access and an FDA that once imposed astounding delays on device approval can do so again. All that may be necessary to undo years of hard work at reforming the FDA is one well-publicized perception of a device failure. In that instance, we might rapidly find the "bad old days" upon us again, and beneficial devices held off the market by a defensive FDA.

The FDA's Trial of Third-Party Review

In November 1998, FDAMA 97 simultaneously terminated the FDA's own existing pilot program and authorized the Agency to recreate the limited third-party 510(k) review program. The original pilot program evolved simultaneously with plans to exempt large numbers of the lowest-risk devices from the revamped, post-SMDA 510(k) process. Now many of those lowest-risk devices reach the market through notification, much as they would have in the original 510(k) process. Practically, that means that incremental advances in the design, or changes in the manufacture or materials, are no longer automatically kept off the market while the FDA grinds through its review process.

Third-party reviewers must be accredited by the FDA, and cannot review Class III devices, or Class II devices that are implantable or require clinical data. The FDA must allow manufacturers to seek 510(k) certification via third parties and offer a choice of reviewers, at the manufacturer's request. Manufacturers must pay for third-party review out of their own pocket, even though third-party approval is no guarantee of FDA approval. The FDA has the authority to accept the reviewer's recommendation, or reclassify the device. In other words, if the third party does not find substantial equivalence, and the FDA accepts this recommendation, then the device cannot be marketed. However, even if the third party recommends approval, the FDA may still reclassify the device as an ineligible Class II or Class III device, blocking market access. It must be understood that the pilot third-party program is meant to be a subcontracting of the FDA at manufacturers' expense, and not an alternative route to market. The third parties are to "assist the Agency in reviewing 510(k)s,"[20] rather than provide a more market-based certification system that could compete with the FDA. Furthermore, the pilot program has specific termination dates: either five years after at least two third parties are available to do 60 percent of the eligible 501(k)s; or four years after accredited bodies have reviewed 35 percent of eligible 510(k)s.

As of the third week in May 1999, there are thirteen accredited third-party reviewers.[21] From the original program's inception in August 1996 to early June 1999, there have been forty-nine submissions to the pilot programs. By comparison, through early June 1999, it is estimated that 1,300 submissions will be made to the FDA in FY 99.[22]

Before either program started, the FDA and the manufacturers were well aware of the weak incentives for manufacturers to use the program. The FDA report of a meeting on June 19, 1996, states,

> Some industry representatives expressed concern...about the limitations of the pilot program that may restrict manufacturers' incentives to participate. In particular they commented that including only low- to moderate-risk devices in the pilot program and limiting third parties' roles to making recommendations rather than final decisions might result in marketing clearances that are no faster, and perhaps slower, than those made by FDA alone.[23]

At the same meeting, some potential third-party reviewers advocated standards-based third-party reviews rather than reviews focused on substantial equivalence; increased harmonization with international standards; and reliance on existing accreditation systems and criteria for potential third parties.[24]

The FDA initially rejected these ideas. FDAMA 97 legally requires the FDA to change its tune, mandating that the FDA find acceptable standards, work to harmonize its accepted standards with international quality standards, and allow manufacturers to meet certain PMA and 510(k) requirements by declaring conformity with the accepted standards.[25] It remains to be seen how effective in practice this new legal requirement is, especially given the FDA's well-established ability to ignore or side-step its legal obligations. In any event, the FDA retains important gatekeeping authority and the ability to withdraw marketing approval.

FDA Modernization Act of 1997

The most recent overhaul of the FDA occurred with the FDA Modernization Act of 1997 (FDAMA 97).[26] FDAMA 97 is a major piece of legislation, requiring large-scale changes. However, in nearly every important particular, it leaves intact the FDA's monopoly control over market access, and does not alter the FDA's incentives to overinvest resources to reduce Type I errors. Rather than alter the fundamental nature of U.S. device certification, the reforms of FDAMA 97 are designed to "streamline the process of bringing safe and effective...medical devices...to the U.S. market."[27] While the FDA will almost certainly operate more efficiently post-FDAMA 97, the twin problems of access monopoly and incentives will remain, and the FDA will continue to block or delay safe and effective medical devices, to the detriment of public health.

Regarding PMAs, FDAMA 97 allows manufacturers to use clinical data from studies of earlier, less-improved versions of a device. Also "PMA applicants shall have...the same access as FDA to data and information submitted to a classification panel...; the opportunity to submit information based on the PMA, through FDA to the panel; and the same opportunity as FDA to participate in panel meetings."[28]

FDAMA 97 altered the approval system for PMA supplements to allow manufacturers to use nonclinical data and data from the original PMA to demonstrate additional capacity following incremental design change. In an important improvement, FDAMA 97 directs the FDA to develop, publish, and adhere to consistent standards and guidance documents "to assure prompt review of a PMA supplement,"[29] and "facilitate the submission of data to support a PMA supplement."[30]

Under FDAMA 97, if the FDA determines that a device is "not substantially equivalent," and therefore not eligible for 510(k), and that the device is Class III, the manufacturer is given the opportunity to request reclassification as Class I or II. The law requires the FDA to review its classification within sixty days. FDAMA 97 is expected to substantially decrease the 510(k) approval process time by exempting many more devices altogether. FDAMA 97 requires the Agency to "*only* request information *necessary*" to determine substantial equivalence, and to "*consider* the *least burdensome* means of demonstrating equivalence," [31] while disallowing withholding 510(k) approval for reasons other than substantial equivalence.

FDAMA temporarily loosens some of the "gag rules" imposed by the agency on manufacturers. Until the law's provision expires in 2006, and under restrictive circumstances, manufacturers can distribute information about "off-label" uses, provided the FDA has already approved the device, the FDA receives a copy of the information, and the manufacturer includes a statement that the use is not cleared by the FDA. The FDA may require the manufacturers to include other information about the "off-label" use at its discretion. Should the Agency determine its restrictions have not been met, the flow of information is again cut off.

In further change, postmarket surveillance studies are no longer automatically required. This has been replaced by a system which allows the FDA to order postmarket surveillance for specific Class II and Class III devices, reducing the burden on manufacturers and health care practitioners.

In a potentially major departure from the status quo, FDAMA 97 sets up a standards-driven initiative for 510(k) devices, designed to promote consistent device approval between Europe and the U.S. It adds a system that permits the FDA to recognize all or part of product review standards established by national or international standards development organizations. The manufacturer decides which FDA-approved standard to use and issues a Declaration of Conformity—that the device under question conforms to the referenced standard. The FDA or the third-party reviewer reviews the declaration and decides whether the standard is the proper standard, and whether everything was submitted in proper form and order. All else being equal, the Declaration of Conformity is sufficient for the FDA to allow market access.

However, the FDA can request supportive data, and "take action" for failure or refusal to provide data—in other words, business as usual, should the FDA resume its long-standing habit of requesting a bewildering amount of information. The FDA may reject the declaration on the basis of inapplicable standard, or that the manufacturer has failed to show conformity. The FDA may also withdraw recognition of specific standards at will.

The FDA's Trial of Third-Party Review May Doom Significant Change of the Current System

FDAMA 97 may be a step forward because of its exemption of many devices, and the expansion of the third-party program, but Congress explicitly states a continuing, dominating role for the FDA[32] in medical device approval.

The FDA's third-party certification pilot program may actually limit the possibility for more far-reaching change. In operation it resembles nothing more radical than a user-fee program for devices. The FDA retains its complete sway over approval, and the FDA has handpicked the devices and third parties so that no clinical and no, or very little, protocol-establishing work will be done.

In practice, the FDA's trial program may block any consideration of alternatives to the FDA's current monopoly. After studying the "feasibility" of such an approach, the agency may conclude that third-party review is a dismal failure or that it is irrelevant because most manufacturers chose to certify through the FDA anyway. In either case, the FDA would report to Congress that third-party review is not effective. While the program is going on, it can be used to delay consideration of any legislative proposals for significant third-party certification. Legislation, it will be said, should be delayed "pending the outcome of the pilot program."

Performance Standards Will Not Eliminate the FDA's Monopoly

Replacing arbitrary command-and-control regulations with written standards and a conformity process, as is contemplated in various instances in FDAMA 97, is a definite improvement over the pre-FDAMA 97 situation. It offers manufacturers something of a known burden of proof.

However, use of performance standards and self-certification as envisioned in FDAMA 97, by itself, will not change the FDA's behavior. The FDA will still possess the legal power to require submission of data and information for its review, dragging out review times until its preferences for minimizing Type I errors are met, and squelching any spark of real change that challenges the FDA's monopoly.

So long as the FDA can deny market access, product performance standards may introduce another bias into research. Given the cost of developing new devices, manufacturers may concentrate their efforts on producing devices that clearly comply with certain product standards and avoid the cost-increasing uncertainty of innovative device development that may involve classification delays or writing a new standard.

Still a further issue arises. How is the FDA to choose the best or most appropriate standard from among the collection of good standards? In the market for other sorts of goods, consumers, by their choices of what to buy, determine the standards for safety, effectiveness, and quality. Many different marketplace standards exist simultaneously, and the market provides a wide range of goods of varying quality. In a monopoly, the monopolist sets the standards; currently, the FDA has a legally protected monopoly. The question is how the FDA (or who) will be able to make the decision about what is best for all people in all circumstances regarding the most appropriate standard. Under the new system, the FDA will recognize a consensus standard. In a specific example, will a consensus standard that requires 70 percent effectiveness for 90 percent of all patients always be better than a standard that is 90 percent effective for 70 percent of all patients? The incentives for the FDA will not have changed, and the FDA will still over-invest in minimizing Type I errors. The FDA will adopt those standards that do not force the agency to be more concerned with Type II errors. If, somehow, the FDA is required to accept standards that seem to necessitate a change in philosophy, it can still find a way to delay, obfuscate, and slow down the approval process. Even in defiance of the law, that is exactly the history of the FDA.[33] There are a nearly infinite number of margins along which the FDA can delay approval, even if it technically breaks the law or neglects to follow executive orders.

The FDA's proponents can argue that the FDA is an independent organization insulated from special interests. Technically, that is true, but the FDA gets its budget and mandate from Congress, which resists few political pressures. What the FDA does depends on the money and mandate imposed by Congress. FDA standards cannot help but reflect that congressional pressure.

The Alternative

Is there an alternative to entrusting a monopoly agency with coercive powers with this power over life and health? Yes, there is. The alternative has a proven record of success. Privatization of the certification of medical devices will save lives and alleviate suffering. It is the efficient, effective alternative to the FDA's current command-and-control approach to regulation. Privatization is widely regarded as a positive step for most areas of government, but many people are reluctant to privatize an agency concerned with health and safety matters. Will the free market work? It works now and certifies the safety and effectiveness of thousands of products. It can work for medical devices, as well.

Unlimited Private Third-Party Certification

What would happen if the FDA were stripped of its monopolistic position over market access? Who would the public turn to for testing and certification of safety and effectiveness? How would the public know medical devices are safe? These questions have answers, leading us to the prospect of an approval process that will be faster and more responsive to the demand for new life-improving therapies and products. Not only can consumers get more speedy and flexible approval of safe devices, but also without sacrificing quality and effectiveness, and at lower cost.

Market-created institutions produce and disperse a vast volume of information about safety and quality every day. For example, *Consumer Reports* and the *Washington Checklist* tell prospective shoppers about best buys; the American National Standards Institute (ANSI) provides manufacturers with standards for manufacturing and safety so the consumer knows that "brand X FM tuner" will work with "brand Y amplifier." There is no compelling reason to believe that the market would not induce that same information flow about the safety and performance of medical devices.

There are reassuring working examples of market solutions to the same types of issues addressed by the FDA. The best-known example is Underwriters Laboratories, Inc. (UL), which has been certifying product safety for more than 100 years, longer than the FDA has been in existence.

Like the FDA, UL is committed to public safety. Both organizations work to safeguard the public from dangerous products. Both are staffed by expert scientists and technicians. UL's actions, like the FDA's, affect millions of consumers and involve billions of dollars worth of products.

Every day, the public buys and uses products that are UL-listed or FDA-approved. We put on our FDA-approved cosmetics after drying our hair with our UL-listed hair dryers. We pour FDA-approved vitamin-enhanced milk over the breakfast cereal we cooked on UL-listed stove tops. Driving home from work, we take FDA-approved aspirin while cooling off with UL-listed automotive air-conditioners. Only the number of products the market produces limits the parallels.

But there are some significant differences. The FDA is a tax-funded public agency, given legal monopoly power over market access and the dissemination of information. Its relationship to Congress leads the FDA to concentrate on approving only those devices that are extremely likely to be safe. The consequence is that many safe and effective devices never reach consumers. UL is a private organization that receives no tax revenue. Its clients, mostly manufacturers, wholly support it. It has no legally created monopoly over market access; it cannot deny consumers choice; it has no incentive to minimize the chance of a Type I error at the expense of Type II errors. UL's market-created incentives are to test products appropriately, optimally reducing the probability of both Type I and Type II errors.

A Case for the Market Solution

A Question of the Right to Contract

Many people accept that consumers and businesses have the right to contract over most goods and services but they deny that right when it comes to medical devices. Two common arguments defending this distinction are based upon information and potential harm. Consumers have good information and can evaluate the quality of most goods, it is claimed, but they have poor information and cannot evaluate the quality of medical devices. Similarly, it is argued that if a consumer makes a mistake about most goods they are unlikely to be caused great harm, which is not the case with medical devices. On the basis of these arguments a consumer's right to contract over medical devices is severely restricted.

However, neither of these premises are correct. Consumers have poor information and face great potential harm about many goods they contract over, like electrical devices and marriage partners. Yet we do not question the right of consumers to contract over electrical devices or marriage partners. Why? In the case of electrical devices although individual consumers may have poor information they contract through distributors who do have good information. The distributors and other informed buyers, along with ex-post threats of liability, cause electrical device manufacturers to produce high quality, safe products. The market commonly operates to economize on the knowledge necessary to make good decisions. Even if few individual buyers have good information the market as a whole operates as if consumers were very highly informed. The same sorts of processes which make the market for electrical devices and other markets operate in a highly "information-rich" manner will also operate in the market for medical devices.

The potential harm argument ignores costs imposed by limiting a consumer's choices. In the case of marriage partners, information is far from perfect and potential harm from poor contracting choices are severe, but potential gains from correct choices are very large. Limiting an individual's right to choose marriage partners on the grounds of avoiding potential harm imposes costs because some potentially beneficial marriages will be delayed or denied. It is true that a poorly chosen medical device could impose large costs on an unsuspecting consumer, but lack of access to medical devices can impose large costs also. As discussed earlier, exclusively focusing on protecting consumers from potential harm from unsafe and ineffective devices does not necessarily improve consumer welfare because it delays or denies consumers' access to some safe and effective devices.

The FDA or some other enforcement arm of the government can protect rights by investigating and prosecuting fraud when it occurs. For example, the marketing of a medical device advertised to consumers as safe and effective but later shown to be unsafe and ineffective is fraud. Manufacturers of fraudulent medical devices are guilty of crimes and should be investigated, prosecuted, and punished. However, fraud does not occur and cannot be established before a product is advertised and marketed; it can only be established after a product has been marketed and evidence exists to prove the fraudulent act in a court of law. The current regulatory process inverts the concept of justice from "innocent until proven guilty" to "guilty until proven innocent." The FDA requires manufacturers to "prove their innocence" by demonstrating that their medical devices are safe and effective before they market those devices, rather than the FDA being required to prove to a court that a manufacturer had engaged in fraud before a product could be legitimately banned from the market.

Since medical devices differ far less than is often supposed from other goods and services where the right to contract is well established the curtailing of individual rights in the marketplace for medical devices is unwarranted and unjustified. Private certification restores the right to contract.

Free Market Certification and Reputation: Ingredients for Profit

Under the watchful eyes of market organizations, consumers are certain that literally thousands of the products they use are safe. Within specified limits, bulletproof glass is, indeed, bulletproof, smoke detectors go off in the event of a fire, and operating a television represents no significant health risk. Magnetic resonance imaging (MRI) machines, artificial hearts, and cardiac-arrest paddles are different from light bulbs, toasters, and cordless telephones. But all are designed to perform specific functions under specified conditions, and they can be certified to work as designed without government monopoly of the certification process. With repeal of the government monopoly on approval, they will reach the market as certified products. Although the market places no restrictions on entry, it places many restrictions on success. Under conditions of free competition, there are no guarantees that a firm will be profitable. Those that prosper are those that provide products and services that perform as advertised. Those products that work well will be purchased and used, and those that do not will languish unsold. And in cases of fraud, the manufacturer will be held liable.

Businesses try to attain maximum profits, and harming customers does not contribute to that goal. Buying and selling are rarely single, isolated transactions where the participants never again have any contact. Most buying and selling takes place as repeated interactions in an environment where reputation is important. Companies maximize profits by having a long-standing repeat customer base, not by taking advantage of every new customer. Though the consumer may be only an occasional customer of device manufacturers' products, the doctors and hospitals who prescribe the products and the pharmacies and drug stores that retail them are repeat customers, usually buying many units of the same device over an extended period of time.

A reputation for honesty, fairness, and quality is necessary for generating profits. The longest established, most profitable companies enjoy good reputations. For example, in the market for home appliances, Maytag, General Electric, and Kitchenaid provide quality products and enjoy good reputations. When buying or replacing a major appliance, many consumers consider the brand of appliance that has a long-standing reputation for quality. When the reputation or product begins to slip, so do the fortunes of the company, as in the case of U.S. carmakers in the 1970s.

That is doubly true when a product requires a long, expensive development and/or a costly production run, as do many medical devices. The concern is not with simple devices like tongue depressors, but with devices of greater complexity and risk, such as implantable devices and diagnostic machines. Reputation is more important in the medical-device market than in many other markets. To earn their return on investment in such devices, manufacturers need to continue operation for a long while. Such devices are not cars or jeans, sold in a market with many different producers and consumers; they are highly specialized products with relatively limited markets. Generating a profit takes time and repeated interactions. The drive for profit creates powerful incentives for businesses to market quality devices.

Protection from Dangerous Devices

Can the private market protect the public from dangerous and ineffective medical devices? Yes, the public can be protected to the extent that members of the public desire protection.

In the absence of the FDA monopoly, devices might be marketed without third-party certification, but consumers and their medical advisers or the retailers who have customer contact could decide whether the promise of the device outweighed its risks, instead of having their decisions dictated by bureaucrats. Having more options, rather than fewer, is normally to the consumer's advantage. Consumers averse to risk could limit purchases to certified devices, and others could, if they chose, purchase uncertified ones, as is now the case with non-medical devices. The lack of compulsory, monopolized certification is not a problem with hair dryers and bulletproof glass, failures of which can be fatal, and there is no reason to expect market certification of medical devices to be any different.

A key argument for FDA regulation of medical devices is that consumers do not have information or the specialized training needed to make good medical decisions. Market certification, however, allows consumers to draw on highly trained and competent assistance. Consumers would rely on the advice of their physicians as to what they should do, just as they do today. In making recommendations, a doctor would rely on the private certification organizations, knowing that a series of bad recommendations would greatly damage his or her practice. Furthermore, in the absence of FDA-sanctioned gag rules that limit what manufacturers can tell physicians about their products, the medical-device companies themselves would become important sources of information, enabling doctors to make better decisions.

Doctors and medical practitioners will be reluctant to rely on devices that lack third-party listing. The only consumers who would use such devices would be those willing to bear a great deal of risk: those people who have few or poor alternatives offered by conventional medicine. Riskier devices, such as implantables, require a doctor for their installation, and complicated diagnostic and treatment devices that require specialized knowledge for their operation are prohibitively expensive to operate outside of a clinical setting. It is difficult even to conceive of a patient being successful in forcing his doctor to implant an unsafe pacemaker or buying a radiation therapy machine for his own unsupervised use. As a final preventative, there is that store of knowledge the FDA has habitually denigrated or denied: the consumer's common sense.

"Fly-by-night" manufacturers, by definition, are not concerned about the long-run effects of reputation on profits. The market cannot prevent such producers from taking devices to market, but their devices will not be certified. Shoddy products will not get the certifier's mark, and will therefore sell for less. Thus, the market will be protecting itself against "fly-by-nighters" by supplying two interrelated types of information: a specific certifier's mark, or lack thereof, and the price. Under the current regulatory scheme, one government-mandated amount of information is supposed to cover all contingencies, and there is no information about effective devices that involve more risk than the FDA has decided to allow. There is much less information under the present regime than consumers or their doctors would have in the free market.

No quality certification scheme can work so efficiently that it never approves an unsafe device. In any testing by any organization, private or public, there is always the chance of certifying an unsafe device. Likewise, there is always the chance that any single copy of any manufactured device will cease to function properly. Perfection cannot be the appropriate standard. The relevant question is whether we should expect more or less failure, specific or categorical, under a free market regime than under a centralized regulatory regime. Because of the incentives faced by private institutions, a market certification process should not result in significantly more frequent categorical failures than in the FDA regulatory system, but market access for safe devices would be faster. This statement is not to marginalize the suffering that results when a device fails or is later found to be unsafe. However, keeping useful devices off the market, banning them, or delaying their market delivery also causes deaths and prolongs suffering. Though unsafe devices will be certified and though samples of safe devices will fail, as also happens under FDA regulation, only market certification provides incentives to optimally reduce the chance of both types of errors.

Supply of Effective Devices

Until now, third-party-certification organizations within the United States have been primarily concerned with safety and not with effectiveness or performance. In contrast, the FDA also evaluates the performance of every device submitted for approval. Can free-market third-party certifiers accommodate wide-scale performance testing?

The certification industry would certainly adapt if the public demanded a general effectiveness mandate in addition to a safety mandate. Adding effectiveness testing will not change the market incentives for third-party organizations. The organizations would strive to be involved in research and development from the earliest stages and to produce flexible, adaptable certification systems. The resulting systems would move to include standards that incorporate effectiveness requirements. The standards, based on defined expectations for performance, would be of the appropriate quality, reflecting the consensus of consumers, manufacturers, and standards authorities. Importantly, those companies would still be dealing directly with their final clients: the consumers and the manufacturers. No special interests or perverse bureaucratic incentives created by congressional oversight would introduce distortions.

Additionally, one would expect the market to generate a range of effectiveness standards, each of which would carry a different type and amount of information reflecting the special conditions of would-be consumers, rather than the current FDA "one-size-fits-all" effectiveness standard. For example, rather than the fixed amount of information conveyed by the FDA, which is nonresponsive to market wants, the market would generate a variety of effectiveness standards. A free-market agency or agencies would certify effectiveness over a range: a particular device is 90 percent effective for 10 percent of the population, or 20 percent effective for 70 percent of the population. This enhanced information flow would improve medical decision making.

Absent any FDA restrictions on the information that manufacturers can make available, the device manufacturers would have a major incentive to contract for performance or effectiveness testing in order to distribute information with their products. The effectiveness data must be strong enough to convince the primary purchasers: the trained

doctors to whom consumers entrust medical decisions or the pharmacy and drugstore owners who depend on frequent, repeated shopping trips by their customers.

Several factors would ensure the accuracy of the manufacturer's
effectiveness data. First, there are the motives of reputation and profit.
Medical devices are purchased to perform certain tasks and not to be
admired on the coffee table. Few doctors prescribe, few retailers stock,
and few consumers buy a device that is not effective, regardless of
whether it is safe or not. Consumers prefer devices that both do not
harm them and that help them. If the devices do not help, there is no
reason to buy. Second, there are sticks to go with the carrot of profit—
that is, tort actions and laws against fraud. The threat of legal action
for deliberate misrepresentation will buttress the profit motive and
induce manufacturers to market effective devices.

Removing the FDA's monopoly on information and market access
will also free another set of market participants who have their own
incentives to qualify the effectiveness of devices. Medical professional organizations and research physicians generate a great deal of
information "for free." In fact, medical practice is steered by distribution of information, whether word-of-mouth presentations at conferences or technical journal articles, and it often results in "off-label"
uses of drugs and devices. A free market for information about devices will spur these activities. Doctors could build their careers independently from the device manufacturers when they submit their clinical results to peer-reviewed journals and professional meetings. A
physician's career, academic standing, and fortune can be built on
documenting a new use for a device, or on replicating successful
trials, or on debunking effectiveness claims. Though consumers may
never read the *New England Journal of Medicine* to access this information, their physicians do.

No "Race to the Bottom"

Competition in the private market creates powerful incentives to
reduce costs. One way to reduce costs is to produce goods or services
of a lower quality. Called a "race to the bottom," this is often cited as
a reason for public rather than private provision of goods and services.
Would private competition in the market for device certification produce a "race to the bottom?"

The executive officers of certification organizations are keenly aware of the fact that competing to lower the certification hurdles is destructive. If the standards are too lax, the third-party listing becomes meaningless to consumers, and therefore meaningless to manufacturers, who would have no incentive to buy the certifier's services. There will be no change in the incentives that certifiers face if they are allowed to certify medical devices.

Just as the market produces low-quality goods, it also produces high-quality goods, and consumers' desires dictate which products remain on the market. The market for standards and certification is no different. The market will generate a range of appropriate standards, each providing the consumer a specific amount and type of information. Consumers will demand at least some high-quality standards and some labs to perform high-quality testing. Furthermore, the individual consumer need not know what the different marks certify. The consumer's doctor will know because he has much more incentive to know.

The empirical experience of the last century has borne out these observations. As competing organizations have come into the market, the testing burden has not become easier for manufacturers, and consumers are still confident about the safety of their products. The adoption of UL's standards by other certifying agencies exemplifies this. UL has been the dominant certifying agency for decades, and it has already incurred the development cost of these standards. Instead of creating new, easier standards, the new competitors to UL have adopted the efficient, accepted UL standards and competed on the basis of testing cost or personal service. The integrity of testing standards and certification has been upheld.

There is, of course, no reason to forbid the FDA to continue in its current role, but without its monopoly. It could compete with private certifiers and manufacturers, and consumers could rely on an "FDA mark" as their chosen standard for safety and effectiveness. Other manufacturers, health professionals, and consumers might prefer other marks.

Appropriately Assign Liability

Some anchor defense of the current regulatory scheme in product liability. The argument states: The possibility of suffering irreparable damage from a liability suit involving medical devices can paralyze research, development, marketing, and distribution. The FDA's public approval and some degree of immunity from liability are necessary to appropriately assign or mitigate liability. In reality, there is no reason to expect such disasters to occur in medical device markets, any more than in markets for fire alarms and fire extinguishers.

Concerning manufacturers' refusals to market devices, Michael Krauss of the George Mason School of Law writes:

> Both economic theory and present-day practice suggest that fear of product liability does not stop manufacturers from producing goods. Manufacturers produce motorcycles and ladders despite the absence of pre-market government approval. They are held liable when their product is defectively designed or manufactured.[34]

Krauss goes on to say that except for recent cases involving Class III devices, "FDA approval does not immunize manufacturers from product liability."[35] Therefore, if fear of liability judgments would prevent manufacturers from producing devices if there were no FDA, it should prevent them from doing so under the current system as well.

Doctors often prescribe FDA-approved therapies for unapproved uses; such "off-label" uses may account for up to 60 percent of all prescriptions written.[36] Writing such "off-label" prescriptions exposes doctors to the standards of common-law negligence principles, by which they can be found liable for their actions; yet they continue to do so. There is no reason to believe that breaking the FDA's approval monopoly would cause radical changes in the common-law standards doctors already face. Without the FDA's approval, a physician would be liable only if the current medical consensus rejected the particular use of a device or if the doctor prescribed a patently unsafe device or a device that could not be made safe for the prescribed usage. Doctors would then rely on the safety mark of the certifier, and the usage guidelines from the manufacturer's information and from medical journals in writing prescriptions. Those guidelines and the safety seal would then be the basis of a doctor's defense in a liability suit.

Expanding third-party certification to medical devices may increase the liability exposure of the certifying organizations. The potential that certifying organizations may be held liable for the manufacturer's products may cause potential certifiers to stay out of the medical device market. However, certifying organizations are not sellers, advertisers, distributors, or manufacturers of products. They do not offer testimonials or underwrite risk. Third-party certification simply states the professional opinion of the certifiers as to the safety and, perhaps, the effectiveness of the good. They can still be sued, but the law does not assign many of the principles of liability to such certification organizations, and there is no principle to hold a certifier liable for an unforeseeable error, provided the certifier was not negligent.

The laws governing fraud and liability protect consumers. Under a free-market certification scheme, an injured consumer still retains all powers of legal redress. Breaking the FDA's legal monopoly on approval of medical devices in no way implies a change in liability law or practice. Currently, the FDA does not especially help or hinder consumers bringing torts before the court, nor does it protect the public by filing individual or class actions on behalf of aggrieved consumers. If the FDA were no longer to exercise monopoly authority, such suits would still be brought, and the relative balance of power between consumers and corporations or physicians would not have changed. The notion that harmed consumers need the FDA to help them collect damages from deep-pocketed medical establishments is specious. Manufacturers of medical devices have never been immune from torts, and removing the FDA blockade to market access will not change that.

The Market in Action: Underwriters Laboratories

UL was founded in 1894 as an independent, not-for-profit organization. It provides certifications of safety for thousands of products and writes standards for manufacturing and performance for hundreds of others. It has been so successful and its market acceptance so complete that consumers scarcely ask themselves if many of the products they buy are safe. They make the rational assumption that they will be because UL and similar organizations certify them.

● UL certifies more than 17,000 different types of products: In 1998, UL issued fourteen billion individual UL marks, the "trademark" symbol affixed to certified items which are UL listed. UL has more than 40,000 clients, including manufacturers, retailers, insurers, code officials, architects, and government agencies.

● Among many other products, UL tests and certifies electrical and medical appliances and equipment, automotive and mechanical products, fire-resistant and other "code" materials, bullet-resistant glass, Occupational Safety and Health Administration (OSHA)-designated "hazardous location" products, alarm systems, and chemicals.

UL writes and maintains 726 different end-use product standards. UL helps
'elop national and international codes and works toward standards harmonization.

UL does not provide the insurance function of underwriting risk. It
produces no testimonials, advertisements, or other marketing support
for its clients. The sole business of UL is disseminating safety and
performance information. UL approval sometimes is conditioned on
manufacturers issuing warning labels, use-and-care booklets, safety
tips, and other consumer information. UL itself distributes informational literature, news releases, and broadcasts public service announce-
ments to educate the public about the meaning of the UL mark. UL
disseminates all this information because the market demands it, not
because the government requires it.

Value Added and No Monopoly

No statutory, regulatory, or court-ordered mandate requires manufacturers to seek UL approval, yet tens of thousands do. Consumers
want to buy safe and effective products. The UL organization acts like
a performance bond. Manufacturers who pay for UL's services are
posting that bond. Consumers recognize this and are willing to buy or
pay more for UL-listed products. Thus, manufacturers who produce a
good product want UL listing. Companies that make a poor, unsafe
product are not listed with UL; many retailers balk at stocking such
products and many consumers think twice before buying them. Product safety is ensured, and the private market has generated value-
adding information without a coercive government monopoly.

Market survival dictates that UL be extremely diligent in avoiding
both Type I and Type II errors and in maintaining independence from
its clients. If UL were a tool of certain manufacturers, UL could not
avoid listing unsafe products. Were that to happen, consumers and
competitors would discover it and the UL mark would no longer add
value to products. As a result, manufacturers would stop paying for
UL and its services.

It is costly for everyone, including manufacturers and UL, to have
poor quality and performance standards and unsafe products. In its
1994 annual report, UL said,

The "real" cost...is compromised safety, which can ultimately result in product
rejection, manufacturing delay, and greater costs. A final result is the loss of the
certification organization's credibility and the manufacturer's product acceptance.

The loss of credibility would spell the end of jobs for UL's management and employees. UL, consumers, and manufacturers all want a reliable and independent UL, and all have incentives to keep it that way.

Unlike the FDA, UL has incentives to reduce Type II errors. If UL in any way unnecessarily delays the marketing of a new product, it lowers the value of the UL mark to producers. That means that UL has powerful incentives to certify a product as quickly as possible without unduly increasing the likelihood of committing a Type I error.

UL operating practices contribute to appropriately rapid certification. UL works closely with the manufacturer's product developers from the earliest stages of research, to help them meet the known burden of the applicable standards. Before a sample product or process is even complete, UL may have been able to certify it.

UL pays its employees out of revenues it earns from providing valuable services for its customers, whereas FDA staff are paid out of tax dollars that all consumers are required to pay. Manufacturers pay for UL's services. Consumers who do not benefit from UL's services do not have to pay for them. UL is free from pressures to comply with special interests; it must satisfy customers directly. In other words, it is not detached from the people who use its services, as tax-supported government agencies are.

Unlike the FDA, UL operates in the private market, and it is not legally protected from competition. Competition in the market for high-quality product safety information has the same effect that competition has in any market. Goods and services produced in a competitive market are produced efficiently, at the lowest cost. Though UL enjoys the widest name recognition in the marketplace, UL has competitors. Among others, these competitors include Electronics Testing Laboratories, a subsidiary of the British conglomerate Inchcape; Factory Mutual of Norwood, Massachusetts; and Canadian Standards Association of Rockville, Ontario. Some competitors use UL standards as the basis of their certification, but others write their own. Some of UL's competitors are for-profit organizations. Others are subsidiaries of other corporate entities. Though UL uses the term "friendly competition,"[37] the competition is there. If UL's standards are inappropriate, or if the public loses confidence in the good name of UL, then there are other organizations ready to serve the market.

UL has incentives to do its job quickly, accurately, and efficiently. If those incentives break down for any reason, the critical point is that even a malfunctioning UL cannot make consumers suffer. Consumers are still able to use the information at hand and make an informed choice. UL tests products and certifies their safety, providing consumers with accurate, timely information, and no more. Consumers can decide for themselves, based on good information, if they want to buy a riskier product or not. No monopolistic government agency prevents consumers from making their own choices.

Government Agencies Use UL

Private consumers are not the only beneficiaries of UL's services. Government agencies also depend on the company. UL is an active participant in development of "building codes" in over 40,000 local jurisdictions around the country. The UL mark is accepted in all 40,000 of those jurisdictions.[38]

OSHA recognizes UL as one of its seventeen Nationally Recognized Testing Laboratories (NRTLs). OSHA's guiding documents specifically state that an NRTL shall certify all electrical workplace products. Many of the standards for certification were developed by other third-party certification organizations—in particular, the American Society for Testing and Materials (ASTM) and the American National Standards Institute (ANSI), but some are UL standards. As an NRTL, UL certifies the safety of products that affect the occupational safety of employees. Most of UL's work as an NRTL involves electrical products, but it also evaluates fire suppressant and elimination products and liquid petroleum gas appliances.[39]

Even medical equipment carries UL's safety certification. UL tests most medical equipment and devices for safety. To be sold as medical devices, the equipment must still be approved by the FDA, at enormous cost, but UL has already certified its electrical safety.

In 1996, the FDA initiated a study of alternatives to its current regulatory program for medical devices, including partial third-party certification. UL is one of the certified third parties in the program. That does not mean that the FDA is one of UL's clients, but it demonstrates that the FDA recognizes UL's competency.

The Food and Drug Modernization Act of 1997 created a system whereby the FDA recognizes certain product performance standards.

Some manufacturers are able to market the lowest-risk medical devices by issuing a Declaration of Conformity, stating their device meets the requirements of the appropriate FDA-approved standard. UL is one of several national and international organizations whose standards have been recognized by the FDA. Specifically, the FDA has recognized some UL standards for photographic and x-ray equipment, as well as other medical and dental equipment.[40]

The Success of Market Certification

In Senate testimony, then-FDA Commissioner David Kessler stated, "The assurance that FDA is there everyday doing its job is so fundamental that we have the luxury of taking it for granted." One implication of his statement is that the FDA is necessary for Americans to feel secure about their medical devices. Extending that logic, do consumers worry that their televisions will start fires, or that they will be injured using their toasters? Is there a strong popular demand for the federal government to certify the safety of consumer products and restrict consumers' access to these products?

There is no such demand because UL and the other competing certifying organizations already fill the role. The market system already produces accurate information about the quality of consumer products.

Conclusion

The U.S. Congress needs to turn over the FDA review and approval of medical devices to independent, privately funded institutions. Legislation has given the FDA a virtual monopoly over the marketing of medical devices, and political pressure forces the FDA to place too much emphasis on preventing the marketing of unsafe and ineffective devices. In doing so, the FDA permanently blocks or delays for years the marketing of safe and effective devices, some of which would save lives if they were available on the market. The cost of FDA regulation of medical devices is higher medical prices, and, more important, unnecessary deaths and suffering.

Reforming FDA processes is not the solution. The reform proposals discussed in Congress have centered on bringing efficiency and accountability to the FDA. They have been designed to force the FDA to adapt to the increasing pace of innovation and the demands of American consumers. Yet the best efforts of congressional and agency reformers fall short. The sad fact is that the reforms insulate the FDA from the market in important ways. The FDA has powerful incentives to drag its feet and request ever more information, delaying approval while people suffer and die. It will continue to demand more information rather than see its power diminish. It will minimize the risk of approving an unsafe device, at virtually any cost, for fear of congressional repercussions. What is most important is that the FDA retains the power to enforce its decisions. The reforms leave intact the FDA's power to prevent new devices from entering the market.

There is an alternative to reform: abandon the current regulatory process and embrace the free market that has worked so well for so long in other fields. Free-market third-party certification promises safe and effective devices—quickly and efficiently—and gives consumers the freedom to choose the amount of risk that best suits them. The market provides consumers with the full remedies and protections of our legal system, and it frees businesses from the crippling costs of undue regulation.

Notes

1.   This paper is a modified version of "Replace FDA Regulation of Medical Devices with Third-Party Certification," Cato Institute Policy Analysis, no. 288 (November 1997). The author gratefully acknowledges the assistance of three Cato interns: Craig Farnham, Matthew Brown and Clay McFaden. The author also thanks Angela Ritzert, Ph.D., of the Joint Economic Committee, for her assistance. Finally, I would like to thank Alex Tabarrok and Roger Feldman for useful comments. The usual caveat applies. The opinions and conclusions expressed in this paper are solely those of the author.
2.   Sam Kazman, "Deadly Overcaution: FDA's Drug Approval Process," Journal of Regulation and Social Costs #1, no. 1 (August 1990): 43.
3.   Alexander Volokh, "Clinical Trials—Beating the FDA in Court," Reason, May 1995, p 23.
4.   Elizabeth Porter, "David Kessler's High-Wire Act on Enforcement," Medical Industry Executive, January 1994, p. 20. See also Robert Higgs, "Wrecking Ball: FDA Regulation of Medical Devices," Cato Institute Policy Analysis, no. 235, August 7, 1995.
5.   Quoted in ibid., p. 36.
6.   Alan M. Slobodin, "The Real Problem with Health Care in America: While Dr. David Kessler Fiddles, Medical Approvals Lag and Americans Die," Legal Backgrounder 9, no. 36 (October 8, 1994): 2, quoting Neergaard, "Is Red Tape Sacrificing U.S. Medicine? Doctors, Companies Battle the FDA," The Legal Intelligencer, August 30, 1994, p. 3.

7.   Tom Hamburger and Mike Meyers, "Losing the Edge: Overseas Patients Reap the Benefits of U.S. Research While Those Here Wait," *Minneapolis Star Tribune*, June 26, 1994, p. 1A.
8.   Robert Goldberg, "The Kessler Legacy at the FDA," *IPI Insights*, January-February 1997, p. 3.
9.   Steve Langdon, "FDA Drug Approval Process May Undergo Surgery," *Congressional Quarterly Weekly*, January 27, 1996, p. 222.
10.   General Accounting Office, "Medical Device Regulation: Too Early to Assess European System's Value as Model for FDA," March 1996, p. 3.
11.   For supporting examples, see Higgs.
12.   Higgs, pp. 14-15 and endnotes.
13.   Former FDA chief counsel Peter Barton Hutt said that the FDA staff reviewers "sent back 510(k)s with so many trivial, unimportant questions that they eventually became the same as a PMA." Quoted in ibid., p. 9 and endnotes.
14.   All submission and approval information for the late 1990s is from the Office of Device Evaluation Annual Report, Fiscal Year 1998.
15.   General Accounting Office, "Medical Devices: FDA Review Time," October 1995.
16.   Ibid., pp. 5-16.
17.   Moreover, Jeffrey Kimball, the executive director of the Medical Device Manufacturers Association, attributes the FDA's success in reducing its backlog to a simple procedure: the FDA now rejects more new device applications. (Steve Langdon, "FDA Drug Approval Process May Undergo Surgery," *Congressional Quarterly Weekly*, January 27, 1996, p. 223) In fact, in the GAO report "Medical Devices: FDA Review Times," the FDA lists "refuse to accept/file policies" as one of the changes instituted to reduce review times. (General Accounting Office, "Medical Devices," p. 75)
18.   Ibid. On-line at *www.cse.org/cse/ia73pt7.htm*.
19.   Ibid. On-line at *www.cse.org/cse/ia73pt8.htm*.
20.   Ibid., p. 17.
21.   See *www.fda.gov/cdrh/modact/accredit.html* for a list of the accredited parties.
22.   Author's conversation with Mr. Eric Reckon, Center for Devices and Radiologic Health, Programs Management Office, on June 3, 1999.
23.   "Information on Medical devices: Third Party Review of Selected Pre-Market Notifications; Pilot Program," www.fda.gov/cdrh/ohipfed.html, September 17, 1996.
24.   Ibid.
25.   Author's conversation with Mr. Tony Rogers, Center for Devices and Radiological Health, Office of Small Manufacturers Assistance on May 25, 1999.
26.   Unless otherwise noted, all information in this section is from U.S. Food and Drug Administration, "Overview—FDA Modernization Act of 1997," update of June 5, 1998. On-line at *www.fd.gov/cdrh/devadvice/371.html*. This document is FDA's "plain English" summary of each section of FDMA 97 relating to medical devices.
27.   Ibid., p. 3.
28.   Ibid., p. 10-11.
29.   Ibid., p. 12.
30.   Ibid.
31.   Ibid., p. 13, italics added.
32.   "The provision maintains a strong, continued role for the FDA in the device approval process....The FDA alone accredits the pool of qualified private par-

ties to conduct the reviews." In addition, the Agency "retains all the authority it has under current law to make final product review decisions...there is no presumption given to the accredited party's recommendation of approvability or classification of a product." Senate Report 105-43, 1997, p. 22; the same is true under the provisions of FDAMA 97.

33. For a discussion on how the FDA breaks statutory law by delaying the approval process, see Higgs, pp. 8-10, where he discusses the FDA's ignoring 1976 amendment requirements to solicit PMA submissions on predicate Class III devices, and to produce performance standards for Class II devices. See also Lydia Verheggen, "FDA Review Times: Not Making the Grade," Issue Analysis, no. 23, Citizens for a Sound Economy, February 20, 1996. Verheggen details the FDA's violation of its statutory deadlines to approve drugs, devices, animal drugs, and food additives.

34. Michael I. Krauss, "Loosening the FDA's Drug Certification Monopoly," George Mason Law Review 4(1996): 457-483 at p. 477.

35. Ibid., p. 477.

36. John Calfee, "The Leverage Principle in FDA's Regulation of Information," in Competitive Strategies in the Pharmaceutical Industry, ed. R. Helms, quoted in ibid., p. 472.

37. Author's telephone conversations with Homer Pringle, UL Legal Department.

38. Underwriters Laboratories, 1994 Annual Report, p. 10.

39. Author's telephone conversation with Roy Resnick, Occupational Safety and Health Administration, December 6, 1996.

40. On-line at *www.fda.gov/cdrh/stdsprog.html* and *www.fda.gov/cdrh/modact/recstand.html*.

Part IV

Health Care Personnel

11

Physician Fees and Price Controls

H. E. Frech, III

Price Controls are Common in Health Care Reform Plans

Some of the more ambitious health care reform plans, which call for national health insurance, have included price controls, typically at two different levels.[1] Important examples from the 1993-94 debate include the Clinton Plan and the Gephardt Plan. The proponents of the plans and the plans themselves often avoided the words "price control" because price control has a bad reputation. Indeed, Clinton administration spokesmen went so far as to deny that the Clinton Plan contained price controls. As a result, euphemisms like global budgeting or limits on balance billing have become common. Unfortunately, even the more responsible print media has generally gone along with these euphemisms.[2] Price control has been described as a law that prohibits "economic activity between consenting adults." This essence of price control is obscured by the use of euphemisms.

The Clinton Plan

I want to focus on the Clinton Plan in particular, in spite of its congressional rejection, because it was the most detailed of the plans and because most of the aspects of Clinton Plan will be live issues for years to come. This is especially true of price controls because they can be implemented in many possible ways.

The Clinton Plan imposes price controls at two levels. First, the monopolistic and mandatory regional health alliances in the Clinton Plan are required to control prices for fee-for-service medicine. Secondly, the Plan requires the alliances to set price controls on the premiums that private health insurance plans can charge. The price control on premiums reinforces the price controls on medical services by increasing political pressure from insurers on the alliances to more tightly control medical service fees.

Let us look at how the price controls in the physician services market emerge from the Clinton Plan. The regional alliances in the Clinton Plan are required to set fee schedules. The setting of fee schedules, in itself, does not necessarily constitute price control. It may simply regulate what the insurer is willing to pay for each service, without regulating the total price in the market. In fact, many private insurers have used fee schedules for years without controlling prices. The French and Australian National Health Insurance Systems also use fee schedules, but they do not control market prices (Rosa and Launois 1990; Burstall and Wallerstein; 1994: 386; Rodwin and Sandier 1993; Altman and Jackson 1991: 136-40).

Some national health insurance plans proposed in 1993-94 for the U.S., add restrictions, or in the case of the Clinton Plan, an absolute ban on balance billing. Balance billing occurs when a consumer and physician agree to a fee for a particular service that exceeds the amount in the fee schedule. The consumer is billed the difference between the total fee and the fee schedule amount that is paid by the insurer—the balance. It is only when the government sets the fee schedule and limits or prohibits balance billing, that price control results.

In part of the U.S. health care system, price control already exists from this approach. In Medicare, the government has, in recent years, imposed tight restrictions on balance billing. Medicare prices are limited to the fee schedule plus a maximum balance bill of 15 percent of the fee-scheduled amount. That is the maximum market price allowed.[3] The Clinton Plan is more extreme—balance billing is absolutely prohibited.

The Gephardt Plan forces many consumers who are currently privately insured into Medicare. Thus, these consumers are forced into a sector that is already price controlled. As the Gephardt Plan shows, the mandatory, monopolistic regional alliances that were in the Clinton Plan are not necessary to impose price controls. This is an important point because the Clintons' mandatory regional alliances were apparently very unpopular and are unlikely to reappear in future proposals. But that does not imply that price controls are unlikely. Price controls, are, as they say in Washington, "still in play." Therefore the analysis of price controls is an ongoing necessity.

The Effects of Price Controls

The Basic Analysis

In most markets, prices are flexible and vary according to the economic forces present. Freely moving prices perform many functions in a market. Unusually high prices signal an industry or sector that is profitable and provide both the information and the incentive for the original sellers to produce more and for other sellers to enter into the market. On the demand side, high prices signal a need to economize further on the good or service. These two effects on both sides of the market tend to increase pressure on prices to decline. Thus, freely moving prices are important to resource allocation and rational decision-making in the long or medium term.

But free prices perform a function that is perhaps even more important in both the long and in the short run—they help ration goods or services among competing buyers. Thus, there is a price, or distribution of prices that clears the market. That is, it allocates goods or services among competing buyers so that there are no left-over buyers who would have liked the good, but can find no sellers and no left-over sellers who would have like to sell the good, but can find no buyers. Even setting aside the effect on resource allocation, price controls ordinarily upset this market-clearing feature of the prices. Price controls set below market-clearing levels lead to excess demand (frustrated buyers), while price controls set above market-clearing levels lead to excess supply (frustrated sellers).[4] In the health insurance or health care markets, I believe that we can ignore the possibility of price controls being set above market-clearing levels.[5]

Price controls set below market levels cause excess demand. Somehow, some of the potential buyers must be rationed out and prevented or discouraged from receiving health care. One possibility is a formal rationing system. But formal systems are unlikely to be politically successful, because they make it so clear to the victims of the nonprice rationing. They are rare in price controlled health care systems. Thus, informal, hidden methods are likely to be used, based on the preferences of the providers and heavily based on consumer waiting time. The resulting waste can be very large, but it is well hidden.[6] Thus, the self-correcting mechanisms of both the market and the political process are likely to be hampered. There are also likely to be subtle costs in lower quality and less incentive to innovate.

Government Price Controls in Health Care

The main effect of price control is nonprice rationing in a particularly inefficient way. This nonprice rationing has hidden costs that are hard to recognize, let alone to measure. In the debate on the Clinton Plan and its alternatives, there has been very little mentioned about these hidden costs of nonprice rationing. The nonprice rationing is probably the most important adverse consequence of price controls in medicine. It has been discussed in Frech and Ginsburg (1975: 36-43) and in path-breaking papers by Patricia Danzon (1992; 1993). If we look at examples from other countries that have strict price controls on fee-for-service medicine, we see major costs imposed by the resulting nonprice rationing. But the costs are very hard to measure.

Japan, for example, has very low price controls in its national health insurance system. They have been set well below market levels. To give some idea of how severe these price controls are, between 1980 and 1992, real fees *declined* by 19 percent, while real wages grew by 11.4 percent.[7] As a result, waiting times are long and doctor visits are brief. Doctors often ask consumers to come back for multiple visits. Appointments are not generally used. Incentives for quality are poor (Rapp and Shibuya 1994; Niki forthcoming; Ikegami 1991: 103-104).[8]

These hidden costs are hard to measure exactly, but we do know that Japanese consumers make about three times as many doctor visits per year as American consumers. Japanese physician visits are short, on average about five minutes, compared to about fifteen to ten minutes in the U.S. (Danzon 1993: 269).

The effects of the price controls on hospital quality in Japan is easier to see, at least in a rough way. The hospital staffing ratio (the average number of employees per patient) is a rough measure of quality, especially the quality of nursing. Japan is by far the lowest of the wealthy countries. International comparisons of this can be tricky because in many countries, including Japan, long-term patients are treated in hospitals. In the U.S., they would be treated in separate nursing homes. A fairer comparison would lump nursing homes with hospitals in the U.S. to compare to all hospitals in Japan. Doing so still leads to a striking disadvantage for Japan. This inclusive staffing ratio is 0.64 in Japan versus 1.49 in the U.S. Another quality dimension is the prevalence of wards and the amount of space per patient. In Japan, unlike the U.S., six and eight-bed rooms predominate. Japanese health insurance only covers rooms with four or more beds. Consumers must pay extra for semi-private or private rooms. The average amount of space per patient is about one-fourth as high in Japan as the U.S., 37.8 square meters versus 147.5 square meters (Niki forthcoming: 18, 19).

The indicators and dimensions of quality discussed so far are inputs into the process of improving health or the quality of life. The most important dimension of the output of the health care industry is the quality of life, especially for the elderly. Another indicator of this that is available in some countries is the percentage of the elderly who are bed-ridden. In Japan, as a result of low levels of nursing support, it is very high. For example, in Japan, 33.8 percent of the institutionalized elderly are bed-ridden versus only 6.5 percent in the U.S. and 4.2 percent in Sweden (Niki forthcoming: Table 4).

Another effect, which is rarely written about, is that Japanese price controls cause a great deal of corruption in its medical system. "Copayment by envelope," bribery and balance billing under the table are common. Based on a careful and clever survey, Ryu Niki estimates that illegal balance bills for hospitals for the aged *average* about 23 percent of the legal price.[9] The legally allowed copayment is only a low 3.9 percent of the legal price. Niki estimates that the total actual copayment, including the balance bills, is 21.7 percent of a true price that is higher. Niki (forthcoming: 21, 22, Table 5) found that virtually all geriatric hospitals accept under the table balance bills. He believes that the government knowingly tolerates this, even though it is illegal, citing the fact that no geriatric hospital has ever been punished for accepting balance bills as evidence. Naoki Ikegami states that a $1,000 to $3,000 "gift" to the attending physician is common at top Tokyo hospitals (1991: 104).[10]

This type of black market copayment is a natural result of regulations that interfere with mutually beneficial trades. Although illegal, black market or "informal" balance billing probably plays an important role in making Japanese medical care more sensitive to consumer values and in providing incentives for quality.[11] Planned reforms in Japan liberalize the regulations to allow more of the balance billing to be legal, though still rather arcane and difficult to observe (Niki forthcoming: 25-27).

Korea has almost the same system as Japan, with similar price controls. In fact, it was explicitly copied from the Japanese. In Korea as well as Japan, waiting times are long. Consumers cannot make appointments. As in Japan, they are often told to come back for return visits. And, even injections of drugs were often split in half to make two visits necessary. That way, the doctor can charge for two office visits and two injection fees. Further, the necessity of two trips raises the time price of the care, helping to reduce the imbalance of quantity demanded and quantity supplied (Jeong Kee Hong 1992).

Canada is in a similar situation although its price controls are not as extreme as Korea or Japan. (That is, the controlled prices are not as far below the market-clearing levels.) But even for Canada, Patricia Danzon estimates that the hidden costs are so large that the Canadian system is roughly as costly as the U.S.

In Quebec in the 1970s, the government instituted price controls by the same means as the Clinton Plan—Universal Provincial Health Insurance with a fee schedule and a ban on balance billing. Especially since the policy was province-wide, this forms a natural experiment to see the implications of price controls on an entire health care system. Shortly after Quebec implemented the Universal Provincial Health Insurance Plan, home visits went down by 63 percent, telephone consults by 41 percent, office visits went up by 32 percent and the time per visit went down by 16 percent (Enterline et al. 1973; 1975). Of course, office visits were relatively better reimbursed than the other services.

This evidence from the Quebec natural experiment is an example to three deleterious results of price controls. First, the convenience and values of providers become relatively more important than those of consumers when providers face more demand than they can satisfy. Second, the types of visits shifted to those that used more of consumers' time, thus helping reduce the excess demand. Third, quality, as measured by the time spent in office visits, declined.

Governmental Price Controls are Fundamentally Different from Negotiated Price Agreements

It is important to make a careful distinction here between price controls in a government system and negotiated prices in competing privately managed care plans. Managed care plans like Preferred Provider Organizations (PPOs) often negotiate reduced prices with doctors, and they often also negotiate an agreement to not balance bill. Superficially, this contractual agreement looks like governmental price control but there are many reasons why it is different.

The biggest problem with price control is the resulting nonprice rationing. But, in private competing PPOs, there are many safety valves for consumers and competitive constraints on what competing PPOs can do in contracting for low prices. A particularly important safety valve is the ability of consumers to select a provider who did not sign the contract. That is, consumers can go out of a plan and get, possibly reduced, but still substantial benefits. They can do that if the nonprice rationing resulting from the price controls is too severe or too insensitive to their tastes and values. Also, going out-of-plan is an important option if the quality of the providers in the plan is too low. Obviously, in a national government system, like the Clinton Plan, consumers cannot go outside of the plan.

Also in a competing PPO system, if a consumer or employer thinks that the price control or nonprice rationing is too strict or too insensitive in his system, he can switch to another PPO or insurance plan. If providers find a particular PPO too restrictive, they can refuse to sign the agreement. These competitive options give PPOs incentives to set up systems that are consistent with consumers' values on average and that are sensitive to individual variations in consumer values.

PPOs and other competing plans may also have other formal and informal nonprice rationing schemes that look superficially like nonprice rationing under governmentally price controlled systems. But again, these controls are very different because consumers have the choice of opting out of the plan and still getting benefits or going to a competing plan, and providers do not have to sign up with the plan in order to treat consumers from the plan.

It is important to remember that when consumers go to providers who are not in a PPO, balance billing is allowed. PPOs do not regulate price for out-of-plan providers. They determine what they will pay for services, but leave the total price up to voluntary agreements between consumers and providers.

Nonprice Rationing in Competing, Voluntary Systems

Again, a critic might say that managed care also has nonprice rationing. So, what is the difference? In fact, one of the arguments used in the debate on the plans is the claim that: "A bureaucrat is a bureaucrat." But this is misleading. The individual bureaucrat may be similar or even the same individual. But it makes a large difference to economic efficiency and consumer welfare whether the bureaucrats are in competing private organizations with market choices and ways of opting out, rather then being in one uniform system that consumers and providers cannot escape. The U.S. Postal Service and Federal Express are both bureaucracies.

At best, the nonprice rationing caused by governmental price controls will follow professional opinions. At worst, it will follow the preferences of the professionals, a very different thing, as evidenced by the experience in Quebec. But, even at best, rationing according to professional opinion will often lead to mistakes and inefficiency.

The Importance of Consumer Values for Efficient Rationing

Even if providers tried to ration altruistically and did so with the best professional motives possible, they would be at a disadvantage. Much of the information that is necessary to decide upon the best treatment is a matter of the individual consumer's taste and values. Typically, the best treatment is not a purely professional matter.[12] The correct treatment depends on the consumer's values and attitudes towards physical risk and financial risk, his attitude towards pain and so on.

One important example is the common and costly coronary artery bypass graft or CABG operation. This operation usually has little or no effect on life expectancy. In some cases, it even has an adverse effect on life expectancy. The main benefit of the CABG operation is that consumer can be free of pain during strenuous physical activities.

For example, the operation would often allow a consumer to continue to ski hard without heart pain. Some consumers would choose such an operation, even if it shortened their life expectancy by a couple of years. But many consumers would not. The choice is not purely, or even mostly, a professional matter. It depends on the values and tastes of the individual consumer.

Another effect of price control is lower incentives for nonprice competition in general, including quality and innovation. Here the innovation affected goes beyond medical technology to include the way that health insurers and plans accomplish their rationing. Thus, innovation includes differing approaches to nonprice rationing and also differing degrees of price rationing. Innovation in price rationing is accomplished by varying the type and level of copayment for differing benefits. There is currently tremendous innovation going on in the U.S. in this area. Things are changing fast. If the U.S. were to adopt price controls, hiding lots of costs from consumers and the media, there would be less incentive to innovate in either new technology or in the financing and delivery of health care.

Rationales for Price Controls

If price control creates these problems, why is it supported? There are two fundamental rationales, corresponding to the two levels of price controls.

Price or Premium Controls at the Plan Level

Let us first look at the regulation of the premiums of health insurance plans. The main rationale for this policy is the idea that the government needs to control the overall level of spending in health care. But, this belief is mistaken. Government control of the level of health care spending is an attack on a symptom, rather than the root cause of spending being too high.

The Current Tax Bias Favoring Excessive Health Insurance

The current tax treatment for employer-based health insurance gives the incentive for excessive insurance. Health insurance costs are deductible to the employer as costs of doing business, while they are not taxable to employees as income in kind. This gives a massive tax subsidy to the purchase of too much insurance. The subsidy can exceed 50 percent for high-income consumers. The incentive is expressed in middle class and wealthy consumers having too much insurance, with too little copayment. In managed care systems, the incentive is expressed by managed care utilization controls that are too loose. The result of these forces is to raise health care costs above the optimal level (Pauly 1986).

To correctly control health care costs, we need to reform the tax system to eliminate the bias to excessive insurance. Intellectually, this problem is not difficult or complex. It is not rocket science. Some of the plans attempt to reduce the tax bias in Byzantine ways, but such complexity is not necessary.

There are two different basic approaches. One taxes the employers for providing excessive health insurance and the other taxes the employees for receiving it. We know that who ultimately pays taxes does not vary with whether the tax is imposed on buyers or sellers.[13] Therefore, it does not matter which approach to tax reform is taken in the long run. But it may matter in the short run for politics and for labor relations.

The simpler approach is to eliminate or reduce the tax deductibility of health insurance for the employers. Following this general approach, the simplest possible policy change would be to eliminate the tax deductibility of employer-based health insurance. To avoid an overall tax increase, other taxes, such as individual or corporate income taxes, should be simultaneously reduced.[14] Slightly more complex would be a policy instituting a cap on the amount that could be deducted, as a cost of doing business, by employers. To improve incentives for most firms, the cap would be set at a level below the cost of most health insurance plans. This would eliminate the subsidy at the margin to excessive health insurance, while retaining a subsidy to the provision of a lean and efficient type of insurance to all employees.

Though eliminating or reducing the tax bias from the employer side is simpler, there are political and labor relations problems with this approach. The change in the incentives is not obvious or transparent to workers. What would be obvious would be an increase in the resistance of employers to providing costly health insurance benefits. This is likely to cause friction in labor relations and worker and union resistance to more efficient, less complete insurance until the workers eventually learn about the new incentives.

The political problem results from the labor relations problem. Employers who now provide relatively generous health insurance benefits are likely to be unable to reduce their benefits immediately, because of the labor relations problems. Thus, these employers are likely to pay higher taxes during the adjustment period, which might be as long as a few years. As a result, these employers are likely to oppose the tax reform politically. Since the firms who pay the most generous benefits tend to be relatively large and well-organized firms, their opposition may be politically important.

The other approach is to tax the health insurance plan premiums as implicit income to workers, as is currently done with many other employee benefits. This is messier in terms of accounting, but far from impossible. Again, to avoid a tax increase when reforming the tax incentives, it would be easy to reduce individual income tax rates simultaneously to offset the increased taxes collected here.

From a labor relations viewpoint, this employee-centered way of reforming taxes would be far better. Employees would immediately see the new, stronger incentives for efficiency in health plans. Far from resisting pro-efficiency changes, they would welcome them. The result would be more harmonious relations during the transition. At the same time, the employees who now receive very generous health benefits are likely to experience a decrease in their net-of-taxes pay while the labor market adjusts. This is probably less serious than the mirror image problem, but it still exists.

Employers are, therefore, much less likely to oppose this type of tax reform politically. On the other hand, there are two reasons why employees may oppose this kind of tax reform. First, as discussed above, some employees temporarily pay more taxes. Second, it appears that many employees do not understand that it does not matter whether employees or employers send the check to the government for employment-based taxes. Thus, they appear to believe that these taxes levied on them would be paid by them and taxes levied on employers somehow would not.

Any of these approaches can, and probably should, be slowly phased in so that union contracts and wages can adjust. A phased adjustment would minimize the income redistribution during the transition, thus minimize the unnecessary political and labor relations problems.

Once the tax system is reformed, the size of the medical care sector would be best decided by Americans as individuals, as consumers, or as employment groups. There is no reason for it to be a matter of government concern. There is no government policy on how much we spend on shoes or music, because the government has not distorted incentives for the purchase of shoes or music.

The Second-Best Argument

One might agree with the analysis of the tax biases to excessive health insurance and health care spending, but still argue for price controls on health plan premiums as a second-best policy. That is, one might argue that it is politically impossible to change the root cause of excessive spending. Therefore, the best policy that is actually possible is price control to offset, at least partially, the harm done by the unchangeable tax policy. I do not agree.

First, I believe the premise—that tax reform is impossible—is incorrect. It simply has not gotten sufficient attention from political leaders. Second, even if tax reform were impossible, I believe that the actual price controls that would emerge from actual government decision-making would be likely to be so far from the second-best optimal price controls that economic efficiency would be harmed, not helped. I would expect the price controls to be set too low, because that would allow the government (and consumers) to exploit providers in the short run. The longer run harm would be less salient politically (Pauly 1981). It is useful to note that price controls at this insurance premium level, no matter how low, are unlikely to cause much wasteful and hidden nonprice rationing in medical care markets, as long as insurers and health plans are free to respond to the low prices by increasing copayment and/or tightening up on competitively determined nonprice rationing.

Price Controls on Individual Physicians and Providers

Now turn to the rationale for price controls on individual physicians or other providers. While the simple idea of reducing costs has some bite here, I think the more sophisticated and powerful idea behind price controls on doctors' services is the view that physician markets are not very competitive. To some extent, this is a matter of seeing the glass as half full or half empty. While the physician market is clearly not perfectly competitive, because of costly consumer information and attenuated incentives, there is a great deal of competition. And the amount of competition is clearly improving under the influence of HMOs and PPOs and also higher copayments in the health insurance market. Competition can be further improved by stronger incentives for HMOs and PPOs to exercise tighter control which would come about through reforming the tax system.

Let me point out one of the ways that consumer information, thus competition, is improved by PPOs. As discussed above, most participating PPO physicians have agreed to a lower price and not to balance bill. So, a PPO consumer knows by asking one question whether a particular physician is a low priced provider. He needs only to ask if the physician is a PPO provider.

Before PPOs, when third-party payors generally took a hands-off approach, to know if someone was a low price provider, the consumer had to know about the relative level of many, perhaps hundreds, of prices. With the advent of PPOs, this complex information is boiled down to the answer to a single question. As PPOs are growing very rapidly, it is becoming easier and easier to know who the low price providers are.

Another Second-Best Argument

Parallel to the second-best argument for price controls on health plan premiums is a similar one for price controls directly on medical care. It goes like this: We know that medical care markets are not perfectly competitive. Price exceeds the competitive price and providers can influence price by their quantity decisions. Therefore, if we cannot make the markets perfectly competitive, the next best policy is an optimal price control.

Like the earlier one, this second-best argument would be correct for an omniscient government with the correct incentives. However, the government is likely to have incentives to set the price controls on medical care too low on average for the same reasons given above: the costs are subtle and long-run, while the benefits, in reduced budgetary costs, are obvious and immediate.

But there is an additional problem here that is even worse for price controls at this level than at the level of insurance premiums. Medical care is differentiated and idiosyncratic. It is more like the wine market than the steel market. Thus, the market naturally and optimally features a wide range of prices for services that differ quite a great deal (Satterthwaite and Dranove 1991; Welch 1991). Any governmental price control system will have to somehow set the prices of all these different services from different providers. It seems implausible that even a well-meaning government with the best interests of consumers and providers at heart could obtain and process the necessary information to control prices in a way that improves on the existing imperfectly competitive market, let alone that it could improve on the more competitive market that is evolving.

Also, price controls directly on medical markets are very likely to cause the type of hidden and wasteful nonprice rationing discussed above. Thus, price controls directly on medical markets are likely to be more harmful than price controls at the level of insurance premiums.

Conclusion

Governmental price controls at any level create major problems and impose large hidden costs, mostly on consumers, through subtle nonprice rationing and changes in quality. These issues have not reached the radarscope of the media during the health care reform debates of 1993-94. The ideal system involves choice among competing health insurers, including managed care systems, many of which inherently provide better information and improve the degree of competition in medical care itself.

The key principle for evaluating the different possibilities that range from national health insurance plans to small changes in insurance subsidies for the poor, is the absence of price control in any form and under any euphemism. There should be no global budgeting targets or limits. Balance billing by providers who choose not to participate in the plan should be absolutely guaranteed. Indeed, the rights of consumers and providers to agree on any price through balance billing is protected in the Australian Constitution (Altman and Jackson 1991: 138). While a constitutional solution might be overkill for the U.S., a strong governmental commitment not to impose price controls on the health care sector would be good policy.

Notes

1.   There is no reason in principle why less ambitious and less costly health care reform plans might not also include price controls. Indeed, after the congressional rejection of the large-scale plans in 1994, the smaller plans are the more likely source of price controls in the future.

2.   The print media, by and large, has done reasonably well with other issues such as budgetary costs.

3.   The Medicare restrictions on balance billing are, in practice, quite tight. The average balance bill before the restrictions were imposed was about 30 percent. Further, for most specialties, the Medicare fee schedule is lower than previous fee allowances were. See Zuckerman and Holihan (1988) and Frech (1988).

4.   For more on the role of prices and the effects of price controls generally, see any standard economics textbook. An example would be Hirshleifer and Galzer (1992: 37, 198-201).

5.   But this is not true in general. Price controls on farm products, electricity, and transportation (for example, airfares) have ordinarily been set above market-clearing prices.

6.   The waste is well hidden in the health care market, but not so well hidden in other markets. For example, in the retail gasoline market during the price controls of 1973 and 1979, long lines of waiting cars made the high costs clear (Frech and Lee 1987).

7.   These real fee and wage changes are calculated from data in Niki (forthcoming: 6, Figure 2).

8.   Eliminating price controls (by explicitly allowing legal balance billing) is a major part of the Japanese health care reforms suggested by Rapp and Shibuya (1994: 660-664). Their rationale stresses improving incentives for quality. The Japanese government has plans to go part way in this direction (Niki forthcoming: 25-27).

9.   The survey of illegal balance billing could hardly proceed by asking the heads of hospitals whether or not they took illegal payments. In fact, Niki used knowledgeable individuals, such as physicians and social workers, with a guarantee of privacy.

10.   I do not wish to give the impression that the Japanese system is not admirable in many ways. Its budgetary costs are low. And while it has tightly controlled prices, it is liberal and efficient in some important ways regarding medical care delivery. For example, Japan permits low tech, low cost hospitals as well as the high tech type of hospitals common in the U.S. This is probably a major source of efficiency. Further, office-based Japanese physicians usually dispense drugs— a major convenience, partially offsetting the long waiting times, inability to make appointments, and short office visits.

11.   Of course, any balance billing, legal or not, undermines the egalitarian idea of one standard of care for all consumers that some people, including Professor Niki, favor. Many observers, on the other hand, would prefer a guaranteed minimum standard of care, but would allow choice of higher levels. For example, see Frech and Ginsburg (1985) or Mark Pauly (1992).

12.   The optimal repair for machines is probably less dependent on the tastes and values of the individual consumer than optimal health care. But, even here, individual differences may be important. Consider the differing decisions that different consumers make on car repair.

13.   This is an issue of basic economics. See any textbook, for example Pindyck and Rubinfeld (1995, p. 305).

14.   There is no need for a general opposition to tax increases to prevent improving the incentives in the tax system. This principle has important implications for policies in other areas, such as environmental policy, as well as for health policy.

References

Altman, Stuart, and Terri Jackson. "Health Care in Australia: Lessons from Down Under." *Health Affairs* 10 (3) (fall 1991): 129-46.

Burstall, Mike, and Konrad Wallerstein. "The Health Care System in France." In *Financing Health Care*, vol. I, eds. Ullrich K. Hoffmeyer and Thomas R. McCarthy, pp. 348-418. Dordrecht: Kluwer, 1994.

Danzon, Patrica M. "Hidden Overhead Costs: Is Canada's System Less Expensive?" *Health Affairs* 11 (1) (spring 1992): 21-43.

Danzon, Patrica M. "The Hidden Costs of Budget-Constrained Health Insurance Systems." In Robert Helms, ed. *Health Policy Reform*, pp. 256-92. Washington, DC: American Enterprise Institute, 1993.

Enterline, Philip E., et al. "Effects of 'Free' Medical Care on Medical Practice—The Quebec Experience." *New England Journal of Medicine* 288 (22) (May 31, 1973): 1152-1155.

Enterline, Philip E., et al. "Physician's Working Hours and Patients See Before and After National Health Insurance: 'Free' Medical Care and Medical Practice." *Medical Care* 13 (2) (February 1975): 95-103.

Frech, H. E. III, "Overview of Policy Issues." In *Regulating Doctors' Fees: Competition, Controls and Benefits Under Medicare*, edited by H. E. Frech III, pp. 1-34. Washington, DC: American Enterprise Institute, 1991.

Frech, H.E. III, and Paul B. Ginsburg. *Public Insurance in Private Medical Markets: Some Problems of National Health Insurance.* Washington, DC: American Enterprise Institute, 1975.

Frech, H. E. III, and William Lee. "The Welfare Costs or Rationing-by-Queuing: Theory and Estimates from the U.S. Gasoline Crises." *Quarterly Journal of Economics* 102 (1) (Feb. 1987): 97-108.

Hirshliefer, Jack, and Amihai Glazer. *Price Theory and Applications.* Englewood Cliffs, NJ: Prentice-Hall, 1992.

Ikegami, Naoki. "Japanese Health Care: Low Cost Through Regulated Fees." *Health Affairs* 10 (3) (fall 1991): 87-109.

Hong, Jeong Kee. "The National Health Insurance in Korea: Excess Demand and Nonprice Rationing." Ph.D. Dissertation, University of California, Santa Barbara, 1992.

Niki, Ryu. "Recent Medical Care Financing Reform for Japan's Aging Society—With Special Reference to the 'First Stage' of Reform." In *First Japan-UK Medical Care Conference: Health Services for Rapidly Aging Societies.* New York: US-Japan-UK Health Policy Institute, forthcoming.

Pauly, Mark V. "Paying the Piper and Calling the Tune: The Relationship between Public Financing and Public Regulation of Medicine." In Mancur Olson, ed. *A New Approach to the Economics of Health Care*, pp. 67-86. Washington, D C: American Enterprise Institute for Public Policy Research, 1981.

Pauly, Mark V. "Taxation, Health Insurance and Market Failure in the Medical Economy." *Journal of Economic Literature* 24 (2) (June 1986): 629-75.

Pauly, Mark V. "The Normative and Positive Economics of Minimum Health Benefits." In *Health Economics Worldwide*, eds. Peter Zweifel and H. E. Frech III, pp. 63-78. Dordrecht: Kluwer Academic Publishers, 1992.

Pindyck, Robert S., and Daniel L. Rubinfeld. *Microeconomics* 3rd ed., Englewood Cliffs, NJ, Prentice-Hall, 1995.

Rapp, Richard T., and Kyoko Shibuya. "The Health Care System in Japan." In *Financing Health Care*, vol. I, eds. Ullrich K. Hoffmeyer and Thomas R. McCarthy, pp. 585-696. Dordrecht: Kluwer, 1994.

Rodwin, Victor G., and Simone Sandier. "Health Care Under French National Health Insurance." *Health Affairs* 12 (4) (fall 1993): 111-31.

Rosa, Jean-Jacques, and Robert Launois. "France." *Advances in Health Economics and Health Services Research*, Supplement No. 1, Jean-Jacques Rosa, guest ed. (1990): 179-95.

Satterthwaite, Mark. A., and David Dranove. "The Implications for Resource-Based Relative Value Scales for Physicians' Fees, Incomes, and Specialty Choices." In *Regulating Doctors' Fees: Competition, Controls and Benefits Under Medicare*, eds. H. E. Frech III, pp. 52-70. Washington, DC: American Enterprise Institute, 1991.

Zuckerman, Stephen, and John Holahan. "Medicare Balance Billing: Its Role in Physician Payment. In *Regulating Doctors' Fees: Competition, Controls and Benefits Under Medicare*, eds. H. E. Frech III, pp. 143-69. Washington, DC: American Enterprise Institute, 1991.

Welch, Finis. "Unexplained Sources of Differences in Physicians' Charges." In *Regulating Doctors' Fees: Competition, Controls and Benefits Under Medicare*, ed. H. E. Frech III, pp. 250-54. Washington, DC: American Enterprise Institute, 1991.

12

The Changing Role of Licensure in Promoting Incentives for Quality in Health Care

Shirley V. Svorny

1. Introduction

The premise of this chapter is that the role of professional licensure, and physician licensure in particular, has been to provide incentives to deter misconduct. By limiting the physician supply, licensing creates a profit or premium stream that increases the losses to a physician when his license is revoked. Training requirements associated with licensure mean that physicians make substantial investments in their human capital, which are also lost if a physician is found guilty of misconduct. As a result of licensing, the incentives facing health practitioners change.

The view I take is that, in the past, the institutional structure of health care provision was such that licensing made sense. Not so long ago, a physician's relationship with a hospital was legally that of an independent contractor. Physicians were held responsible by the courts for their own actions and those of health professionals under their supervision. There was little or no institutional liability. Under the circumstances, given the lack of institutional oversight, it served patients to have a licensing system that generated additional penalties for misconduct.

365

The system has evolved, however, to one in which responsibility is shared among health professionals. Much of the liability that once rested with physicians has been assigned to hospitals and other institutional providers. This has changed the nature of monitoring arrangements, putting individuals with the wherewithal to assess physician performance—individuals running hospitals and health maintenance organizations—in the position of being unable to turn their backs on misconduct. Given that monitoring costs have declined, and the increased probability of observing misconduct, it is my view that the potential for medical licensure to contribute to social welfare has been diminished.

I am not alone in taking this view of the declining importance of state medical licensure. Ginsberg and Moy (1992) have made a similar point with respect to evolving health care markets and the implications for medical licensure. Stevens (1986) suggests that the move to capitation as a method of payment will have a profound effect. Because captation encourages the formation of multispecialist groups, Stevens argues that it provides both the incentives and the structure for monitoring physician performance.

This chapter begins with a discussion of state medical boards, who they serve, and the relationship between medical licensure and physician service quality. In section 3, alternative methods of deterring improper behavior on the part of physicians are discussed and compared to licensure. Section 4 describes changes in the medical marketplace—institutional liability, peer review, and access to disciplinary records—which reduce the value of state licensing functions.

Section 5 discusses the value of licensure in today's markets. The line of analysis in section 4 leads to the conclusion that licensure is of greatest value where physicians continue to practice independently, removed from institutional liability and peer review. Yet, these areas, because they are generally the least well served, have little interest in maintaining a system that limits supply, suggesting the potential for widespread gains from the elimination of licensure arrangements.

Section 6 addresses current policy issues. These issues have one thing in common—each has the potential to influence incentives for quality care, and it is in that context that they are discussed. The issues include the extension of prescriptive powers, "any-willing-provider" clauses, requirements for due process appeals in dismissing physicians from group practice, public access to the National Practitioner Data Bank records, and standards of evidence to which state medical boards are held as the basis for disciplinary actions.

2. State Medical Boards and Medical Licensure

Concerns regarding strong informational asymmetries in health care markets underlie most arguments for licensure. Because consumers are unable to assess the quality of care they receive, it is argued that government intervention is justified (see Arrow 1963).[1]

Critics, however, are quick to point out how unfathomable it is that licensure leads to informed choice (see, for example, Young 1987, Goodman 1980, Benham 1991, or Rayack 1982). First, licensure does not restrict physicians to practice in a particular area of medicine; it is not against the law for an ophthalmologist to perform heart surgery. Second, it is hard to argue that passing a standardized exam (perhaps after several sittings) offers much information about physician competence years or even decades later. Finally, critics note licensure exams clearly cannot screen out individuals who might defraud patients.

As Friedman (1962) argued, consumers do not need to be trained in medicine to choose a physician. Specialty certification provides consumers with some information, but most consumers choose a physician on the basis of referrals from friends or other medical professionals.

The disparity in incomes across physicians suggests that judgments about physician quality are made all the time. That judgments are made about physician quality is also mirrored in the employment of foreign-trained physicians. The International Medical Graduates who entered this country in the early 1970s in response to particularly liberal immigration restrictions, and huge Medicare-related increases in demand, were disproportionately employed in long-term care facilities and residency positions not affiliated with medical schools. Being licensed did not make them equals in the medical market (see Svorny 1979).

Medical Licensure as a Cartelizing Device in the Market for Physician Services

Many observers argue that licensure is a cartelizing device—benefiting physicians by limiting competition in the market for physician services—and providing few advantages to consumers. Reuben Kessel (1958) painted a damning picture of the medical societies, suggesting that their actions to limit the supply of physicians were typical of cartel behavior. Kessel argued that the cornerstone of the American Medical Association (AMA) monopoly power was its ability (delegated by the individual state legislatures) to accredit medical schools, as only graduates of accredited medical schools were eligible to be licensed to practice. Kessel argued that the power to accredit gave the AMA the power to limit both the number of schools and the rate of production of physicians.

As additional evidence of cartel behavior, Kessel pointed to AMA efforts to enforce monopoly pricing (what economists call price discrimination) and medical society-enforced prohibitions on advertising.

Consumer Interest Models of Medical Licensure

In response to cartel allegations, Leland (1979, 1980) attempted to show that it is possible for minimum quality standards to enhance welfare. Leland's work is based on the premise that patients have difficulty distinguishing qualified from less qualified physicians. When consumers can't identify high quality physicians, he argues that all physicians must charge the same fee (equal to the average quality). As a result, the most talented individuals choose other professions (where their superior ability can be revealed and rewarded more easily). Under these conditions, Leland shows that minimum quality standards raise not only the average price, but the quality of the product as well. The intuition is that barriers to entry increase earnings, attracting more able individuals to the market. Leland emphasizes that his work should be seen as a counter-example to the cartel hypothesis; showing that it is not true that minimum quality standards can *never* improve welfare.

Two alternative explanations for licensure rest on its ability to solve the common principal-agent problem as it applies to the delivery of patient care. In health care, the patient is the principal, the medical practitioner the agent. The disparity in their self-interests causes problems for the principal in assuring that the agent will act competently.

Carl Shapiro (1986) describes how licensure might be seen as a means to resolve the incentive problem associated with the agency relationship in health care. He argues that physicians who have made investments in medical education are able to produce high quality services with less effort, and that this reduces physician incentives to shirk on providing quality services. The intuition is that, because it is easier for physicians to do a good job, they do so more often. Following this line of thought, consumers can avoid costly monitoring costs by using a physician who has made substantial investments in medical education. Shapiro justifies standardized training requirements (often seen as evidence of AMA control) on the basis that it is otherwise costly to reveal one's investment.

Despite their efforts to find benefits to consumers from licensing, both Leland and Shapiro conclude that a system of certification would be better. Certification is similar to licensure, except that non-certified individuals are allowed to sell services to anyone who chooses to buy them. Economists have long favored certification over licensure (Friedman 1962). Certification is preferred because consumers can use it as a guide, but may purchase care from non-certified practitioners if they so choose. As Leland notes, under certification "buyers have a wider range of choice...they can buy low-quality goods or services if they wish" (p. 283).

Licensure vs. Certification

There are two standard arguments in support of licensure over certification (see Leffler 1978). First, there may be significant externalities associated with the consumption of physician services. If the bad care that one person receives makes someone else worse off—as is the case if infectious disease is not treated properly—then constraints on the sale of physician services may be useful in preventing the spread of infectious disease. The second traditional argument for licensure is that people are not smart enough to make their own choices. That the government should, therefore, make choices for them, sits well with some social activists.

A third justification for licensure over certification is in Svorny (1987, 1992). Like Shapiro, I see licensure as valuable in resolving the agency problems in health care markets. But I stress that the main value of licensure is in the abnormal profits that are created and in the required investments in medical training. Both leave the physician with a potentially large capital loss were she to suffer the loss of her license to practice medicine. A physician's access to the profits created by limiting entry lasts only as long as she acts in ways that are deemed appropriate by the state medical board.

Certification does not produce the same incentives. Under a system of certification rather than licensure, non-certified individuals compete with certified practitioners, making it impossible to maintain the abnormal profits that discourage physician misconduct.

Incentive-producing profits or premium streams of the type created by licensure have been described in a number of different markets as a means by which to assure quality (see Lazear 1981 and Klein and Leffler 1981). In labor markets, "efficiency wage" arrangements involve paying workers a wage above their value elsewhere, producing a premium stream that is lost upon malfeasance. The higher wage and potential for loss create incentives for workers to act in the interest of the firm, to self-monitor. Workers know that if they are caught shirking their duties, they will be fired and lose the present value of the premium stream. Such arrangements are thought to prevail when monitoring costs are high. Even though the firm pays the worker a higher wage, the incentives for performance make the arrangement a useful one from the point of view of the firm; productivity is higher and the firm saves money on monitoring workers on a day-to-day basis.

In dismissing licensure, economists have overlooked the potential for such arrangements to improve the quality of services in the market for physician services.[2] A malfeasant physician loses not only the return of his or her required investment in training, but also the profits generated by restricting entry.

Taking the view that profits in the market for physician services are welfare-enhancing, one can argue that restrictions on advertising (described by Kessel as evidence of cartel activity) are desirable as they protect the profits generated by restrictions on entry. Following the same logic, state requirements that physicians be U.S. citizens (now illegal) may have served the purpose of maintaining profitability in the market for physician services by discouraging physician immigration. Obviously, protection of physicians' profits comes at a cost to society. It is an empirical question as to whether the gains outweigh the added costs.

The price-fixing schemes that Kessel found so offensive may actually have been socially useful. In contrast to profits created by limiting the quantity of services provided, price discrimination increases physician income in an efficient way. Price discrimination transfers wealth from consumers (consumer surplus) to physicians without affecting resource allocation. At the extreme, perfect price discrimination (where each consumer is charged the most he or she is willing to pay), allows large wealth transfers with no social cost or deadweight loss. Quantities sold are as they would be in a competitive market.

The Political Equilibrium

The simple cartel view of medical licensure is also rebuked by work that suggests both consumer and professional interests are represented in medical board policy. A useful model for thinking about how conflicting pressures influence public policy is in Peltzman (1976). Peltzman's model of the political process places the regulator in the position of seeking support from both producers and consumers.

When there is an increase in demand for a product whose price or supply is regulated, Peltzman's regulator experiences an increase in the total "surplus" over which he has control. The predicted response, because both producer and consumer support is attractive to the regulator, is to redistribute a portion of the new surplus to both parties. One solution is to allow prices and profits to rise, but by less than they would if regulators' interests simply reflected the interests of producers.

Evidence from the mid-1960s suggests that Peltzman's model of the determination of regulatory equilibrium may be more useful for analyzing the market for physician services than the simple cartel model. The passage of Medicare and Medicaid legislation in the mid-1960s significantly increased the demand for physician services by subsidizing the health care consumption of the elderly, the disabled, and the poor. Regulators responded by eliminating restrictions on physician immigration.[3] Physician earnings rose, but by an amount less than they would have had there been no increase in the number of physicians entering the United States.[4]

Because physician groups have much to gain from restricting licensure, economic theory tells us that even if there is an identifiable, socially optimal level of entry restrictions, a democratic political process will overshoot it. Physicians will lobby strongly to go beyond optimal supply restrictions and consumers, relatively less organized, will be no match for their lobbying efforts.[5] Groups that can easily organize and lobby will have a disproportionate influence over the final policy choice, especially when the regulatory costs are spread broadly across a large group of consumers (Stigler 1971).

What little empirical evidence there is seems to confirm the joint influence of consumers and physicians over medical board policies. Leffler (1978) finds licensing laws to be most restrictive in states where consumer demand for quality would be expected to be high, evidence that consumer interests influence the political decision-making process. There is evidence that, at one time, physician interests were the stronger of the two; Svorny (1987) finds licensure restrictions greater than those that would be optimal for consumers.

The choice is not between socially optimal regulation and an unregulated market, but between sub-optimal regulation leaning toward the interests of one group or another and an unregulated market. Neither is perfect. If, for example, physicians dominate the medical regulatory process, we can expect that supply will be constrained by an amount that is greater than is optimal from the point of view of society as a whole. But eliminating licensure reduces incentives for quality. The choice is between an imperfect regulatory outcome and an imperfect market outcome. Critical to the choice is the extent to which market constraints deter misconduct. Changes over time in the incentives and costs of third parties who monitor physician practice could make licensure less preferred than an unregulated market outcome.

3. Deterring Physician Malfeasance

In addition to licensure, a variety of alternative mechanisms have the potential to deter fraudulent and incompetent service providers. The market penalizes malfeasant physicians through loss of reputation. With fewer customers and fewer physician referrals, physicians suffer the consequences of inappropriate practice. There are, however, problems with relying on reputation alone. First, new entrants have little to lose in the way of reputation. Second, reputation loss may not be large enough a loss to achieve social goals for optimal deterrence.[6] To increase the potential loss upon malfeasance in some markets, companies or workers are "bonded." Money is set aside that can be obtained by the customer if the service is provided poorly.

Nonmarket penalties for malfeasance include legal liability and criminal penalties (fines and prison). In each case, individuals face incentives to self-monitor to avoid a penalty. But, because legal liability and fines require that individuals have sufficient wealth, they will not always work. For individuals or institutions with few assets (such as newly licensed physicians), or for individuals who can hide their assets, the incentives to self-monitor may be insufficient. Finally, using imprisonment as a deterrent is not a particularly useful solution, as real resources are used when individuals are imprisoned (Posner 1977). Lost is the output of the incarcerated individual, as well as the resources spent securing prisons.

An advantage of licensure over these other methods of control is that loss of the premium stream creates a significantly large penalty that cannot be avoided by hiding one's wealth. Also, it is useful in motivating individuals with few physical assets, as license revocation threatens the value of their human capital.

4. Recent Developments

Despite having just set forth the benefits associated with licensure, it is my view that, due to recent developments in the provision of health care, the value of medical licensure arrangements in assuring physician quality has diminished. Today, hospitals, health care providers, and even firms that purchase health care for their workers are held liable for physician malfeasance by the courts. Large-scale provision of care (through HMOs and other providers) and the ability of computers to store and retrieve information about physicians make it easier to monitor physicians than ever before. Also, reputation is becoming increasingly important in assuring quality in the market for physician services. Together, these developments limit the value of maintaining existing licensing arrangements.

Liability

The biggest changes have to do with liability for misconduct. A series of court decisions have increased hospital liability for physician malpractice. For many years, hospitals had no legal liability for what transgressed on their premises. Physicians alone were liable—both for their own actions and those of nurses and other medical professionals working under their supervision. Under such circumstances, one could argue that self-monitoring on the part of physicians was important, providing an agency-based justification for licensing.

Initially, the judicial doctrine of charitable immunity protected hospitals and administrators from claims of malpractice.[7] But this particular form of protection was lost in the 1940s and 1950s, as hospital care expanded and hospitals were perceived as providing non-charitable services.

After the loss of charitable immunity, hospitals relied on the independent contractor status of physicians as a defense against malpractice liability. Under the legal doctrine of respondent superior—"let the master answer"—hospitals could only be held liable for torts caused by individuals directly employed by the hospital. If physicians were independent contractors—and most were—the hospital could not be held liable. Two other legal doctrines—"captain of the ship" and "borrowed servant"—put the liability for other medical professionals with the physician in charge.

Over the last twenty years or so, however, hospital protection from immunity has eroded, principally because the nature of the delivery of care has changed. Many physicians are no longer independent contractors, but directly employed by hospitals, limiting the ability of the hospital to use the independent contractor defense against negligence. Also, judicial attitudes have changed—courts have been willing to find employment relationships (between hospitals and physicians) based on facts that would not have been interpreted as an employment arrangement in the past (Southwick 1988).

Because physicians are increasingly members of teams of health professionals, with no one individual exercising direct control, modern courts have rejected the "captain of the ship" and "borrowed servant" doctrines that held physicians liable for the actions of other health professionals. And because patients see hospitals as providing comprehensive care rather than as a setting for independent physician practice, courts have applied the doctrine of "apparent agency," increasing hospital liability for professional malpractice.

The courts' assignment of corporate liability to hospitals has added yet another layer of liability. Under the doctrine of corporate liability, hospitals are held directly liable for negligence. Hospitals have a duty to select and retain competent doctors, formulate policies to ensure quality care, and, in some jurisdictions, oversee the work of all practitioners.

Whether this increased liability is justifiable, or just a search for a deep pocket, is debatable. Southwick (1988) suggests that the true basis for assigning vicarious liability to the hospital is that hospitals tend to have insurance coverage or superior financial means. He cites a general trend toward court decisions that facilitate the recovery of damages for personal injury.

An obvious justification for shifting liability to the hospital is that it creates incentives for hospitals, which are probably best equipped to monitor physicians, to do so. Rutchik (1994) states that "The threat of corporate liability is a useful and positive tool that gives hospitals great incentives for self-monitoring and diligent, careful operation" (p. 548).

The shift in liability to include the hospital changes things dramatically. Specific individuals are responsible for selecting physicians and monitoring their performance. Furrow (1993) writes, "patterns of poor medical practice will be deterred by placing liability on institutions rather than individuals, since organizations have superior data collecting abilities and tools for managing risks" (p. 187).

The vast majority of physicians who behave inappropriately will find it difficult, if not impossible, to obtain staff privileges. Although no system can offer perfect protection from physician misconduct, the incentives associated with institutional liability seem extremely useful in this regard.

Although most of what has been written focuses on hospital liability, hospitals are not alone in increasingly being held accountable for physician services. Health Maintenance Organizations, Preferred Provider Organizations, Independent Practice Associations, and other providers are being held responsible for ascertaining the quality of professionals associated with the organization (Johnsson 1990, Geyelin 1990).

Peer Review

The movement to physicians practicing in groups with capitated payment arrangements has led to increased incentives for physicians to seriously question their peers whose practice patterns lie outside the normal bounds. An individual physician can harm the group's reputation substantially, to the detriment of all involved. Those familiar with capitation and group practice report that physicians are willing to question physicians whose practice patterns seem unusual and that peer pressure is a powerful tool toward improving care (Montague 1994b, 1994c). Montague (1994b) reports, "the interests of hospitals and physicians are converging in integrated capitated systems. Outliers' practices didn't used (sic.) to cost their peers anything, but capitation means outliers will influence their peers' compensation" (p. 51).

Also, the increase in institutional liability makes peer review a serious matter. According to Kearney and McCord (1992), "New forces of liability have made the accuracy, and therefore, the candor, of peer review discussions more critical than ever" (p. 33).

This contrasts sharply with the traditional perception of physicians as unwilling to point out the deficiencies of a colleague to patients or hospital boards (Kessel 1958). Incentives have surely changed. In the past, an individual doctor had little to gain by spending his or her time trying to evaluate the work of another physician. If he or she were uncertain about the skills of another professional, simply refraining from referring patients to that physician would have been the most likely choice of action.[8]

Data

The shift in liability toward hospitals and other groups has been accompanied by a development that facilitates the monitoring of physician performance by these newly responsible entities. The growth in low-cost computer data management has facilitated record-keeping, making it harder for practice outliers to escape notice and disciplined physicians to hide their past records of malpractice.

It is now possible to keep track of physician practice patterns and compare them to those of their peers. Such profiles are extremely useful in modifying physician behavior. Remarkably, just making physicians aware of how their practice patterns differ from those of other physicians is sufficient to cause changes in their behavior (Montague 1994b).

Once disciplinary actions have been taken, records of these actions are kept in data banks maintained by the Federation of State Medical Boards, the American Medical Association, individual state medical boards, and the federal government. Hospitals are required by law to check the NPDB at the time practitioners apply for hospital privileges and every two years thereafter (Department of Health and Human Services 1993). It is no longer the case that a malfeasant physician can escape her record by moving to another state.

Ready access to data on state disciplinary actions and actions taken by hospitals (such as loss or suspension of staff privileges) clearly facilitate a hospital's ability to evaluate a potential staff physician prior to granting privileges. Combined with hospital liability, these sources of data provide the means to protect consumers from repeated infractions by incompetent, careless, or fraudulent practitioners.

Brand Name

If the new world is one in which individual physicians act as part of a team of health care providers, and this is certainly the case in hospitals, HMOs, and other similarly structured practice arrangements, brand name will become increasingly valuable to consumers in determining the point of care choice. Dolan (1980) made this point. He stressed that the changing nature of the market for physician services would provide protection for consumers through reputation. "If institutions become the locus of medical care," he wrote, "brand-name identification would inevitably follow" (p. 42). He suggested that institutions would develop identities based on service quality, convenience of obtaining service, cost, and even therapeutic ideology.

Once this happens, brand name becomes a valuable asset, easily diminished at the first media report of physician misconduct or ineptitude. To protect this asset, stakeholders in institutions that provide health care to consumers will take steps to avoid such outcomes. So valuable is brand name to stakeholders, its very existence creates strong incentives to monitor service quality at every point.

5. Residual Value to Licensure

Given the changes in health care delivery patterns, which increasingly provide protection from malfeasant physicians, it is reasonable to ask whether we still need the penalties generated through licensing health professionals. As the probability of being caught and penalized increases, theorists suggest that the size of the optimal penalty declines (Posner 1977).[9] Clearly, due to increased institutional liability, concern over brand name, peer review, and physician tracking data systems, the chance of being caught and penalized has increased. This means that the penalty can be reduced. The value of holding the loss of license up as a penalty for misconduct has diminished.

But not all communities have made the same changes in health care delivery. Evidence suggests that the western region of the United States has led the nation in shifting toward managed and capitated care (Montague 1994a). There is more integration in the delivery of health care services in urban areas than in suburban or rural areas. A majority of groups in rural areas report only "slight" competition with other group practices, unlike groups in urban and suburban areas, which report moderate to intense competition. Cooperation/collaboration with HMOs is least likely for group practices in rural areas, in the south, and for small to medium size groups.

This means that not every community will benefit equally from the quality-inducing side effects of competition, reputation, and institutional liability. Where significant numbers of doctors continue to practice independently, removed from institutional oversight, licensure would appear to remain a useful or efficient means of quality control.

But it is in just these areas that the negative supply effects of licensure are the most felt. Observers have long lamented the lack of physicians in rural and isolated communities. Each effort to shift care to these communities—subsidies to physicians who locate there, increased immigration of foreign trained physicians—has failed to eliminate the problem of "under served" communities. In the debate over scope-of-practice legislation (which would allow physician assistants and nurse practitioners to practice independently and to provide services heretofore restricted to physicians), again, it has been argued that independent NPs and PAs could practice in areas where practice profitability is insufficient to attract physicians.

The strong negative supply effects of licensure in rural communities make it hard to argue the merits of licensure in any circumstance. If the supply consequences of licensure requirements are so severe as to preclude treatment in the least populous areas, requiring exceptions to scope-of-practice legislation, clearly the merits of licensure escape this under-served, generally poor population. Regulations that create incentives for service quality among physicians that never practice in their communities are of little value to these remote consumers, and we can hardly hang an argument for extending licensing arrangements on the lack of institutional oversight in rural areas.

6. Related Policy Issues

The following public policy issues share a common theme. Like licensure, each has the potential to impact incentives for service quality in the market for physician services.

Prescriptive Powers

An issue directly related to licensure has to do with the prescription of controlled substances. As things stand now, many states permit nurse practitioners and physician assistants to prescribe drugs, although there are limits to the type of drugs that may be prescribed. This is a change from prior rules, which vested prescriptive powers with physicians. By 1993, fourteen states had granted independent nurse practitioners prescribing authority that included controlled substances (Pearson 1993).

This is an interesting issue because one major use of medical licensure over time has been to penalize individuals who prescribe drugs inappropriately (see Svorny 1993). Assuming it is in society's interest to regulate drug consumption, there may be some value to confining prescriptive powers to a limited number of health professionals so as to create a premium profit stream to deter opportunistic behavior. Because constraints on entry and required investments are less onerous for allied health professionals than for physicians, they have less to lose upon the revocation of their license than do physicians. Perhaps recognizing this, several states require physician supervision when granting other health personnel prescriptive powers.

Any-Willing-Provider and Due Process Requirements for Dismissal

In order to deter managed care plans from choosing a set of physicians and excluding others (a closed panel), physician groups have supported "any-willing-provider" legislation. Under this legislation, plans must accept all qualified health providers willing to accept their rates and rules. Prodded by state medical societies, many states have adopted "any-willing-provider" legislation (Leone 1994).

Along the same lines, legislation was proposed by the American Medical Association to afford physicians a due process appeal when dismissed from service by an HMO or other health care provider. The question is whether plans should be prohibited from terminating physicians without showing cause (Brostoff 1994).

From the perspective of generating incentives for physician quality, this type of legislation is not desirable. Benefits derived from the shift to hospital and institutional provider liability are lost (or substantially attenuated) if it is difficult for a hospital or HMO to disassociate itself from a physician.

Access to National Practitioner Data Bank Records

Public access to the National Practitioner Data Bank and state data bank records is the focus of public policy debate. One clear benefit from allowing the most widespread access to the data is that penalties for malfeasance would be enhanced. It has been reported that hospitals, dealing with substandard care, can use the threat of an NPDB report to get physicians to agree to monitoring and reviews of their performance (Montague 1994d).

Standards of Evidence

Another issue related to quality incentives is the standard of evidence to which the state medical boards are held as the basis for disciplinary actions. Many states constrain their boards by requiring relatively strong standards of evidence in disciplinary hearings. According to Swankin and Cohen (1992), fifteen states require "clear and convincing evidence"—strong evidence to find a physician guilty. Twenty-eight states require only a "preponderance of evidence"; there need only be more evidence backing the board's position than backing the physician's position.

Standards of evidence have been the focus of legislative battles in more than one state. Critics say that the clear and convincing standard protects physicians at the expense of the public. With respect to service quality, adopting the weaker standard will increase physician incentives for self-monitoring and should improve the overall quality of care in a state.

Conclusion

The focus of this paper has been on incentives for quality in medical labor markets. Quality care results when millions of individual decisions are made in ways that benefit patients. Quality care can be encouraged with incentives for performance and penalties for misconduct. Society benefits when quality assurance is accomplished efficiently, minimizing the associated costs.

Changes in the medical marketplace suggest it is time to revise state policies with respect to medical licensure. Improvements in the incentives for others to monitor physicians due to shifts in liability, the growth in group practice, and peer review, and the increased ease with which this monitoring can be performed, suggest a diminished value for licensure arrangements.

Variations across states in regulatory mechanisms offer a chance to judge the relative merits of different approaches. Innovations, such as increased roles for non-physician providers, weaker standards of evidence in disciplinary hearings, or variations in direct hospital liability for physician malpractice, will provide information about the costs and benefits of alternative policies. By studying the consequences of innovations in various jurisdictions, lawyers, economists, and health professionals can contribute to the development of an efficient system of quality assurance in the market for physician services.

Notes

1. Even Arrow, who is often quoted as favoring government intervention in assisting consumers in the market for physician services, said "insofar as this is possible" (p. 966).
2. For exceptions, see Blair and Kaserman (1980) and Gellhorn (1956).
3. Modifications of immigration policy and a ruling by the U.S. Secretary of Labor that physicians were in short supply in the United States opened the U.S. borders to physicians trained abroad.
4. See Svorny (1991) for an estimate of what physician earnings would have been had there been no change in immigration restrictions in the mid-1960s.
5. However, the representation of consumer interests in the medical marketplace by health maintenance organizations and other large-scale service providers suggests that consumers may be gaining in their influence over public policy with respect to health care licensing.
6. Also, those who are harmed are not compensated (Rutchik 1994).
7. This discussion of hospital liability is based on material in Rutchik 1994, Southwick 1988, Kinney 1992, Furrow 1993, and Kearney and McCord 1992.
8. Consistent with these perceptions, recent empirical work shows a positive relationship between group practice presence and physician disciplinary actions across states (Svorny and Feldman 1997).
9. This is because the expected penalty is equal to the penalty times the probability of being penalized.

References

Arrow, Kenneth J. "Uncertainty and the Welfare Economics of Medical Care." *American Economic Review*, VOL NO?? December 1963, pp. 941-73.
Benham, Lee. "Licensure and Competition in Medical Markets," in *Regulating Doctors' Fees: Competition, Benefits, and Controls Under Medicare*, edited by H. E. Frech III. Washington, DC: American Enterprise Institute for Public Policy Research, 1991, pp. 75-90.

Blair, Roger D., and D. L. Kaserman. "Preservation of Quality and Sanctions within the Profession," in *Regulating the Professions: A Public Policy Symposium*, edited by R. D. Blair and Stephen Rubin. Lexington, MA: Lexington Books, 1980, pp. 185-98.

Brostoff, Steven. "AMA Backing 'Anti-HMO' Legislation. *National Underwriter*, No. 22, 98th Year, May 30, 1994, pp. 1, 23.

Dolan, Andrew K. "The Potential of Institutional Licensing and Brand-Name Advertising in the Medical Care System." *Journal of Contemporary Business*, Vol. 9, No. 4, 1980, pp. 35-43.

Eaton, B. Curtis, and William D. White. "Wealth—The Support of Institutions and the Limits of Control." The Hoover Institution, Palo Alto, Calif., E-86-26, June 1986.

The Federation of State Medical Boards of the United States. *The Exchange: Section 3, Physician Licensing Boards and Physician Discipline*. Fort Worth, Texas, 1992-1993.

Friedman, Milton. *Capitalism and Freedom*. Chicago: University of Chicago Press, 1962.

Furrow, Barry R. "Quality Control in Health Care: Developments in the Law of Medical Malpractice." *Journal of Law, Medicine and Ethics*, Vol. 21, No. 2, summer 1993, pp. 173-92.

Gellhorn, Walter. *Individual Freedom and Governmental Restraints*. Baton Rouge: Louisiana State University Press, 1956.

Geyelin, Milo. "HMOs' Malpractice Immunity is Fading." *Wall Street Journal*, 1 February 1990, B1, B6.

Ginsberg, Paul B., and Ernest Moy. "Physician Licensure and the Quality of Care." *Regulation*, fall 1992, pp. 32-39.

Goodman, John C. *The Regulation of Medical Care: Is the Price Too High?* San Francisco: The Cato Institute, 1980.

Johnsson, Julie. "Managed Care Involvement Increases Liability Exposure." *Hospitals*, March 5, 1990, pp. 40-44.

Jones, P. Eugene, and James F. Cawley. "Physician Assistants and Health System Reform." *Journal of the American Medical Association*, Vol. 271, No. 16, April 27, 1994, pp. 1266-1272.

Kearney, Kerry, and Edward McCord. "A New Era for Hospital Liability." *Risk Management*, Vol. 39, No. 9, September 1992, pp. 28-33.

Kessel, Reuben A. "Price Discrimination in Medicine." *Journal of Law and Economics*, October 1958, pp. 20-53.

Kessel, Reuben A. "The A.M.A. and the Supply of Physicians." *Law and Contemporary Problems*, spring 1970, pp. 267-83.

Kinney, Judith M. "Expansion of Hospital Liability Under the Doctrine of 'Corporate Negligence'." *Temple Law Review*, Vol. 65, 1992, pp. 787-802.

Klein, Benjamin, and Keith B. Leffler. "The Role of Market Forces in Assuring Contractual Performance." *Journal of Political Economy*, August 1981, pp. 606-20.

Lazear, Edward P. "Agency, Earnings Profiles, Productivity, and Hours Restrictions." *American Economic Review*, September 1981, pp. 606-20.

Leffler, Keith B. "Physician Licensure: Competition and Monopoly in American Medicine." *Journal of Law and Economics*, April 1978, pp. 956-67.

Leland, Hayne E. "Minimum-Quality Standards and Licensing in Markets with Asymmetric Information," in *Occupational Licensure and Regulation*, edited by Simon

Rottenberg. Washington, DC: American Enterprise Institute for Public Policy Research, 1980, pp. 165-284.

Leland, Hayne E. "Quacks, Lemons and Licensing: A Theory of Minimum Quality Standards." *Journal of Political Economy,* December 1979, pp. 1328-46.

Leone, Peter R. "New developments in 'any willing provider' laws." *Health Care Financial Management,* May 1994, pp. 32-35.

Montague, Jim. "Precision Maneuvers." *Hospitals & Health Networks,* Vol. 68, No. 1, 1994a, pp. 26-33.

Montague, Jim. "Profiling in Practice." *Hospitals & Health Networks,* Vol. 68, No. 2, 1994b, pp. 50-51.

Montague, Jim. "Capitation and Physicians." *Hospitals & Health Networks,* Vol. 68, No. 7, 1994c, pp. 30-35.

Montague, Jim. "Should the Public Have Access to the National Practitioner Data Bank?" *Hospitals & Health Networks,* Vol. 68, No. 11, 1994d, pp. 52-56.

Pearson, Linda J. "1992-93 Update: How Each State Stands on Legislative Issues Affecting Advanced Nursing Practice." *Nurse Practitioner,* Vol. 18, No. 1, January 1993, pp. 23-38.

Peltzman, Sam. "Toward A More General Theory of Regulation." *Journal of Law and Economics,* August 1976, pp. 211-40.

Posner, Richard A. *Economic Analysis of Law.* Boston: Little, Brown and Co., 1977.

Rayack, Elton. "The Physician Services Industry," in *The Structure of American Industry,* edited by Walter Adams. New York: Macmillan Publishing Co., Inc., 1982, pp. 188-226.

Risen, James. "Kaiser Wins Break from Health Reform Clause." *Los Angeles Times,* 28 July 1994, D2.

Rutchik, David H. "The Emerging Trend of Corporate Liability: Courts' Uneven Treatment of Hospital Standards Leaves Hospitals Uncertain and Exposed." *Vanderbilt Law Review,* Vol. 47, No. 2, March 1994, pp. 535-71.

Shapiro, Carl. "Investment, Moral Hazard, and Occupational Licensing." *Review of Economic Studies,* Vol. 53(5), No. 176, 1986, pp. 843-62.

Southwick, Arthur F. *The Law of Hospital and Health care Administration,* 2nd edition. Ann Arbor, MI: Health Administration Press, pp. 539-82.

Stevens, Rosemary A. "The Future of the Medical Profession" in *From Physician Shortage to Patient Shortage: The Uncertain Future of Medical Practice,* ed. Eli Ginzberg. Second Conference on Health Policy, Cornell University Medical College. Boulder, Colorado: Westview Press, 1986.

Stigler, George J. "The Theory of Economic Regulation." *Bell Journal of Economics,* spring 1971, pp. 3-21.

Svorny, Shirley. *Foreign-Trained Physicians and Health Care in the United States,* Ph.D. Dissertation, University of California, Los Angeles, 1979.

Svorny, Shirley. "Physician Licensure: A New Approach to Examining the Role of Professional Interests." *Economic Inquiry,* Vol. 25, No. 3, July 1987, pp. 497-509.

Svorny, Shirley. "Consumer Gains from Physician Immigration to the U.S.: 1966-1971." *Applied Economics,* Vol. 23, No. 2, February 1991, pp. 331-37.

Svorny, Shirley. "Should We Reconsider Licensing Physicians?" *Contemporary Policy Issues,* Vol. 10, January 1992, pp. 31-38.

Svorny, Shirley. "Advances in Economic Theories of Medical Licensure." *The Federation Bulletin: The Journal of Medical Licensure and Discipline,* Vol. 80, No. 1, spring 1993, pp. 27-32.

Svorny, Shirley, and Roger Feldman. "The Changing Structure of the Market for Health Services: Implications for Physician Discipline," draft paper, Department of Economics, California State University, Northridge, June 1997.

Swankin, David A., and Rebecca A. Cohen. "A Resource Guide for Responding to Attempts to Weaken State Medical Licensing Boards by Legislating a Higher Standard of Evidence." *Federation Bulletin: The Journal of Medical Licensure and Discipline*, Vol. 79, No. 6, December 1992, pp. 206-18.

U.S. Department of Health and Human Services, Office of the Inspector General. *National Practitioner Data Bank: Usefulness and Impact of Reports to State Licensing Boards*. Boston, March 1993.

Young, S. David. *The Rule of Experts: Occupational Licensing in America*. Washington, DC: The Cato Institute, 1987

13

Liability Reform: Traditional and Radical Alternatives

Patricia M. Danzon

Introduction

Liability reform for medical providers is an issue of ongoing concern at both the federal and state levels. Most of the major health care reform bills introduced in 1994 included at least some liability reform measure, of which the most common were: traditional tort reform (caps on awards for pain and suffering, collateral source offset, limits on attorneys' fees, etc.); mandatory but nonbinding alternative dispute resolution (ADR); and demonstration projects for enterprise liability, which would transfer liability from individual physicians to the health plan that financed or the hospital that provided the patient's care. Other promising (and many not-so-promising) reforms have also been proposed.

Federal health care reform should be viewed as an opportunity, not a necessary precondition for nationwide change in the liability system. However, most previous changes have occurred at the state level, where further experimentation may continue. Following the sharp increases in liability insurance premiums in the mid-1970s and 1980s, most states enacted changes in their rules of tort liability for medical providers. Liability insurance markets have been relatively stable for over a decade, which has removed the immediate pressure for change.

However, certain features of the current liability system are dysfunctional and unnecessarily costly.

Moreover, the health care delivery system is being fundamentally restructured, in response to market pressures for cost control and without waiting for Washington. The underlying trend is a shift from passive fee-for-service reimbursement of providers to active controls and/or capitation forms of payment that shift risk to providers and hence radically change their incentives to eliminate excess.[1] At minimum, the liability system should not obstruct these changes. At best, liability reform could take advantage of these changes in the health care delivery system to offer consumers more choice over rules of liability and compensation and lower costs.

The medical malpractice reforms enacted by states over the last two decades span a wide range, including caps on awards, collateral source offset, shorter statutes of limitations, screening and mediation panels, etc. Some of these reforms have moderated the growth in claims and awards (Danzon 1984, 1986; Zuckerman et al. 1990), but fundamental criticisms of the tort system remain. Proposals for more radical change include enterprise liability (for example, Weiler 1991; Weiler et al. 1993; Abraham and Weiler 1994); an administrative fault-based system (AMA 1988); no-fault systems of compensation, modeled in part on the no-fault schemes of Sweden and New Zealand; and increased contractual options (Havighurst 1995; Danzon 1997).

This chapter evaluates both traditional tort reform and the major alternatives, drawing on simple economic theory and a considerable body of empirical evidence. To define a framework for the analysis, section 1 outlines the ideal functioning of the liability system from an economic perspective, and section 2 examines the shortfalls between this ideal and the actual operation of the malpractice system. Sections 3, 4, and 5, review traditional tort reforms, the Swedish and New Zealand no-fault schemes, enterprise liability proposals, the American Medical Association's proposal for an administrative fault-based system, and contractual options. Section 6 concludes.

1. The Theory of Tort Liability

In theory, the law of medical malpractice holds health care providers liable only for medically caused (iatrogenic) injuries that are caused by negligence; adverse outcomes that are consistent with the normal risks of customary medical care are the burden of the patient.

Tort liability has two primary functions. First, it provides a source of compensation for persons injured. Second, by imposing sanctions on persons found negligent, it is intended to deter future negligent behavior. [2] It is this second deterrent function that must be viewed as primary, if the tort system is evaluated by the criteria of economic efficiency. If judged as a system of compensation and insurance, tort liability is grossly inefficient—and arguably also inequitable—compared to either public or private first-party insurance systems. Roughly forty cents of the malpractice insurance premium dollar reach the patient as compensation, compared to over ninety cents for large first-party health insurance programs. Much of the difference—about forty cents of the liability insurance dollar—is spent on litigation, equally divided between plaintiff and defense attorneys. Tort liability also entails other, unmeasured costs, including time and anxiety costs borne by the litigants and liability-induced distortions in medical practice, so-called "defensive medicine." These measured and unmeasured overhead costs of the liability system result from the attempt to determine causation and assign responsibility for injuries. These overhead costs are *only* worth incurring if assignment of fault induces offsetting benefits, by increasing incentives for injury prevention and hence deterring future injuries. Thus, by the criteria of economic efficiency, the tort system can *only* be justified, *if at all*, as a system for deterring negligence and preventing injuries.

In designing tort liability or any other risk reduction program, economists generally assume that the social objective is to minimize the total societal cost of injuries, which includes not only the compensated and uncompensated costs of injuries, but also expenditures on prevention, litigation, and other overhead.[3] The efficient or socially optimal investment in prevention requires that the costs of prevention be weighed against the benefits, in terms of averting costs of injury, compensation, and overhead. At the margin, an additional dollar spent on injury prevention should save at least a dollar of expected injury-related costs. The optimal level of prevention thus defined minimizes the total societal cost of injuries. Moreover, optimal policy should recognize that the liability system is part of a network of systems for controlling risk and compensating victims, which include market forces and regulation for controlling risk, and other private and public insurance systems. Each of these systems should be used where it is most cost-effective.

For product risks and defects that are clearly evident to the consumer, market forces are sufficient to deliver the quality that consumers prefer and are willing to pay for. For example, if I buy a rotten apple, I cannot sue the greengrocer for compensation. But if consumers cannot readily observe or understand risks, then reliance on markets alone leads to nonoptimal injury rates and nonoptimal insurance (Spence 1977, Shavell 1980). Asymmetric information about risks between consumers and producers provides the economic rationale for the professional liability of learned professionals, including physicians, lawyers, and accountants, and for product liability of manufacturers with respect to latent risks. In the case of medical care, if patients misperceive the benefits and risks of alternative treatments and cannot readily monitor the quality of care delivered, then market forces alone with a rule of *caveat emptor* would likely result in too many risky procedures and too little care per procedure.[4]

In theory, a negligence rule of liability can create incentives for providers to take the level of care that patients would want if they shared the provider's information. Sufficient (but not necessary) conditions for a negligence rule to lead to optimal outcomes include the following: courts set the standard of care at the efficient level, at which the marginal benefit from additional care is just equal to the marginal cost; damages are set at optimal levels; providers are liable for failure to obtain informed consent; and suits are brought and compensation awarded if and only if negligence occurs.[5]

Efficient deterrence incentives can in theory sometimes also be achieved by a rule of strict liability, whereby producers are liable for all injuries caused by the product or service, regardless of negligence. However, strict producer liability is not an efficient liability rule if potential victims can affect the risk of injury by their own precautions. This is clearly relevant to many product and workplace injuries; it is also relevant to some medical injuries. Strict liability is often advocated on grounds that it extends compensation to all victims who suffer an injury as a result of the activity in question, without regard to provider fault. However, if the social objective is compensation, as noted earlier, this can be achieved at much lower overhead cost through other public and private insurance mechanisms.[6]

The evidence suggests that the malpractice system performs these deterrence and compensation functions imperfectly, at best, and at high cost. The shortfall between the negligence system in theory and in practice arises primarily because the decision-makers—courts, doctors, patients, liability insurers—lack the perfect information that is assumed by the theory.[7] Because courts lack good information about appropriate care, the standards applied in practice are unpredictable and possibly systematically biased. With uncertain legal standards, a negligence rule may create nonoptimal deterrence incentives (Craswell and Calfee 1986); many valid claims are not filed and many invalid claims are filed. With uncertain legal standards, doctors cannot protect themselves simply by taking the required level of care. Unpredictable legal standards lead to "defensive" practices to reduce the probability of liability and create the demand for comprehensive liability insurance. Liability insurance would not interfere with deterrence if it were perfectly experience-rated. But in practice experience-rating is crude and infrequently used, both because insurers lack the necessary information and possibly because providers already face significant uninsured time and embarrassment costs of being sued and therefore prefer policies with full coverage of monetary losses. A rule of strict liability in theory eliminates the need for courts to make a finding of negligence. But determining whether an injury was caused by medical care, rather than by the underlying disease, would require a similar inquiry, as would the no-fault rules that exclude "normal risks" of medical care. Thus, in practice the choice is between imperfect alternatives on the basis of less than complete empirical evidence.

2. Criticisms of the Liability System

Overall Costs of Liability

The common argument, that liability costs are a significant contributor to growth in total health care costs, is clearly wrong, at least in its simplest form. A full accounting of the impact of liability on health care spending must include all liability-induced costs and offsetting compensation and deterrence benefits. Reliable measures of most components of costs and benefits are unavailable. Malpractice premiums are less than 1 percent of health care costs. There is no reliable estimate of the cost of "defensive medicine" and those that do exist do not always use a meaningful definition. "Defensive medicine" should be defined as liability-induced change in medical practice that is intended primarily to reduce the provider's risk of liability and that fully informed patients would not be willing to pay for, given their insurance coverage. This definition excludes cost-justified deterrence, that is, changes in medical practice that cost less than the expected benefits, which tort liability is intended to encourage. The definition also excludes care that is not cost-justified but that occurs because of insurance-induced moral hazard on the part of patients and providers. This insurance-induced excess care resulted from the incentives of fee-for-service insurance, and has been mislabeled defensive medicine. One purpose of capitation and other managed care strategies that are replacing open-ended fee-for-service payment of providers is to reduce this insurance-induced excess care. This potential efficiency gain from managed care may be undermined if courts hold managed care plans to the excessive norms developed under fee-for-service medicine, imposing liability whenever coverage for costly services is denied. More on this below.

Even harder to measure are the deterrence benefits of the liability system—the reduction in risk of injury that results because liability makes providers more careful. Casual evidence confirms this liability-induced care in many forms: quality assurance and risk management programs have proliferated, patients are informed of risks, record-keeping is more careful, to name only the most obvious. These and other measures have surely reduced the number of injuries. However, because we lack precise measures of benefits and costs, whether the overall benefits outweigh the costs remains an unanswered question.

High Overhead Costs

Perhaps of greater concern than total cost is the high cost of litigation and consequently the high overhead loading on liability as a patient compensation system. There are two real questions here: first, are the pure administrative costs of determining fault and liability outweighed by deterrence benefits? If so, the liability system yields positive net benefits despite high overhead costs, assuming that the compensation paid to victims is valued at cost. Second, even if the net benefits are positive, could the system be made more cost-effective, by reducing the costs without commensurate reduction in deterrence benefits?

Although the first question—whether the deterrence benefits outweigh the overhead costs—cannot be answered with the available data, rough calculations suggest that it may be (see Danzon 1985).

The only credible estimates are based on the New York data on medical injuries, as analyzed in Weiler et al. (1993). This study found that the proportion of injuries attributable to negligence was lower in hospitals facing a higher probability of being sued, given a negligent injury.[8] The conclusion of this analysis is that negligent injury rates would be significantly higher, were it not for the threat of tort liability, and that the deterrence benefits of the malpractice system may well outweigh its costs, even ignoring such intangible benefits as retribution or fairness. Moreover, although other quality assurance and professional monitoring systems are often proposed as alternatives to tort liability, in practice these other mechanisms have been strengthened in response to tort liability, making them complementary to rather than substitutes for liability.

Nevertheless, even if the current liability system does yield positive net benefits, the design of cost-effective reforms remains an important concern.

High and Volatile Costs of Claims

Since the 1970s, the frequency of malpractice claims (claims per 100 physicians) has been high relative to historical norms and relative to other countries. This is often cited as evidence of system malfunction, although of course it may not be if the higher claim rates are offset by greater deterrence benefits. Medical malpractice liability has existed for centuries, but such actions were rare until the late 1960s. From the early 1970s to the mid-1980s, malpractice claim frequency increased at more than 10 percent a year, and claim severity (average payment per paid claim) increased at twice the rate of general inflation. Claim frequency stabilized at about thirteen claims filed per 100 physicians per year in the 1990s, down from a peak of sixteen in the mid-1980s. The unexpected surge in claim costs precipitated sharp increases in liability insurance premiums in the mid-1970s and mid-1980s, which, in turn, led many states to adopt tort reforms. Of these, caps on awards, collateral source offset and shorter statutes of limitations appear to have had some success in slowing the rate of growth in costs (Danzon 1984, 1986; Zuckerman et al. 1990), although other factors no doubt also contributed to the stabilization of costs.

During the 1980s, claim frequency and severity rose at least as rapidly in the U.K. and Canada as in the U.S., but absolute levels remain lower because these countries started from much lower levels than the U.S. In 1987, physicians in the U.S. were still five to six times more likely to be sued than physicians in Canada and the U.K. and awards for comparable injuries were several times larger in the U.S. (Danzon 1990).[9] The increase in malpractice premiums outpaced the increase in claims costs in the U.K. and Canada, particularly for surgeons, as the medical defense unions introduced rate differentials across specialties and attempted to shift from pay-as-you-go to funding of incurred liabilities. The squeeze of sharply rising premiums but constrained provider incomes under public health systems generated intense political pressures. In the U.K., the National Health Service agreed to indemnify doctors for the costs of their malpractice insurance premiums. This indemnity undermines the deterrent function of liability, reducing it to a costly and inequitable social insurance program.

There is an important lesson in this U.K. experience, should the U.S. adopt global budget caps and physician fee regulation, as proposed in 1994, while retaining an open-ended liability system. If liability awards increase, because of changing social norms, but provider revenues are capped, the cost of paying for the more generous social insurance is borne by providers who cannot pass on the costs in higher fees.[10] This is unfair and is likely to be politically intolerable.

Mismatch Between Claims and Injuries

Although malpractice claim frequency has risen, the number of claims appears to fall far short of the number of negligent injuries.[11] Two detailed reviews of hospital records in California (Mills et al. 1977) and New York (Weiler et al. 1993, hereafter Harvard study) concluded that the incidence of negligently caused injury is just under one per hundred hospital admissions. However, both studies use an extremely broad definition of injury. For example, the Harvard study defined as an iatrogenic injury "any disability caused by medical management that prolonged the hospital stay by at least one day or persisted beyond the patient's release from hospital." This implicitly assumes that the reviewers had perfect information about the appropriate duration of stay and expected outcome, given the patient's condition, and that all deviations from these expected values were attributable to medical error. More plausibly, some deviations from average are to be expected, reflecting unobserved medical factors that cannot be determined from a retrospective chart review and purely stochastic differences in patient response to a given treatment.

These studies also use legal or medical definitions of negligence, whereas the relevant definition for policy purposes is the economic definition, based on the notion of the socially optimal level of care, which defines negligence as failure to take precautions with social costs less than expected benefits.[12] Given the broad definitions of injuries and negligence used, it is perhaps not surprising that almost 60 percent of the identified "injuries" were minor, or that the number of claims filed was less than one-tenth of the number of negligently caused injuries as defined by the study. The ratio of claims to negligent injuries was much higher for serious injuries: roughly one claim is filed for every three such injuries and one in six is paid (Weiler et al. 1993). Using data from several studies, White (1994) calculates that, given an iatrogenic injury, the probability of suit is substantially greater if negligence occurs. This much higher probability of suit for negligent treatment than for non-negligent treatment should provide a significant deterrent effect, even if there is a high overall error rate in claiming.

Even if the number of malpractice claims were to fall short of the number of negligently caused injuries, appropriately defined, this would not necessarily imply that deterrence incentives and compensation provided through tort liability are too low, once other quality-control and insurance systems are taken into account. If providers face market incentives and regulatory pressures to practice with care, or if they are risk averse with respect to tort claims and also face high nonmonetary time and embarrassment costs of being sued, then a one-for-one match between tort claims and negligent injuries is not necessary to achieve adequate incentives overall for appropriate care.[13] Similarly, since other public and private insurance mechanisms are less costly to operate, compensating small claims through the tort system may not be cost-effective. In general, determining whether incentives for care are too high or too low is very difficult, once we recognize that the net impact reflects nonmonetary and monetary incentives from market, regulatory, and liability systems.

Although the Harvard study concluded that many of the claims filed lacked evidence of a medically caused injury, this may partly reflect the limited information available to the reviewers. In other studies using more complete information, independent reviewers have concluded that negligence was certainly present in roughly 31 percent of cases and not present in 44 percent, with the remainder uncertain (Farber and White 1991). For claims with negligence, the probability of payment was .64, and the average payment was $258,000; for claims without negligence, the probability of payment was only .24 and the average payment was $65,900. This suggests that the most extreme criticisms of the tort system as a random lottery are exaggerated.

Unequal Compensation

It is often argued that tort awards are unfair, because patients with similar injuries receive unequal compensation. This criticism ignores the dual function of the tort system. Although equal compensation for similar injuries might be appropriate if compensation were the sole purpose of tort liability, deterrence requires unequal compensation for two similar injuries if one is caused by negligent care and the other reflects other factors, including the patient's underlying condition. Theory and empirical evidence suggest that the settlement process roughly adjusts payments for the degree of defendant negligence (Danzon and Lillard 1983; Farber and White 1991), consistent with efficient deterrence and with one definition of fairness. Nevertheless, predictability of the outcome for a given degree of negligence is far from certain. This contributes to imperfect deterrence, incentives for defensive medicine, and volatility in liability insurance markets. Thus, improving accuracy and predictability of the disposition process should be a major goal of liability reform.

Inappropriate Compensation

A valid concern is that awards for pain and suffering, which account for a large fraction of the total payout on malpractice claims, may exceed levels necessary for optimal compensation.[14] Theory cannot determine optimal compensation for an irreplaceable loss (Cook and Graham, 1977), but tort payments for pain and suffering in the U.S. are almost certainly too high (Danzon, 1984b). Compensation for pain and suffering is not included in compensable benefits in any other private or social insurance program where patients or taxpayers are faced with the explicit trade-off between the generosity of the insurance benefits and the cost. Uncertainty and delay in receiving compensation for pain and suffering further undermines its value as insurance to patients, since the purpose of insurance is to provide a reliable level of income if a loss occurs. Moreover, awards for pain and suffering probably have little if any impact on deterrence, but nevertheless contribute significantly to the average cost and volatility of liability insurance premiums, because they account for such a large fraction of insurer losses. For these reasons, scheduled limits on awards for noneconomic loss, as exist in several other countries, could contribute significantly to the cost-effectiveness of the liability system, as discussed below.

3. Traditional Tort Reforms

Most of the defects of the current liability system—imperfect deterrence, imperfect compensation, high litigation costs, and imperfect experience-rating of liability insurance—are at bottom attributable to imperfect information on the part of courts, plaintiffs, and providers. With perfect information, courts could costlessly make accurate findings of negligence, which would create incentives for providers to take due care but no more (no "defensive medicine"), and liability insurance premiums could be perfectly experience-rated. Simply changing the liability rule or amount of damages does not, of itself, create better information. However, rules can be designed to make better use of the information that is available, reduce abuses, and prevent waste.

In evaluating proposed reforms, recall that the objective assumed here is to minimize the total social cost of injuries, including the utility costs of injuries (after optimal compensation), prevention, litigation, and other overhead. Providing optimal compensation to patients is implied by this criterion, as a necessary condition for minimizing the utility cost of injuries. Reducing the cost of liability insurance premiums, which has been the goal of most actual reform proposals, may simply shift costs with no net efficiency gain.[15]

Limits on Awards for Pain and Suffering

Limits on awards for nonmonetary loss ("pain and suffering") are consistent with optimal patient insurance and would reduce litigation costs with minimal if any loss in deterrence. A schedule based on the injury severity and the plaintiff's life expectancy, as exists in Sweden and some other European countries, is superior to a single cap for all cases, which is the more common variant in state tort reform legislation in the U.S.[16] Such schedules can be designed to yield socially desired levels of compensation; they also reduce overhead by reducing the parties' ability to influence the outcome through expenditure on litigation. Limits on noneconomic damages are unlikely to affect deterrence, since the very large losses are typically insured and typically are not used for experience-rating of individual (as opposed to class) premiums, because they are viewed as random bad luck, beyond the control of the insured.

Evidence from several studies (Danzon 1984, 1986; Zuckerman et al. 1990) shows that damage caps are the single reform that does reduce the average cost per claim and insurance premiums. Although only the few very large awards are affected, since 5 percent of claims account for roughly 50 percent of the total dollars paid (Danzon and Lillard 1983), a reduction in these few very large payments can significantly affect the total payout and hence reduce malpractice insurance premiums.

Although pain and suffering caps are the only reform that has been shown to reduce malpractice costs, and cost reduction was the leading rationale given for including liability reform in the 1994 health care reform proposals, caps on awards were not included in the Administration's Health Security Act (HSA) or the House or Senate Leadership bills.[17]

Periodic Payments

Periodic payment of compensation for future damages enables the defendant to provide the patient's compensation through an annuity. This minimizes the cost to the defendant of assuring whatever level of compensation the court intends for the plaintiff. Note, however, that to preserve incentives for rehabilitation, the amounts of such future payments should be fixed at the time of claim disposition, to preserve incentives for cost-conscious use of care and rehabilitation. Periodic payment provisions were included in most of the leading health care reform bills, but sometimes only at very high dollar thresholds. Again, structuring the award as a periodic payment may reduce the plaintiff attorney's contingent fee, compared to the fee payable on a simple lump sum award, unless the fee contract is written to prevent this.

Collateral Source Offset

Collateral source offset deducts from tort feasor's liability to the plaintiff any compensation available from designated private first-party or public insurance programs. The goal of preventing double compensation of the plaintiff can be achieved either by reducing the tort award (collateral source offset) or by subrogation, which transfers (part of) the plaintiff's claim to his or her other insurers.[18]

For purposes of deterrence, subrogation is preferable because the tort feasor pays in full for all costs. Collateral source offset, by reducing the potential tort recovery, could significantly reduce plaintiff incentives to bring claims and hence undermine deterrence. The empirical evidence tends to support this concern. Collateral source offset rules have not only reduced claim severity but also claim frequency, consistent with this feedback effect (Danzon 1984). Nevertheless, because subrogation may entail higher transaction costs, the optimal mechanism for eliminating double compensation remains an unresolved empirical question.

Collateral source offset for medical malpractice claims was included in the Health Security Act. It was not in either the House or Senate Leadership bills.

Limits on Contingent Fees

Several states have imposed limits on the plaintiff attorney's contingent fee percentage, typically as a sliding scale that decreases with the size of the award. The rationale for this approach is weak. If the goal is to reduce large awards, this is better achieved by directly imposing scheduled limits. Contingent fees provide a potentially efficient risk-sharing arrangement for bearing the costs of investment in litigation with an uncertain pay-off. If the goal is to reduce litigation expenditure and payments to attorneys, this is better achieved by reducing uncertainty and the ability of litigants to influence the outcome, which would reduce incentives to invest in litigation. If the goal is to reduce large awards, this is better done directly by scheduled limits as described above.

If the goal is to reduce frivolous litigation, the English rule for shifting costs to the losing party is a promising approach. However, in order to protect risk-averse plaintiffs and make the system even-handed in application, defense costs should be applied against the plaintiff's attorney rather than against the individual plaintiff. Such a rule would expose plaintiff attorneys to greater uncompensated expense in the event that they take a case and lose. This would make them more reluctant to bring cases of marginal merit, and on most cases the fee percentage would likely be increased to compensate the attorney for the added risk. Thus, a ceiling on the contingent fees would obstruct the implementation of an English rule for cost shifting.

Limits on plaintiff attorneys' contingent fees were included in several of the 1994 health care reform proposals. But since the proposed limit was often simply one-third of the award or settlement (as in the HSA, for example), and this is the most common market-determined percentage, the statutory limit would not be binding in the majority of cases. A flat limit of one-third might be binding on cases with small potential recovery, because the fixed costs of litigation tend to lead to a higher percentage on smaller cases. Discouraging filing of low-stakes cases is surely not one of the objectives of fee limits.

Alternative Dispute Resolution (ADR)

Alternative dispute resolution (ADR) is a popular proposal and was included in most of the health care reform proposals. However, if ADR is to reduce delay and litigation costs, it must speed settlement or substitute for a formal trial in a large percentage of cases. This implies that if the ADR system is formal arbitration, it should be binding. For less formal procedures, the parties should face significant penalties for going on to trial. This can be achieved by applying the English rule of cost-shifting to post-ADR litigation, within limits. Thus, a party who rejects an ADR finding and who receives the same or less at court could be required to pay the other side's legal costs of going to trial. Because most plaintiffs would be risk averse and in any case could not pay the court costs of both sides, the English rule should be applied to the plaintiff's attorney, who should be permitted to increase the contingent percentage to reflect the added risk.

One of the most promising forms of ADR is early neutral evaluation (ENE), which has been adopted in other types of litigation in northern California (Rosenberg and Folberg 1994). If combined with a system of early binding offers and a fee-shifting rule for frivolous rejection of an offer and going on to trial, ENE could significantly reduce the costs and delay of claim disposition. The ENE is designed to provide a prompt, well-informed neutral evaluation of the case. The early binding offer system, combined with the English rule, creates incentives for each party to act on their true information, with penalties for bluff and strategic manipulation.

By contrast, adding nonbinding arbitration, or screening and mediation panels, without significant penalties for appeal, may simply increase costs. For example, the HSA and House and Senate Leadership bills all proposed systems of nonbinding arbitration, the results of which were not admissible as evidence at trial and with no penalties for proceeding to trial. This approach simply adds the costs and delay of an additional step in the litigation process.

4. Foreign Models of "No Fault" Systems

Even if the most extreme criticisms of the tort system are exaggerated, the question remains whether alternatives would be more cost-effective. The Swedish model has been adopted in Norway and Finland and has been suggested in Canada and the U.K. (Fenn 1993). The Swedish and New Zealand models are often cited as illustrating the potential savings from switching from a negligence rule of liability to a no-fault (causation-only) test of compensability. The analogy is drawn (for example, Weiler 1991) to the workers' compensation system, which compensates for all injuries and illnesses arising out of employment, regardless of the fault of the employer. As shown below, analogies between the Swedish and New Zealand systems and workers' compensation or proposals for strict enterprise liability for medical malpractice are misplaced. The low reported overhead costs in these countries are misleading and in any case are not due to the use of a causation-only test for compensation. Nevertheless the experience of these two systems is instructive for other countries considering similar alternatives, including the U.S.[19]

The Swedish Patient Compensation Insurance (PCI)

The PCI was established in 1975 by voluntary contract between medical providers and a consortium of insurers, to preempt the threat of statutory expansion of tort liability.[20] Although patients retain the choice to sue in tort under traditional negligence rules, tort claims have been extremely rare since the PCI was established, at least until recently. Key features of the Swedish model include the elimination of the concept of negligence or fault and decoupling of patient compensation from deterrence or any sanctioning of providers. Patient compensation is provided by the Patient Compensation Insurance (PCI), while the discipline of medical providers is handled by the Medical Responsibility Board (MRB). No information is transmitted between them, in order to obtain the doctors' cooperation with the PCI. The PCI is administered by a consortium of insurers, with appeal to a special advisory panel and ultimately to arbitration.

The Swedish model has attracted interest other countries because of its relatively low budget cost, low overhead rate, and widespread acceptance by medical providers. Claim frequency has stabilized at about twenty-one per 100 physicians per year, compared to thirteen-sixteen claims per 100 physicians in the U.S. The higher rate in Sweden is not surprising, given the lower costs of filing, somewhat broader criteria of compensability and less reason to oppose payment of marginal claims (see below). Roughly 40 percent of these claims receive compensation in both countries. But the PCI costs roughly $2.38 per capita, or 0.16 percent of health care costs in Sweden, whereas medical malpractice insurance premiums are about 1 percent of higher health expenditures in the U.S. Thus, the per capita budget cost of the Swedish PCI appears to be roughly one-tenth of U.S. malpractice premiums. Administrative overhead is 14-18 percent of total PCI premiums, compared to roughly 60 percent in the U.S. This low overhead rate is often cited as evidence of the potential savings from eliminating negligence in favor of a no-fault (causation-only) rule of compensability for medical injuries (Weiler 1991), analogous to the strict liability of employers for workplace injuries under workers' compensation.

However, these inferences are based on a misunderstanding of the PCI. The low budget cost of the PCI, despite the higher claim frequency, reflects primarily two factors. First, the collateral offset rule shifts most of the wage loss and medical expense of iatrogenic injuries to other social insurance programs. In fact, such cost-shifting does not reduce and may actually increase the social costs of injuries, by undermining cost internalization, which undermines general and specific deterrence.[21] Because most of the economic loss related to iatrogenic injury is shifted to these other social programs, the PCI budget vastly understates the true cost of compensating iatrogenic injuries in Sweden.

Second, awards for noneconomic loss are below those in most other European countries and roughly one-tenth of those in the U.S. [22] The low PCI payment level relative to the U.S. is possible because Sweden's tort system is much less favorable to plaintiffs than the U.S. tort system, offering even lower payments than the PCI.[23] Since the PCI is a voluntary alternative to tort that patients elect on a case-by-case basis, the PCI must offer plaintiffs an expected payoff that at least matches their expected tort recovery, net of costs, in order to deflect tort claims. Thus, other countries that have more generous tort systems could not adopt the Swedish model or any other voluntary contractual alternative and expect to realize costs as low as in Sweden, unless they also adopted significant tort reform.[24] Indeed, if a Swedish-style PCI were offered as a voluntary alternative to tort in the U.S. as it is in Sweden, it would not offer significant gains over those that can be realized through out-of-court settlement, which already provides a voluntary, contractual alternative that operates in the shadow of the tort system.

The PCI's low overhead percentage is not the result of using a causation-only test for compensability. Although the PCI is often called no-fault, this is misleading. From the patient's perspective, the criteria of compensability are quite similar to a traditional negligence rule based on customary practice. Under the PCI, an injury is compensable if (1) it occurred with "substantial probability" as a direct consequence of medical intervention, and (2) either the treatment was not medically justified or the injury could have been avoided by performing the treatment differently. Thus, although the terminology of fault and negligence has been eliminated, compensation requires some notion of "error." Adverse outcomes caused by medical care are explicitly excluded, if the treatment was medically justified.

But from the provider's perspective, the PCI is truly no-fault in the sense of no liability. The PCI eliminates all reference or inquiry into fault or negligence, does not require the patient to identify a particular provider who failed in a duty of care, and entails neither financial nor reputational consequences for individual providers. This "no-liability" scheme bears no resemblance to strict liability, as applied in workers' compensation and product liability, or as proposed for strict enterprise liability of hospitals (Weiler 1991), since the strict enterprise liability proposal retains the basic rule that the liable defendant should pay for the damages, in the interests of deterrence.

The low litigation expense of the PCI reflects several features of the system that are unlikely to be acceptable in the U.S. These include the elimination of all links between patient compensation and provider liability and deterrence, and the modest level of patient rights, compared to a U.S. tort plaintiff (although not necessarily compared to a tort plaintiff in Sweden). Because physicians are not liable and have no personal stake in the outcome, they generally cooperate rather than opposing compensation of an injured patient. Patients have little to gain from appeal to the review panel or to arbitration. Both are closed to the press and public, and the panel has ruled in favor of the insurers in 90 percent of cases.[25]

Thus, the low litigation rates reflect primarily the fact that neither plaintiffs nor physicians have strong incentives to oppose or appeal the insurers' adjudication of claims. Other contributing factors are the simple claim filing process; administration by a monopoly consortium of insurers, which eliminates insurers' incentives to vigorously oppose plaintiff claims or to experience rate premiums; and lack of competition and provider-specific accountability for costs in the health care system, which makes providers more willing to tolerate flat-rated premiums,[26] despite significant geographic differences in claims experience. It remains to be seen whether the PCI will survive the recent reforms of the Swedish health care system, which have introduced more competition and provider accountability, and the opening up of liability insurance markets to more competition as a result of Sweden's entry into the EU.

The deterrence function, to the extent that it exists, was assigned to the Medical Responsibility Board. Patients can file a claim with the Medical Responsibility Board if they feel that their treatment was negligent or contrary to the statutory code of medical practice. They bear their own filing costs and receive no compensation. Providers may receive a reprimand or warning, but this has no financial consequence and probably at most a minor reputation effect. There are roughly six MRB claims per 100 physicians per year, of which one in six receives some sanction. Thus, the ratio of MRB sanctions to paid PCI claims is less than one in ten—a rough measure of the loss in potential deterrence that results from decoupling compensation from medical discipline. Although the PCI database on iatrogenic injuries might in theory be used to identify and control persistent sources of risk, in practice the information collected is insufficient. Moreover, although clinics and hospitals are informed about their claims experience, the responsible individuals and sometimes even the nature of the injury are not identified.

Conclusions. The main lesson from the Swedish PCI experience is that a sufficient and possibly a necessary condition for low overhead costs is to forego all links between compensation and deterrence or injury prevention. Whether this results in more iatrogenic injuries with social costs that outweigh the reduction in litigation costs is an unanswered empirical question. The answer would probably differ across countries, depending on the costs and benefits of their tort systems and on the costs and effectiveness of other systems of quality control, including market-based incentives for quality.

The New Zealand Accident Compensation Corporation (ACC)

The New Zealand Accident Compensation Corporation (ACC) was established in 1974 as a comprehensive no-fault compensation system for victims of "personal injury by accident," including "medical misadventures." The establishment of the ACC eliminated normal tort rights for such injuries, in contrast to the Swedish PCI, where tort actions remain an option. Claims are administered by the ACC, with appeal to a special ACC Authority. Compensation was set at a relatively high percentage of wage loss for workers, plus scheduled lump sum payments for noneconomic loss. Nonworkers received only the lump sum payments. Medical costs were borne by the National Health Service (NHS), except that the ACC paid directly for services in private hospitals, co-payments and services not covered by the public system.

Between 1975 and 1989 total expenditures under the ACC grew at a nominal rate of over 20 percent a year, or roughly 6 percent a year after adjusting for inflation. This exceeds the average rate of increase of U.S. malpractice premiums over the same period. Note, however, that the New Zealand figure reflects compensation for injuries from all causes, including employment, automobile, etc., in addition to medical injuries. A strict comparison of trends in costs of compensating iatrogenic injuries is not possible because the ACC has not categorized iatrogenic injuries separately. Financing was hidden in payroll and general taxation, with no separate assessment of medical providers.

Dissatisfaction with this cost explosion, the inequity of the incidence of costs (low risk employers and drivers subsidizing high risks) and the neglect of injury prevention led to significant reforms of the ACC in 1992. The new rules for compensation for medical injuries are remarkably similar to traditional negligence rules, although there is no interest in restoring the tort system for adjudicating claims. The problems under the original ACC that led to these reforms are instructive.

"Personal injury by accident" was broadly defined by the original ACC statutes to include "physical and mental damage caused by medical, surgical, dental, and first aid misadventure." The intent was to exclude illness and normal risks of medical care but to include medical injuries that fall outside the realm of normal risk, including but not limited to those caused by negligence. In practice, adverse outcomes that have either very low probability or unexpected severity have been considered compensable. This definition of compensability is similar to the criterion of "unintended and unexpected" adverse consequences proposed by Weiler (1991), which was rejected by the architects of the PCI as unworkable (Oldertz 1988).

Defining compensability in terms of an event that is unexpected or of unexpected severity suppresses but does not eliminate the need to determine whether the care was appropriate. If "expected" is defined in terms of statistical probability, the probability distribution depends on the level of care, which thus begs the question of the appropriateness of care, given the patient's medical condition. Moreover, even if an appropriate level of care is implicitly or explicitly assumed, this leaves open whether the expected outcome is to be defined on subjective or objective grounds. Rulings and commentary in New Zealand have differed on this point, creating the potential for inconsistent and arbitrary outcomes.

Difficulties in implementing this definition led to numerous proposals for change. Some urged use of ICD-9 definitions of injuries, others urged extending the system to include all incapacity. Logically, in a compensation system that eliminates defendant-specific liability and hence makes no attempt at deterrence, there is no equitable justification selecting some victims for compensation, on grounds of the cause of their injuries, while denying compensation to others in similar condition but from other causes. Thus, there is a fundamental inequity in any system that provides tax-financed compensation to those injured in the course of medical care, while denying compensation to others with similar injuries but from other causes, if there is no deterrence rationale for the distinction.

The 1992 ACC reforms adopted a far more restrictive definition of compensability that goes a long way toward restoring a negligence standard. "Medical misadventure" is now defined as "personal injury resulting from medical error or medical mishap." "Medical error" is "the failure ... to observe a standard of care and skill reasonably to be expected in the circumstances." "Medical mishap" is determined largely on the basis of "rarity and severity" of the outcome, specifically, less than a 1 percent probability of occurring, provided that the injury severity exceeds a specified threshold. This category specifically excludes abnormal reactions and complications of procedures, and injuries related to lack of informed consent, misdiagnosis or treatment omissions, unless resulting from negligence.

The 1992 reforms require the ACC to pay for all medical costs incurred by compensated victims, effectively restoring the traditional collateral source rule, in the interests of accountability and internalization of costs to those causing injuries. This change recognized that the previous practice of not paying for NHS treatment costs incurred by ACC beneficiaries undermined the ACC's incentives to control the amount and duration of expenditures.

Like the Swedish PCI, the New Zealand ACC is often acclaimed for low overhead costs (less than 10 percent of total expenditures) and prompt payment of compensation. However, far from indicating efficiency, this simply reflects the ACC's practice of accepting over 80 percent of claims as filed, relying largely on physicians as gatekeepers to certify that a claim is a "personal injury by accident" and, in cases of permanent disability, that continued benefits are necessary. But physicians have no incentive to oppose claims; indeed physicians could personally benefit from endorsing a patient's claim for compensation from the ACC, since the ACC paid higher fees than did the NHS and compensation through the ACC would preempt the patient from filing a tort claim.

Thus, the ACC cut overhead costs by eliminating measures to screen out invalid claims, which in turn contributed to the rapid escalation of total costs. Similarly, data collection costs have been kept low. But because this meant elimination of detailed information on the causes of injuries—for example, the failure to identify iatrogenic injuries or detail on causation for any injuries—the database cannot be used for prevention and risk management. Overall, the ACC experience suggests that saving on overhead may be "penny wise but pound foolish": skimping on the visible overhead component can lead to higher real social costs of injuries.

The 1992 reforms authorize the ACC to establish a medical misadventure account, funded by premiums levied on registered health care professionals, with experience rating and no-claims bonuses. This is consistent with the intended increase in autonomy and accountability of health care providers under the overall health care sector reforms.[27] The 1992 reforms also authorized the ACC to report potentially negligent medical misadventures to the appropriate disciplinary body. However, these changes have remained discretionary.

Conclusion. The New Zealand experience under the original ACC structure illustrates pitfalls to be avoided rather than a useful prototype that other countries might adopt. The original definition of a compensable event was difficult to implement and raised ethical issues, leading almost inevitably to proposals to expand the system to cover incapacity more generally. However, the difficulty of defining compensable events and the potentially huge budget costs of such a system led to the restoration of a quasi-negligence criterion of patient compensation. But, as in the PCI, the terminology of fault has been eliminated and so far individual providers are not accountable for the injuries that they cause.

As in the Swedish PCI, the low reported administrative costs of the ACC are not an indicator of efficiency. Rather, low overhead reflects the elimination of all links between compensation and deterrence. The causes of medical injuries are not investigated and there is no feedback to the individual providers that are responsible for the injuries. If the proposed introduction of experience-rated premiums for providers were implemented, providers would have more incentive to oppose claims and litigation costs would likely increase. As in Sweden, the elimination of all provider liability, explicit or implicit, is key to the nonadversarial adjudication of claims. In addition, in New Zealand the very low reported overhead percentage reflects the rubber stamping of claims, with the result that claims costs and total costs have exploded, despite—and in part because of—low overhead costs. The true overhead cost of any insurance or accident compensation scheme includes not only the reported overhead but also the unmeasured deadweight loss from unnecessary injuries and inappropriately compensated claims (Danzon, 1992). This is not observable, but in the ACC it is likely to be very high.

5. Proposed Alternatives to Tort Liability in the U.S.

The number of proposals for radical alternatives to traditional tort liability in the U.S. is too numerous to review. Here we focus on those three that have received significant attention and are reasonably practical—elective strict liability, an administrative fault-based system, and contractual alternatives. Each of these comprehensive reform proposals would simultaneously change many dimensions of the traditional tort system. It is worth noting that some of these component changes could be applied within the traditional tort system, while retaining its other features. For example, an administrative mechanism of claim disposition could replace traditional trial by judge or jury; scheduled damages could replace traditional damage rules while retaining the fault-based rule of liability. Thus, some or even much of the potential benefit of these comprehensive proposals might be obtained by selective adoption of some of their less radical features.

Enterprise Liability

Proposals for enterprise liability call for shifting of liability entirely from individual physicians to larger enterprises, either hospitals or health plans. Some courts already add hospitals and sometimes managed care plans as additional defendants under theories of vicarious and agency liability (see Danzon 1997). Weiler (1991), Weiler et al. (1993), and Abraham and Weiler (1994) argue for holding the hospital strictly liable for injuries arising out of care by physicians on their staff, including injuries that occur outside the hospital, without regard to fault, similar to strict employer liability for workplace injuries. The elective strict liability (ESL) proposal would empower hospitals and other health care organizations to elect to offer an alternative, administrative system of compensation in return for a waiver from common law tort liability. Following experience with a voluntary, elective system, it might be implemented more widely.

The arguments for ESL are that it would improve efficiency of deterrence, because hospitals are best placed to coordinate injury prevention programs; provide more accurate experience rating and hence better internalization of costs, because of greater statistical credibility of the claims experience of large enterprises; and reduce the costs of legal defense.

Under ESL medical causation is a necessary but not a sufficient condition for compensation. Excluded are injuries resulting from the normal risks of medical care and imperfect cures of the underlying condition. Thus, in contrast to some earlier no-fault models, more recent variants of ESL recognize some of the many difficult causation issues that arise in attributing an adverse medical outcome to medical care. The patient enters the health care system in imperfect health. Some adverse health outcomes or imperfect cures reflect the inevitable course of the underlying disease, even with appropriate medical care. Moreover, appropriate care may even increase some risks—for example, risks related to invasive surgery—in order to treat the underlying condition. A simple causation-only strict liability system would create incentives for providers to avoid high-risk patients and treatments, unless they could charge differential fees to reflect the higher liability costs. Retaining a fault principle for errors of omission might reduce the incentive to avoid high-risk treatments but the incentive to avoid high-risk patients would remain. Thus, although strict liability in principle eliminates the need for courts to investigate negligence, in fact, a very similar inquiry would be necessary to determine whether an injury was the result of normal and appropriate care, and hence not compensable. Without such an inquiry, all imperfect cures would be potentially compensable.

Weiler (1991) argues that the causal inquiry is far less difficult than is the additional fault judgment, referring to evidence from Sweden and New Zealand: "in Sweden and New Zealand, the two countries that have provided no-fault compensation for medical injuries...it has been possible to draw a causal dividing line without any pronounced administrative burden for the no-fault programs as a whole." As argued above, the low administrative costs in Sweden and New Zealand result from abandoning provider-specific liability and any attempt at deterrence, not from use of a causation-only test for compensability. In fact, compensation requires evidence of some error in care, in addition to causation. Moreover, because ESL retains provider-specific liability for damages, with experience-rated premiums, litigation and administrative costs under ESL would certainly be higher than under the PCI or ACC.

Any overhead savings under ESL would result primarily from the use of an administrative disposition process and scheduled damage payments. These changes can be made without switching from fault to a strict liability rule. Similarly, if channelling liability from the individual doctor to the health care enterprise offers real efficiency savings, this could be done by voluntary contract within the context of a fault-based rule. The Kaiser HMOs already assume liability for all practitioners; adjudication of patient claims by arbitration rather than tort is specified as part of the contract of insurance coverage. Not surprisingly, such contractual election of enterprise liability is confined to fully integrated, exclusive HMOs, whose providers treat only HMO patients and whose patients receive all their treatment from HMO providers. In looser, nonexclusive independent practice (IPA) or network HMOs, placing enterprise liability on the health plan could add administrative costs and reduce accountability, contrary to requirements for efficient deterrence and the intent of the ESL proposal. Yet these looser systems are more common and growing more rapidly, reflecting patients' willingness to pay slightly higher premiums in return for greater choice of providers.

Conclusion. Enterprise liability is likely to be efficient only for fully integrated health care systems such as staff model HMOs, where the health plan has the information and authority to manage all providers of care. In this case, liability should fall on the health plan, not individual hospitals within the plan. If enterprise liability were mandatory for all health plans, it would probably accelerate the formation of exclusive provider networks. Since this would run counter to current market trends, it would probably reduce overall consumer well being.[28]

The AMA Administrative Fault-Based System

The American Medical Association has proposed an administrative fault-based system (AFS) that would remove medical malpractice claims from the courts to a specialized administrative "Medical Malpractice Review Board" in each state (AMA 1988). The AFS retains a fault-based rule of liability, with the modified standard of care defined in terms of a "range of reasonableness," based on the standards of a prudent and competent practitioner in the same or similar circumstances. The traditional contributory negligence rule is replaced by comparative negligence. Whereas traditionally compensation is in principle denied if the relative contributions of the patient's underlying condition and the provider's actions were 55 percent and 45 percent, respectively, under the proposed standard the provider would pay 45 percent of the damages. Apportioning damages would compensate more patients, and could be considered more equitable to patients and providers; it is also consistent with efficient deterrence of injuries.

Payments for noneconomic loss would be based on a schedule, depending on the patient's life expectancy, with amounts indexed to preserve real value. Collateral source offset is included. Future damages would be annuitized, with future payments determined at time of claim disposition to preserve incentives for rehabilitation.

The administrative procedures for claims adjudication are intended to be less costly, permitting greater access to those with valid claims, while screening out non-meritorious claims. Nevertheless, the adversarial structure of proceedings is retained, with free attorney assistance for patients whose claims are deemed valid on initial screening. In order to encourage settlement, both the plaintiff and defendant(s) would be required to make blind settlement offers prior to the hearing, and would be subject to sanctions if they rejected an offer that is not significantly bettered at the hearing. The hearing resembles a traditional trial, except that it is adjudicated by an examiner experienced in medical malpractice claims, rather than judge or jury; appeal is to the appellate courts, but on rules of law only. Thus, the court cannot review the facts or the finding of liability in a particular case or set medical standards; the Board has ultimate authority over these functions.

To strengthen professional discipline, the Board would operate a clearinghouse for reports from several sources, including settlements and awards in malpractice cases, hospital reviews, reports from other physicians (who are required to report suspected incompetence, impairment, and drug or alcohol dependence of their colleagues), and other state disciplinary actions. The Board can also investigate reports of substandard performance from members of the public and others and, following a full due process proceeding, may impose sanctions including fines and license revocation.

The AFS proposal does not specify in detail how the system would be financed. Financing by premiums payable by providers, as in the status quo, would be possible in principle but might weaken physician support for the system, due to the potential for expanded liability and proposed strengthening of the other disciplinary mechanisms. To the extent that the AFS does expand provider liability and include elements of pure social insurance, by offering free legal aid to patients whose claims pass the initial screen, there may be a case for some tax financing or subsidy.

Conclusion: The AFS Compared to the PCI. The administrative fault-based approach resembles in some ways the Swedish PCI, but with important differences. Both limit compensation to injuries caused by medical error ("avoidable" injury in the case of the PCI), defined relative to customary medical practice. Both use written clarification of the criteria of compensability, although the PCI rules are much more detailed. By adopting a comparative negligence standard, the AFS adopts a more expansive definition of causation and hence expands the number of potentially compensable injuries relative to traditional tort rules.

However, the AFS retains a link between patient compensation and provider sanctions and deterrence, unlike the PCI. Because of this, providers would have incentives to oppose AFS claims. In addition, the AFS gives much broader rights to patients than the PCI, paralleling the more pro-plaintiff U.S. tort system. Unlike the PCI, the AFS process would be open and subject to public scrutiny. For all these reasons, the AFS approach would incur higher per capita budget cost and overhead costs than the PCI. However, in return for these higher costs and expanded patient rights, the AFS would almost certainly provide stronger deterrence and greater equity to plaintiffs. These added benefits might more than outweigh the higher costs, yielding higher *net* benefits. In any case, political requirements for reform in any country require potential gains to both sides, relative to the status quo in that country. As noted earlier, a Swedish-style PCI would not meet this criterion in the U.S. By contrast, the AFS could benefit patients, reduce overhead costs per claim, reduce incentives for defensive medicine and prove more acceptable to providers.

6. Concluding Comments

The available data are—and are likely to remain—inadequate for a full evaluation of whether the benefit of the current malpractice system outweighs its cost. My reading of the evidence is that this is possible but not assured. Certainly, both extreme criticism and unquestioning defense of the current system are exaggerated. However, there is little doubt that the status quo system could be made more cost-effective by some simple reforms. Several of the more radical alternatives are worth considering, in part or in whole, at least as demonstration projects.

There is no simple perfect solution to the problems of professional liability and patient compensation. Fundamentally, the rationale for professional liability arises because patients and other third parties have less information than providers. But simply changing the liability rule does not per se create better information. The traditional malpractice system functions imperfectly because courts and liability insurers cannot accurately assess the actual level of care or the optimal level of care. This leads to incentives to file invalid claims, errors in findings of liability and damages, defensive medicine and incentives to expend resources to influence the outcome.

Reforms should be designed to improve the accuracy of the decision-making process, with incentives to use the information available, sanctions for abuse and strategic behavior, and benefits based on sound insurance principles. Reforms that merely attempt to reduce the more visible budget costs are likely to result at best in cost shifting, at worst in higher real social cost of injuries.

My personal judgment is that the most valuable changes to the existing system include: a schedule for noneconomic damages, based on injury severity and age of the plaintiff; periodic payments of future damages; written clarification of the standard of care and rules for determining economic loss, including inflation and discount rates; and a system of early neutral evaluation, combined with early settlement offers and the English rule of cost shifting for pursuing litigation, applied to the plaintiff's attorney. A more radical alternative would replace trial by jury with an administrative system of adjudication, while retaining the fault-based rule of liability, scheduled payments for noneconomic loss, written clarification of the standard of care and rules for economic damages, and possibly the English rule of cost-shifting. Both of these alternatives could be combined with an elective enterprise liability option, with either a negligence or strict liability rule, initially on an experimental basis. All of these alternatives maintain cost internalization to parties responsible for injuries and hence preserve deterrence incentives, while reducing some of the uncertainties of the traditional common law rules that encourage wasteful litigation and expense.

In general, the trend in health care markets towards formation of comprehensive networks of care offers new opportunities for change and experimentation in liability rules. The system of claims disposition, criteria of compensability and levels of compensation could be specified as terms of the health plan contract. Consumers could then express their willingness to pay for liability alternatives, just as they do for other dimensions of quality and quantity of services. Given the active role of employers and public purchasers in monitoring and selecting among plans, the concern that consumers might consistently be misled on quality is much diminished relative to the traditional, atomistic, fee-for-service medical market place.

Of most immediate concern is the potential expansion of liability of managed care plans, both for denial of payment for costly procedures and for the negligence of providers affiliated with the plan, under principles of vicarious or agency liability. Managed care offers the potential for a more cost-effective alternative to traditional fee-for-service insurance coverage, reducing some dimensions of choice in return for lower cost. The market evidence shows overwhelmingly that some variant of managed care is preferred by many patients. However, if managed care plans are held to the same standards of customary care that have developed under fee for service, this potential for cost reduction and efficiency gain will be preempted. A detailed discussion of appropriate liability rules for managed care is beyond the scope of this paper and is provided elsewhere (Danzon, 1997). However, addressing the issues specific to managed care is a critical part of any serious attempt at liability reform.

Notes

1. With fee-for-service reimbursement, providing more services generates additional net revenue, whereas for a capitated provider ordering or providing more services increases costs with no additional revenue. Danzon et al. (1995) analyze the causes and likely effects of restructuring.
2. See, for example, Brown (1973), Shavell (1980).
3. See Calabresi (1963) for an early explicit statement of this principle. "Optimal" and "efficient" are used here in this technical sense. They have normative content only to the extent that efficiency is a major goal of social policy, without implying that it is or should be the only policy objective.
4. This prediction assumes that providers act as self-interested income-maximizers. Altruism, professional or ethical concerns, or other quality monitoring mechanisms may modify the result (Danzon 1991, 1994b).

5.   Liability for lack of informed consent is necessary to control the rate of risky procedures. These conditions are sufficient but not necessary. For example, a shortfall in claims relative to negligent injuries could be offset by higher damage awards, by partially effective market forces, or by regulatory or other controls.

6.   Under strict liability all iatrogenic injuries would be compensable through tort. But if compensation is the sole objective, using tort liability is inefficient because of its higher administrative costs than other first-party compensation programs. Under a perfect negligence system, in theory there should be no negligence and no claims, since by definition it is cheaper to prevent injuries that would be deemed negligent than to pay for the resulting damages (Shavell 1982). Injuries that optimally are not prevented could be covered through private first-party or social insurance.

7.   These arguments are developed in detail in Danzon (1991a, 1998).

8.   Weiler at al. (1993) did not find statistically significant evidence that a higher risk of suit reduces the absolute number of negligent injuries. For statistical reasons, such an effect may be hard to detect.

9.   The difference in net compensation to patients is less than the difference in gross awards, because the attorney's contingent fee (typically one-third of the award) is subtracted from the award in the U.S. and because medical costs are covered by public health care systems in the U.K. and Canada. Fenn (1993b) reports 10.5 new claims per 100 hospital doctors in the U.K. This is not directly comparable to the U.S. rate of 13 claims per 100 doctors, since the U.S. figure applies to all medical specialties, including primary care doctors who are much less likely to be sued than hospital based specialists.

10.   The pass-through of average premium costs is not inconsistent with deterrence, if the bad apple physician who incurs higher than average liability costs is unable to pass on costs in excess of the average for his specialty, location, and patient mix.

11.   For other countries there is no evidence on number of negligent injuries, but since the number of claims is lower while quality assurance programs are generally weaker, the shortfall between claims and negligent injuries is probably even greater than in the U.S.

12.   Mills et al. (1977) defined a negligent injury as one that would be likely to lead to a jury verdict for the plaintiff, in the opinion of the reviewers who were experts in legal medicine. The Harvard study used a medical rather than an economic definition of appropriate care. Judgments about the *ex ante* appropriateness of the care may also be biased by the fact *ex post* the outcome is known.

13.   Spence (1977) shows that the optimal tort award for deterrence is lower if market forces or other quality assurance mechanisms are partially effective. With costly litigation, it may be optimal to have a low probability of suit but high penalties.

14.   "Optimal compensation" is defined as the level of compensation consumers are voluntarily willing to pay for if given the choice, including altruistic willingness to pay for others as well as willingness to pay for oneself.

15.   The economic rationale for these reforms is discussed in detail in Danzon (1984b, 1985).

16.   Written criteria or scheduled limits on major components of economic loss would also be useful. Such schedules could, for example, specify guidelines for determining quasi-wage loss benefits for minors or homemakers; the discount

and inflation factors to be used in calculating future values; and guidelines for potentially open-ended costs such as private nursing and education. Written criteria would reduce uncertainty and ability to influence the outcome, and hence would reduce expenditure on litigation.

17. Limits on awards reduce the contingent fee payable to the plaintiff attorney by the same percentage and the attorney's net revenue after costs by an even larger percentage, assuming that the fee is a flat percentage of the plaintiff's award. Plaintiff attorneys strongly oppose limits on awards.

18. Alternatively, the patient/plaintiff could be required to compensate other insurers out of the tort award for funds already paid. This latter practice is unlikely to be enforceable. Subrogation is currently available, but the extent to which it is used is unknown.

19. For a more detailed description of the Swedish and New Zealand systems, see Danzon 1994a, 1994c.

20. Proposals for statutory expansion of liability grew out of concern that very few patients (roughly ten a year) received compensation under traditional tort liability for malpractice.

21. "General deterrence" refers to the internalization of injury costs to the responsible activity or industry; it operates via effects of prices and demand elasticity. "Specific deterrence" refers to internalization to the individual responsible; it operates by changing individual incentives for prevention.

22. In 1987, the mean payment for noneconomic loss under the PCI was $3,800; the maximum was $117,070. Nevertheless, payments for noneconomic loss account for roughly 74 percent of total PCI payments, because economic loss is heavily covered through collateral sources.

23. Among other obstacles, plaintiffs allegedly have difficulty obtaining the expert testimony required to support a claim for negligence under the custom-based negligence rule.

24. If a PCI model were adopted in place of the tort system, with no right to appeal to tort, then the need to match tort compensation would not constrain the payment levels that could be set under the PCI.

25. Since 1992, major decisions of the review panel and all arbitration decisions will be published.

26. The PCI is financed by premiums paid by the county councils, who are responsible for financing and provision of the public health care system in Sweden, and by private physicians, dentists, and other paraprofessionals. For each provider category, premiums are assessed on a flat per capita basis, regardless of claims experience.

27. Like the 1989 reforms of the U.K. NHS, the goal of the NZ NHS reforms was to separate financing and provision of hospital care. Hospitals were reorganized as "Crown Health Enterprises (CHEs)," with autonomous boards, and must compete to provide services to regional health authorities.

28. For a more complete discussion of tort liability for managed care plans, see Danzon (1997).

References

Abraham, Kenneth S., and Paul C. Weiler. 1994. "Enterprise Medical Liability and the Evolution of the American Health System." Harvard Law Review 108:381-438.

American Medical Association (AMA). 1988. *A Proposed Alternative to the Civil Justice System for Resolving Medical Liability Dispute: A Fault-Based Administrative System.* Chicago: American Medical Association/Specialty Society Medical Liability Project.

Brown, John P. 1973. "Toward and Economic Theory of Liability," Journal of Legal Studies 2:323.

Coase, Ronald. 1963. "The Problem of Social Cost," Journal of Law and Economics 3:1.

Cook, P. J., and D. A. Graham. 1977. "The Demand for Insurance and Protection: The Case of Irreplaceable Commodities," Quarterly Journal of Economics 91:143-56.

Craswell, Richard, and John Calfee. 1986. Deterrence and Uncertain Legal Standards. Journal of Law, Economics and Organization 2(2):279-303.

Danzon, Patricia M. 1984a. "The Frequency and Severity of Medical Malpractice Claims," Journal of Law and Economics 27:115-48.

Danzon, Patricia M. 1984b. "Tort Reform and the Role of Government in Private Insurance Markets," Journal of Legal Studies 13 (3):517-49.

Danzon, Patricia M. 1985. *Medical Malpractice: Theory, Evidence and Public Policy.* Cambridge, MA: Harvard University Press.

Danzon, Patricia M. 1986. "New Evidence on the Frequency and Severity of Medical Malpractice Claims," Law and Contemporary Problems 5(49): 57-84.

Danzon, Patricia M. 1990. "The "Crisis" in Medical Malpractice: A Comparison of Trends in the United States, Canada, the United Kingdom and Australia," Law, Medicine and Health Care 18 (1-2).

Danzon, Patricia M. 1991a. "Liability for Medical Malpractice," Journal of Economic Perspectives 5(3): 51-69.

Danzon, Patricia M. 1992. "Hidden Overhead Costs: Is Canada's System Really Less Expensive?" Health Affairs, spring 11(1): 21-43.

Danzon, Patricia M. 1994a. "The Swedish Patient Compensation System: Myths and Realities." International Review of Law and Economics 14:453-66.

Danzon, Patricia M. 1994b. "Alternative Liability Regimes for Medical Malpractice: Results From Simulation Analysis." Journal of Risk and Insurance 61(2): 219-44.

Danzon, Patricia M. 1994c. "Tort Reform: The Case For Medical Malpractice" Oxford Review of Economic Policy 10(1): 84-98.

Danzon, Patricia M. 1997. "Tort Liability: A Minefield for Managed Care?" Journal of Legal Studies XXVI(2) (Pt.2): 491-519.

Danzon, Patricia M. 1998. "Medical Malpractice." In *The New Palgrave Dictionary of Economics and the Law.* London: Macmillan (forthcoming).

Danzon, Patricia M., and Lee Lillard. 1983. Settlement out of Court: The Disposition of Medical Malpractice Claims. Journal of Legal Studies 12: 345-77.

Danzon, Patricia M., Laura G. Boothman, and Paul Greenberg. 1995. "Consolidation and Restructuring: the Next Step in Managed Care." In Harvey Jolt (ed.) *Health Care Management: State of the Art Reviews* 2(1): 1-15.

Farber, Henry S., and Michelle White. 1991. Medical Malpractice: An Empirical Analysis of the Litigation Process. RAND Journal of Economics 22:199-217.

Fenn, Paul. 1993. "Compensation for Medical Injury: A Review of Policy Options," in C. Vincent, M. Ennis, and B. Audley, eds. *Medical Accidents. New York:* Oxford University Press.

Havighurst, C. C. 1995. *Health Care Choices: Private Contracts as Instruments of Health Reform.* Washington, DC: The AEI Press.

Mills, D. H., J. S. Boyden, and D. S. Rubsamen. 1977. *Report on the Medical Insurance Feasibility Study* (sponsored jointly by California Medical Association and California Hospital Association). San Francisco: Sutter Publications.

Oldertz, Carl. 1988. "The Patient, Pharmaceutical and Security Insurances." in Carl Oldertz and Eva Tildefelt, eds. *Compensation for Personal Injury in Sweden and Other Countries.* Juristforlaget: Stockholm. 51-78.

Rosenberg, J. D., and H. J. Folberg. 1994. "Alternative dispute resolution in a civil justice reform act demonstration district: findings, implications and recommendations." Stanford Law Review 46.

Shavell, Steven. 1980. "Strict Liability vs. Negligence." Journal of Legal Studies 9: 1-25.

Shavell, Steven. 1982. "On Liability and Insurance." Bell Journal of Economics 13:120-32.

Sloan, Frank A., and Randall R. Bovbjerg. 1989. *Medical Malpractice: Crises, Responses and Effects* HIAA. Washington, DC.

Spence, Michael. 1977. Consumer Misperceptions, Product Failure and Product Liability. Review of Economic Studies. 64:561-572.

Weiler, Paul C. 1991. *Medical Malpractice on Trial. Cambridge, MA:* Harvard University Press.

Weiler, Paul C., Howard H. Hiatt, Joseph P. Newhouse, William G. Johnson, Troyen A. Brennan, and Lucian Leape. 1993. *A Measure of Malpractice: Medical Injury, Malpractice Litigation and Patient Compensation.* Cambridge, MA: Harvard University Press.

White, Michelle J. 1994. "The Value of Liability in Medical Malpractice." Health Affairs 13(4): 75-87.

Zuckerman, Steven, Randall R. Bovbjerg, and Frank A. Sloan. 1990. "Effects of Tort Reforms and Other Factors on Medical Malpractice Insurance Premiums." Inquiry 27:167-82.

About the Editor

Roger Feldman is the Blue Cross Professor of Health Insurance in the Center for Health Services Research at the University of Minnesota and research fellow at The Independent Institute in Oakland, California. Dr. Feldman was a Marshall Scholar at the London School of Economics and holds a Ph.D. in Economics from the University of Rochester. His research interests include competition among doctors, hospitals, and health maintenance organizations. Recently, he completed a study of national HMO mergers. Dr. Feldman's experience in health care policy includes serving on the Senior Staff of the President's Council of Economic Advisers, where he was lead author of a chapter in the 1985 Economic Report of the President. From 1988 to 1992, he directed one of the four national research centers sponsored by the Health Care Financing Administration (HCFA). Dr. Feldman is on the editorial board of *Inquiry*, and he is a regular contributor to journals in health services research and economics. His paper, "Effect of HMOs on Premiums in Employment-Based Health Plans," was selected as Best Article of 1993 by the Association for Health Services Research and "The Effect of Market Structure on HMO Premiums" (with Douglas Wholey and Jon Christianson) was selected for the 1995 Research Award by the National Institute of Health Care Management. He is the co-author of several books including the most recent, Competitive Pricing for Medicare (with Bryan E. Dowd). Professor Feldman is currently advising the HCFA on implementing a demonstration of competitive pricing for Medicare.

About the Contributors

Noel D. Campbell is assistant professor of business administration (economics) at North Georgia College and State University. He received his Ph.D. in economics from George Mason University in 1997. He has written extensively on health care issues for the Cato Institute and the National Center for Policy Analysis. He has published articles on land settlement issues in the *Journal of Real Estate Finance and Economics*, and on political entrepreneurship in the *Review of Austrian Economics* (forthcoming).

Patricia M. Danzon is the Celia Moh Professor of Health Care Systems and Insurance and Risk Management at the Wharton School at the University of Pennsylvania. Having received her Ph.D. in economics from the University of Chicago, she is a member of the Institute of Medicine and the National Academy of Social Insurance. Professor Danzon has previously held positions as adjunct professor at Duke University, visiting professor at the University of Chicago, senior research fellow at the Hoover Institution and research economist at the RAND Corporation. She is an internationally recognized expert in health care systems, pharmaceuticals and medical liability, and has served as a consultant to international agencies and governments as well as to private institutions in the U.S. She is associate editor of the *Journal of Health Economics*, and past associate editor of the *Journal of Risk and Insurance* and the *American Economic Review*. She is the author of *Pharmaceutical Price Regulation: National vs. Global Interests; Medical Malpractice: Theory, Evidence and Public Policy,* and *Responsible National Health Insurance* (with M. Pauly, P. Feldstein and J. Hoff), plus numerous articles in scholarly journals.

Richard A. Epstein is the James Parker Hall Distinguished Service Professor of Law at the University of Chicago. A member of the

American Academy of Arts and Sciences and the California Bar, he is an editor of the *Journal of Law and Economics* and a member of the Board of Advisors of The Independent Institute. A graduate of Oxford and Columbia Universities, Professor Epstein received his LL.B. cum laude from Yale Law School in 1968. His many books include *Principles for a Free Society: Reconciling Individual Liberty with the Common Good, Mortal Peril, Simple Rules for a Complex World, Takings, Forbidden Grounds, The Bill of Rights in the Modern State, Modern Products Liability Law,* and *Torts* among others. He is the author of over 160 articles and reviews in journals such as the *University of Chicago Law Review, Harvard Law Review,* the *Yale Law Journal, Stanford Law Review,* and the *New England Journal of Medicine.*

H. E. Frech, III, is professor of economics at the University of California at Santa Barbara. He received his Ph.D. in economics from UCLA and has taught at Harvard University and the University of Chicago. He is an adjunct professor at Sciences Po de Paris and an adjunct scholar at the American Enterprise Institute. He is the editor of several books including, *Health Economics Worldwide* (with Peter Zweifel), *Health Care in America,* and *Regulating Doctor's Fees,* as well as the author of, *Public Insurance in Private Medical Markets* (with Paul B. Ginsburg), *Taxing Energy* (with Robert Deacon, Steven DeCanio, M. Bruce Johnson), *Competition and Monopoly in Medical Care* and *The Productivity of Health Care and Pharmaceuticals* (with Richard Miller). He is also North American editor of the *International Journal of the Economics of Business.* Professor Frech is the author of over eighty articles in scholarly journals, and he has served as a consultant to many public and private organizations.

Ronald Hamowy is emeritus professor of History at the University of Alberta. He received his Ph.D. from the University of Chicago under the late Nobel Laureate economist and philosopher, Friedrich A. Hayek, and has taught at City University of New York, Stanford University, and Simon Fraser University. Dr. Hamowy is the author of *Canadian Medicine: A Study in Restricted Entry* and *The Scottish Enlightenment and the Theory of Spontaneous Order.* In addition, he has edited and annotated Trenchard and Gordon's *Cato's Letters* and is the editor of *Dealing With Drugs: Consequences of Government Control.* His articles have appeared in numerous publications, including the *William and Mary Quarterly,* the *History of Political Thought, Philosophy of the Social Sciences, and* the *New Republic.*

Ronald W. Hansen is senior sssociate dean for faculty and research at the William E. Simon Graduate School of Business Administration at the University of Rochester. From 1986 to 1988 he was associate professor, Merrell Dow Professorship, at the College of Pharmacy, the Ohio State University. He was a member of the National Advisory Council on Health Care Technology Assessment, Department of Health and Human Services (1985-1988) and a study committee member, "Children's Vaccine Initiative," Institute of Medicine, National Academy of Sciences, 1992-1993. He helped to establish the Center for the Study of Drug Development, formerly at the University of Rochester and now at Tufts University. He is a member of the editorial board of the *Journal of Research in Pharmaceutical Economics.* His articles have appeared journals including in the *Journal of Health Economics,* the *Journal of Risk and Insurance* and the *Journal of Pharmaceutical Economics.* He is a contributor to numerous books including *Principles of Pharmacoeconomics, Competitive Strategies in the Pharmaceutical Industry, Care and Cost,* and *Issues in Pharmaceutical Economics.*

Clark C. Havighurst is the William Neal Reynolds Professor of Law at Duke University, having received his J.D. from Northwestern University. His research has covered most phases of regulation in the health services industry, competition in the financing and delivery of health care, medical malpractice, and private contracts as instruments of health reform. He is a member of the Institute of Medicine of the National Academy of Sciences and served for some years as chairman of the executive committee of the Journal of Health Politics, Policy and Law. Professor Havighurst has served as resident consultant at the RAND Corporation in Santa Monica, at the Federal Trade Commission, and at Epstein, Becker & Green and is a former editor of the journal, *Law and Contemporary Problems.* He is the author of *Health Care Law and Policy, Health Care Choices,* and *Deregulating the Health Care Industry.* He is a contributor to over twenty volumes, and the author of over fifty articles and reviews in scholarly journals.

Gail A. Jensen is professor in the Department of Economics and Institute of Gerontology at Wayne State University, and also a fellow of the Employee Benefit Research Institute and the National Center for Policy Analysis. She received her Ph.D. from the University of Minnesota, and was previously assistant professor in the School of Public Health, University of Illinois at Chicago, and economist at the American Hospital Association and Abt Associates. She has contributed to many volumes in health care policy, including *American Health Policy, Rescuing American Health Care,* and *Managed Care and Changing Health Care Markets.* Her many journal articles and reviews have appeared in such places as *Health Affairs, Inquiry, Medical Care, Journal of Health Economics, Journal of Regulatory Economics, Journal of Risk and Uncertainty,* the *Milbank Quarterly, Journal of Risk and Insurance, Regulation,* and *Review of Economics and Statistics.*

Michael A. Morrisey is professor at the Department of Health Care Organization and Policy in the School of Public Health and director of the Lister Hill Center for Health Policy at the University of Alabama at Birmingham. He has been a senior economist at the American Hospital Association, and visiting research specialist at the Battelle Human Affairs Research Center. He received his Ph.D. in economics from the University of Washington in 1979. Dr. Morrisey is the author of three books including *Cost Shifting in Health Care: Separating Evidence from Rhetoric,* and over 100 articles on health economics and health insurance issues. His research has appeared in the *Review of Economics and Statistics, Journal of Health Economics, Journal of Law and Economics,* and *Medical Care,* among others. He is on the editorial boards of three health policy and health services research journals including *Health Affairs,* and is a fellow of the Employee Benefit Research Institute.

Paul H. Rubin is professor of economics and law at Emory University in Atlanta and editor in chief of *Managerial and Decision Economics.* Dr. Rubin received his B.A. from the University of Cincinnati in 1963 and his Ph.D. from Purdue University in 1970. He has been an adjunct scholar at the American Enterprise Institute, the Cato Institute, and the Georgia Public Policy Foundation, and former vice president of the Southern Economics Association. Dr. Rubin has been senior staff economist at President Reagan's Council of Economic Advisers, chief economist at the U.S. Consumer Product Safety Commission, director of advertising economics at the Federal Trade Commission, and vice president of Glassman-Oliver Economic Consultants, Inc., a litigation consulting firm in Washington. He has taught economics at the University of Georgia, City University of New York, Virginia Tech University, and George Washington University Law School. Dr. Rubin has written or edited seven books, and published over one hundred academic articles and chapters on economics, law, and regulation. He has also contributed to the *Wall Street Journal*. Recent books include *Managing Business Transactions* and *Tort Reform by Contract*. He has consulted widely on litigation related matters, and has addressed numerous business, professional, policy and academic audiences.

Barbara A. Ryan is vice president of Capital Economics where she specializes in antitrust and regulatory issues in health care and other industries. She received her Ph.D. in economics from George Mason University in 1994, and has served as economic advisor to the chairman of the U.S. International Trade Commission, lecturer in economics at George Mason University, Manager of Arthur Young & Company, research associate at Evans Economics, Inc., and economist at The National Bank of Washington. Her research in health care concerns the competitive consequences of mergers and acquisitions in the hospital and related industries.

Shirley V. Svorny is professor of economics at California State University, Northridge. She received her Ph.D. in economics from the University of California, Los Angeles, and she has served as vice president and senior economist at Security Pacific National Bank and economist at Getty Oil Company. She has written extensively about medical licensure and discipline. She is the author of more than a dozen articles in scholarly volumes and journals.

Charlotte Twight is professor of economics at Boise State University. She received her J.D. degree from the University of Washington in Seattle in 1973 and her Ph.D. from the same institution in 1983. Her articles have appeared in *Public Choice,* the *Journal of Economic Behavior and Organization,* the *Journal of Theoretical Politics*, the *Journal of Public Policy*, and many other scholarly journals. She serves on the Academic Advisory Board of the Institute for Health Freedom. Her forthcoming book is *Dependence by Design: The Rise of Federal Control Over the Lives of Ordinary Americans.*

Index

AALL. *See* American Association for Labor Legislation

AARP. *See* American Association of Retired Persons

Abell, Irvin, 23

ACC. *See* New Zealand Accident Compensation Corporation

Access, 9, 110, 161, 329; enhancing, 113; market, 325, 334, 337; monopoly on, 313, 322, 325, 334, 337; quality of, 172

Accountability, 87, 110, 115, 163, 405, 406

ADA. *See* Americans with Disability Act

Adams, David: on aspirin advertising, 288-89

Administrative fault-based system (AFS), 409-11; and PCI compared, 411

Admissions, price per, 237, 241

ADR. *See* Alternative dispute resolution

Advertisements, ix, 2, 7, 330; banning, 288, 301; consumer direct, 302-6, 307; cost of, 303; criticism of, 302; deception in, 294-99, 302, 306; educational value of, 290, 297-98; FDA and, 286, 288, 296-97; pharmaceutical, 7, 290-92, 307, 309n19; physicians and, 301; price reductions and, 306; regulation of, 7, 303, 309n19, 310n35; review of, 295, 300, 301, 302; risk of, 286, 288-89, 292; standards for, 296-97, 300; treatment and, 305; TV, 303-4

Aetna Life Insurance Company, insurance plan by, 34

AFL-CIO, 27, 91; COPE and, 62n78

AFS. *See* Administrative fault-based system

AIDS virus/therapies, 211, 212, 276-77, 281

Aid to Permanently and Totally Disabled (APTD), 41

Alternative dispute resolution (ADR), 385, 398-99

Alternative treatments, 275; benefits/risks of, 388; MSAs and, 127, 128

AMA. *See* American Medical Association

Amazing Aspirin (pamphlet), 285

Amendments to the Food, Drug and Cosmetics Act (1962), 271

American Academy of Actuaries, 206

American Association for Labor Legislation (AALL), 17; AMA and, 18; health insurance plan by, 19; opposition to, 20-21

American Association of Retired Persons (AARP), 50, 209

American College of Surgeons, prepayment plans and, 63n79

American Farm Bureau Association, 27

American Federation of Labor, health insurance and, 20, 22

American Hospital Association, 173, 182

American Medical Association (AMA), 28, 376; AALL and, 18; AFS by, 409-11; Committee on Social Insurance and, 19; compulsory health insurance and, 23, 25; control by, 369; due process and, 379; Eldercare and, 34, 64n102; fault-based system and, 386; King-Anderson bill and, 29-30, 33-34; membership in, 239; monopoly pricing and, 368; opposition from, 27, 31; prepayment plans and, 63n79; Wagner-Murray-Dingell bill and, 25

American Medical Political Action Committee (AMPAC), 29, 62n78

American National Standards Institute (ANSI), 327, 340

427